Early Intervention for At-Risk and Handicapped Infants, Toddlers, and Preschool Children

Early Intervention for At-Risk and Handicapped Infants, Toddlers, and Preschool Children

Second Edition
1989

Diane D. Bricker, Ph.D.

VORT Corporation
Palo Alto, California

First edition published 1986 by Scott,
        Foresman & Co.
Copyright © 1986, 1989 Diane D. Bricker

Published by:
  VORT Corporation
  PO Box 60132
  Palo Alto, CA 94306

ISBN 0-89718-140-9

To my parents

CONTENTS

ACKNOWLEDGEMENTS

This book reflects the synthesis of many years of involvement in the field of Early Intervention. The quality of the book comes from the many written and verbal interactions with colleagues and parents as well as observations of children in a variety of intervention programs. These observations and interactions have directed my thinking. The flaws in the book and the approach come from my limitations to have learned all that I should have from these observations and interactions.

Part One

Theory and Foundation

1.
Overview

THE NEED

I am often alarmed at the apparent lack of understanding by the layman and the professional community about intervention efforts surrounding infants and young children who are at-risk and handicapped. This statement is not meant to be critical, but rather it is meant to underline the need for analysis and reanalysis of the field of early intervention. My observations of programs and comments by those who operate these programs, those who are consumers, and those who support these programs through their tax dollars lead me to believe that the early intervention enterprise is poorly understood, both as a science and as a therapeutic venture.

To the observer, whether legislator, community agency personnel, or interested citizen, early intervention programs for infants and preschool-age children who are at-risk and handicapped seem to be thought of as exceptional caregiving facilities. The enrolled children and their families are obviously valued and the program personnel are dedicated to assisting the participating children and families in a number of areas. Staff members of these programs are often referred to as "angels of mercy." Rarely does one hear comments that suggest the observer appreciates the rigor and structure that is necessary for an effective program. Perhaps the comments are not forthcoming because, in fact, the rigor and structure are not present. If the profession of early intervention is to be viewed by the outside world as a sound educational enterprise based on objective findings, then we must begin to demonstrate, through our actions and words, that such an evaluation is warranted.

It may be fair to say that informed citizens, allied health professionals, and others associated with the development of social policy see our efforts as mainly in the category of *cannot hurt and might help*; conversely, other people are indiscriminately supportive of all early intervention efforts whether valid or not. That is, how can providing services for children who are at-risk and handicapped be bad? All too often we, as professionals in the field, do not make effective moves to counter such opinions whether internally or externally held. If the early intervention enterprise expects to become respected as a sound educational and scientifically rigorous undertaking, then a first step is for the early intervention professional to adopt a position that will lead to the systematic development of effective procedures and content based on sound theoretical premises. We cannot hope to change and shape outside opinion if we do not have our own house in order.

We face a challenging decision. We can pursue the path of many ventures that are a part of public education in which the administrative and teaching staff have side-stepped their responsibility to America's children and fostered mediocrity rather than excellence. The alternative is to accept that responsibility and move forward in the development of effective early intervention programs for infants and children who are at-risk and handicapped. The field of early intervention is new and thus not yet laden with tradition and folklore. This reality provides us with an exceptional opportunity to build a field that responds to fact, not fancy; sound theory, not whimsey; and structure, not fad. We have the excitement and the opportunity, and now we must continue to garner the necessary financial and personnel resources to develop a field that does, indeed, maximize the growth and learning potential of children who are at-risk and handicapped.

To meet such a challenge is the purpose of this book. The field of early intervention requires a range of competent professionals. We cannot afford to operate, nor can the children afford to be served by, programs with personnel who are not knowledgeable about relevant content and procedures, and who do not undergird their daily intervention activities with objective evaluations of effectiveness. The premise of this book is that early intervention programs must be staffed by well-trained professionals and, unlike mushrooms, such professionals do not appear overnight. This book provides those in the field and those still in training with a resource that will assist in achieving knowledgeable and competent professionals. This book presents a comprehensive overview of the field of early intervention and, while doing so, points out information that is anchored in fact as well as that which remains largely speculative. Ample information exists to allow the field to move forward on what currently must be considered "best practice" with the clear understanding that in the future, current best practice may be replaced by more effective approaches and content.

PERSPECTIVES

The approach to early intervention described in this book is guided by four major perspectives: developmental, transactional, family involvement and comprehensive. An appreciation of these perspectives is fundamental to understanding the present approach as well as best practice in the field of early intervention.

Developmental Perspective

Most children follow developmental guidelines or at least logical progressions that move the child to increasingly more complex response repertoires. That is, infants learn to roll over before they can sit up, sit up before they stand, stand before they walk, and walk before they run or climb stairs. Development can be visualized as an inverse pyramid with the basic building blocks acquired by the infant being gradually differentiated into increasingly higher-level responses.

Figure 1-1 presents an example of the potential sequence of development for early communication taken from norms found in the literature. As illustrated in Figure 1-1, infants are first able to produce sounds that indicate pleasure or discomfort. At this level, infants can also respond to environmentally produced sounds; however, responses may vary from increasing activity to becoming still and attempting to locate the sound source. Entry into the second level is indexed by the production of vowel sounds and the ability to respond to familiar sounds by infants. At the next level, infants can vocalize to the human voice, produce a variety of speech sounds, and play simple games (e.g., "peek-a-boo") with caregivers. By the next level, infants have learned to use their voice to attract attention; imitate a variety of sounds; correctly identify familiar objects, people, and events when named; and use objects to attract caregivers' attention. These responses, in turn, evolve into the production and comprehension of words and familiar phrases.

The model presented in Figure 1-1 probably does not accurately reflect developmental change in children. Rather, as Kagan, Kearsely, and Zelazo (1978) point out, a better analogy is to view early development as a canvas upon which certain impressions are made. As the artist works on the canvas, these initial strokes are blended into increasingly more complex images that often do not reflect any vestiges of the initial form. The building-block model presented in Figure 1-1 should be viewed likewise in that early response forms are blended and modified into behaviors that may not reflect their origin. Even with this caveat, a variety of criticism has been directed toward the use of the developmental model.

Many critics will be quick to indicate that although an outlined sequence, such as the one in Figure 1-1, is appropriate for nonhandicapped children, rarely do such hierarchies reflect the sequence of development seen in disabled populations—particularly those with motor and/or sensory impairments. Some authorities suggest the presence of specific pathologies may impact emergent response forms in ways that produce significant deviations in the developmental path followed by an

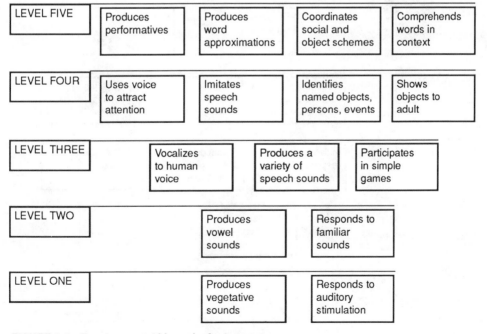

FIGURE 1-1. Developmental hierarchy for language.

infant or child (Guess, 1980). Indeed, this is often the case with children who are more severely impaired. However, even for children who experience deviations as well as delays, a developmental perspective seems useful if response classes are defined as general hierarchical sequences. For example, if the response classes contained in Figure 1-1 are rewritten to be more generic, as shown in Figure 1-2, then the developmental hierarchies would seem appropriate for most infants or children who are handicapped. These hierarchies, although general in nature, can still provide a useful set of guidelines for the interventionist.

Critics of using a developmental perspective with infants and children who are handicapped also question whether using developmental hierarchies leads to the most efficient training sequence. Indeed, the question is asked, in particular for children who are more severely disabled, whether sufficient time is available to move a child systematically through so many levels of learning or instruction (Sailor, Guess, Goetz, Schuler, Utley & Baldwin, 1980). The argument is made, that rather than working on apparent precursors such as crawling prior to walking or vocalizing prior to producing words, training should begin with the higher order skill (e.g., walking or producing words). This approach may teach children specific skills but does not appear to produce generalized responses. The child may learn several words and use them under the training conditions (e.g., when the teacher says, "What is this?") but the child may fail to develop a generalized word-learning and word-using skill. By assisting the child in acquiring some basic speaker/listener rules and communication requirements such as establishing joint topics, the child may eventually develop a communication system that can be used across settings, people and events.

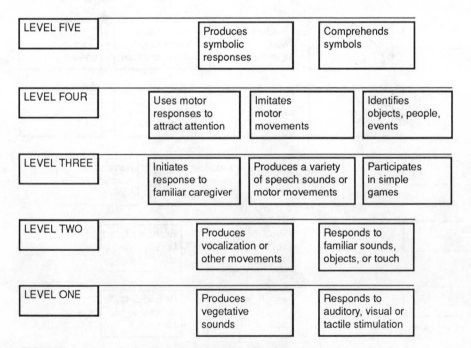

FIGURE 1-2. *Generic developmental hierarchy for language.*

A final word in defense of using developmental hierarchies with disabled populations is concerned with the rigidity with which such models of development are followed. Looking at a road map to find a route from city A to city B (given each is of adequate size) generally reveals the availability of several different routes between the two destinations. One route may be more direct and thus the one most commonly followed between the two cities. However, for a variety of reasons, people may choose to substitute one of the less traveled routes. Using a set of developmental hierarchies should be viewed in a like manner. That is, most children follow the specified route, but that does not mean that the interventionist cannot or should not consider variations when a child has a disability that appears to preclude moving along the common route. The developmental model is useful only when viewed and applied with a fundamental understanding of individual differences. Its value comes from providing a general overview of how development proceeds in important behavioral domains. That value can be neutralized unless the interventionist acknowledges the need for individual tailoring of intervention that is often necessary when dealing with infants and young children who are at-risk and handicapped.

Transactional Perspective

The transactional perspective that underlies the approach to early intervention described in this book is based on the important chapter published in 1975 by Sameroff and Chandler. In that chapter, Sameroff and Chandler's review of pertinent literature leads to the inescapable conclusion that the outcome for infants and children is directly dependent upon their organismic integrity and the quality of their caregiving environment. These authors propose viewing the infant along two continua of risk: one called *reproductive risk* and one called *caregiver risk*. The continuum of reproductive risk refers to the genetic and biological constitution of the infant. Infants with Down syndrome have a genetic condition that renders their development at serious risk. So, too, infants who suffer severe asphyxia at birth are at considerable risk for the development of serious problems. The continuum of caregiver risks refers to the social and physical environment experienced by infants. If the environment is appropriate, the chances of infants prospering are increased, while caregiving environments that are abusive or neglectful of infants increase the chances that infants will not develop without problem.

Thus, where these two continua of risk bisect for each infant determines the quality of life that can be expected. In a general sense, the more biologically competent the infant, the more the infant can compensate for the effects of a poor caregiving environment. The child that survives an abusive home and becomes an outstanding university student most likely had the biological competence to compensate for a poor caregiving environment. The brother or sister of this individual may have been born several weeks premature and thus developed associated problems that precluded offsetting the negative impact of an inadequate caregiving environment; thus, this individual may spend time in special education classes and never become fully self-sufficient. There are infants and children with biological insults so great that no amount of appropriate environmental caregiving can completely compensate. Effective environmental stimulation may reduce the impact of the disability; but for the moderately to severely handicapped individual the effects of major biological insults, such as cerebral palsy, hydrocephalus, or Down syndrome, cannot be completely erased. On the other hand, even the most biologically competent child may suffer from the effects of particularly abusive homes, if only in the sense that whatever potential the child had will never be fully realized.

The transactional perspective described is focused on the on-going exchanges between the continua of reproductive and caregiving risk. An equally important aspect of the transactional model to be considered by early intervention personnel is the daily transactions that occur between infants or children and their environments. These transactions form the substance of the intervention provided to the child who is at-risk and handicapped. Understanding this perspective and incorporating it into the interventionist's philosophical approach to intervention are essential.

Several years ago, the predominant theoretical position on the environment-child interaction was unidirectional—that is, investigators primarily examined the effect the environment had on the infant or young child and not the children's effect on their environment (Bell, 1974). For example, in a series of influential investigations (e.g., Bowlby, 1973; Dennis, 1963), findings suggested the depressive effects of institutional environments on young children. This research was unidimensional in that the focus was on the effects of inconsistent caregiving or mothering on the young child. These studies did not examine the impact of the child on the environment.

In the 1960s, another group of investigators began examining the social environment's impact on the infant. For example, Rheingold, Gerwirtz, and Ross (1959) found that responses like vocalization were affected by social consequences provided by caregivers. Although such investigations demonstrated that environmental manipulations could control affective forms of behavior, the focus remained unilateral in that the investigators examined only the effect of the caregiver's behavior on the infant's behavior.

In spite of Piagetian theory, the interactionist model did not come into vogue until the early 1970s. During this period, many investigators (see e.g., Lewis & Rosenblum, 1974) began considering the child-caregiver relationship as one in which both participants affected the behavior of the other. Reciprocal exchanges governed by each participant's response became the focus of attention and study. Patterns of social interaction governed by the partner's response to each other formed a circular feedback system, which initially was pictured as a rather simplistic system. Lewis and Lee-Painter (1974) have discussed the problems associated with the position that child-caregiver interactions form a simple interactive network, and these investigators have offered a more complex model in which both the child and caregiver are actively involved and "significantly influence each other."

The daily exchanges between children and their environment serve as the foundation of the intervention approach described in this book. The intervention procedures and content are formulated to take advantage of the reciprocal interaction between children and their environment; therefore, inherent in the approach is concern not only for the child's behavioral repertoire but also for how that repertoire impacts the environment over time. Adopting such an approach requires attention both to the reciprocal exchanges between the caregivers and the child and to the larger social context in which the child and caregiver reside. In effect, one is required to examine the transactions that occur between the child-caregiver, caregiver-family, and family-community.

Family Involvement Perspective

Although attention to caregivers and families will be addressed in detail in Chapter 7, it seems important to provide the reader with the basic philosophy toward families adopted in this book. Family involvement is considered fundamental to the success of early intervention with infants and young children. The greater the family's involvement, the greater the probability that the child's problems will be minimized and progress maximized. The passage of P.L. 99-457 has provided legislative credence to family involvement and has emphasized to all agency personnel delivering services to young children the importance of including family members in planning, executing and evaluating programs of intervention.

To be effective in intervention efforts with infants and young children, early intervention personnel must begin to formulate their input on the basis of the larger social context in which the family resides. Sameroff (1982) and Simeonsson (1988) have articulated the need to take into account the resources, stresses, values, and desires of family members before developing elaborate intervention plans that the family may find unsuitable or even distasteful. In a review chapter, Parke and Tinsley (1982) have assembled evidence that strongly suggests intervention efforts with infants who at-risk and handicapped are significantly enhanced when the primary caregiver (generally the mother) receives adequate support from her spouse and when both parents, in turn, receive adequate community support, whether from extended family members, organizations (e.g., church), or friends.

Thus, it seems imperative that the transactions that occur between the caregiver/interventionist and the child should be, in turn, placed in the larger social context of the family. The approach described in this book reflects this position, and thus, the transactional model presented in Figure 1-3 has been expanded to include this perspective.

Comprehensive Intervention Perspective

Another important perspective underlying the approach presented in this book is the breadth of intervention. The approach is designed to permit the interventionist to focus on arranging environmental contingencies to produce change in the infant or child. The key concept is taking action to produce change in the child and family. This perspec-

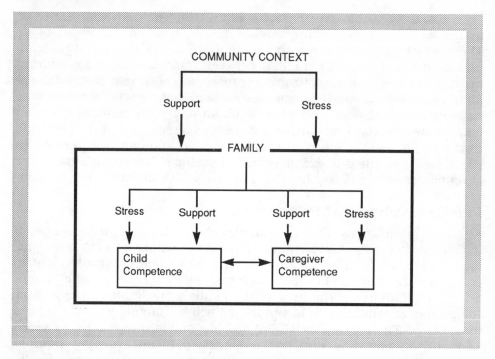

FIGURE 1-3. Transactional model in environmental context.

tive requires that intervention be defined in its broadest sense and does not refer exclusively to programming of skills more traditionally thought of as educational in nature (e.g., reading and writing). Rather, in the present approach, the focus is on any skill or behavior that can be acquired through some form of environmental manipulation.

A comprehensive approach provides the interventionist with a broad array of domains to consider as potential intervention targets. For example, working in tandem with an orthopedist and physical therapist to assist a child in learning to properly use a prosthetic device would be considered an appropriate goal. So, too, assisting a mother in acquiring more effective intervention strategies would be considered within the purview of intervention efforts. Even assisting the family in acquiring social services that might indirectly impact on the care of the child would be an appropriate target within the present approach.

During the past few years there has been a major reinterpretation of the importance of play for the young child (see Chance, 1979), and a number of investigators have suggested the importance of play for the child who is handicapped as well (McHale & Olley, 1982; Fewell & Kaminski, 1988). Thus, the area of play which may have been previously thought of as recreation for young children is coming to be viewed as activity essential to their growth and development. This reevaluation of the merits of play suggests that these activities be considered within the early intervention enterprise as well. Consequently, the approach here considers acquiring skills such as manipulation of toys, interactional skills with peers, imitation, and imaginary play behaviors to be important to the development of the young child whether handicapped or not, and thus legitimate intervention targets.

The only areas not dealt with directly in this approach would be techniques that attempt to alter the basic anatomy of the child, for example, surgery to repair a structural deficit. However, even in cases where medical intervention is required, it may be necessary to work on some corollary behavior that is considered educational. The child with hydrocephalus may require the surgical implant of a shunt to drain off excess spinal fluid; but if that child has suffered some neurological damage associated with the hydrocephalus, then some form of intervention may be required to assist the child in functioning as normally as possible.

The point to be emphasized is that the approach described is comprehensive in nature and is focused on a *wide range* of skills that will enhance children's independence and adjustment to their environment.

From Research to Application

This book has been written primarily for the broad range of personnel in training or currently delivering services to children who are at-risk and handicapped; thus, a section on research issues might seem somewhat off target. However, I do not share this position and feel strongly that interventionists, program developers, therapists, and any others associated with delivering quality services to young children and their families should be concerned with information developed by the research community and how to apply such information, when appropriate, to service delivery efforts.

Many researchers and practitioners assume that information flows unilaterally from the laboratory to field application for the enhancement of general knowledge or for the implementation of specific rehabilitative procedures for the benefit of specific populations. Some writers have questioned whether the unilateral flow from researcher to practitioner produces the greatest positive clinical change. In fact, several writers have emphasized that the practitioner need not play the role of an empty vessel waiting to be filled with selected information provided by the research community (Butterfield, 1978). Rather, the interventionist or educator should actively seek and apply a variety of therapies and procedures as they appear useful and relevant to the problems at hand—even if such procedures lack a strong empirical or scientific base. The generation of ideas, information, and strategies that may enhance the quality of life for individuals and groups comes from both the practitioner and researcher.

Communication is a second source of difficulty leading to the long-standing gap between knowledge and practice. Researchers and practitioners, with rare exceptions, form camps whose inhabitants talk and write predominately for each other. As Baumeister (1981) commented, communication among colleagues tends to be horizontal rather than vertical. Rather than crossing borders into the other camp, conversations tend to occur among individuals with similar thoughts and modes of operation.

Although it is probably safe to surmise that barriers to the flow of information and communication have hindered the research-practice exchange, the literature does contain examples of productive reciprocity between researcher and practitioner. For example, Tyler and Kogan (1977) conducted an investigation in which eighteen preschool children with cerebral palsy were used and the focus was on providing the participating mothers with a special training program to enhance mother-child interactions. The content of the training program was derived from previous clinical observations of increasing negative behavior by the child and decreasing positive interactions between mother and child over time. By implementing an intervention program under controlled conditions, these investigators were able to produce a positive impact on behaviors that have clinical importance to young children who have cerebral palsy and their mothers. Conversely, procedures developed under controlled conditions have found relevant and useful clinical application. For example, Eilers, Wilson, and Moore (1977) developed a procedure to examine speech discrimination in infants. This operant procedure, termed *visually reinforced infant speech discrimination* (VRISD), has subsequently been adopted for hearing evaluations of infants in clinical settings (Northern & Downs, 1978). Work in the development of early communication has also found application. Information discovered by investigators such as Stern (1981), whose research addressed the infant's readiness to communicate has been subsequently integrated into communication intervention programs designed for children who are at-risk and handicapped (see e.g., Bricker & Schiefelbusch, 1984.)

A third major barrier to effective transactions between the research and practitioner communities is the lack of articulate and credible individuals to function as translators of research and clinical findings. Most professionals working in the area of early intervention consider themselves to be either researchers or practitioners and not both. The research community tends to be interested in the controlled and systematic manipulation of selected variables while the practitioner community is interested in producing verifiable change in their target population. Neither group accepts as a primary role the description of research outcomes to the applied community or the description of practical problems to the research community.

Even if people were available to discuss research findings and barriers to clinical practice, few mechanisms exist to facilitate the systematic movement of useful research outcomes into the practitioner's realm or the reverse. The advent of journals such as *Topics in Early Childhood Special Education, Journal of Early Intervention* and *Infants and Young Children* have been helpful in addressing this problem as they do provide vehicles for establishing a researcher-practitioner dialogue. The availability of these journals and conferences specifically focused on early intervention helps considerably in bridging the research-to-practice chasm; however, the literature on child development, intervention and relevant environmental factors remains vast and scattered, requiring considerable effort by researcher and practitioner alike to

maintain currency with the array of information that may be potentially relevant and useful to their respective activities.

The perspective of this book is that, first, interventionists are
capable of digesting and understanding information generated by the
research community. Second, that interventionists are interested in any
information, whatever the source, that will enhance intervention efforts
with infants and children who are at-risk and handicapped. Third, that
interventionists recognize that one way to increase the effectiveness of
the field is to apply state-of-the-art knowledge and then collect systematic information on the effectiveness of the approach or content with
specified populations of infants and children. We can do no less if we are
to become a respected profession built on fact, not fancy.

SUMMARY

This book has blended relevant research outcomes into a comprehensive
and cohesive intervention approach for infants and young children who
are at-risk and handicapped. An attempt has been made to present the
major theoretical underpinnings that direct our current intervention
efforts and to use those conceptual underpinnings as the basis for formulating the practical knowledge contained in this book.

The first part of this book addresses two critical areas: (1) selected
major theoretical issues facing early interventionists and (2) selected
research findings on general efficacy and more specific intervention
parameters. Part Two discusses the application of the theory and
research presented in Part One. There is nothing to preclude the reader
from reading one part without the other or selected chapters; however,
the book has been constructed to present a unified approach.

This book presents a description of one general approach which is
comprehensive in nature. An attempt has been made to present the
approach in a balanced manner, but no attempt has been made to
describe the many competing and complementary procedures or content
currently available.

The past history of the early intervention enterprise has been short
and eventful. The future appears full of opportunity to advance our
knowledge and practice.

References

Baumeister, A. (1981).   Mental retardation policy and research: The unfulfilled promise. *American Journal of Mental Deficiency, 85,* 449-456.

Bell, R. (1974).   Contributions of human infants to caregiving and social interaction.   In M. Lewis & L. Rosenblum (Eds.), *The effect of the infant on its caregiver.* New York: Wiley & Sons.

Bowlby, J. (1973). *Attachment and loss: Separation, anxiety, and anger.* New York: Basic Books.

Bricker, D., & Schiefelbusch, R. (1984). *Infants at risk.* In L. McCormick & R. Schiefelbusch (Eds.), Early language intervention. Cols., OH: Merrill.

Butterfield, E. (1978).   Behavioral assessment of infants: From research to practice.   In F. Minifie & L. Lloyd (Eds.), *Communicative and cognitive abilities: Early behavioral assessment.* Baltimore, MD: University Park Press.

Chance, P. (1979). *Learning through play.* New York: Gardner Press.

Dennis, W. (1963).   Environmental influences upon motor development. In W. Dennis (Ed.), *Readings in Child Psychology* (2nd ed.). Englewood Cliffs, NJ: Prentice-Hall.

Eilers, R., Wilson, W., & Moore, J. (1977).   Developmental changes in speech discrimination in infants. *Journal of Speech and Hearing Research, 20,* 766-780.

Fewell, R., & Kaminski, R. (1988).   Play skills development and instruction for young children with handicaps.   In S. Odom & M. Karnes (Eds.), *Early intervention for infants and children with handicaps.* Baltimore, MD: Paul Brookes.

Guess, D. (1980).   Methods in communication instruction for severely handicapped persons. In W. Sailor, B. Wilcox, & L. Brown (Eds.), *Methods of instruction for severely handicapped students.* Baltimore, MD: Paul Brookes.

Kagan, J., Kearsley, R., & Zelazo, P. (1978). *Infancy: Its place in human development.* Cambridge, MA: Harvard University Press.

Lewis, M., & Lee-Painter, S. (1974).   An interactional approach to the mother-infant dyad.   In M. Lewis & L. Rosenblum (Eds.), *The effect of the infant on its caregiver.* New York: Wiley & Sons.

Lewis, M., & Rosenblum, L. (Eds.). (1974). *The effects of the infant on its caregiver.* New York: Wiley & Sons.

McHale, S., & Olley, G. (1982).   Using play to facilitate the social development of handicapped children. *Topics in Early Childhood Special Education, 2,* 76-86.

Northern, J., & Downs, M. (1978). *Hearing in children.* Baltimore, MD: Williams & Wilkins.

Parke, R., & Tinsley, B. (1982).   The early environment of the at-risk infant.   In D. Bricker (Ed.), *Intervention with at-risk and handicapped infants: From research to application.* Baltimore, MD: University Park Press.

Rheingold, H., Gerwirtz, J., & Ross, H. (1959). Social conditioning of vocalizations in the infant. *Journal of Comparative Physiological Psychology, 52,* 68-73.

Sailor, W., Guess, D., Goetz, L., Schuler, A., Utley, B., & Baldwin, M. (1980). Language and severely handicapped persons: Deciding what to teach to whom. In W. Sailor, B. Wilcox & L. Brown (Eds.), *Methods of instruction for severely handicapped students.* Baltimore, MD: Paul Brookes.

Sameroff, A. (1982). The environmental context of developmental disabilities. In D. Bricker (Ed.), *Intervention with at-risk and handicapped infants: From research to application.* Baltimore, MD: University Park Press.

Sameroff, A., & Chandler, M. (1975). Reproductive risk and the continuum of caretaking casualty. In F. Horowitz, M. Hetherington, S. Scarr-Salapatek, & G. Siegel (Eds.), *Review of child development research* (Vol. 4). Chicago: University of Chicago Press.

Simeonsson, R. (1988). Unique characteristics of families with young handicapped children. In D. Bailey & R. Simeonsson (Eds.), *Family assessment in early intervention.* Cols., OH: Merrill.

Stern, D. (1981). The development of biologically determined signals of readiness to communicate which are language "resistant." In R. Stark (Ed.), *Language behavior in infancy and early childhood.* New York: Elsevier.

Tyler, N., & Kogan, K. (1977). Reduction of stress between mothers and their handicapped children. *The American Journal of Occupational Therapy, 31,* 151-155.

2.
Early Experience

INTRODUCTION

Before discussing the approach to early intervention proffered in this book, it will be useful to discuss in some detail the essential philosophical premises on which the early intervention enterprise has been built. Too often those of us working in the area take for granted the importance of early experience for the developing child. We often suggest that if the infant or young child gets off to the right start, future success is assured. The discussion that follows calls into question that assumption and offers a more comprehensive and considered perspective on early experience.

Early intervention with infants and children who are either at-risk or handicapped as a result of medical or environmental factors has become big business. Considerable resources have been captured and deployed to support a variety of programs to enhance the growth and development of infants and children suffering from biological or environmental conditions that predispose them to contemporary or future problems. What have been the evolutionary paths which have moved our thinking from a philosophy of predeterminism and the constancy of the IQ to the general acknowledgement of the importance of early experience and the plasticity of the infant and young child?

Early intervention is predicated on the belief that early experience is instrumental in the child's future development. Even theorists who do not view development as a continuous process admit that early experience is important for children (Kagan & Klein, 1973). This view is based on the premise that: Early experience is essential to later development because continuity exists between early behavior and subsequent behavior. It is "as the twig is bent so grows the tree" philosophy. Prior to exploring the historical roots for the importance of early experience, a discussion of the concept of continuity will be useful.

CONTINUITY

As Anne Pick notes:

> We assume and believe that there is continuity of development, but, as both Horowitz and Scott document, our present measures provide meager evidence for our assumptions. Nevertheless, a belief in continuity is the basis for attempting to carry out early assessment for problem remediation and prevention in the first place (Pick, 1978, p. 107).

As indicated in the quote, the notion of continuity is fundamental to prevention and early intervention. Continuity suggests some basic consistency to intellectual and personality variables in the development of the child into an adult. The infant who begins as a placid, easygoing baby is thought to develop most likely into a relaxed adult. It is not uncommon to hear an individual's parents comment that, "John has been that way since he was a baby." So too, we tend to believe, given a normal environment, that the bright, active toddler will grow into a capable, productive adult. Most people seem to hold the belief that there is a strong relationship between personality and intellectual functioning of the child and the type of adult the child becomes. How often when an adult performs some particularly outstanding or bizarre event (e.g., appears to murder without provocation) do we look for the roots of such behavior in the person's early experiences? In fact, Freud's theory of the cause of the adult's maladaptive behavior can be traced to some early traumatic event that the child/adult has repressed. Through psycho-analysis this event is brought into the person's consciousness to be confronted and thus eliminated or put into perspective (Freud, 1978).

The belief in continuity—that is, behavioral repertoires evolve in consistent ways set by the early experiences of the child—underlies the early intervention effort. If infants and young children who are handi-capped or at-risk for developing a problem can be set on a positive devel-opmental path, then the outcome for the child should be enhanced. However, if deviations from normal patterns go unchecked or become too pronounced, then subsequent outcomes are more likely to be negative (e.g., the child remains or becomes maladaptive). Keeping the concept of continuity in mind will help the reader understand the historical and the contemporary view of the impact of early experience. The final section of this chapter presents a reinterpretation of the importance of early experience.

HISTORICAL PERSPECTIVE

Ramey and Baker-Ward (1982) have indicated that since World War II the belief in the primacy of early experience has been the pervasive model for viewing and interpreting normal and atypical development. These writers argue that until recently the early experience model has colored and influenced both "educational practices and social policy" to the exclusion of most other perspectives. How did this occur? To understand, let us look first at the development of the concept of predeterminism.

The concept of predeterminism is based on the belief that develop-ment is genetically determined. Developmental outcomes and rate are seen to be exclusively controlled by maturation. This position became popular in the 1900s and according to Hunt (1961), had its modern roots in the Darwinian theory of natural selection. An early advocate of pre-determinism was Frances Galton, whose writing argued that physical traits and mental abilities are largely inherited. In an edited volume on the topic of individual differences (Jenkins & Peterson, 1961), Galton's article entitled "Classification of Men According to Their Natural Gifts" puts forth the premise that humans come with mental abilities which are normally distributed and which are relatively resistant to training. Some children are born with great gifts, some born with average skills and others, who Galton labeled as "idiots and imbeciles," are born with little ability (1961). This view was consonant with the notion of the constancy of the IQ held by a number of influential educators and psychologists at the turn of the century (Hunt, 1961). These leaders argued that a child's measured IQ, which they believed reflected true mental ability, remained constant over time. Little could be done to modify the child's basic mental capacity and thus the IQ.

A corollary of the position of the heritability of mental abilities is that the environment has little impact on the developing child. Those who believed in predeterminism argued that the infant came genetically well-equipped or poorly equipped, and thus the environment could do little to counter or enhance the youngster's developmental outcome. Interestingly, investigators supporting the predeterminism position during this early period failed to recognize, or perhaps refused to acknowledge, that those children that tended to perform well came from adequate homes while those children who did poorly tended to reside in circumstances of poverty. The view that environmental stimulation produces minimal change provided little hope that intervention during the early years could affect the ultimate path of the child. Action more consistent with the philosophy of predeterminism was to remove individuals with limited capacity from society and provide them with custodial care (Wolfensberger, 1969).

Given the apparent strength of the predeterminism position, what factors were responsible for the development of the position in which the primary determiner of the individual's competence shifted from sole reliance on the genetic contribution to a belief in the primacy of the environment? In approximately four decades, a dramatic change has occurred in the view of environmental influences and the primacy of early experience.

THE PENDULUM SWINGS: MORE CONTEMPORARY VIEWS

A number of factors appear to be responsible for the shifting view of the importance of environmental impact on a child's development and the primacy of early experience. These factors include: (1) environmental influences; (2) psychoanalytical influences; (3) animal research on the impact of early experience; and (4) reanalysis of environmental impact on humans.

Environmental Influences

The philosophy of John Locke is frequently cited as antithetical to the position of predeterminism. Locke believed that all men were free to set their own developmental paths and destinies (Kagan, Kearsely, & Zelazo, 1978). Perhaps because this position is more consonant with many of the ideals reflected in the democratic philosophy of this nation, it gradually increased in popularity. The predominate view became "nurture" over "nature." That is, the child begins as a neutral being and the environment determines the direction and rate of the child's future growth. Thus, the better the child's start during the early years, the greater the probability of future success. Children experiencing poor beginnings might never be able to compensate for lost time or experience. Adoption of such a philosophy provides pervasive support for the impact and importance of early experience.

Psychoanalytical Influences

Based on the work of Freud and others sharing his psychoanalytical orientation, a view that emotional or mental disturbance often had its roots in some traumatic experience of infancy or early childhood evolved. The psychoanalytical perspective has been characterized by Anderson (1963):

1. The child is passive and responds to all the stimulation to which he is exposed without action or selection on his part;

2. The child is so delicate and tender that he must be protected at all costs, and must have exceptional amounts of love, affection, and security;

3. The child carries forward all his memories and experiences to later behavior, and is particularly affected by so-called "traumatic" episodes or single intense experiences (Anderson, 1963, p. 312).

According to Anderson (1963), analytic writings are filled with examples of supposed traumatic events, often sexual in nature, that affect later development. This position presupposes the importance of the child's early environmental experiences. If raised in a loving home, the child would develop into a well-adjusted adult, while children raised in settings where they experienced some intensely unpleasant events are marred for life. For example, the work of Spitz, as reviewed by Hunt (1961), attributes decreases in the developmental quotients of institutionalized infants to the lack of consistent mothering. Depriving these infants of the necessary early emotional relationship with their mothers produces a traumatic reaction that affects all aspects of the infant's development.

The psychoanalytical position can be seen represented in the more contemporary work of Kennell and Klaus. These investigators have assembled findings that they interpret as showing, "the importance of the first few minutes and hours of human maternal-infant contact . . ." (Kennell, Voos, & Klaus, 1979). Mothers who, following birth, were allowed immediate and extended contact with their infants were reported to have developed better bonding with their infants than did mother-infant dyads separated briefly following birth. The underlying premise was that immediate contact permitted mother and infant a positive early experience that set the course for future development. As evidence, Kennell et al., (1979) reported that initial differences between control and experimental dyads were maintained over several years.

The psychoanalytical position has had and continues to have an impact on how the early developmental period is viewed. This position holds that, although the individual's biological proclivities are important, the early experiences of infants and young children are critical to the development of balanced, well-adjusted adults.

Animal Research

A variety of investigations conducted on young animals have also lent support to the view of the primacy of early experience (Denenberg, 1970). Although criticized for the extrapolation from animal to human (see Clarke & Clarke, 1976), a number of writers have employed animal research findings to build a circumstantial case for the importance of early experience for the developing child. For example, when Mason (1970) wrote, "Radical deprivation can thus lead not merely to developmental arrest but to functional disintegration of established systems" (pp. 35-36), he was basing this conclusion on research conducted with animals. The implications of this statement for human infants seemed clear in a climate which emphasized the primacy of early experience.

The effect of social isolation on young animals was illustrated in a series of classic studies conducted by Thompson and Melzack (1956). Scotty puppies were divided into two groups: one group was raised normally in a home setting while the other group was isolated in small cages, one puppy per cage. The isolated puppies never saw their keepers. A series of experiments was conducted with both groups of puppies between the ages of seven and ten months. In every experiment the isolate-reared puppies behaved differently from the home-reared puppies. Thompson and Melzack characterized the isolate-reared puppies as immature, and in situations that required learning or problem solving, their performances were significantly inferior to the home-reared dogs. For example, in learning to avoid a toy mechanical car that delivered a shock when touched, the home-reared puppies learned to avoid the car after receiving an average of six shocks, while it took the isolate-reared puppies an average of twenty-five shocks to learn to avoid the car. Based on their work, Thompson and Melzack's conclusion was "that a rich and stimulating environment in early life is an important condition for normal development. Restriction of experience during this crucial period can result in enduring retardation . . ." (p. 6).

Deprivation studies conducted with other animal species often produced comparable outcomes. Depriving kittens of the opportunity to move freely in the environment results in deficient motor behavior (Held, 1965).[1] The classic work of the Harlows with rhesus monkeys is well known. The Harlows reported that rearing infant monkeys in situations where the mother or peers are unaccessible results in aberrant adolescent and adult animals (Harlow & Harlow, 1966). However, except for the animals that experienced long-term social deprivation (e.g., six to twelve months), placement with other monkeys produce a rehabilitative effect over time. Nonetheless, the Harlows concluded:

> Both normal mothering and normal infant-infant affectional development are extremely important variables in the socialization of rhesus monkeys and presumably of the higher primates (p. 272).

The impact of early environments has also been demonstrated with animals who are provided enriched early experiences. Rats, dogs, cats,

---

[1] Campos, Svejda, Campos, and Bertenthal (1982) report that independent ambulation affects a human infant's perception as well.

and primates raised in enriched environments out perform control animals when confronted with problem-solving tasks. For example, rats exposed to a variety of play things during the early developmental periods are better at running mazes than rats who have not experienced such a variety of objects in their cages. According to Denenberg (1970), basic animal research has demonstrated that, "Stimulation and experiences during early development can have profound and permanent effects upon the behavioral and physiological capabilities of the organism" (p.2).

In 1949, Donald Hebb published a detailed description of his theory on the neuropsychological basis of thought. An important aspect of Hebb's theory was the postulate that the more brain cortex that is used for associative functioning (that is, those responses that are acquired through learning), the more adaptive the animal; that is, the human has a larger associative area than the dog. A second postulate was that the size of the associative area is directly influenced by early experience (Hunt, 1961). According to Hebb, the associative areas are made up of "cell assemblies" that are the primary neurological linkage that permit intelligent behavior. Early sensory experience was thought to be particularly significant for the formation of cell assemblies (Ramey & Baker-Ward, 1982). Thus, Hebb's theory provided a rich and plausible explanation of the effects of early experience on young animals. When young animals or infants are deprived of appropriate environmental stimulation, the organism is unable to develop the necessary underlying neurophysiological basis for maximum adaptive behavior.

Human Research: Reanalysis of Environmental Impact

In 1961, the book *Intelligence and Experience* was published in which Hunt reevaluated and reinterpreted the data on the concept of predeterminism, the constancy of the IQ, and the impact of early experience on the developing child. This reinterpretation focused, in part, on earlier work using animals which had purported to show that experience had little impact on development. Hunt's analysis led him to conclude the opposite. In addition, he reviewed works such as the Kirk (1958) study which involved children. This study examined the impact of early intervention on a group of community-based and institutionalized preschool retarded children. Hunt reported the Kirk findings to be positive both in terms of immediate impact after the conclusion of intervention and upon follow-up. (This conclusion was not shared by everyone; see Clarke and Clarke, 1977.) Such studies taken in concert with other findings, such as those on the relationship between environments and the performance of twins, led Hunt to suggest a reinterpretation of the impact of early experience. This reinterpretation was dramatically different from views held by those who believed that hereditary was the overriding variable in determining a child's outcome.

Other important investigations designed to demonstrate the impact of early experience on the infant and young child were conducted by Wayne Dennis and his colleagues. One of the more pertinent studies involved 174 children whose ages ranged from one to four years and who lived in three Iranian institutions. The children were generally found to be significantly retarded in the onset of motor milestones (Dennis, 1963).

The more impoverished the institution, the greater the children's retardation. Dennis concluded:

> The data here reported also show that behavioral development cannot be fully accounted for in terms of the maturation hypothesis. The important contributions of experience to the development of infant behavior must be acknowledged. (Dennis, 1963, p. 94)

In another intriguing study, Dennis and Dennis (1951) reared two fraternal female twins from the age of two to fourteen months. The experimenters provided all the care and the twins saw no other children and few other adults.[2] The infants were not rewarded or punished for any response nor were they provided any instruction. Finally the environment, although healthy, was relatively sterile. The Dennises took extensive notes and tested the infants periodically. They reported that the twins acquired most of the early motor responses (e.g., smile, vocalizes, reaches, sits) gradually over time; however, many more advanced behaviors such as rolling, kneeling, creeping, and standing were significantly delayed in their onset. In addition, one twin never acquired several important behaviors, such as standing and stepping alone, during the duration of the study. These findings led the Dennises to conclude that many motor responses that develop after the first months require stimulation and practice if such responses are to appear in the infant's repertoire at the expected time.

Another interesting finding which stimulated evaluation of environmental impact on test performance was the study of the army recruits who failed to perform satisfactorily on the Army General Classification Test during World War II. All prospective recruits for military service during World War II were required to take a general intelligence test called the Army General Classification Test. Ginzberg and Bray (1953) found that 716,000 men between the ages of eighteen and thirty-seven years were rejected from the service on the grounds of mental deficiency determined by their test performance (Masland, Sarason, & Galdwin, 1958). This figure was astounding given that these men were not recruited from institutional settings but were presumably functioning appropriately within society. The poor performance of these recruits appeared to reflect, in part, a mismatch between information required to survive in their environment and information requested on a standardized intelligence test.

A forerunner to this important study was conducted by Alper and Boring (1961), who compared intelligence test scores of Northern and Southern whites with those of black recruits in 1918. The findings led Alper and Boring to conclude, "that it is the Negro's educational disadvantage and not actually his color which handicaps him in these tests" (p. 550). Following this same line of inquiry, Masland et al. (1958) reported that the rejection rates for military service were significantly different for varying geographical sections of the country. For example, ninety-seven recruits were rejected per one thousand from the South, while only ten per one thousand were rejected from the West. Such out-

---

[2] Conduct of such a study today would be prohibited by research ethics governed by institutional research boards.

comes convinced Masland et al. (1958) that cultural and educational influences clearly affected the recruits test taking performances.

Regardless of theoretical bent, no responsible investigator has denied that the level and quality of the functioning of the mentally retarded reflects social and cultural factors. What has not been systematically studied is how these kinds of factors operate so as to have an interfering effect on development. The question of the degree of influence of these factors cannot be answered until we understand how and when they exert their influence (Masland et al., 1958, p. 392).

By the late 1950s and early 1960s, the weight of the various pieces of evidence had moved the pendulum from viewing nature as the dominate force to viewing nurture as the deciding factor. The overriding importance of the environment, the reduced influence of hereditary factors, and thus the primacy of early experience became the popular view. These perspectives were responsible for two powerful movements. First, the war on poverty was begun and with it the development of the Head Start programs that were designed to provide children in circumstances of poverty with an enriched environment (Zigler & Cascione, 1977). The second major move was the application of the experimental analysis of behavior to institutionalized populations (Bricker & Bricker, 1975).

PRIMACY OF EARLY EXPERIENCE

During the 1970s, several questions emerged that suggested a reinterpretation of the primacy of early experience was needed. First, a number of investigators had found essentially no correlation between the scores infants attained on intelligence tests before age two years and scores attained in later developmental periods. For a group of 252 children who were tested periodically between twenty-one months and eighteen years, Honzik, MacFarlane and Allen (1963) reported that predictions became increasingly poor as the time interval between tests increased, the correlation between test scores at twenty-one months and eighteen years being .07. The lack of predictive validity between performance on intelligence tests before age two and performance of adolescence called into question the continuity between early and late forms of behavior and further suggested that the infant's early environment, whether adaptive or maladaptive, can be offset by subsequent intervening variables (McCall, 1979; Seifer,& Sameroff, 1982).

The animal and human research that appeared to provide evidence of the impact of early environmental enrichment or deprivation was reexamined. In a number of instances, it was found that what appeared to be permanent effects of early experience could be eliminated with subsequent intervention. As mentioned earlier, many of the monkeys undergoing social deprivation—if the deprivation were not too extreme—came to develop normal adult behaviors when removed from isolation (Novak & Harlow, 1975). In a cross-cultural study, Kagan and Klein (1973) reported that infants raised in a remote Indian village in Guatemala appeared listless, fearful, and quiet. When the performances of such infants were compared to American infants along a number of dimensions, three months' retardation was generally evidenced by the Guatemalan infants. Yet by eleven years of age the children of the village conducted themselves in responsible ways meeting the demands of their society in a competent and acceptable manner. Further, these children were able to perform a number of cognitive tasks in ways similar to patterns shown by middle-class American children. Kagan and Klein concluded:

> If the first environment does not permit the full actualization of psychological competence, the child will function below his ability as long as he remains in that context. But if he is transferred to an environment that presents greater variety and requires more accommodations, he seems more capable of exploiting that experience and repairing the damage wrought by the first environment than some theorists have implied. (1973, p. 960)

Even in situations where great deprivation is experienced, many reports exist that suggest the resiliency of children and the reversibility of early effects. Marie Mason (1963) described the changes she observed in a young child who had been raised in isolation by her handicapped, uneducated mother for six and one-half years. When admitted to the hospital, the child could not talk or walk and had few socialized behaviors. After two years of habilitative efforts, both educational and medical, the child made a "striking social adjustment" and was considered to be of normal intelligence (Mason, 1963). In the Clarke and Clarke book, *Early Experience: Myth and Evidence* (1976), a number of case studies are presented in which children made remarkable recoveries from situations in which they experienced extreme forms of deprivation. Also Dennis and Najarian (1963) found that significant retardation during the first year of life in institutionalized infants did not necessarily predict that these children would perform poorly at age six. These investigators concluded that their findings did not support the "permanency of early environmental effects." The Kauai longitudinal study, which followed a multiracial cohort of children from the prenatal period to adulthood, also contributes support to this argument (Werner, 1986). This important study found that many children exposed to adverse biological and environmental conditions can grow into successfully-coping adults.

A final source of information causing questioning of the primacy of early experience came from early intervention efforts. In some notable cases, the experimental children who participated in early intervention programs did not show performances superior to those of controls (Blatt & Garfunkel, 1969), or initial differences in favor of the experimental children dissipated over time. According to Clarke and Clarke (1977), Kirk's work was one such project in which the initial superior performances of the children attending a preschool program were lost after the control children completed one year of school. The Clarkes contended that the outcome of the Kirk study (1958) accurately predicted the "washout" effects reported for the Head Start programs (Ramey & Baker-Ward, 1982). And thus, for many "experts," the Head Start programs became the target of arguments against short-term and nonecological approaches (e.g., failure to include family members, failure to examine other relevant environmental variables such as living conditions, subsequent school expectations) to the war on poverty

(Bronfenbrenner, 1975). As the evidence accumulates, a growing need for yet another reevaluation of the early experience model seems in order.

A REINTERPRETATION OF EARLY EXPERIENCE AND CONTINUITY

The previous discussion has reflected the shifting views of early experience since the late 1800s. Through the arguments presented in the previous discussion, the reader should have gained a sense of the changing perspectives surrounding early experience. These historical perspectives serve as an important foundation for understanding today's view of early experience held by a number of theoreticians, researchers, and interventionists (see e.g., Ramey & Baker-Ward, 1982; Pick, 1978; McCall, 1979, 1981; Clarke & Clarke, 1976; and Kagan et al., 1978; Brownell & Strauss, 1984; Werner, 1986; Sameroff, Siefer, Barocas, Zax & Greenspan, 1987).

Reading and analyzing contemporary writings on early experience leads to the following conclusions:

1. Early experience is important;

2. Subsequent experience is also important;

3. An enriched early experience does not protect children from subsequent poor environments; and

4. A deprived early environment does not have to doom children to retardation or maladaptive functioning if corrective action is taken (e.g., child's environment changes in positive ways.)

This set of assumptions, if correct, provides early interventionists with a useful model in which early experience is seen as but one link in the chain of growth and development (Brownell & Strauss, 1984). However, given the assurance of a reasonable environment, the better an infant or young child's beginnings, the more likely is future success (Sameroff & Chandler, 1975). This caveat may be particularly pertinent for children who are handicapped for whom a good start may assist in attenuating the impact of the handicapping condition. Parents, early interventionists, program developers, and policy makers should respect the early developmental periods and create effective programs for infants and young children who are handicapped and at-risk. However, we must not forget that our efforts can be eliminated or diminished if subsequent programs fail to measure-up to the quality of the early services.

So what of continuity of behavioral development? Although the concept of continuity appears to have weak empirical support, it is important to recognize that support for discontinuity is based primarily on the inability to make long-term predictions from early to later behavior. In addition, to view development as discontinuous is, as Lewis and Starr (1979) note, unattractive for two reasons. First, the level of analysis may tend to make development appear either to be continuous or discontinuous. To view superficially the evolution of the caterpillar into a butterfly, the impression would be that development is discontinuous. However, studying cellular changes would lead to the conclusion of developmental continuity. The second reasons derives from logic.

"Speaking of a given behavior pattern as being without developmental antecedents gives us little in the way of useful knowledge" (Lewis & Starr, 1979, p. 655). Studying a completely baked cake will provide useful information about its structure and contents, but to fully understand the process it would be important to be aware of the initial ingredients and the composition of the batter prior to the baking. Thus, it seems that in the case of the child there is intuitive logic to the notion that at least some continuity exists over time. But what is the nature of that continuity? What variables affect it? Finally, of what relevancy is continuity for early interventionists?

The relationship between behavioral continuity and early intervention is important. If early behavioral repertoires are directly linked to future motor and conceptual development, logic would argue for the importance of early experience for the child's subsequent development. If, however, behavior is discontinuous, then early experience may be of less importance to the child's future as Clarke and Clarke have suggested (1976). The continuity dilemma hinges, in part, on the length of time one would expect to be able to predict behavioral continuity. Further, it would seem that some amount of the predictability is predicated on the relative continuity of the individual's environment. Even those strongly committed to the continuity position recognize that dramatic changes in an environment would tend to produce significant changes in a child's behavior.

The continuity issue will no doubt remain a controversy for many years; however, for present purposes a reasonable resolution might be to accept the notion of contiguous continuity. That is, the current behavioral repertoire provides the foundation for the development of the next succeeding stage, which, in turn, directly affects the next subsequent stage or level of development. This perspective is not new; see, for example, Honzik et al. (1963). The developmental curves presented in Figure 2-1 illustrate the notion of contiguous continuity.

Curve A represents a normal growth curve in which there is a direct correspondence between mental age and chronological age. The dotted lines indicate the expected convergencies between these two variables. Such a curve permits accurate predictions from adjacent periods (e.g., age one to two years) as well as nonadjacent periods (e.g., age two to twelve years). Curve B illustrates growth that began slightly better than expected then gradually tapered off. Reasonable predictions can be made to adjacent periods (e.g., age one to two *or* six to seven years), but predicting across several periods would not be accurate (e.g., from age two to six *or* age three to twelve years). Curve B might represent the growth reported for many Down syndrome children whose behavior moves further from the norm as they grow older (see Ludlow & Allen, 1979). Curve C again demonstrates the possibility of correctly predicting from adjacent periods but the inability to make accurate predictions across nonadjacent periods.

The knowledge that prediction diminishes over time, especially for young children, is certainly not new (see e.g., McCall, 1979). However, little apparent thought has been given to the relationship between longevity of program impact and the diminishing capability to predict

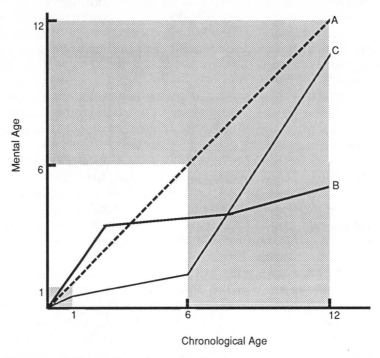

FIGURE 2-1. Hypothetical growth curves.

later development from earlier performance. Recognition of the number of variables that may affect children's development should lead to great caution in predicting future performances or the longevity of a program's impact.

While attempting to predict long-term effects is difficult, demonstrating the immediate impact of the child's current behavioral repertoire on the acquisition of subsequent new response forms is clear. Therefore, it is more sensible to demonstrate successive impact over time rather than attempting to predict much later behavior based on the preschool years. It seems rather remarkable that investigations have been able to report long-term effects such as those described by Lazar, Darlington, Murray, Royce, and Snipper (1982), and Gurnalnick and Bricker (1987). However, these global outcomes suggest the importance of attempting to study the environments of children to determine what aspects have maintained the original gain or what changes have occurred to reduce or dilute the initial experimental and control differences.

The collection of such information will no doubt reflect the interactive nature of development, as has been proposed by a number of major theorists (Piaget, 1970; Uzgiris, 1981; Sameroff & Chandler, 1975; Lewis & Rosenblum, 1974; Werner, 1986). Development is systematically shaped by the transactions between the organism and the environment. An intricate web of reciprocal transactions occurs that leads to the transformation of the child's behavioral repertoire. Unless the child's biology and environment remain relatively constant, one would be correct to predict variable outcomes for individual children. When investigations report that experimental groups maintain their superiority over time, one might speculate that the early intervention has affected not only the child but also influenced other important environmental factors as well (e.g., the parent).

What then is a reasonable expectation for program impact? A simple answer seems unlikely. Rather, program impact is most likely determined by a number of variables. The length, quality, and content of an early intervention effort will doubtlessly affect the longevity of the impact. The Early Training Project developed by Gray and Klaus (Gray, Ramsey, & Klaus, 1982) documented the change of the experimental and control children enrolled in this project over a period of eighteen years in tandem with attempting to examine changes in the environments of the children and their families. The outcomes of this investigation accurately reflect the issues raised in the preceding discussion. That is, one cannot reasonably hope to evaluate the long-term impact of early intervention efforts in a vacuum. Rather, the continuity or discontinuity of development mirrors environmental change. Early intervention programs cannot protect children who are at-risk or handicapped from the future. Such programs may be able to enhance the child's development, but these enhancements are surely not automatically retained. Rather, children's progress will depend upon their current repertoire and the transactions that occur with subsequent environments.

SUMMARY

Early experience is important, but to leave that statement unqualified leads to the somewhat misleading conclusion of the primacy of early development. There is ample evidence that even children who experience seriously neglecting and abusive environments can recover normal functions when placed in a positive and supportive environment. However, it is not clear how well these children may have developed if they had not experienced such negative early environments. These children may have recovered because of particularly powerful innate endowments, and had they been placed in a reasonable early environment, they might have developed outstanding capabilities. We simply do not know.

Although children with apparent normal capabilities can compensate for early deprivation, it is less clear how adverse environments affect children who are handicapped. As a group, infants and young children who are handicapped by definition have fewer resources with which to compensate for poor environmental input. It may be appropriate to assume that neglecting and abusive parents may have a greater and more enduring impact on children who are handicapped. Children who begin with a disadvantage, whether physical, sensory or intellectual, are less well equipped to compensate for yet further deficits produced by uncaring or ill-informed adults.

Until the field of early intervention is able to generate more definitive findings on the impact of early environments for infants and young children who are at-risk and handicapped, it seems wise to assume that quality early intervention is necessary to assist these children in the acquisition of adaptive responses that lead to independent functioning. Further, there appears to be a direct relationship between behavioral repertoires sampled at adjacent periods that provides support to the concept of contiguous continuity. These beliefs form a basis for intervening early and continuing some form of intervention until the child provides clear evidence of being able to cope effectively with environmental demands without special support.

References

Alper, T., & Boring, E. (1961). Intelligence-test scores of northern and southern White and Negro recruits in 1918. In J. Jenkins & D. Paterson (Eds.), *Studies in individual differences*. New York: Appleton-Century-Crofts.

Anderson, J. (1963). Personality organization in children. In W. Dennis (Ed.), *Readings in child psychology* (2nd ed.). Englewood Cliffs, NJ: Prentice-Hall.

Blatt, B., & Garfunkel, F. (1969). *The educability of intelligence*. Washington, D.C.: The Council for Exceptional Children.

Bricker, W., & Bricker, D. (1975). Mental retardation and complex human behavior. In J. Kauffman & J. Payne (Eds.), *Mental retardation: Introduction and personal perspectives*. Columbus, OH: Charles E. Merrill.

Brownell, C., & Strauss, M. (1984). Infant stimulation and development: Conceptual and empirical considerations. In M. Frank (Ed.), *Infant intervention programs: Truths and untruths*. New York: The Haworth Press.

Bronfenbrenner, U. (1975). Is early intervention effective? In B. Friedlander, G. Sterritt, & G. Kirk (Eds.), *Exceptional infant: Assessment and intervention* (Vol. III). New York: Brunner/Mazel.

Campos, J., Svejda, M., Campos, R., & Bertenthal, B. (1982). The emergence of self-produced locomotion: Its importance for psychological development. In D. Bricker (Ed.), *Intervention with at-risk and handicapped infants*. Baltimore, MD: University Park Press.

Clarke, A., & Clarke, A. (1976). *Early experience*: Myth and evidence. New York: The Free Press.

Clarke, A., & Clarke, A. (1977). Prospects for prevention and amelioration of mental retardation: A guest editorial. *American Journal of Mental Deficiency, 81*, 523-533.

Denenberg, V. (1970). Introduction. In V. Denenberg (Ed.), *Education of the infant and young child*. New York: Academic Press.

Dennis, W. (1963). Environmental influences upon motor development. In W. Dennis (Ed.), *Readings in child psychology* (2nd ed.). Englewood Cliffs, NJ: Prentice-Hall.

Dennis, W., & Dennis, M. (1951). Development under controlled environmental conditions. In W. Dennis (Ed.), *Readings in child psychology* (2nd ed.). New York: Prentice-Hall.

Dennis, W., & Najarian, P. (1963). Development under environmental handicap. In W. Dennis (Ed.), *Readings in child psychology* (2nd ed.). Englewood Cliffs, NJ: Prentice-Hall.

Freud, S. (1978). The origins and development of psychoanalysis. In R. Corsiri (Ed.), *Readings in current personality theory.* Itasca, IL.: Peacock Publishers.

Galton, F. (1961). Classification of men according to their natural gifts. In J. Jenkins & D. Peterson (Eds.), *Studies in individual differences.* New York: Appleton-Century-Crofts.

Ginzberg, A., & Bray, D. (1953). *The uneducated.* New York: Columbia University Press.

Gray, S., Ramsey, B., & Klaus, R. (1982). *From 3 to 20: The early training project.* Baltimore, MD: University Park Press.

Guralnick, M., & Bricker, D. (1987). The effectiveness of early intervention for children with cognitive and general developmental delays. In M. Gurnalnick & F. Bennett, (Eds.), *The effectiveness of early intervention for at-risk and handicapped children.* New York: Academic Press.

Harlow, H., & Harlow, M. (1966). *Learning to love.* American Scientist, 54, 244-272.

Hebb, D. (1949). *The organization of behavior: A neuropsychological theory.* New York: Wiley & Sons.

Held, R. (1965). Plasticity in sensory-motor systems. *Scientific American, 213,* 84-94.

Honzik, M., MacFarlane, J., & Allen, L. (1963). The stability of mental test performance. In W. Dennis (Ed.), *Readings in child psychology* (2nd ed.). Englewood Cliffs, NJ: Prentice-Hall.

Hunt, J. McV. (1961). *Intelligence and experience.* New York: Ronald Press.

Kagan, J., Kearsley, R., & Zelazo, P. (1978). *Infancy: Its place in human development.* Cambridge, MA: Harvard University Press.

Kagan, J., & Klein, R. (1973). Cross-cultural perspectives on early development. *American Psychologists, 28,* 947-961.

Kennell, J., Voos, D., & Klaus, M. (1979). Parent-infant bonding. In J. Osofsky (Ed.), *Handbook of infant development.* New York: John Wiley.

Kirk, S. (1958). *Early education of the mentally retarded.* Urbana, IL: University of Illinois Press.

Lazar, I., Darlington, R., Murray, H., Royce, J., & Snipper, A. (1982). Lasting effects of early education: A report from the consortium for longitudinal studies. *Monographs of the Society for Research in Child Development, 47* (Serial No. 195).

Lewis, M., & Rosenblum, L. (1974). *The effect of the infant on the caregiver.* New York: Wiley & Sons.

Lewis, M., & Starr, M. (1979). Developmental continuity. In J. Osofsky (Ed.), *Handbook of Infant Development.* New York: John Wiley.

Ludlow, J., & Allen, L. (1979). The effect of early intervention and preschool stimulus on the development of the Down's syndrome child. *Journal of Mental Deficiency Research, 23,* 29-44.

Masland, R., Sarason, S., & Gladwin, T. (1958). *Mental subnormality.* New York: Basic Books.

Mason, M. (1963). Learning to speak after years of silence. In W. Dennis (Ed.), *Readings in child psychology* (2nd ed.). Englewood Cliffs, NJ: Prentice-Hall.

Mason, W. (1970). Early deprivation in biological perspectives. In V. Denenberg (Ed.), *Education of the infant and young child.* New York: Academic Press.

McCall, R. (1979). The development of intellectual functioning in infancy and the prediction of later IQ. In J. Osofsky (Ed.), *Handbook of infant development.* New York: Wiley & Sons.

McCall, R. (1981). Nature-nurture and the two realms of development: A proposed integration with respect to mental development. *Child Development, 52*(1), 1-12.

Novak, M., & Harlow, H. (1975). Social recovery of monkeys isolated for the first year of life. *Developmental Psychology, 11,* 453-465.

Piaget, J. (1970). Piaget's theory. In P. Mussen (Ed.), *Carmichael's manual of child psychology* (Vol. I). New York: Wiley & Sons.

Pick, A. (1978). Discussion summary: Early assessment. In F. Minifie & L. Lloyd (Eds.), *Communicative and cognitive abilities: Early behavioral assessment.* Baltimore, MD: University Park Press.

Ramey, C., & Baker-Ward, L. (1982). Psychosocial retardation and the early experience paradigm. In D. Bricker (Ed.), *Intervention with at-risk and handicapped infants: From research to application.* Baltimore, MD: University Park Press.

Sameroff, A., & Chandler, M. (1975). Reproductive risk and the continuum of caretaking casualty. In F. Horowitz, M. Hetherington, S. Scarr-Salapatek, & G. Siegel (Eds.), *Review of child development research* (Vol. 4). Chicago: University of Chicago Press.

Sameroff, A., Seifer, R., Barocas, R., Zax, M., & Greenspan, S. (1987). Intelligence quotient scores of 4-year-old children: Social-environmental risk factors. *Pediatrics, 79*(3), 343-350.

Seifer, R., & Sameroff, A. (1982). A structural equation model analysis of competence in children at risk for mental disorder. *Prevention in Human Services, 1,* 85-96.

Thompson, W., & Melzack, R. (1956, January). Early environment. *Scientific American* (reprint) 1-6.

Uzgiris, I. (1981). Experience in the social context. In R. Schiefelbusch & D. Bricker (Eds.), *Early language: Acquisition and intervention.* Baltimore, MD: University Park Press.

Werner, E. (1986). A longitudinal study of perinatal risk. In D. Farran & J. McKinney (Eds.), *Risk in intellectual and psychosocial development.* New York: Academic Press.

Wolfensberger, W. (1969). The origin and nature of our institutional models. In R. Kugel & W. Wolfensberger (Eds.), *Changing patterns in residential services for the mentally retarded.* President's Committee on Mental Retardation, Washington, D.C.

Zigler, E., & Cascione, R. (1977). Head Start has little to do with mental retardation: A reply to Clarke and Clarke. *American Journal of Mental Deficiency, 82,* 246-249.

3.
History and Rationale for Early Intervention Programs

In this chapter three major areas are addressed: (1) the historical development of early intervention programs for children who are environmentally at-risk, biologically at-risk and handicapped; (2) a rationale for the provision of early intervention programs for at-risk and handicapped populations; and (3) the philosophy that provides the foundation for the intervention procedures described subsequently in this book.

A BRIEF HISTORY OF PROGRAM DEVELOPMENT

Programs for the child who is handicapped appear to have evolved, in part, from a more general set of programs for young children who suffered primarily from conditions stemming from poverty. When preschool programs were initiated in the late 1800s, the primary strategy for dealing with children who were handicapped was institutionalization in a large residential facility often located in remote rural areas (Wolfensberger, 1969). The historical philosophy and concern that led to the development of programs for young children is important to appreciate because a similar philosophy and concern seems to continue to undergird the expansion of social and educational services for the youth of this country today (for a detailed review of early treatment of the handicapped, see Hewett & Forness, 1977). An appreciation of the evolution of services for the young children of this nation assists in understanding current legal mandates, such as P.L. 94-142 and P.L. 99-457, that exist in the United States. Examining the historical context should help convince the reader that such legal and legislative precedents are based on a firm commitment to assist those who, through poverty or organic defects, need protection and additional support to ensure equal access to societal benefits.

According to Lazerson (1972), the historical roots of early childhood education in this country are intertwined with three major themes. The first is that early schooling can be instrumental in social change. Thus, much of the historical and current emphasis in education has been focused on social reform for the poor. Second is that the early developmental period is unique and important. Third is that early childhood programs have been viewed by some as a means to reform rigid and narrow educational approaches often found in the public schools.

A philosophical basis for the importance of the early childhood period existed before the 1900s; however, the actual catalyst for the development of early educational programs appears to have been the concern for children growing up in the squalid conditions of poverty. According to Maxim (1980), important educational reforms for young children were stimulated by a number of concerned individuals living in different countries. For example, programs for young children living in poverty were initiated in the late 1800s-early 1900s by Robert Owen in Scotland, Friedrich Frobel in Germany, Margaret McMillan in England and Montessori in Italy and appear to have borne some interesting similarities. Owen, McMillan and Montessori, in particular, began programs because of their concern for the health and abuse of young children living in poverty. These programs were developed to offer poor children the opportunity to thrive physically and intellectually.

Inspired in particular by the work of Frobel, kindergarten programs were introduced in the United States in the mid-1800s, and by 1900, public school kindergartens were well established (Maxim, 1980). In Lazerson's view (1972), the growth of kindergarten programs in this country was intimately tied to social reform. That is, workers such as Jane Addams, Robert Woods, and Kate Wiggin saw the need to assist city children who were growing up in conditions of extreme poverty. An underlying philosophy appeared to be that to develop a sense of middle class values, the child of poverty must be apprehended and educated early. A second goal of these initial kindergarten programs was to influence the family life of slum dwellers through education of the parent (Lazerson, 1972), a theme that gained support once again in the 1960s.

Although the nursery school movement in this country also had European roots and its development was subject to many of the same forces, nursery school programs developed separately from the kindergarten movement (Maxim, 1980). As with kindergartens, nursery schools were originally developed to serve children living in poverty. During the 1920s, few nursery school programs were available, but following the Great Depression, a significant growth in programs occurred largely because of support from the federal government to create jobs. The operation of nursery schools provided jobs for unemployed teachers and also provided facilities where working mothers could leave their children. Day care was also begun so women could join the work force and later to permit welfare recipients to return to work (Belsky, Steinberg & Walker, 1982).

Following on the heels of the Great Depression came World War II, which produced a need for child-care facilities so women could join the war effort. However, these day-care programs were custodial in the sense that little attention was given to the children's educational needs (Maxim, 1980). After the war, federal support for day care was discontinued, while support for programs from private agencies began to grow. This shift meant that many of the programs for young children began serving privileged rather than underprivileged children. During the postwar era, little was done in the way of program development for poor or young children who were handicapped.

In the 1960s, two important moves began: a new view of young children and a renewed attack to direct the impact of poverty on young children. A burgeoning area of research on infants and young children began to suggest that the young human was a more capable learner than was generally believed. Researchers began to report that infants could perform sophisticated discrimination and memory feats (see Schaffer, 1977). Such data provided strong support for the view that learning could begin early in the child's life. Further, in 1964 Bloom published his influential work that indicated much of the child's cognitive growth occurred during the first four years of life. Of course, many authorities question the validity of this position today.

Paralleling these findings, a number of writers were beginning to argue in favor of the plasticity of a child's intellectual growth and the enormous impact of the environment on the child (Hunt, 1961). In addition, influential work by Bowlby (1973) and Spitz (1946) pointed to the catastrophic effects of placing infants in nonstimulating environments, which added fuel to the argument of the importance of early experience and the long-term impact of early environments.[1] These two positions— the ability of the young child to learn and the impact of the environment—along with political motivation provided the foundation for the development of a massive social program labeled "The War on Poverty," which was designed to salvage the young child being raised in poverty (Beller, 1979).

Precursors to Contemporary Programs

Wayne Dennis (1976) and his colleagues were able to observe the effects of what he termed a "natural experiment." Before 1956, a Lebanese social agency called the Creche had kept foundling children assigned to their care from birth to 16 years. A new policy, which required placement of foundlings in adoptive homes within a few years (preferable before two), was instituted. A comparison of children who had remained in the Creche for an extended period with those that were placed in adoptive homes before age two was made:

> It was found that, as a group, children adopted from the Creche within the first two years of life overcame their initial retardation and soon reached a mean I.Q. of approximately 100, which was maintained (p. 123).

However, children adopted after the age of two did not overcome this preadoption retardation. Further, Dennis's findings indicated the longer the child remained in the institutional environment, the greater the retardation.

A similar and more widely known study conducted by Skeels and his colleagues reported findings similar to those of Dennis. This longitudinal study focused on two groups of infants who grew up in extremely different environments. Initially, both groups of infants were residents of an orphanage, and their generally functioning was in the retarded or low-normal range (Skeels, 1966).

Thirteen of these infants were placed in an institution for the retarded as "house guests" of a group of retarded females and the ward staff. These 13 children came to constitute the experimental group who, because of marked improvement, were placed in adoptive homes. The

---

[1] As discussed in Chapter 2, not until sometime later was the impact of early experience placed in perspective to the child's longitudinal growth.

contrast group was composed of those children who remained wards of the state and resided in an institutional environment. The initial differences reported between the experimental and control groups were subject to violent attack by a number of prominent psychologists (see Goodenough & Maurer, 1961). These critics were inclined to defend the relative constancy of the IQ and asserted "that the differential patterns of gains and losses upon retest shown by children whose initial IQ's fell at the extremes of the distribution is a statistical rather than an educational phenomenon" (Goodenough & Maurer, 1961). After a considerable hiatus, Skeels and his co-workers began to track the progress of the experimental and contrast groups (Kirk, 1977). In a thirty-year follow-up study Skeels (1966) reported:

> All 13 children in the experimental group were self supporting and none was a ward of an institution, public or private. In the contrast group of 12 children, one had died in adolescence following continued residence in a state institution for the mentally retarded, and four were still wards of institutions, one in a mental hospital, and the other three in institutions for the mentally retarded. In education, the disparity between the two groups was striking. The contrast group completed a median of less than the third grade. The experimental group completed a median of the 12th grade (p. 55).

The early work of Dennis, Skeels, and their colleagues has had a significant impact on the field of early intervention. These "natural" experiments suggested two important possibilities. First, that young children's growth and development is dependent, in part, upon their early environment thus making the context and arrangement of events of importance during the formative years. Second, that early repertoires are susceptible to changing environmental conditions that can eliminate early deficiencies or deficits.

Children who have problems or the strong potential for developing problems can be conveniently divided into three groups: those who are at-risk for environmental reasons, those who are at-risk for biological reasons, and those who are handicapped. Contemporary programs for these three groups have evolved from different philosophies and consequently can be usefully separated in terms of their recent program development. The separation of children into these different programs serves us well in terms of discussion, but it should be remembered that many infants or children can be appropriately classified into more than one of these categories. For example, the premature infant from a low-income family is often biologically and environmentally at-risk.

Programs for Environmentally At-Risk Children

Without doubt the major early intervention effort in this country for the environmentally at-risk child has been Head Start; yet according to Zigler and Cascione (1977), "Since its inception, Head Start has been a program shrouded in confusion and misunderstanding" (p. 248). Thus, it may be useful to review the goals of this important social-educational program for young children. In 1964, President Johnson's administration created the Office of Economic Opportunity. A major program developed by this federal agency was Operation Head Start. Head Start funds were deployed to local community action groups throughout the country to develop preschool programs for children living in poverty, and the specific goals included the following:

1. Improve the child's physical health and physical abilities.

2. Help the emotional and social development of the child by encouraging self-confidence, spontaneity, curiosity, and self-discipline.

3. Improve the child's mental processes and skills with particular attention to conceptual and verbal skills.

4. Establish patterns of expectations of success for the child which will create a climate of confidence for his future learning efforts (Maxim, 1980 p. 22).

Summarily, Zigler and Cascione (1977) emphasized that the goal of the Head Start programs "should be the enhancement of the participants' social competence . . ."

Not only have the goals of Head Start been poorly understood but the outcomes or impact of this massive federal program have been hotly debated (see e.g., Clarke & Clarke, 1977; Zigler & Cascione, 1977; Cicerelli, Evans, & Schiller, 1969; Peters & Deiner, 1987). A source of this conflict must be, in part, the variety of programs subsumed by the Head Start umbrella. Approaches vary in terms of curricular focus, staffing patterns, structure, and service delivery models. Attempting to arrive at some meaningful consensus given such variety of programs is probably not realistic. It is rather more likely that some Head Start programs are effective in meeting the established goals while others are not.

In 1972, the Head Start legislation was amended to ensure that 10 percent of the Head Start enrollment be handicapped (Ackerman & Moore, 1976). This legislative change has created an exceptional opportunity for many children with handicaps to participate in mainstreamed programs during their preschool years. In 1973, it was reported that the Head Start programs served approximately 30,000 children who were handicapped. By 1984, 99 percent of all Head Start programs had enrolled at least one child with handicaps, and by 1985, approximately 62,000 children with handicaps were being served each year (Peters & Deiner 1987).

Studies investigating the impact of early intervention programs have produced mixed results. For example, the results of a study undertaken approximately at the same time the Head Start program was initiated were published in 1969 by Blatt and Garfunkel. A group of fifty-nine preschool-age children from low-income homes were randomly assigned to experimental and nonexperimental groups. The experimental group attended a structured intervention program, while the nonexperimental group did not. Extensive evaluation of the children's performances found that:

Disadvantaged children are influenced more by the home setting than by the external manipulation of their school environment. In light of what we believe to have been the face validity of an enriched preschool program, the inability of this program to produce measurable differences between experimental and nonexperimental children causes us to suggest that it is not enough to provide preschool disadvantaged children with an enriched educational opportunity. (Blatt & Garfunkel, 1969, p. 119-120)

This conclusion suggests that other factors present in children's homes can outweigh the impact of even sound school-based intervention. More attention to elements within the home environment appear essential to ensure maximum impact of early intervention.

A number of other early intervention efforts developed during the early phases of Head Start report more positive outcomes than Blatt and Garfunkel (1969). For example, Gray and Klaus's (1976) Early Training Project reported a seven year follow-up of eighty-eight black children from low-income homes in rural Tennessee. These children were assigned to two experimental groups that differed in length of intervention. In addition, there were local and distal control groups who received no intervention. Comparisons of performances for these four groups are reported for 1962 to 1968 when these children completed the fourth grade. In Gray and Klaus's words:

Intervention caused a rise in intelligence which was fairly sharp at first, then leveled off, and finally began to show decline once intervention ceased. The control groups on the other hand tended to show a slight but consistent decline with the single exception of a jump between entrance into public school and the end of first grade.

As noted by Gray and Klaus, the remarkable feature of the project may be the sustaining impact on the experimental children over a considerable time period given the relative brevity of early intervention, rather than the fact that the differences between experimental and control children diminished over time. A subsequent follow-up of this project has been published (Gray, Ramsey & Klaus, 1982).

The results reported from this seventeen-year follow-up are complicated and difficult to summarize. Gray et al. (1982) report that initial differences between experimental and control groups on school performance measures did not maintain over time, but some other differences were retained (e.g., better social adjustment). Although these data may appear to indicate lack of success of the early intervention efforts, Gray et al. (1982) take an alternative position. They argue that any difference that can be retained for such extended time periods reflects the potential powerful effect of early experiences.

Undoubtedly the most impressive contemporary longitudinal study of children from low-income environments is the consortium effort coordinated by Irving Lazar. "In 1976, 12 investigators who had independently designed and implemented infant and preschool programs in the 1960's pooled their original data and conducted a collaborative follow-up of the original subjects . . ." (Lazar, Darlington, Murray, Royce & Snipper, 1982). This collaborative effort permitted assessment of program effects across a number of projects and follow-up of a substantial group of children through high school. The population enrolled in these twelve projects were infants and young children from low-income homes. The individual projects varied in philosophy and approach; however, adequate similarity existed to permit pooling the findings on four dependent variables: school competence, developed abilities (as measured by achievement and intelligence tests), children's attitudes, and impact on family.

A monograph (Lazar et al., 1982) describes the procedures, analysis and results in detail;[2] only the primary outcomes will be highlighted here. The most salient outcome was that significantly fewer children who participated in preschool programs were assigned to special education classes and retained in a grade than children who did not participate in preschool programs. Other findings are less supportive of program impact except that mothers of experimental children were more satisfied with their children's school performance and had higher expectations for the children than mothers of control children.

An extensive review of seventeen early intervention programs designed for environmentally at-risk children conducted by Bryant and Ramey (1987), reinforces earlier interpretations of program impact.

> . . . intellectual benefits can be derived by children when compensatory education is begun at various points during the preschool years. Although the data are not perfectly clear on this issue, it appears that significant benefits can be obtained whether programs are begun in infancy, early childhood, or during the preschool years (p. 71).

Summary

The past intervention work that has been conducted with environmentally at-risk populations is encouraging and discouraging. If society is willing to make the economic investment in what Bronfenbrenner (1975) and others have termed long-term ecological intervention, then the results of studies by Lazar et al. (1982) and others suggest that the majority of young children in poverty can be given the necessary boost to function well within the public schools and subsequently as productive, contributing citizens. Without comprehensive intervention efforts that include the family, outcomes appear considerably less optimistic.

Programs for Biologically At-Risk Children

Infants and children assigned to the category of biologically at-risk can display a broad range of problems that develop during the prenatal, perinatal, or neonatal periods. These problems can stem from a variety of causes (e.g., genetic, trauma, infection, prematurity), can be manifest in numerous ways, and can impact the infant's respiratory system, size, weight, or tone (Werthmann, 1981). However, the condition most often associated with biologically at-risk infants is a preterm birth; a shortened gestation period usually associated with a low birth weight. The more premature the infant, the lower the birth weight and increased frequency of other associated problems (Bennett, 1987).

As medical science becomes more sophisticated, smaller and sicker infants are surviving, creating other dilemmas such as deciding upon

---

[2] This monograph is highly recommended to those readers interested in an in-depth description of the consortium activities. A recent comprehensive description of another consortium project is provided by Karnes et al. (1981) as well. This report is particularly relevant because the intervention group contained handicapped children. Beller (1979) also presents a comprehensive review of programs for environmentally at-risk children.

optimal care for these often tiny, fragile newborns. As Kopp (1983) points out, the infant mortality rate has dropped dramatically during the past 100 years, and yet the World Health Organization reported that in 1984, the infant morality rate for the United States was 10.6, which is higher than many European countries (Miller, 1987).

Initially, early care of the biologically or medically at-risk infant (most often the preterm infant) was provided by obstetricians. Gradually, care for the preterm and sick infant was shifted to the new speciality area of pediatrics. Today, care of the biologically at-risk infant is primarily handled by neonatologists who are trained specifically to care for distressed newborns. Most major medical facilities have neonatal intensive care units (NICU), which are designed to provide special medical care and contain sophisticated equipment to monitor and maintain distressed newborns. NICUs are generally staffed with a cadre of neonatologists and specially trained nurses. Hospitals that do not have NICUs refer newborns with serious problems to a metropolitan or regional medical facility that has an NICU.

With the advent of NICUs and increased medical knowledge which permits successful handling of smaller and sicker newborns, two issues have taken on growing attention. The first issue concerns the ethics involved in the saving and maintenance of newborns who are severely damaged, and the second issue concerns the type of care or stimulation that will maximize biological or psychological growth in the biologically at-risk infant.

The first issue requires serious consideration by medical and educational personnel as well as by society in general (Lyons, 1985). At least two factors need to be confronted. First, what is the quality of life for those infants saved through heroic efforts of the medical community? Second, what is the cost of such care? The future quality of life is currently difficult to predict. In many cases there appears to be little relationship between the state of the infant during the early months and subsequent developmental outcomes. As Sigman, Cohen and Forsythe (1981) note, the "prediction from early medical complications to later mental performance is poor" (p. 313). As these investigators suggest, the great plasticity in the early stages of development taken in conjunction with the significant impact possible from the caregiving environment can lead to considerable fluidity in the subsequent repertoires displayed by biologically at-risk infants. Thus, we are currently in a poor position to make sound judgements about the developmental outcomes of biologically at-risk infants.

The cost of care and of increasing survival rate of the biologically at-risk infant is a growing concern. A report published by the U.S. Congress's Office of Technology Assessment (Budetti, Barrand, McManus, & Heinen, 1981) found that in 1978 the cost ranged from $1800.00 to $40,000.00 per patient. An analysis examining cost by birthweight indicated that the average cost for infants less than one thousand grams (under 3 pounds) was $22,508.00, and the cost per survivor was $46,340.00. As the weight increases, the cost decreases. As significant as these costs appear, they do not reflect the cost of similar care in an NICU today.   More infants are being saved, but the cost is reaching astronomical proportions.

The second major issue that has been raised by increasing the survival rate of the biologically at-risk infant concerns the form of care or stimulation provided the infant once the baby's medical status becomes stable.   During the 1960s and 1970s, a variety of intervention strategies were undertaken.   Cornell and Gottfried (1976) have classified these as two basic types.   One strategy entailed designing interventions to make up for presumed sensory deficits; for example, providing additional auditory stimulation (e.g., heart beat) or movement (e.g., rocking).   The other strategy was to provide the preterm infant with "extraordinary" stimulation; for example, extra handling, talking, and auditory or visual stimulation.   In an analysis of the impact of these various intervention strategies on the biologically at-risk infant, Cornell and Gottfried (1976) concluded: "In summary, the most pervasive trend involves what may be generally described as motor development.   The performance of stimulated or experimental-group infants tended to exceed that of control-group infants on measures of sensorimotor and motor skills, as well as muscle tones" (p. 37).   However, these authors caution drawing generalizations because of the diversity of the populations, treatments, and measures employed in the investigations.

From the original work that focused on stimulation of the preterm or at-risk infant evolved a perspective which changed the focus from the infant to the infant-caregiver relationship (Barnard, 1976), or what many writers refer to as bonding and attachment.   As researchers studied the interactions that occurred between caregivers (primarily mothers) and their infants, it became clear that caregivers are the primary presenters and interpreters of environmental input to their young infants.   As the importance of the early environment provided by the caregiver became increasingly clear to researchers and practitioners, programs to encourage and enhance the attachment of the parent to the infant increased (Barnard, 1976).

Much of the underlying rationale for the increased attention to attachment and bonding was stimulated by the work of Klaus and Kennell and their colleagues (1976).   These investigators argued that shortly after birth there was a critical and hightened period for establishing maternal attachment.   Delivering a preterm or sick infant who was subsequently removed to an NICU separated mother and infant during this period, thus affecting maternal-infant bonding.   Many intervention programs conducted in NICUs attempted to attenuate the disruption by encouraging parents to be present as often as possible and to assist in the care of the infant; thus affecting maternal and infant bonding less significantly.   Studies of early maternal-infant separation have generally not focused on the possible negative or long-term impact on maternal-child relationships (Kopp, 1983).   This is not to indicate, as Ramey, Zeskind, and Hunter (1981) remark, that having a premature or sick infant is not a significant event; rather, it suggests that when separation occurs the outcomes are not uniformly predictable.

Influenced in large part by the maternal-bonding research, a number of investigators became interested in studying caregiver-infant interactions. Models were proffered that attempted to better explain outcomes of the at-risk population. In particular, the transactional model described by Sameroff and Chandler (1975) has received considerable attention. Based on transactional or interactional theory, a series of studies were conducted that attempted to examine mother-infant interaction of term and preterm and/or sick infants (Kopp, 1983, reviews a number of these investigations). In particular, investigators compared the behavior of at-risk infant-mother dyads with "normal" infant-mother dyads to isolate differences in the interactional patterns, as well as to look at selected factors (e.g., amount of maternal verbal responding) as predictor variables. As Kopp (1983) notes, "difference between term and pre-terms emerged but many of the differences were of low magnitude and some could have been accounted for by other variables" (p. 105).

A number of longitudinal studies of at-risk infants (primarily preterms) have been conducted. Four of the more ambitious are the San Francisco study (Hunt, 1981), Springfield study (Field, Dempsey, & Shuman, 1981), Staten Island study (Caputo, Goldstein, & Taub, 1981) and Los Angeles study (Sigman, Cohen, & Forsythe, 1981). These outcomes were analyzed by Sameroff (1981) who reported that in three of these four longitudinal studies "The single most potent factor influencing developmental outcome turns out to be the cultural environment of the child, as expressed in socioeconomic status and parental educational level" (p. 392). Further, Sameroff notes that "No single factor, either birth weight alone or accompanying physical problems, clearly predict a specific developmental outcome" (p. 392).

Nonetheless, when taking preterm infants or infants having other conditions placing them at-risk as a group, the outcomes are less positive than for well, term infants. This finding has served as a basic rationale for continuing to develop early intervention programs for the at-risk infant both during their stay in the NICU and after discharge (Field, 1983).

In spite of our inability to predict which at-risk infants will thrive and those that will not and the equivocal outcomes of intervention efforts (Cornell & Gottfried, 1976; Kopp, 1983; Gibson & Fields, 1984), a number of researchers and clinicians see value in offering early intervention programs to infants at-risk. Taft (1981) indicates two reasons he favors intervention programs: First, the considerable plasticity of the nervous system during the early developmental periods and, second, many of the positive outcomes of intervention have not yet been measured (e.g., family comfort and satisfaction with the child).

Contemporary intervention approaches for at-risk infants are designed to be conducted in the NICU, after discharge of the infant, or both. Current NICU intervention programs differ in target populations, period of intervention, staffing, service delivery systems, and intervention goals (Sweet, 1982).

Most NICUs have established criteria for determining the population to be served or for isolating selected subgroups of infants (e.g., those at extreme risk). Programs also vary in when or how long they intervene with the target population. Some states, such as Florida and California, provide developmental assessment during the first year for infants meeting certain risk criteria (Sweet, 1982).

Some intervention programs are conducted by the nursing staff, some by social workers, and some by specially trained educators (Cole & Gilkerson, 1982). Those conducted in the NICU are largely in the form of assisting the parent, when possible, to provide the infant with appropriate stimulation. In addition, support groups for parents are often available. Once the infant is discharged, the program may provide home visitation, a center where the family can bring the infant, or both. These programs generally assist parents in coping with infants, many of whom may be irritable and difficult during the first weeks at home. Many intervention programs initially focus on helping the parents feel comfortable with their infants and developing the assurance that they can satisfactorily manage and meet the infant's needs (Bromwich, 1981). Once the parent feels comfortable and in control, strategies for enrichment of the infant's environment are often suggested. For those readers interested in reading about specific intervention programs for at-risk infants, see Field, Sostek, Goldberg, & Shuman, 1979; Kopp, 1983; Tjossem, 1976; Badger, 1977.

Summary

This section has provided a global review of the changing perspectives on at-risk infants. In a brief period, these babies have become an important target for research in the development of better medical and education information and technology. Today, smaller and sicker infants are surviving. This reality requires thoughtful consideration by the medical, educational, and general population of the care to be provided and the associated responsibility for that care.

The intervention approaches for at-risk infants have changed from focusing exclusively on the infant to a general concern for the infant's ecology. Intervention efforts today are designed to account for medical and environmental factors to maximize the infant's growth and the family's adjustment.

Programs for the Handicapped Child

Concerns for the child coming from circumstances of poverty have been paralleled by concerns for the child who is handicapped. There has been increasing focus on the rights of children and recognition by legislators, courts, and program implementers of the need to eliminate discriminatory practices against the handicapped individual (Garwood, 1987; Garwood, Fewell & Neisworth, 1988). Kirk (1978) suggested that two major events following World War II acted as triggers for the development of educational programs for the child who is handicapped:

> First, a number of states that previously had not supported programs of special education in the public schools passed laws to subsidize such programs...The second major impetus was the parent movement. (Kirk, 1978, p. 6)

The historical roots of educational programs for the handicapped were perhaps initiated in part by the work of Alfred Binet. As Kirk has noted (1977), contrary to popular belief, Binet did not believe in the fixed nature of intelligence nor did he construct his original test to measure a fixed entity. Rather, Binet was interested in differentiating between children who would benefit from special instruction. He began classes for the mentally retarded in Paris in 1909; thus Kirk has dubbed Binet the father of "modern special education" (Kirk, 1977).

Before Binet's work, Itard conducted an experiment with a young adolescent boy found unattended in the woods. Victor, as this child came to be known, was originally unable to speak and had no socialized behaviors. Leading authorities declared Victor an incurable idiot, but Itard believed the boy could be trained. During a 4 year period, a highly structured sensory training program was developed and implemented with Victor. Because Victor failed to acquire many of the skills Itard had set out to teach, he considered the "experiment" a failure; however, a more realistic view of changes in Victor's repertoire has lead others to conclude the intervention devised by Itard was clearly successful (Ball, 1971). A remarkable aspect of Itard's work is the sophistication of the training offered to Victor at a time when few research or educational resources existed.

An early attempt at ameliorating mental retardation through early education was conducted by Kirk. Kirk indicated he had become interested in such a venture because of his long time association with Harold Skeels and because "In 1946, I read a number of articles published in the *Reader's Digest*, *The Ladies Home Journal*, and in a psychological monograph, which intimated that feeblemindedness could be cured" (Kirk, 1977, p. 6). In 1948, Kirk received support to begin an experiment that was the first formal attempt to provide an early intervention program to a group of preschool-age children with mental retardation.

The Kirk investigation included eighty-one mentally retarded preschool children between the ages of three to six years with IQs that ranged from 45 to 80. The subjects were from four different groups: a community experimental group in which the children attended a community-based preschool program; community contrast group which attended no preschool program; institutional experimental group which attended an institutional preschool program; and an institutional contrast group that attended no preschool program. Upon completion of the preschool experience, the experimental subjects in both the community and institutional preschool groups outperformed the contrast subjects. A follow-up after the first year of elementary school found that the initial differences between contrast and experimental community subjects tend to "wash out" through either an acceleration in the contrast subjects or limited change in experimental subjects, or both. Nevertheless, according to Kirk (1977), "The conclusion we drew from this experiment was that intervention at the preschool level accelerates the rate of mental and social development, while no intervention at that age level tends to allow the rate of mental and social development to slow" (p. 7).

An extremely interesting monograph was published by the State of California's Department of Mental Hygiene (Rhodes, Gooch, Siegelman, Behrns, & Metzger, 1970). The study reported was a follow-up to some work completed by Stedman and Eichorn (1964), which compared the development of a group of ten home-reared Down syndrome children with that of ten institutionalized Down syndrome children. Most comparisons favored the home-reared children and thus a further experiment was formulated to see if changes in the institutional program and environment could produce changes in the Down syndrome children.

Changes were made in the children's physical setting, staff were trained, and a comprehensive training program was initiated in which language training was the focus. The reported results indicated that positive changes were seen in language behavior, intellectual growth, and social skills of a population previously thought by many to be uneducable (Rhodes, et al., 1970).

In 1968, the United States Congress enacted the Handicapped Children's Early Education Program (HCEEP). The purpose of this federal program for preschool-age handicapped children was "to demonstrate the feasibility of early education to the American public" (Ackerman & Moore, 1976, p. 669).

> The Act provided monies for demonstration programs, insisted that such programs be geographically disperse, mandated the involvement of parents, and ordered dissemination of the results to the communities that surrounded the preschool programs. Furthermore, the Act insisted that programs be coordinated with other existing programs and that they be evaluated in order to show others their worth (Ackerman & Moore, 1976, pp. 669-670).

Until recently, the appropriations for the HCEEP steadily increased, resulting in an increased number of programs and children being served. An article by Swan (1980) indicates the success of this federal program in terms of the number of programs that have been continued in communities using local or state funds. In addition, an evaluation report issued by the Littlejohn Associates for Special Education Programs indicates the enormously positive impact of these programs. To highlight a few outcomes noted by the Littlejohn report:

- Projects have been active in every state and in several territories.

- 55 percent of the children who leave HCEEP demonstration projects are placed in integrated settings with non-handicapped children which is less expensive than more specialized placements.

- 80 percent of the 280 projects (studied by this report) are still continuing to serve children independent of HCEEP funding.

- More than 30,600 children have been served in continuation projects at no cost to the HCEEP.

- Replication programs are known to have served 107,850 children.

- More than 3,000 products have been developed by HCEEP projects .

- Twenty-one HCEEP projects have been approved for dissemination by the Joint Dissemination Review Panel of the Department of Education on the basis of evidence of effective programming and in cost of replication (Roy Littlejohn Associates, 1982 p. 146-147).

The Roy Littlejohn Associates report concludes that: "The accomplishments of the HCEEP projects as shown by the survey results are greater and more varied than for any other documented education program we have been able to identify" (p. 149). Others may not share the enthusiasm for the HCEEP found in the Littlejohn report, but there seems little doubt that from both a historical and a contemporary perspective, the impact of this federal program on the development of early intervention programs for infants and preschool-age children who are handicapped has been significant. A recent survey of HCEEP supports this conclusion (Karnes & Stayton, 1988).

Toward the end of the 1960s and the early 1970s, other events occurred that encouraged the development of early intervention programs for preschool children who are handicapped. A few states began passing legislation that mandated community services for selected preschool handicapped populations, and P.L. 94-142 was signed into law in 1975.

The final link to contemporary programs can be found in a number of exemplary programs developed in the 1970s—many of which were supported by HCEEP funds. Descriptions of many of the notable programs that lay the ground work for what we do today can be found in the influential volumes edited by Friedlander, Sterritt, and Kirk (1975) and Tjossem (1976). This latter volume was the product of an important conference held in Chapel Hill, North Carolina in May, 1974. This conference and the book have been of great importance because, for many of us working with young children who are handicapped, this was the first opportunity to learn about other professionals working in the area and to share ideas and ideals.

Summary

A comparison of the historical background of programs for children who are handicapped with programs for children who are environmentally and biologically at-risk shows considerable philosophical and pragmatic overlap. The major difference may be in the area of impact. Given appropriate and long-term programs, the prognosis for the environmentally and biologically at-risk child seem excellent; to date such optimism for children who are handicapped should be tempered with the technological and knowledge constraints facing interventionists dealing with infants or children who have sensory, motor, and cognitive impairments. Our history indicates genuine progress in learning how and what to offer children who are handicapped and their families; nonetheless, too often information and technological limitations find us falling short of the goal of independent functioning for handicapped populations.

THE RATIONALE FOR EARLY INTERVENTION

Certainly since the introduction of J. McV. Hunt's book, *Intelligence and Experience* (1961), contemporary psychologists and educators have come to acknowledge the importance of the environment on the development of children. For a number of years, many investigators placed such an emphasis on environmental variables that the genetic or organic contribution from the individual was overlooked or, at least, undervalued. Fortunately, the work of investigators such as Sameroff and Chandler (1975) has rekindled interest in the organism-environment interaction. Acknowledgement of genetic and biological limitations with the acceptance that the child's potential for development can be reduced or enhanced by environmental variables appears the preferred position now, and this position generates a number of potent theoretical arguments to support early intervention (Sameroff, 1982).

The following rationale for early intervention is composed of four major arguments. These arguments for early intervention include: (1) maximizing the child's developmental outcomes; (2) preventing the development of secondary disabilities; (3) providing support for families; and (4) cost-effectiveness. These arguments tend to be formulated using logic rather than empirical support because of the limited objective data available on the impact of early intervention.

The first basic argument for early intervention is derived from the premise of environment and child interaction and suggests that early learning lays the foundation for subsequent development of more complex behavior (Bricker, Seibert & Casuso, 1980). Piaget's (1970) theory of early development supports such a position with the belief that the systematic interaction of early responses with the environment produces increasingly more complex behavior. A logical underlying assumption of this position is that without the early simple response forms, children do not have the building blocks from which to evolve more complex understanding or knowledge of their world. Without systematic early intervention, many children who are handicapped will not acquire even simple sensorimotor responses albeit more complex response forms (Snyder-McLean, McLean & Etter, 1988). A few examples may serve to make this point.

Infants who have difficulty coordinating basic schemes, such as movement of the arm/hand to retrieve a visually located object, will be generally delayed in exploring and manipulating their environment. In order to systematically retrieve interesting or desired objects, coordination of the visual and auditory system with reaching is generally required, except when the infant makes contact by happenstance. Reduced physical exploration of the environment generally depresses the onset of these important behaviors. For example, the blind infant's understanding of the concept of objects appears to be acquired more slowly than for nonvisually impaired children (Fewell, 1983). Unless at some future point the infant can make up such deficits, a gradually increasing gap between the expected and actual repertoire occurs.

The absence or significant delay in the onset of critical responses appears generally to have cumulative effects over time. Consequently, to minimize these deficits, intervention should be offered to children when such deficits are identified. In most cases, to wait or delay treatment produces more pervasive and complex problems that are more difficult and costly to remedy.

This argument in no way suggests the primacy of early experience or a continuing overpowering effect on subsequent development. Rather, in agreement with Clarke and Clarke (1976), this argument sees early experiences as one segment in the life of the developing organism and their importance determined, in part, by the child's constitution and subsequent environmental experiences.

Many infants and children who are at-risk or handicapped are inclined, without proper handling, to develop a variety of undesirable behaviors (Risley & Wolf, 1966; Baumeister & Forehand, 1973), or fail to respond in a manner that is reinforcing or satisfying to the caregiver (Field, 1983). Such behaviors are not inevitable accompaniments of a handicapping condition but appear rather as the result of inappropriate handling.

Thus, a second argument for intervening early with children who are at-risk or handicapped can be labeled as preventative. That is, family members can attenuate or inhibit the development of secondary or associated disabilities in their infant or child *if* they are provided the necessary information and instruction to acquire effective coping strategies (Bricker, Bailey & Bruder, 1984).

The reciprocal nature of caregiver-child interactions assumes an underlying time-sequence frame. That is, one partner's response generally precedes the other's. The timing, or synchrony, of the caregiver's response to the baby appears to have the potential of seriously affecting the quality of their relationship even during the very early phases of development (Osofsky, 1976). Synchrony of responding refers to the caregiver's ability (and to a lesser extent the child's capacity) to monitor the state, mood, or needs of the child and to respond in a facilitating manner according to the child's needs. For example, if a baby is thrashing and crying vigorously, an appropriate move on the part of the caregiver is to respond with behaviors that are soothing to the infant; for example, the caregiver might lift the child, rock him, and talk quietly to him. If the baby were in an awake, alert state, an appropriate response might be to offer some form of stimulation the baby might find interesting; for example, showing the baby a bright-colored toy, tickling her toes or returning her coos and gurgles.

Such synchronous responding to infants and young children takes the form of "doing what comes naturally" to most caregivers. Fortunately, most babies and their caregivers arrive at a reasonable synchrony of their reciprocal responses; however, a number of investigators (Brazelton, Koslowski, & Main, 1974; Bell, 1974; Denenberg & Thoman, 1976) have noted that some babies exceed the ability of their caregivers to cope. The development of an asynchronous relationship can result from having a difficult-to-manage child (e.g., autistic child) or a caregiver with little sensitivity to the state or needs of the child. In examining caregiver's sensitivity, Brazelton et al. (1974) reported the differential effects produced by mothers on two similarly tense, overreactive infants. The mother who was able to modulate or synchronize her behavior to the infant helped the baby become more responsive, while in the other case, the infant learned to escape his mother's increased stimulation by tuning her out. These two parallel cases demonstrate that a mother's behavior "must not only be reinforcing and contingent upon the infant's behavior, but that it must meet more basic 'needs' of the infant in being aware of his capacity to receive and utilize stimuli" (Brazelton, Koslowski, & Main, 1974).

Although the quality of the early caregiver-child interaction is probably more dependent upon the sensitivity of the adult, asynchrony in the relationship can be produced by the infant as well. Denenberg and Thoman (1976) discuss a case in which the infant's irritable and unresponsive behavior apparently made it extremely difficult for a mother to respond appropriately. An investigation of the state or mood changes of this infant revealed that this baby shifted states significantly more often than other infants of comparable age. The erratic behavior of this infant made it difficult for the mother to modulate her responses appropriately, and the amount of time the mother spent with her infant was observed to gradually decrease over time. Decreasing the amount of interaction between the child and his or her parent may eventually lead to an even more ineffectual relationship.

A second facet of the prevention argument is the apparent irreversible nature of some disabilities if steps are not taken for correction during the formative years. For example, without proper exercising and positioning, the child with severe spasticity may develop contractures that are permanent. Hearing-impaired children may not learn to use their residual hearing unless trained to do so early in life (Horton, 1976). Children with major disabilities may never function completely within the normal range across a number of behavioral domains, but there are data to suggest that such disabled children can be assisted in becoming more adaptive and independent (Bricker, Bailey, & Bruder, 1984; Simeonsson, Cooper, & Scheiner, 1982; Guralnick & Bricker, 1987).

The third argument for early intervention focuses on the needs of families who have special needs children. Often family members appear to undergo considerable stress (Roos, 1978; Gallagher, Beckman, & Cross, 1983; Beckman & Pokorni, 1988). Early intervention may be a valuable resource for parents and siblings in three areas. Early intervention programs can be instrumental in helping family members to adjust and cope with their child who is handicapped. There seems little question that the advent of an infant who is at-risk or handicapped produces trauma, fear, and stress for most parents or families (Singer & Irvin, 1989). Descriptions of the phases or cycles that parents move through in the adjustment process abound in the literature (Gabel, McDowell, & Cerreto, 1983). Accompanying reflections offered by many parents facing such adjustment processes was the dismay they felt toward professionals, friends, or family who could not or did not offer constructive help or support and the gratitude they felt toward those who were supportive and helpful (Turnbull & Turnbull, 1978).

A second aspect of this argument for the potential value of early intervention for families is that these programs can assist caregivers in acquiring the necessary skills for managing and instructing their child (Bricker, Bailey & Bruder, 1984). Most infants and young children tend to spend more time with family members; however, increasingly, parents are seeking alternative out-of-home day care arrangements (Klein & Sheehan, 1987). Thus, it seems imperative if the child's learning opportunities are to be maximized and are to generalize across environments, then caregivers should have the management and intervention skills that will make them able to cope with and teach the child.

A third aspect of this particular argument for early intervention indicates that programs can assist families in obtaining support such as counseling, social services (e.g., food stamps), appropriate medical assistance, or child care (Hanson, Ellis, & Deppe, 1989). Not all families require such assistance, but many do. In our own experience with parents, we have noted that parents frequently ask staff and other parents for help in solving a specific problem with their child. For example, do you know a dentist who is willing to work with a difficult-to-manage child? Parents who may be feeling unusually helpless can be assisted by a staff member in locating a counseling service that is appropriate and affordable. Without such essential supports for the families, the probability of alienation from the child increases, with the effect that neither child nor family members make or maintain an adequate adjustment to each other. Early intervention programs may be pivotal for many families in the evolution of an acceptable relationship with the member of their family who is handicapped. Such acceptance should lead to maintaining the individual who is handicapped in the community and obviate institutionalization.

A fourth argument some early interventionists cite as a rationale for early intervention is cost (see, e.g., the Colorado Department of Education report entitled, "Effectiveness of Early Special Education for Handicapped Children"). The cost of providing special education exceeds the cost for regular education. The average annual cost per child for regular education has been reported to range from $1,148 to $2,060.[3] Based on the lowest reported cost figure, the average cost per child for regular education to age 18 (for years 1978-79) is $13,776 and $16,072, including two years of preschool. The average cost per child for special education to age 18, when beginning intervention at birth, age two, and age six is: $37,273, $37,600, and $46,816 respectively (Interact, 1981).

The cost of early education varies according to the types of service offered (Barnett, Escobar & Ravsten, 1988). The cost of special education also varies as the age of beginning special education is postponed. For example, based on 940 children ranging from mild to severely handicapped, the median cost of special education (per child per year) was reported to be $2,021 for infants, $2,310 for preschoolers, and $4,445 for elementary and secondary students (Interact, 1981). These figures are no doubt confounded by such factors as length and intensity of various programs and type and severity of handicapping conditions.

In some cases, early special education services enable school-age children to attend regular education classes. For example, many graduates from the Mama Lere Parent Teaching Home (Horton, 1976), an early intervention program for children with hearing impairments, ages birth to six, were enrolled in elementary school classes. The average cost per child per year for children with hearing impairments attending regular

---

[3] Information in this section came from a variety of sources, and cost data were aggregated to estimate average cost of special and regular education and cost savings of early intervention. For an explanation of data sources, procedures for calculating costs, assumptions, and limitations for these figures, see Interact (1981).

classes was $847 as compared with the average cost for special education classes for the hearing impaired, which was $1,710 per child per year. A considerable savings was realized when children who are handicapped are able to attend regular classes.

The cost to operate an early intervention program is far less than the cost of residential (or institutional) services. For example, the Child Development Units Program (Texas) provided classroom programs for ninety-seven preschool children who were handicapped. The cost of operating this ten-month program was $3,908 per child. Had this program not been available, many of the children would have qualified for enrollment in a state residential school. The average cost for residential school services ranged from $12,888 to $29,868 per child per year (Liberman, Barnes, Ho, Cueller, & Little, 1979).[4] The cost of institutional care was also greater than the cost for special education programs in public school settings. As mentioned earlier, the average cost for special education classes for children with hearing impairments was $1,710 per child per year. The average cost per child per year at the State School for the Deaf was $5,107 (Horton, 1976).[5] Compared with the costs of regular education for one year in Ypsilanti, Michigan, a special education self-contained classroom increases the cost of schooling by 143 percent. Institutional care increases the cost of schooling (school district contribution) by 187 percent (Schweinhart & Weikart, 1980).

In addition to direct savings when children are placed in regular education programs and being maintained in the community, other economic advantages have been reported. The economic analysis of the Perry Preschool Project (Weber, Foster, & Weikart, 1978) suggests that the benefits of early intervention outweighed the costs. The total economic benefit for two years of preschool was estimated to be $14,819 per child, a 248 percent return on the original investment of $5,984 per child. Three sources contributed to the derived economic benefit calculations: decreased education costs (fewer children needing special education services); increased lifetime earnings (projected earnings); and the value of parents' released time while their children attended preschool (Schweinhart & Weikart, 1980; Barnett & Escobar, 1988).

A follow-up study of children who had participated in the INREAL program for three-to-five-year-old children who were language impaired and bilingual (Spanish) indicated early intervention is cost effective. Three years after completing the program, children required fewer special education services (e.g., speech and language therapy, special education classes) than did children who had not been in the program. The need for later special education services resulted in considerable savings of educational costs. A savings of $1,283.76 per child was realized for language-impaired children, and a savings of $3,076.16 per child was realized for bilingual children (Weiss, 1981).

The more traditional rationale of maximizing development outcomes, preventing associated disabilities, and supporting and instruct-

---

[4] These figures are outdated but nonetheless reflect the comparative costs of regular and special education and community versus residential care.

[5] Again these figures are dated but still provide useful comparisons between public school and residential costs.

ing families becomes more persuasive when economic benefits are considered. At the very least, significant savings can be realized if early intervention only prevents the need for residential or institutional care. However, reducing the probability of custodial care is only one economic advantage of providing early intervention services to children who are at-risk or handicapped and their parents. There is considerable savings in educational costs if early intervention increases the likelihood of regular educational placement. A savings is also realized for children who need long-term special education services if intervention begins before school age. In some cases early intervention enables parents to become more self-sufficient. In general, the accrued economic benefits appear to outweigh, or at least justify, the expenditures required to ensure the availability of services for children who are at-risk or handicapped and their parents.

SUMMARY

As a prelude to the approach to early intervention advocated in this book, this chapter has offered a brief history of the early education movement that was begun in the 1800s. Discussion of selected contemporary programs targeting environmentally and medically at-risk and handicapped populations served to illuminate the issues that continue to require attention and innovative solutions. Finally, a multifaceted rationale that has been garnered from the available literature and clinical experience was discussed in some detail. In large measure, the arguments favoring early intervention programs are relative to the weight given to such variables as long-term versus short-term investments, selected criteria to determine success or adequate progress, and the importance attached to every human being regardless of the potential for normalcy.

References

Ackerman, P., & Moore, M. (1976). Delivery of educational services to preschool handicapped children. In T. Tjossem (Ed.), *Intervention strategies for high risk infants and young children*. Baltimore, MD: University Park Press.

Badger, E. (1977). The infant stimulation/mother training project. In B. M. Caldwell & D. J. Stedman (Eds.), *Infant education: A guide for helping handicapped children in the first three years*. New York: Walker & Company.

Ball, T. A. (1971). *Itard, Sequin & Kephart: Sensory education—A learning interpretation*. Columbus, OH: Charles E. Merrill.

Barnard, K. (1976). Nursing: High risk infants. In T. Tjossem (Ed.), *Intervention strategies for high risk infants and young children*. Baltimore, MD: University Park Press.

Barnett, W., & Escobar, C. (1988). The economics of early intervention for handicapped children: What do we really know? *Journal of the Division of Early Childhood, 12*(2), 169-181.

Barnett, W., Escobar, C., & Ravsten, M. (1988). Parents and clinic early intervention for children with language handicaps: A cost effectiveness analysis. *Journal of the Division of Early Childhood, 12*(4), 290-298.

Baumeister, A., & Forehand, R. (1973). Stereotyped acts. In N. Ellis (Ed.), *International review of research in mental retardation* (Vol. 6). New York: Academic Press.

Beckman, P., & Pokorni, J. (1988). A longitudinal study of families of preterm infants: Changes in stress and support over the first two years. *Journal of Special Education, 22*(1), 55-65.

Bell, R. (1974). Contributions of human infants to caregiving and social interaction. In M. Lewis & L. Rosenblum (Eds.), *The effect of the infant on its caregiver.* New York: Wiley & Sons.

Beller, E. (1979). Early intervention programs. In J. Osofsky (Ed.), *Handbook of infant development.* New York: Wiley & Sons.

Belsky, J., Steinberg, L., & Walker, A. (1982). The ecology of day care. In M. Lamb (Ed.), *Nontraditional families.* Hillsdale, NJ: Lawrence Erlbaum.

Bennett, F. (1987). The effectiveness of early intervention for infants at increased biologic risk. In M. Guralnick & F. Bennett (Eds.), *The effectiveness of early intervention for at-risk and handicapped children.* New York: Academic Press.

Blatt, B., & Garfunkel, F. (1969). *The educability of intelligence.* Washington, DC: The Council for Exceptional Children.

Bloom, B. (1964). *Stability and change in human characteristics.* London: John Wiley.

Bowlby, J. (1973). *Attachment and loss: Separation, anxiety, and anger.* New York: Basic Books.

Brazelton, B., Koslowski, B., & Main, M. (1974). The origins of reciprocity: The early mother-infant interaction. In M. Lewis & L. Rosenblum (Eds.), *The effect of the infant on its caregiver.* New York: Wiley & Sons.

Bricker, D., Bailey, E., & Bruder, M. (1984). The efficacy of early intervention and the handicapped infant: A wise or wasted resource? *Advances in Developmental and Behavioral Pediatrics* (Vol. V). Greenwich, CT: JAI Press.

Bricker, D., Seibert, J., & Casuso, V. (1980). Early intervention. In J. Hogg & P. Mittler (Eds.), *Advances in mental handicap research.* London: Wiley & Sons.

Bromwich, R. (1981). *Working with parents and infants: An interactional approach.* Baltimore, MD: University Park Press.

Bronfenbrenner, U. (1975). Is early intervention effective? In B. Z. Friedlander, G. M. Sterritt, & G. E. Kirk (Eds.), *Exceptional infant* (Vol. 3). New York: Brunner/Mazel.

Bryant, D., & Ramey, C. (1987). An analysis of the effectiveness of early intervention programs for environmentally at-risk children. In M. Guralnick & F. Bennett (Eds.), *The effectiveness of early intervention for at-risk and handicapped children.* New York: Academic Press.

Budetti, P., Barrand, N., McManus, P., & Heinen, L. (1981, August). *The implications of cost-effectiveness analysis of medical technology. Case Study #10: The cost and effectiveness of neonatal intensive care.* Office of Technology Assessment, Washington, DC

Caputo, D., Goldstein, K., & Taub, H. (1981). Neonatal compromise and later psychological development: A 10-year longitudinal study. In S. Friedman & M. Sigman (Eds.), *Preterm birth and psychological development.* New York: Academic Press.

Cicerelli, V., Evans, J., & Schiller, J. (1969). *The impact of Head Start on children's cognitive and affective development: Preliminary report.* Washington, DC: Office of Economic Opportunity.

Clarke, A., & Clarke, A. (1976). *Early experience: Myth and evidence.* New York: The Free Press.

Clarke, A., & Clarke, A. (1977). Prospects for prevention and amelioration of mental retardation: A guest editorial. *American Journal of Mental Deficiency, 81,* 523-533.

Cole, J., & Gilkerson, L. (1982). Developmental consultation: The role of the parent/infant education in a hospital/community coordinated program for high risk premature infants. In A. Waldstein (Ed.), *Issues in neonatal care.* WESTAR/TADS.

Colorado Department of Education (no date). *Effectiveness of early special education for the handicapped children.* (Report commissioned by the Colorado General Assembly.)

Cornell, E., & Gottfried, A. (1976). Intervention with premature human infants. *Child Development, 47,* 32-39.

Denenberg, V., & Thoman, E. (1976). From animal to infant research. In T. Tjossem (Ed.), *Intervention strategies for high risk infants and young children.* Baltimore, MD: University Park Press.

Dennis, W. (1976). Children of the Creche: Conclusions and implications. In A. Clarke & A. Clarke (Eds.), *Early experience: Myth and evidence.* New York: The Free Press.

Fewell, R. (1983). Working with sensorily impaired children. In G. Garwood (Ed.), *Educating young handicapped children.* Rockville, MD: Aspen Publications.

Field, T. (1983). High-risk infants "have less fun" during early interactions. *Topics in Early Childhood Special Education, 3*(1), 77-87.

Field, T., Dempsey, J., & Shuman, H. (1981). Developmental follow-up of pre- and postterm infants. In S. Friedman & M. Sigman (Eds.), *Preterm birth and psychological development.* New York: Academic Press.

Field, T., Sostek, A., Goldberg, S., & Shuman, H., (Eds.). (1979). *Infants born at risk.* New York: Spectrum.

Friedlander, B. Z., Sterritt, G. M., & Kirk, G. E., (Eds). (1975). *Exceptional infant: Assessment and intervention.* New York: Brunner/Mazel.

Gabel, H., McDowell, J., & Cerreto, M. (1983). Family adaptation to the handicapped infant. In G. Garwood & R. Fewell (Eds.), *Educating handicapped infants*. Rockville, MD: Aspen Publications.

Gallagher, J., Beckman, P., & Cross, A. (1983). Families of handicapped children: Sources of stress and its amelioration. *Exceptional Children, 50*, 10-19.

Garwood, S. (1987). Political, economic and practical issues affecting the development of universal early intervention for handicapped infants. *Topics in Early Childhood Special Education, 7*(2), 6-18.

Garwood, S., Fewell, R., & Neisworth, J. (1988). *Topics in Early Childhood Special Education, 8* (1), 1-11.

Gibson, D., & Fields, D. (1984). Early stimulation programs for Down's Syndrome: An effectiveness inventory. In M. Wolraich (Ed.), *Advances in Behavioral and Developmental Pediatrics* (Vol. 5). Greenwich, CN: JAI Press.

Goodenough, F., & Maurer, K. (1961). The relative potency of the nursery school and the statistical laboratory in boosting I.Q. In J. Jenkins & D. Paterson (Eds.), *Studies in individual differences*. New York: Appleton-Century-Crofts.

Gray, S., & Klaus, R. (1976). The early training project: A seventh-year report. In A. Clarke & A. Clarke (Eds.), *Early experience: Myth and evidence*. New York: The Free Press.

Gray, S., Ramsey, B., & Klaus, R. (1982). *From 3 to 20: The early training project*. Baltimore, MD: University Park Press.

Guralnick, M., & Bricker, D. (1987). The effectiveness of early intervention for children with cognitive and general developmental delays. In M. Guralnick & F. Bennett (Eds.), *The effectiveness of early intervention for at-risk and handicapped children*. New York: Academic Press.

Hanson, M., Ellis, L. & Deppe, J. (1989). Support for families during infancy. In G. Singer & L. Irvin (Eds.), *Support for caregiving families*. Baltimore, MD: Paul Brookes.

Hewett, F., & Forness, S. (1977). *Education of exceptional children*. Boston, MA: Allyn & Bacon.

Horton, K. (1976). Early intervention for hearing-impaired infants and young children. In T. Tjossem (Ed.), *Intervention strategies for high risk infants and young children*. Baltimore, MD: University Park Press.

Hunt, J. (1981). Predicting intellectual disorders in childhood for preterm infants with birthweights below 1501 gm. In S. Friedman & M. Sigman (Eds.), *Preterm birth and psychological development*. New York: Academic Press.

Hunt, J. McV. (1961). *Intelligence and experience*. New York: Ronald Press.

Interact (1981). *Early intervention for children with special needs and their families. Manuscript prepared by Interact: The national committee for services to very young children with special needs and their families.* WESTAR.

Karnes, M., Schwedel, A., Lewis, G., Ratts, D., & Esry, D. (1981). Impact of early programming for the handicapped: A follow-up study into the elementary school. *Journal of the Division for Early Childhood, 4,* 62-79.

Karnes, M., & Stayton, V. (1988). Model programs for infants and toddlers with handicaps. In J. Jordan, J. Gallagher, P. Hutinger, & M. Karnes (Eds.), *Early childhood special education: Birth to three.* Reston, VA: Council for Exceptional Children.

Kirk, S. (1977). General and historical rationale for early education of the handicapped. In N. Ellis & L. Cross (Eds.), *Planning programs for early education of the handicapped.* New York: Walker & Co.

Kirk, S. (1978). The federal role in special education: Historical perspectives. *UCLA Education, 20,* 5-11.

Klaus, M., & Kennell, J., (Eds.). (1976). *Maternal-infant bonding.* St. Louis: Mosby.

Klein, N., & Sheehan, R. (1987). Staff development: A key issue in meeting the needs of young handicapped children in day care settings. *Journal of the Division of Early Childhood, 7*(1), 13-27.

Kopp, C. (1983). Risk factors in development. In M. Haith & J. Campos (Eds.), *Infancy and the biology of development,* Vol. 2—from P. Mussen (Ed.), *Manual of child psychology.* New York: Wiley & Sons.

Lazar, I., Darlington, R., Murray, H., Royce, J., & Snipper, A. (1982). Lasting effects of early education: A report from the consortium for longitudinal studies. *Monographs of the Society for Research in Child Development, 47* (Serial No. 195).

Lazerson, M. (1972). The historical antecedents of early childhood education. *Education Digest, 38,* 20-23.

Liberman, A., Barnes, M., Ho, E., Cuellar, I., & Little, T. (1979). The economic impact of child development services on families of retarded children. *Mental Retardation, 17,* 158-159.

Lyon, J. (1985). *Playing god in the nursery.* New York: Norton.

Snyder-McLean, L., McLean, J., & Etter, R. (1988). Clinical assessment of sensorimotor knowledge in nonverbal, severely retarded clients. *Topics in Early Childhood Special Education, 8*(4),1-22.

Maxim, G. (1980). *The very young: Guiding children from infancy through the early years.* Belmont, CA: Wadsworth.

Miller, C. (1987). *Maternal health and infant survival.* Washington, D.C.: National Center for Clinical Infant Programs.

Osofsky, J. (1976). Neonatal characteristics and mother-infant interaction in two observational situations. *Child Development, 47,* 1138-1147.

Peters, D., & Deiner, P. (1987). The reality of early childhood: Head Start and the child development associate. *Topics in Early Childhood Special Education, 7*(3), 48-58.

Piaget, J. (1970). Piaget's theory. In P. Mussen (Ed.), *Carmichael's manual of child psychology* (Vol. 1). New York: Wiley & Sons.

Ramey, C., Zeskind, P., & Hunter, R. (1981). Biomedical and psychosocial intervention for preterm infants. In S. Friedman & M. Sigman (Eds.), *Preterm birth and psychological development.* New York: Academic Press.

Rhodes, L., Gooch, B., Siegelman, E., Behrns, C., & Metzger, R. (1970). A language stimulation and reading program for severely retarded mongoloid children. *California Mental Health Research Monograph,* No. 11, State of California.

Risley, T., & Wolf, M. (1966). Experimental manipulation of autistic behaviors and generalization in the home. In R. Ulrich, T. Stachnik, & J. Mabry (Eds.), *Control of human behavior.* Glenview: Scott, Foresman & Co.

Roos, P. (1978). Parents of mentally retarded children - Misunderstood and mistreated. In A. Turnbull & H. Turnbull (Eds.), *Parents speak out.* Columbus, OH: Charles E. Merrill.

Roy Littlejohn Assoc., Inc. (1982, November). *An analysis of the impact of the Handicapped Children's Early Education Program.* Prepared for Special Education Programs, U.S. Dept. of Education.

Sameroff, A. (1981). Longitudinal studies of preterm infants: A review of chapters 17-20. In S. Friedman & M. Sigman (Eds.), *Preterm birth and psychological development.* New York: Academic Press.

Sameroff, A. (1982). The environmental context of developmental disabilities. In D. Bricker (Ed.), *Intervention with at-risk and handicapped infants: From research to application.* Baltimore, MD: University Park Press.

Sameroff, A., & Chandler, M. (1975). Reproductive risk and the continuum of caretaking casualty. In F. Horowitz, M. Hetherington, S. Scarr-Salapatek & G. Siegel (Eds.), *Review of child development research* (Vol. 4). Chicago: University of Chicago Press.

Schaffer, H. (Ed.). (1977). *Studies in mother-infant interaction.* New York: Academic Press.

Schweinhart, L., & Weikart, D. (1980). Young children grow up: The effects of the Perry preschool program on youths through age 15. *Monographs of the High/Scope Educational Research Foundation,* Number seven.

Sigman, M., Cohen, S., & Forsythe, A. (1981). The relation of early infant measures to later development. In S. Friedman & M. Sigman (Eds.), *Preterm birth and psychological development.* New York: Academic Press.

Simeonsson, R., Cooper, D., & Scheiner, A. (1982). A review and analysis of the effectiveness of early intervention programs. *Pediatrics, 69,* 635-641.

Singer, G., & Irvin, L. (1989). Family caregiving, stress, and support. In G. Singer & L. Irvin (Eds.), *Support for caregiving families.* Baltimore, MD: Paul Brookes.

Skeels, H. M. (1966). Adult status of children with contrasting early life experiences. *Monographs of the Society for Research in Child Development, 31*(3, Serial No. 105).

Spitz, R. (1946). Hospitalism: A follow-up report. *Psychoanalytic Study of the Child, 2,* 313-342.

Stedman, D. J., & Eichorn, D. H. (1964). A comparative study of the growth and development trends of institutionalized and noninstitutionalized mongoloid children. *American Journal of Mental Deficiency, 69,* 391-401.

Swan, W. (1980). The handicapped children's early education program. *Exceptional Children, 47,* 12-16.

Sweet, N. (1982). New faces and approaches in the intensive care nursery: The roles of the developmental/education specialist. In A. Waldstein (Ed.), *Issues in neonatal care.* WESTAR/TADS.

Taft, L. (1981). Intervention programs for infants with cerebral palsy: A clinician's view. In C. Brown (Ed.), *Infants at risk.* Johnson & Johnson Baby Products Company Pediatric Round Table Series, 5.

Tjossem, T. (Ed.). (1976). *Intervention strategies for high risk infants and young children.* Baltimore, MD: University Park Press.

Turnbull, A., & Turnbull, R. (Eds.). (1978). *Parents speak out.* Columbus, OH: Charles E. Merrill.

Weber, C., Foster, P., & Weikart, D. (1978). An economic analysis of the Ypsilanti Perry Preschool Project. *Monographs of the High/Scope Educational Research Foundation,* Number five.

Weiss, R. (1981). INREAL intervention for language handicapped and bilingual children. *Journal of the Division for Early Childhood, 4,* 40-51.

Werthmann, M. (1981). Medical constraints to optimal psychological development of the preterm infant. In S. Friedman & M. Sigman (Eds.), *Preterm birth and psychological development.* New York: Academic Press.

Wolfensberger, W. (1969). The origin and nature of our institutional models. In R. Kugel & W. Wolfensberger (Eds.), *Changing patterns in residential services for the mentally retarded.* President's Committee on Mental Retardation, Washington, DC.

Zigler, E., & Cascione, R. (1977). Headstart has little to do with mental retardation: A reply to Clarke and Clarke. *American Journal of Mental Deficiency, 82,* 246-249.

4.
The Impact of Early Intervention Programs on Children and Families

Those of us working with children who are at-risk and handicapped should take seriously the role of advocate. Often, those intimately associated with an area tend to forget that others may not share their enthusiasm for an endeavor to which they are professionally committed. An individual who knows little about the devastating effects of physical, mental, and behavioral impairments cannot be expected to understand the need for intervening early when a child with such a defect is identified. Further, uninformed people do not automatically understand or accept that infants and young children can benefit from intelligently designed intervention programs.

Obviously, professionals working in early intervention programs have a responsibility to provide services to children and families; they have a secondary responsibility, perhaps not so obvious, to inform the community about the importance of providing these services to young at-risk and handicapped populations. As well-informed spokespersons, we may be able to assist the larger community in gaining an understanding and appreciation for the needs of young children who are at-risk or handicapped and their families.

To be an effective spokesperson, one should be armed with logical arguments and relevant information about the effectiveness of early intervention programs. In Chapter 3, a rationale for early intervention was presented; in this chapter, selected outcome data on the impact of early programming for infants and children who are at-risk or handicapped and their families is discussed. The intent is to provide the reader with a rich source of information for becoming an effective advocate for programs that serve young at-risk and handicapped populations.

THE ISSUE: IS EARLY INTERVENTION EFFECTIVE?

Many interventionists hold that the value of early intervention is obvious and has been demonstrated (Hayden & McGinness, 1977); critics, even those predisposed philosophically towards the benefits of early intervention, argue that the efficacy of early intervention efforts still awaits objective verification (Clarke & Clarke, 1976; Ferry,1981; Gibson & Fields, 1984). In all probability, however, the supporters are too easily convinced of the value and the critics too harsh in their judgement, given current knowledge and resources available for studying program impact.

A complex array of variables affects the development of young children. Evidence that will enhance our understanding of biological growth factors is needed and salient environmental variables that may significantly affect developmental outcomes must be determined. For example, in the Down syndrome population, the precise impact that oral-motor problems (e.g., mouth cavity is small, motor coordination of lips and tongue is poor) have on language acquisition and production is still not known. Nutrition of pregnant women is important but the impact of certain dietary deficiencies during the fetal growth period on a child's subsequent learning is poorly understood. How much a responsive environment can offset neurological damage experienced by asphyxiated infants is yet to be determined (Campbell, Leib, Vollman & Gibson, 1989). Understanding the genetic-environment interplay can be compared to weaving a tapestry in which threads emanating from a variety of sources are woven into a pattern. The pattern is influenced by the quality of thread and the weaver's ability to create the conceptualized design. So with children, the outcome is determined by the quality of genetic-biological constitution and by salient environmental determinants (Sameroff & Chandler, 1975).

Appreciation of this interaction is important to interpretation of efficacy outcomes and the complexity of the task. A number of review articles and chapters have addressed the efficacy of early intervention programs. These reviews examined studies that met certain inclusion criteria with the express purpose of reaching some general conclusion about the efficacy of early intervention programs (Dunst & Rheingrover, 1981; Simeonsson, Cooper & Scheiner, 1982; Odom & Fewell, 1983; Hanson, 1987; Guralnick & Bennett, 1987). Although an over-simplification, these reviews report that participation in early intervention is associated with positive effects for children; however, the reviewers consistently identify a number of issues which seriously compromise these outcomes. First, studies vary greatly along dimensions of population, methodology, assessment tools and procedures, program characteristics, parent involvement and staff training and experience (Guralnick, 1988). This variability makes the drawing of generalized conclusions difficult. Second, apart from standardized tests of development, the field lacks adequate tools to measure program impact on children and on families. Third, experimental designs acceptable to the scientific community are often difficult to implement in programs designed to deliver services to children and their families.

Taking a different approach, Casto and his colleagues have examined the effectiveness of early intervention using meta-analysis (Casto & Mastropieri,1986; White, Mastropieri, & Casto, 1984). Meta-analysis refers to an analytical procedures which permits the combining of results of individual studies to produce a generalized outcome. Reported meta-analysis outcomes tend to support the efficacy of early intervention when examining changes in children's test scores and these analysis also find that longer, more intense programs produce better outcomes. Less optimistic results are reported for meta-analysis of age-at start, parent involvement, and degree of structure. Casto and Mastropieri (1986) report their meta-analysis indicated that parents are not "essential to intervention success," that beginning programs earlier is not better, and that more structured programs do not necessarily produce better outcomes.

Critics of these meta-analytical results have questioned the drawing of general conclusions by pooling studies that are very different (Strain & Smith, 1986; Shonkoff, Hauser-Cram, Krauss & Upshur, 1988). The outcome from a meta-analysis conducted by Shonkoff and Hauser-Cram (1987) on a smaller, more select group of studies on parental involvement lends substance to this criticism. The more selective meta-analysis conducted by Shonkoff and Hauser-Cram found that higher levels of parent participation was associated with greater child progress—a conclusion different from that of Casto and Mastropieri.

Despite conceptual and methodological problems, critics and supporters of early intervention continue to examine efficacy issues. The goal of this chapter is to discuss outcome data from selected early intervention programs serving different populations of children. In addition, summary conclusions about these studies are presented.

EARLY INTERVENTION PROGRAMS

Major developments in early intervention programs have occurred since the early 1970s and have been directed toward two populations: biologically impaired children and children at-risk for medical or environmental reasons.[1] The distinctions between these two populations are important. The biologically impaired child shows clear evidence of some significant structural or behavioral deficit or deficiency usually identifiable early in life. This group includes children with genetic abnormalities (e.g., Down syndrome), metabolic disorders (e.g., phenylketonuria), neurological disorders (e.g., cerebral palsy), and sensory impairments (e.g., visually impaired, hearing impaired). The children classified as at-risk for medical or environmental reasons, or both, include those who are born premature or suffer some medical difficulty early in life (e.g., respiratory distress syndrome), who have caregivers with questionable competencies (e.g., teenage mothers), or who are in abusive or neglecting environments. The reader should acknowledge the distinctions between these populations in terms of etiology, homogeneity (e.g., similarities and dissimilarities), incidence, prognosis, and the possible need for differing intervention approaches. Chapter 6 discusses these differences in detail.

The programs reviewed in this chapter were selected because the authors presented objective outcome data on program impact; because the results were published in generally accessible sources (e.g., journals or books as opposed to unpublished or inhouse reports); and because intervention efforts were formalized approaches used with more than one child. The review of the intervention effectiveness includes representative studies and is not comprehensive.

---

[1] This distinction is admittedly arbitrary. Children with medical difficulties could be classified as biologically impaired; however, the present text has not chosen to do so for two reasons. First, many medically at-risk infants recover without enduring problems. Second, the efficacy literature makes a distinction between the organically handicapped and medically at-risk infants.

Programs for Children with Down Syndrome

The biologically impaired population receiving considerable attention by intervention researchers is the child with Down syndrome. This population holds appeal because the majority of these children: (1) are identifiable at birth; (2) have a common genetic aberration; and (3) constitute the largest population with a specific genetic abnormality (Hayden & Beck, 1982). These commonalties have lead to the conclusion that Down syndrome individuals constitute a homogeneous population, and consequently, treatment effects on individuals or population sub-groups have been largely ignored. This tendency probably has masked a wide range of variability in this population (LaVeck & Brehm, 1978). Data on the infant with Down syndrome has indicated ranges in intellectual impairment from mild to severe (Bricker & Carlson, 1982; Bricker & Sheehan, 1981), emotional and social interactional differences (Cicchetti & Sroufe, 1976), and differences in motor development and tone (Harris, 1981). In addition, many of these youngsters have heart defects, hearing impairments, and other serious difficulties that interfere with development (Pueschel, 1984). Such defects and population variability affect treatment outcomes; however, intervention researchers appear to have given little attention to these important variables.

Early in the 1970s, Alice Hayden and her colleagues began a project that has produced a decade of information and material on the child with Down syndrome (Hayden & Dmitriev, 1975; Hayden & Haring, 1976; Dmitriev, 1979; Hayden & Haring, 1977). In 1977, Hayden and Haring reported program impact data on three groups of children with Down syndrome: those involved in the Model Preschool Project (N=53); those who formerly attended the program but were now in public schools (N=13); and those who did not participate in the early intervention project (N=28). Demographics for the three groups were similar; however, the age ranges for the three groups differed, making the analysis of outcome data difficult to interpret. A comparison of the performances on the Down Syndrome Performance Inventory of model program children with performances of nonparticipating age matches using a cross-sectional analysis suggests that the model program children initially functioned higher and maintained this advantage. Further, analysis in which comparisons were made on rates of development suggests that the developmental rate declines for the model program children and increases for the nonparticipating children. Final analyses conducted between performance level and rates of progress are interpreted by Hayden and Haring to indicate the value of early intervention.

Alternative interpretations of these analyses conducted by Hayden and Haring are less favorable. First, the rates of growth reported for the model population on the Down Syndrome Performance Inventory often exceed those of a normal population. This rate renders the Down Syndrome Performance Inventory suspect because a group of children with Down syndrome exceeding the projected normal rate of development seems highly unlikely. Second, the most interpretable data indicate, as the authors themselves note, ". . . that the model preschool program is not changing the basic developmental patterns of its children, but simply maintains the same developmental patterns at a higher overall rate" (p. 134). It seems plausible that a selection factor was operating. That is, more concerned caregivers sought early programming for their children—and this early advantage was maintained over time. Whether the model program was instrumental in creating and maintaining the early advantage is unanswerable with the available data.

An investigation conducted by Ludlow and Allen (1979) reflects a similar phenomenon. In this study, the progress of three groups of children with Down syndrome was compared over a ten-year period. Group A (*N*=72) was composed of children living at home who attended at least two years of preschool before their fifth birthday and whose parents received counseling. Group B (*N*=79) was composed of children living at home who had no preschool experience and whose families received no counseling. Group C (*N*=33) was composed of children with Down syndrome placed in a residential placement before their second birthday. Using the Griffiths Scale, the children's development was compared from birth to ten years. Testing the children at the same age was not possible and thus interpretation of scores was required.

A rapid decline in development for all groups during the first three years was reported. For Group A, development continued to decline slightly until age ten. For Group B, development declined until age five and then stabilized until age ten. For Group C, the initial sharp decline was modified but the downward trend occurred to age ten. Group A scored approximately 10 IQ points higher initially and maintained this superiority over Group B until approximately age eight. The mean difference in Group C's performance dropped from 10 IQ points initially to approximately 23 IQ points by age ten when compared with Group A. Similar though less dramatic differences are reported on the Stanford-Binet. A measure of personal-social development and speech development found Group A functioning significantly better than Groups B and C. Perhaps the most significant finding reported was that the percentage of Group A children attending public schools at ages five and ten was much higher than for Group B children.

These optimistic outcomes should be tempered by several factors. First, the initial superior performance of Group A (in the range of 10+ IQ points) strongly suggests these children may have come from a more concerned, responsive home environment. Ludlow and Allen suggest this may not be so because no selection was made in terms of family/children included in the early intervention and counseling. Second, Groups A, B, and C ". . . showed remarkable homogeneity on the variables examined (e.g., social class, parent education)." The investigators' explanation of the early difference is the probable impact of the early programming and counseling. Nonetheless, although the program did not discriminate or select, the parents themselves may have. Another potential contaminant recognized again by the investigators was the possibility of biased testing because the investigators did a significant portion of the assessments.

Addressing the same issue of the effects of early training on children with Down syndrome, Aronson and Fallstrom (1977) conducted a less global, better controlled investigation. Sixteen Down syndrome children ranging in age from twenty-one to sixty-nine months living in a small residential home were matched for CA (chronological age) and sex and divided into training and no training groups. Although the investigators were unable to match individual children for MA (mental age), the mean MA for each group was 20.6 months. All children participated in a preschool program, and the training group received an additional fifteen minutes to one hour of specialized training twice a week for eighteen months. The children were tested every six months during this period plus a' follow-up test twelve months after training was completed. The Griffiths Scale revealed an average increase in MA of 10.5 months for the trained group and 3.5 months for the controls, a reliable difference. The 12 month follow-up found no statistically significant differences between groups; however, this comparison was marred somewhat because one pair was not included because of the death of a child and because eight of the children had moved to other institutions. Determining the effect of subject attrition is impossible. However, when the performances of the remaining matched pairs were compared at follow-up, the children receiving the training outperformed the control children in six out of seven pairs.

Clunies-Ross (1979) assessed the impact of a structured intervention program on three groups of infants with Down syndrome. The three groups were composed of children from successive yearly intakes into the program (in 1976, $N=16$, mean CA=16.2 months; in 1977, $N=13$, mean CA=15.5 months; in 1978, $N=7$, mean CA=11.2 months). In addition to the structured classroom program for the infants, parents were required to attend a ten-week course focused on child development and management. The children were assessed at four-month intervals using the Early Intervention Development Profile (Rogers, D'Eugenio, Brown, Donovan, & Lynch, 1977); other measures were used periodically. Data were reported for six test points for the 1976 group, four test points for the 1977 group, and two test points for the 1978 group. A review of these data indicate steady progress for each group in similar increments over test periods. The 1978 group for which training was begun earliest show the highest developmental index (DI).

To illuminate this finding, Clunies-Ross (1979) performed a second analysis. Eight children from each successive enrollment year with at least four completed test periods were assigned to a birth-to-eleven month, twelve-to-twenty-three months or over-twenty-four months group depending upon their age at enrollment. The performances of the eight children in each of these age groups was compared. This comparison revealed the DI of the youngest group was initially highest. Perhaps the most important aspect of these data is the consistent report of accelerating development. This result, as the investigator notes, is in direct conflict with much of the previous reported data on the child with Down syndrome, which previously has shown a decelerating rate of development.

Hanson (1976; 1977) conducted an intervention program similar to that of Clunies-Ross. The intervention was structured, directed towards building specific skills, and parents were included as an integral part of the program; however, the Hanson project delivered services in the home. The interventionist also kept systematic data on the infant's acquisition of developmental milestones. The data were then compared with developmental data on normal infants and home-reared infants with Down syndrome not enrolled in early intervention programs. "These comparisons show that, in general, infants in the intervention program achieved developmental milestones at a slightly later age than the norms (i.e., normal infants) but consistently earlier than the infants with Down syndrome not involved in an intervention program" (Hanson & Schwarz, 1978). The differences reported for the intervention infants and the nonintervention infants with Down syndrome are quite dramatic. For example, a mean difference of ten months was reported when 50 percent of the intervention infants could drink unassisted from a cup; a mean difference of seven months for independent walking was reported. In other areas differences were minimal. Direct comparisons between investigations conducted in different settings must be made carefully, as done by Hanson and Schwarz (1978). The use of differential criteria for attainment of the milestone behaviors could significantly affect the comparisons.

An intervention study with infants with Down syndrome conducted by Piper and Pless (1981) yielded less optimistic outcomes. For this study, 37 infants with Down syndrome under the age of twenty-four months were recruited. Twenty-one infants were assigned to the experimental group, while the remaining sixteen infants composed the control group. Assignment to groups was made on the basis of referral dates. The experimental infants received center-based biweekly, one-hour therapy sessions. Stimulation activities were demonstrated to the parents. At the initiation of the intervention program, the Griffiths Scale and the Home Observation for Measurement of the Environment Inventory (Caldwell, 1978) were administered and again in six months, at the program's termination. A discriminant analysis found the experimental and control groups to be reliably different only on one subscale of the Home Inventory. Change scores from pretest to posttest were not significantly different for the experimental and control groups; however, although mean developmental quotients declined for both groups over the six-month period, the control group declined less.

Piper and Pless acknowledged that this investigation has some limitation. For example, the experimental and control subjects were assessed at different times of the year, which may have produced a bias. In addition, the length of intervention, the intensity, and the location may have affected the outcome. Finally, Piper and Pless indicated an inability to determine the frequency or fidelity with which the parents conducted the prescribed therapy.

This investigation has a number of problems; for example, as noted by Bricker, Carlson, and Schwarz (1981), an infant may have received as little as twelve hours of training during a six-month period. Furthermore, the concordance between the intervention and the chosen outcome measure seems questionable. In the Clunies-Ross (1979) and Hanson (1977) investigations, the length of intervention was considerably longer, the content more comprehensive, and the measurement instruments more relevant to the focus of training.

A more focused intervention project was conducted and reported by Harris (1981) in which twenty infants with Down syndrome ranging in age from 2.7 to 21.5 months were provided neurodevelopmental therapy. The Bayley Scale of Infant Development (Bayley, 1969) and the Peabody Developmental Motor Scales (Folio & DuBose, 1974) were administered before and after treatment. Based on the initial assessment, individual neurodevelopmental treatment plans were developed for each infant. Equivalent groups of infants were formed, then randomly assigned to a treatment or no-treatment group. Forty-minute therapy sessions were conducted three times per week in the infant's home (except for one child) for a period of nine weeks. The no-treatment infants were enrolled in early intervention programs. There was a statistically reliable difference between groups on the attainment of the treatment objectives. However, a t-test comparison found no differences between groups on the Bayley and the Peabody Developmental Motor Scale. At first glance, these findings might seem inconsistent, but probably are not because treatment was focused on specific objectives and only a few items on the Bayley or Peabody tests reflected the treatment emphasis.

An extensive report on an early intervention program has been provided by Kysela and his colleagues (Kysela, Hillyard, McDonald, & Ahlster-Taylor, 1981). This program had a home-based component which provided educational services for twenty-two infants who had a mean age of 13.5 months at the initiation of the program. Nineteen of these infants had Down syndrome. The center-based component served eight Down syndrome toddlers whose mean age was 28.4 months upon entry into the program. Parents involved in the home-based component were required to complete a formal training program, followed by visits to the families by a home specialist on a weekly or biweekly basis. The toddlers attended a half-day session four or five days per week. The investigators provided a detailed description of the conceptual and programmatic aspects of the program.

Results for the home-trained infants and center-based toddlers are reported in terms of progress in the expressive and receptive language program (a primary training target for all infants). These data are difficult to summarize, however, Kysela et al. (1981) suggest the results indicate that the children from both groups ". . . acquire[d] complex language skills with a rapid rate of learning and very few errors" (p. 370). On the whole, data from this project indicate that the program had a positive effect on the participating children even though, as the investigators note, controls were unavailable for comparison purposes.

In 1968, Rynders and Horrobin (1975; 1980) initiated a family-center early intervention project for infants with Down syndrome. From the point of referral until thirty months, the instruction was conducted in the infant's home with daily structured play sessions. When infants reached thirty months of age they were enrolled in a preschool program. The focus of this program was on concept utilization and communication. At age five years, the children moved into a public school program.

To assess the impact of the program, Rynders and Horrobin (1980) created a distal control group from another city. There were eighteen control and seventeen experimental children; all were diagnosed as having trisomy 21 and were matched on several demographic and physical variables. Comparisons were made at sixty months using the Boehm Test of Basic Concepts, an experimental language sampling instrument, the Stanford-Binet, and an adapted version of the Bruininks-Oseretsky Motor Test.

Interestingly, these investigators report no differences between the control and experimental subjects on the language measure and the Boehm test, but reliable differences were found favoring the experimental subjects on the Binet and Bruininks-Oseretsky Test. These findings were somewhat unexpected because the focus of the experimental program had been on concept formation and communication. The measure chosen to sample these areas did not reflect superiority of performance by the experimental subjects. Rather, the experimental subjects outperformed the controls on the more global measures of intelligence and motor behavior.

This investigation is one of the better controlled investigations of early intervention. Although random assignment of control and experimental subjects was not possible, an effort was made to recruit a group of distal controls who looked similar to the intervention subjects on a number of important variables. In addition, these infants did not perform differently on the Bayley Scales at twelve months of age but did diverge on an IQ measure at sixty months. Similar results were reported by Connolly, Morgan, Russell, and Richardson (1980), who compared two groups of children with Down syndrome matched on CA and parental education. The group participating in an early intervention program outperformed the nonintervention group on measures of IQ and SQ.

A description of an early intervention program was published in 1975 by Bidder, Bryant, and Gray. The approach used was to train mothers of infants with Down syndrome whose mean CA was twenty-four months and mean MA was approximately fifteen months. The mothers were divided into an experimental (*N*=8) and control group (*N*=8). The eight mothers in the experimental group received twelve two-hour training sessions during a six-month period. The training focused on teaching the mothers to employ behavior modification principles to assist the child in gaining desired behaviors. The experimental mothers were able to attend a discussion counseling group. The Griffiths Scales were administered before and after. Significant differences were reported for the experimental children for the language and performance scales; however, no differences were found for the other scales or overall scores. In addition, the experimental mothers reported increased knowledge about their children and improved morale.

A more recent study summarizes the findings of the research discussed above. Berry, Gunn, and Andrews (1984) evaluated the development of thirty-nine Down syndrome children using the Bayley Scales of Infant Development and the Merrill-Palmer Scale. These children attended a variety of private and public early intervention programs throughout Australia. Berry, Gunn, and Andrews' independent longitudinal assessment of the children's performance indicated ". . . that development in these children is consistently proportional to their chronological age and there is no evidence of plateaus during this period" (p. 167). The authors attribute consistent proportional mental growth observed in this population to their participation in early intervention programs.

Summary

Many studies have focused on determining the impact of early intervention on the Down syndrome population; however, only those with objective evaluative outcomes were reviewed. This review leads to several general conclusions:

1. Significant variability exists in the length and nature of proffered intervention services for the children and their families. These variances make drawing general and valid conclusions difficult. That is, do programs with different emphases and intervention time produce different effects? For specification and comparison of this variability see Guralnick and Bricker (1987) and Bailey and Bricker (1985) as well as Chapter 8.

2. Analyses have examined total program impact, thus the relative importance of specific elements (e.g., family participation, curricula employed, staff) is unknown.

3. A variety of instruments have been employed to assess program impact. Attempting to compare children's performances across measures is questionable because of content and administration differences.

4. The most common measures employed have been standardized intelligence tests. Use of these tools presents problems. First, the measures have not been standardized on handicapped populations; second, the test content may not reflect the instructional objectives emphasized by the program; and third, some children with handicaps may be penalized by standardization procedures.

5. Intervention researchers are faced with a number of changing variables that are difficult to control (e.g., child's health, family participation, child attrition, fidelity of treatment). Most experimental designs are not adequate to manage the uncontrolled and shifting variables facing the intervention researchers (Baer, 1981).

6. The generally positive effects reported across children and programs suggest that early intervention with young Down syndrome populations does have an impact.

7. Instruments, designs and methods of analyses are improving for evaluating the impact of early intervention; however, further work in these areas is needed.

Programs for Children Who are Biologically Impaired and Non-Down Syndrome

Shifting from intervention projects focused exclusively on the child with Down syndrome, we find a sizeable descriptive literature is available. Most of these reports tend to be descriptive and provide little material for objective evaluation of program impact. However, a few studies are available that provide, if not totally satisfactory, at least limited objective information on aspects of program impact.

In 1975, an early intervention program was begun at the University of Miami (Bricker & Dow, 1980). The focus of this program was on the child who was severely and profoundly handicapped, birth to five years of age. During the three years of this program, fifty children met the criteria for inclusion in the evaluation analysis. Of these fifty children, thirty-five were classified as severely/profoundly retarded, thirteen as moderately retarded, and two as mild or not retarded (but with severe motoric disabilities). These children attended a daily, full-day, center-based program. The program was structured to assist each child in acquiring critical skills in the areas of motor, communication, social, self-help, and cognition. Daily/weekly probe data were gathered on individual children's progress toward specific objectives. For an overall assessment of program impact, the Uniform Performance Assessment System (White, Edgar, Haring, Affleck, Hayden, & Bendersky, 1980) was administered. A correlated t-test comparison of pretest and posttest performance indicated a significant improvement ($p<.001$) for each of the four developmental domains and for the overall score in terms of the percent of items passed.

Given the serious problems of this population, these findings were encouraging even though adequate controls were lacking. In addition, upon graduation from this program, 88 percent of these children were placed in the public school at a time before P.L. 94-142 was being systematically enforced.

Bricker and Sheehan (1981) reported findings from a project located at the University of Oregon. This program operated a half-day, four days per week. Children were assessed and then IEPs developed to address cognitive, motor, communication, and social deficiencies. An activity-based training approach was used with the children's educational objectives embedded in daily group activities. Child-initiated behavior and parental involvement were major goals for all participants.

During Years 2 and 3 of the project, the Bayley Scales of Infant Development were administered to eighteen (mean CA = 20.0 months) and seventeen (mean CA = 15.7 months) infants, respectively, in the fall and again in the spring. The analysis revealed a reliable difference from pretest to posttest for the entire group as well as for subgroup analyses of infants classified as mild, moderately, and severely handicapped (with the exception of two subgroups). The McCarthy Scales for Children's Abilities (McCarthy, 1972) were used with children whose CA exceeded thirty months. Twenty-four children (mean CA = 46.8 months) were included in the Year 2 analysis, while thirty-two children (mean CA = 45.9 months) were included in the Year 3 analysis. The pre-post comparison made with the General Cognitive Index and mental age showed a significant difference. In addition, the subgroup analyses for Years 2 and 3 were generally significant. Two criterion-referenced instruments were used: the Uniform Performance Assessment System (White et al., 1980) and the Student Progress Record (Oregon State Mental Health Division, 1977). All pre-post comparisons using these two measures for Years 2 and 3 were significant.

Using a similar approach, but with an increased emphasis on parental involvement and the programming of functional skills using daily activities, Bailey and Bricker (1985) report data from a three-year early intervention program supported by the Handicapped Children's Early Education Program. The outcome data for Years 2 and 3 were reported for two groups of children: toddlers served in center-based classes and infants served at home. During Year 2, thirty-six children were enrolled with a mean age of one-year-six-months, while during Year 3, forty-six children were enrolled with the same mean age. Pre-posttest five-month interval comparisons were conducted using a standardized test (the Gesell) and a programmatic assessment (Comprehensive Early Evaluation and Programming System). Because the program was developmentally integrated, a total group and subgroup analysis for the normal, at-risk, mild, moderate, and severe groups was conducted when an adequate N was available. For the Gesell, the pre-post comparisons using the MA scores were significant for Years 2 and 3 for the total groups. The subgroup analysis found reliable differences for the nonhandicapped, mild, and moderate groups for Years 2 and 3. The pre-post difference was significant for the at-risk and severe groups for Year 3 (the small N during Year 2 did not permit a comparison). The pre-posttest comparisons on the programmatic measure for total groups and subgroups, where adequate N permitted calculation, were all significant.

An analysis of a subsequent three year Oregon-based early intervention program was completed by Bricker and Gumerlock (1988). An activity-based approach with parental involvement similar to the previous project was used. Program impact data were presented for 21 infants and 25 toddlers. Pre- and posttest comparisons on the Bayley Scales and Gesell were statistically significant for the infants. These same comparison were significant for those toddlers given the Gesell but not for those assessed with the Binet. The Evaluation and Programming System: For Infants and Young Children (Bricker, Gentry, & Bailey, 1985) was used to assess the children's quarterly progress toward IFSP goals and objectives. All pretest to posttest comparisons were highly significant.

These investigations can be criticized because they lack adequate controls; however, the uniformity of results across years and across instruments suggests the reported change was a real phenomenon. That such change would have occurred without the benefit of an early intervention program seems remote but must remain a plausible possibility.

A project described by Rosen-Morris and Sitkei (1981) is similar in many ways to the Bricker and Dow (1980) investigation in that a highly structured classroom program was developed for infants and young children who were severely handicapped. Subjects in the Rosen-Morris project ranged in age from eighteen months to six years. Approximately 50 percent had cerebral palsy, while the remainder had a combination of sensory impairments, Down syndrome, and epilepsy. Three measures were used to assess program impact: the Bayley Scales of Infant Development, the Student Progress Record, and the Preschool Attainment Record. Testing was done in the fall and then nine months later. Bayley mental- and motor-age equivalency scores were reported on eleven children. A t-test on the raw score indicated a reliable change. Thirty students were included in the pre-post analysis of the Student Progress Record and Preschool Attainment Record.

The results indicated a significant change on both measures. Given the nature of the target population, i.e., severely handicapped, the uniformly positive outcomes are encouraging. However, qualification of these results is necessary. First, the investigators indicated the need to adapt presentation of the Bayley items. Although this undoubtedly was necessary, it is unclear how such modifications of the testing instrument affected the results. Also, the t-test appears to have been computed on the raw scores rather than the age equivalencies. Finally, although the differences were reported as significant, the actual change in scores or age equivalencies are minimal. This small percentage change was true for the Bricker and Dow (1980) investigation as well. A relevant question then becomes, How much change is necessary for the effect to be considered educationally significant? More global reviews of programs and their impact on children who are severely handicapped have been conducted by Bailey and Bricker (1984), and Guralnick and Bricker (1987).

In a program with a center-based approach, sixteen multiply handicapped children between sixteen and sixty months of age received concentrated training in language, social, motor, and problem solving. To evaluate the program impact, Bagnato and Neisworth (1980) employed a variety of measures using a pre-post design. Multiple assessments were conducted every twelve weeks from four to twenty-four months (depending on child's length of enrollment). An intervention-efficiency index was calculated for each child and showed an average developmental gain of 1.11 months for each month of participation. Bagnato and Neisworth (1980) report that nine of the children showed a monthly gain in excess of one month.

The Portage Project (Shearer & Shearer, 1976) delivered educational services in the home rather than in a center. A home teacher visited participating families for 1.5 hours per week. An individual program was developed, and the teacher instructed the parents in its implementation. Child progress was monitored through the use of activity charts and progress reports that parents completed weekly. Unfortunately, general evaluation results were only summarized. Shearer and Shearer (1976) reported results from the Cattell Infant Test and the Stanford-Binet indicated that "The average child in the Project gained fifteen months in an eight-month period, as measured by these pre-post assessment tools." A second analysis entailed a comparison between a group of children enrolled in the Portage Project and a group of randomly selected children from a program for low-income children. The Binet, Cattell, Alpern-Boll Developmental Profile, and the Gesell Developmental Schedules were administered before and after to both groups. "A multiple analysis of covariance was used to control for IQ, practice effect, and age." Portage project children were reported to have made significantly greater gains in mental age, IQ, language, academic, and socialization skills.

In another article, Shearer and Shearer (1972) reported significant mean IQ gains on the Binet and Alpern-Boll Tests when ". . . children served as their own control." The lack of specificity in the reported results makes evaluation difficult. The number of children for whom the evaluation data are presented is not specified nor is the time interval for test administration. The nature of the analysis is described in only the most global fashion. However, Revill and Blunden (1979) also reported positive outcomes when employing the Portage model with a diverse group of nineteen handicapped children and their families. The subjects served as their own control, and the intervention began after a two-month baseline period. Although outcomes were variable, children's performances on the Griffiths Scale improved after intervention.

Soboloff (1981) reported a project in which fifty cerebral-palsied children seen in a clinic setting from 1952 to 1965 but who were not enrolled in any early intervention program were compared with fifty cerebral-palsied children seen between 1965 to 1978 who were enrolled in an early intervention program. No systematic attempt was made to match these two groups; rather, individuals with complete clinic records were included in the comparison. Records of the one-hundred children were evaluated independently by an orthopedic surgeon, a physical therapist, a nursery school teacher, and a speech therapist.

A number of comparisons were made. First, the percentage of children having some form of corrective surgery was examined, and the results indicated that in the group who had early intervention, 19 percent had surgery, while only 9 percent of the nonintervention group had surgery. Second, the records indicated that the early intervention group developed mobility and ambulation earlier. Comparison of family reactions also favored the early intervention group. Finally, the number of individuals from the two groups functioning in normal social settings (mainstreamed) was not different.

These findings led Soboloff (1981) to conclude, "In the present study there was no question that early stimulation was effective . . ." (p. 265). However, this conclusion warrants caution for several reasons. A number of significant changes in treatment variables could have occurred between the times that the two samples were drawn. In addition, the type of cerebral palsy in the two groups differed. Finally, the study was confounded by age because therapy was begun for the early intervention group considerably earlier than for the comparison group. This difference alone could have accounted for the discrepancies reported between the groups. Nonetheless, this investigation is one of the few attempts to evaluate the impact of early intervention on a population of motorically impaired children. Harris (1987) provides a review of a variety of intervention programs designed for children with motor disorders.

Preschool programs for sensory impaired children can be found in most public schools, and yet objective documentation of program impact is limited. Simmons-Martin (1981) reported outcome data on forty-four deaf children who entered an early intervention program at an average age of twenty-six months. The Scales of Early Communication Skills were used to evaluate child progress. The children were given the measure twice a year, and all children were tested over a two-and-one-half year span, receiving five separate communication skill ratings. Simmons-Martin reported that across these five ratings, the children's performance reliably improved. Unfortunately, one has no way to link this change directly to program impact rather than to maturation or other environmental variables. A variety of other early intervention programs for the child with hearing impairments have attempted to examined program impact. Many of these programs have been reviewed by Meadow-Orlans (1987).

A longitudinal study of ten blind infants provides limited comparative data on this population (Fraiberg, 1975). The intervention focused on providing support and guidance for parents as well as techniques for assisting the infant in acquiring adaptive behavior. Homes were visited twice per month and narrative records kept on the infants' progress. These records of behavioral progress were compared with norms in a previous study of sixty-six blind infants on select items in which the criteria used to determine successful acquisition were similar (Adelson & Fraiberg, 1975). On these items, which represent important bench marks (e.g., sits, stands, walks), the early intervention group reached criteria ahead of the comparison group. For early occurring responses, a difference of two months was reported, but this difference increased over time until a seven to thirteen month difference separated the groups. As the investigators noted, such a comparison must be carefully qualified; however, the differences in the acquisition of later motor skills were so dramatic as to strongly suggest a program impact.

Beside Fraiberg's work, there appears to be few investigations of the effects of early intervention on infants and young children who are visually impaired. Olson (1987) has reviewed the few investigations that address this population.

Summary

Many of the conclusions presented after the section on efficacy studies with Down syndrome children can be reiterated for the present group of studies:

1. Again, diversity is the rule because population served, program length, instructional content and approach vary considerably across programs.

2. Again, design problems exist because researchers were often required to make comparisons without adequate controls. Few children per cell as well as violations of assumptions of homogeneity make use of some statistical procedures questionable.

3. In addition to the more common methods for assessing program impact (e.g., standardized tests), some investigators used strategies designed to measure more qualitative outcomes (e.g., anecdotal accounts of program impact, family reactions, placement in regular education programs).

4. Finally, at least one research group conducted analyses of sub-groups of the total population to determine if program impact was differential for at-risk, mildly, moderately or severely impaired children.

Programs for At-Risk Children

Better controlled intervention studies have been conducted on populations of at-risk children than on biological impaired children for several reasons: First, larger numbers of at-risk children exist; second, less heterogeneity is found is this population; third, the formulation of nonintervention controls raises fewer ethical concerns than in populations of biologically impaired children.

Four of these programs have been selected for discussion. Each of these programs was chosen because it represented a specific population (e.g., premature, low-income), was a well-controlled study, and offered a different perspective on the effects of early intervention.

In an early study conducted by Scarr-Salapatek and Williams (1973), thirty premature (mean gestation thirty-two weeks), low-birth-weight infants (1300 to 1800 grams) born to young Black mothers from poverty circumstances were randomly assigned to an experimental ($N=16$) and control group ($N=15$). The experimental infants were placed in a special nursery and were provided designed stimulation activities (mobiles in the isolettes, extra handling). The controls received standard care for low-birth-weight infants. After discharge, a visitor made weekly visits to the homes of the experimental infants. Systematic input on handling and stimulation were provided to the mother. A follow-up at one year tested nine control (four children were lost and two parents refused to bring their infant in for testing) and fifteen experimental subjects with the Cattell Infant Intelligence Scale.

The results indicated the experimental group's performance was near normal levels and significantly different from the control infants. The random assignment and independent assessment leave little doubt, as the authors conclude, that this early intervention program produced a significant advantage in the behavioral functioning of the participating infants. An obvious concern with this investigation is the attrition in the control group.

The Scarr-Salapatek and Williams (1973) investigation confounded the variables of poverty and low birth weight. An investigation by Leib, Benfield, and Guidabaldi (1980) evaluated a special neonatal treatment using a population of preterm infants from white middle class homes. Twenty-eight preterm infants (mean gestation age = 32 weeks) were assigned to a control or experimental group. No significant differences were found between the groups prior to treatment. Treatment consisted of placing a mobile in the isolette, tactile/kinesthetic stimulation during feedings, and auditory stimulation (playing a music box). The control group received standard nursery care. The Brazelton Scales were administered prior to treatment and prior to discharge. The experimental infants performed significantly better on items reflecting inter-active processes (e.g., responses to social stimuli such as cuddliness and consolability) but were not different from the controls on motor and organizational processes. In addition, no significant differences between groups in weight gain were found. At six months, the Bayley Scales of Infant Development were administered. The treated infants' developmental status on the mental and motor scale was significantly higher than the untreated infants. The authors suggest this prescribed intervention program for high-risk preterm infants appeared to have enhanced the quality of development in the experimental group. Extensive reviews of intervention effects with medically fragile infants have been completed by Cornell and Gottfried (1976); Bricker (1984); Holmes, Reich and Pasternak (1984); and Bennett (1987).

A sizeable number of early intervention programs for infants or children from low-income families have been reported in the literature (e.g., Garber & Heber, 1981; Fowler, 1975; Gray, Ramsey, & Klaus, 1982; Karnes, et al., 1981). A number of excellent reviews of these programs exist (Bronfenbrenner, 1975; Beller, 1979; Ramey & Bryant, 1982; Bryant & Ramey, 1987) and, thus, only one representative program will be discussed here.

One of the most thoroughly researched project on the effects of early intervention on infants from poverty has been conducted by Ramey and his colleagues (Ramey & Campbell, 1979; Ramey, Farran, & Campbell, 1979). This project, called Abecedarian, had four yearly cohorts of 121 biological normal infants from low-income homes who were randomly assigned to experimental or control groups. The experimental infants attended a day-care program with a comprehensive curriculum. Attendance in the program began by three months of age, and the infants attended full-time, five days per week, fifty weeks per year. The Bayley Scales were used until the infants were eighteen months old, then the Stanford-Binet, McCarthy Scales, and Wechsler Preschool Scale were used from twenty-four to sixty months. The major goal of this project ". . . has been the prevention of a decline in intellectual development in the experimental group of high-risk children" (Ramey & Campbell, 1979, p. 14).

At twelve months, no differences between groups were found on the Bayley, but from then on significant differences in the range of 10 to 15 IQ points have been reported between control and experimental groups. These investigators also reported differences in language development and social confidence in favor of the experimental children (Ramey, MacPhee, & Yeates, 1983). A later companion project, called CARE, has also produced a wealth of information on the effects of different intervention approaches with children from low-income environments (Ramey, Bryant, Sparling,& Wasik, 1985).

Hunt (1980) provides a fascinating description of an early intervention project conducted in an orphanage in Tehran. For ethical reasons, this project had no simultaneous controls but rather looked at the effect of social and environmental changes by noting the ages the infants acquired selected behaviors. The foundling infants were studied in groups or "waves" from successive years. The first wave (N=15) received the usual institutional care and were tested routinely until age three. The second wave (N=10) received auditory and visual enrichment through tape recorders and mobiles which the infant could activate. The third wave (N=10) received "human enrichment" in which the infant-caregiver ratio was reduced and the staff responded to the infants as they deemed appropriate. The fourth wave (N=20) replicated the second wave but was implemented with more care. Wave five (N=11) received human enrichment, but the staff was trained to deliver systematic intervention. Testing with the Uzgiris-Hunt Scales (1975) indicated that each successive intervention subsequent to wave two hastened development of the infants, with the wave five intervention producing the greatest effect. Hunt also noted qualitative differences in language and social-responsiveness in favor of the wave five infants.

Summary

For several reasons, some of the previously discussed methodological and design problems facing the researcher using populations who are handicapped are absent when examining program effects with at-risk groups. First, control groups are easier to establish because there are no ethical constraints similar to those associated with withholding treatment from handicapped populations. Second, the availability of controls and larger numbers of infants make possible employing more traditional designs and analyses. Third, standardized instruments can be more appropriately used because the at-risk group does not deviate as far from norms as handicapped groups. Fourth, because the at-risk population does not generally suffer from significant chronic organic impairments, growth and development may occur more rapidly, permitting assessment of short-term intervention efforts. This constellation of variables permit the conduct of better controlled studies with at-risk populations. The consistent findings suggest early intervention can have a major and sustaining impact on at-risk groups, particularly the economically at-risk (Bryant & Ramey, 1987). The major criticism generally directed at these investigations is reliance on measures of child intelligence without examining effects on health, social skills or impact on the child's family.

Follow-Up of Contemporary Programs

Evaluation of long-term effects of early intervention programs with children who are handicapped are limited. There are probably two explanations. First, the conduct of longitudinal research is difficult and costly. Second, if one accepts the perspective that the developing child is affected at each stage in life and that hundreds of variables intercede between childhood and later life, there might be little reason to expect an early advantage to be maintained over time.

Descriptions of follow-up studies by Field, Dempsey, and Shuman; Sigman, Cohen, and Forsythe; Hunt; and Caputo, Goldstein, and Taub in an edited volume by Friedman and Sigman (1981) provide a rich source of longitudinal data on the sick, premature, and low-birth-weight child. Sameroff (1981) has summarized the findings of these four investigations. First, by entry into school, many at-risk children have developed problems. Second, "The single most potent factor influencing developmental outcome turns out to be the cultural environment of the child, as expressed in socioeconomic status and parental educational level"

(Sameroff, 1981, p. 342). This latter finding provides powerful support for early intervention efforts to: (1) reinforce families already providing an enriching environment for the infant, and (2) assist parents who provide unsatisfactory physical and social environments in acquiring more facilitative strategies for interacting with their infant.

One of the more impressive contemporary longitudinal study of children is a consortium effort directed by Irving Lazar. "In 1976, 12 investigators who had independently designed and implemented infant and preschool programs in the 1960's, pooled their original data and conducted a collaborative follow-up of the original subjects . . ." (Lazar, Darlington, Murray, Royce, & Snipper, 1982). This collaborative effort permitted assessment of program effects across a number of projects and follow-up of a substantial group of children through high school. The population enrolled in these twelve projects were infants and young children from low-income homes. The individual projects varied in philosophy and approach; however, enough similarity existed to pool their results.

The most salient outcome of this longitudinal follow-up project was that significantly fewer children who participated in an early program were assigned to special education classes, and fewer were retained in a grade than the control children. No significant differences between experimental and control children on measures of achievement and intelligence were found (Lazar, et al., 1982).

Two notable investigations initiated in the late 1960s and early 1970s also focused on children from low-income families and have produced outcome data that supplement the consortium finding. Long-term differences in IQ and other academic and achievement measures in favor of the experimental groups were reported (Garber & Heber, 1977; Ramey & Campbell, 1979).

A follow-up study conducted by Moore, Fredericks, and Baldwin (1981) focused on nine-, ten-, and eleven-year-old children who were moderately to severely handicapped and enrolled in trainable mentally retarded public school classes. This group of children differed in that some (*N*=68) had no preschool experience, some (*N*=35) had one year and some (*N*=48) had two years of preschool experience. A statewide assessment instrument, the Student Progress Record, was used to compare performances in language, academics, self-help, and motor skills of these three groups of children. The results indicated that those children enrolled in preschools for two years performed significantly better on the language, academic, self-help, and motor scales. The performance of the group with one year's preschool experience was not reliably different from the group with no experience. Such results must be considered tentative because this was a retrospective investigation with all the problems inherent in such an approach. Furthermore, a selection factor may have been operating because concerned families may be more apt to seek a preschool placement earlier for their children; thus, the differences may stem not so much from the preschool experience but the family's handling of the child.

Follow-up of the federally funded Handicapped Children's Early Education Programs(HCEEP) has been conducted to determine its national impact. Stock, Wnek, Schenck, Gabel, Spurgeon and Ray (1976) followed children from 32 programs and reported progress greater than could be expected by maturation. In 1982, an analysis of the HCEEP by Littlejohn Associates reported that 55 percent of the children who leave HCEEP are placed in integrated settings; and 67 percent perform in the average or above average range.

These investigations can be seen as parallel to the Lazar et al. (1982) consortium project except the focus was on children who were handicapped. Three major differences exist, however. First, the HCEEP follow-up did not have control groups for comparison. Second, the HCEEP follow-ups provided no information on these children's progress and adjustment during adolescence and the early adult years. Third, HCEEP follow-ups combined a variety of programs and obtained information in a less rigorous method. Even with these constraints, the outcomes reported by these independent research agencies must be seen as encouraging. In addition, a few other investigators have reported information on enrolled children upon entry into the public schools; for example, Zeitlin (1981) and Weiss (1981).

Summary

Conducting follow-up or longitudinal research is an arduous task reflected by the paucity of studies contained in the literature. The methodological and design problems identified in the earlier summary sections also create barriers to the conduct of longitudinal research, and most likely these problems are compounded by the passage of time during which a complex array of variables may change and become realigned. Nonetheless, there continues to be a significant need for longitudinal studies on organically impaired populations.

PROGRAM IMPACT ON FAMILIES

The evaluation made of early intervention programs has been primarily focused on addressing child outcome variables. Attempts to examine program impact on other social agents in the child's life have been sparse (Clarke-Stewart, 1981) largely because programs have lacked the necessary resources and tools to conduct such research. The family members' comfort with their child who is at-risk or handicapped as well as their ability to manage the child may often be more important to maintaining the child in the home and community than whether or not the child reaches specific developmental objectives. The program-impact information that has been collected on families has been reviewed elsewhere (see e.g., Baker, 1984; Walker, Slentz & Bricker, 1985; Rosenberg & Robinson, 1988), and thus, only a few representatives studies will be described. These studies can be conveniently categorized into three areas: (1) acquisition of instructional skills by parents; (2) interaction between the caregiver and child; and (3) quality of life changes in the families.

Acquisition of Instructional Skills

One of the early research investigations on the effects of training parents as interventionists was conducted by Baker and his colleagues (Baker & Heifetz, 1976; Baker, Heifetz, & Murphy, 1980). One-hundred-sixty families with children who were mentally retarded between the ages of three and fourteen participated in this study. The parents were divided into four groups, each having a different training format. A fifth group received delayed training and served as a control. The parents were assessed on a Behavioral Vignettes Test (Baker & Heifetz, 1976) before and after training. The training focus of each group was to assist parents in the acquisition of behavior modification techniques (e.g., use of systematic praise, planned ignoring). Four different approaches were used: (1) training manual; (2) training manual and biweekly phone calls; (3) training manual and group meetings; and (4) training manuals, group meetings, and home visits. All methods required the parents to teach specific skills to their children. The training lasted approximately twenty weeks and was completed by 87 percent of the families.

All the mothers involved in training demonstrated a significant improvement on the Behavioral Vignettes Test when compared to control mothers (Baker & Heifetz, 1976). The results for the fathers were related to the type of training they received. The children of trained parents improved significantly in skill acquisition over the control group, suggesting that the child change was directly related to the parent acquisition of behavioral teaching skills.

A study conducted by Bidder, Bryant, and Gray (1975) with the mothers of infants with Down syndrome reported similar findings to the Baker and Heifetz study. After training of the mothers, significant differences were found in favor of the treatment group on the language and performance scales of the Griffiths, and positive trends on the loco-motor and eye-hand scales.

A few investigations employing single-subject analyses report that parents have successfully learned to use specific intervention procedures such as task analysis (Filler & Kasari, 1981), shaping techniques (Adubato, Adams, & Budd, 1981), reinforcement strategies (Petrie, Kratochwill, Bergan, & Nicholson, 1981) and use of more appropriate antecedents (Chelsedine & McConkey, 1979). Each of these investigations reports that parents acquired the targeted behavioral teaching strategy and found that parents were able to employ the acquired skills to effectively instruct their child.

The studies reviewed in this section clearly indicate that parents of children who are handicapped can acquire intervention skills. In addition, the acquisition of these skills appear to produce positive outcomes in their children's development.

Interactional Change

The Carolina Abecedarian Project has reported that participation in this intervention program enhanced the mother-infant relationship in a population of rural poverty Black families (Ramey, MacPhee, & Yeates, 1983). Likewise, the Milwaukee Project found that the mildly retarded urban poor mothers involved in their project changed the manner in which they interacted with their children by becoming more responsive and verbal (Garber & Heber, 1977). Similarly, Johnson (1975) and Johnson, Breckenridge and McGowan, (1984), described a project involving Mexican-American families living in poverty. After the second year of intervention, the experimental mothers, when compared with a non-intervention control group, were found to be significantly warmer and less intrusive, and to use more play materials with their infants. The experimental children also scored significantly higher than the control children on the Stanford-Binet.

Gordon and Kogan (1975) intervened with mothers of cerebral palsy children to change interactional patterns. After baseline interactional patterns were determined, parents were divided into an intervention group and a delayed intervention group. The delayed group received training eight weeks after the first group. The intervention included an interview discussing specific behavioral strategies and an interaction session between parent and child. After the intervention period, both groups of mothers improved their interactional style, and significantly more positive behaviors were displayed by both mothers and children. This study was replicated by Tyler and Kogan (1977) and again, the intervention was found to significantly reduce negative interactions between mothers and their children.

Christophersen and Sykes (1979) reported a study using three parent-child dyads. The preschool-age children were moderately retarded. A parent-child interactional code was used to measure the effectiveness of intervention. The parents were trained to reward appropriate behavior, and to use time out or a verbal reprimand for inappropriate behaviors. All subjects showed: (1) an increase in positive parent-child interactions; (2) a decrease in negative interactions for two subjects; (3) a decrease in parent nonattending; and (4) increase in child compliance.

These investigations, focused on affecting the interactional dimensions of the parent-child relationships and conducted with children who were handicapped or environmentally at-risk, taken in tandem with studies conducted on at-risk infants (Minde, Shosenberg, Marton, Thompson, Ripley, & Burns, 1980; Bromwich & Parmelee, 1979; Field, Widmayer, Stringer, & Ignaloff, 1980), have produced encouraging outcomes. Projects designed to enhance positive dimensions of parent-child relationship seem feasible and effective (Rosenberg & Robinson, 1988).

Quality-of-Life Changes

A comprehensive evaluation of the effects of early intervention on families was undertaken by Rescorla and Zigler (1981). Originally, eighteen children, age birth to three years, from low-income families participated in this study. Parents of the children were visited in the home twice a month for the first year of the project and monthly thereafter. The focus of the visit was the parents' social and economic needs. These parents were also given free medical care, and day care was provided. Child progress was assessed at periodic intervals for the experimental and matched comparison group. An evaluation of the program found that twelve of the seventeen mothers in the experimental group sought further education during the program and eight of these mothers continued their education. There was a decline in the number of experimental parents seeking welfare. An analysis of the five-year follow-up data indicated a significant difference favoring the experimental group on socioeconomic status, number of children (fewer), employment, and general quality of life. The children in the experimental group also had significantly higher scores on the Peabody Picture Vocabulary Test than control children.

The Milwaukee Project collected data on quality-of-life changes in participating families (Garber & Heber, 1977; Garber & Heber, 1981). More mothers from the experimental group were employed, and of those who were working, there was an average difference of nearly forty dollars for weekly salary in favor of the experimental mothers. A significantly greater portion of experimental mothers were literate. Ramey and his colleagues (Ramey, MacPhee, & Yeates, 1983) also reported educational and employment changes in project parents. Though the groups were educationally equivalent at the time of the child's birth, the experimental mothers had acquired significantly more formal education by the time their children were fifty-four months old. As might be expected, more of the experimental mothers held semiskilled or skilled jobs than the control mothers.

Field (1981) compared the effects of two intervention approaches with teenage mothers and their preterm infants. The mothers and infants of the control group were assessed every four months for a year, while the intervention groups participated in either a home-visit program for a year or a center-based nursery program for six months. The intervention groups received the same type of informational input; however, the center-participating mothers served as paid staff members in the nursery program and as such were expected to care for other infants besides their own. Post-intervention results indicated that the infants attending the center-based program performed better on growth and developmental measures and that their mothers found employment more frequently than the mothers in the other groups. The incidence of repeat pregnancy was also lower among the center mothers.

The Carolina Abecedarian Project, the Milwaukee Project, and the Field project (1981) reported favorable attitudinal changes in participating parents. However, two studies reporting attitudinal changes in parents of children who were handicapped are conflicting. Hetherington, Suttill, Holmlund, and Frey (1979) measured the attitudes of sixty parents of children who were severely developmentally delayed (mean age = 5.6 years). Thirty of these parents participated in an intervention project. After two years of intervention, participating parents had more "negative attitudes" towards their child who was severely handicapped than before intervention and than the control group. The authors suggest the lack of progress by the children during intervention may have caused discouragement in the parents. On the other hand, Spiker (1982) reported that thirty-two mothers of children with Down syndrome were positive about their experiences when participating in intervention programs.

The few studies reviewed in this section suggest that early intervention programs can assist families in improving the quality of their lives. Early intervention personnel are well advised to broaden their focus and become concerned with affecting important aspects of children and their families' lives.

Summary

The review of efficacy programs focused on parents leads to several conclusions:

1. Comparatively little empirical work determining program impact on parents has been reported.

2. The major thrust of the reported work has been on teaching parents behavior management and interactional skills. The results indicate that parents can acquire specific management and interactional skills. However, what is less clear is the parents' ability to generalize these skills in functional ways.

3. The impact of programs on a number of important variables concerning quality of life have been studied infrequently and more research in these areas is needed.

As will be discussed in Chapter 7, the involvement of parents in intervention programs has changed dramatically during the past decade. As partially reflected in the efficacy literature reviewed, researchers are shifting from measuring program impact exclusively on children to measuring program impact on parents. An additional change has been to expand the research focus from investigations of instructional and management skills to studying interactional and quality-of life-variables.

ISSUES ASSOCIATED WITH EFFICACY OUTCOMES

Two important issues are associated with determining the effect of early intervention programs on young children: the longevity of program impact and expectancies. Each of these issues is discussed below.

Longevity of Program Impact

A serious criticism of early intervention efforts is that the effects produced on enrolled children tend to disappear or "wash out" over time (Clarke & Clarke, 1977). The investment of resources in early intervention programs are questioned when initial reported superiority of the experimental subjects is not maintained over time. Taken at face value such criticism would seem valid; however, at least two factors need consideration.

I remember Sue Gray saying that early intervention is not an inoculation against future educational practice, and she has reaffirmed this position (Gray, Ramsey, & Klaus, 1982). Yet critics seem to expect early gains made by children should be maintained regardless of the child's future circumstances. Ample evidence exists that indicates without subsequent proper environmental arrangements (e.g., reinforcement of a learned response), acquired behavior will not necessarily be maintained and new responses may not be developed as expected. The literature is replete with examples in which children have acquired behavior that does not generalize to other settings or is not maintained. Does this mean that the intervention should never have occurred? Or, rather, does it suggest that additional attention should be given to subsequent environments to ensure the generalization and maintenance of learned skills? Research from longitudinal intervention programs suggests that by continuing systematic educational intervention, gains made during the preschool period can be maintained into the elementary years (Bryant & Ramey, 1987).

A second dilemma that arises when studying the longevity of effect is the notion of continuity (see also Chapter 2 for a discussion of continuity). The controversy surrounding continuity of behavior has long been a favorite topic of developmental specialists (see e.g., Kagan, Kearsley, & Zelazo, 1978). Some theorists argue that human behavior is continuous. That is, earlier behavior provides the foundation for subsequent development, and that clear regularities in growth and development are apparent for individuals over time (Lewis & Starr, 1979). Others argue that there is little evidence of continuity for children, as indicated by such factors as the poor predictive power of an infant's performance on a standardized test for later development (McCall, 1979). Rather, the data appear more supportive of a transactional explanation in which both the child's constitution and the environment play critical roles (Warner, 1986).

The relationship between behavioral continuity and early intervention is important. If early behavioral repertoires are directly linked to future motor and conceptual development, logic would argue for the importance of early experience for the child's subsequent development. If, however, behavior is discontinuous, then early experience may be of less importance to the child's future as Clarke and Clarke have suggested (1976). The continuity dilemma hinges, in part, on the length of time one would expect to be able to predict behavioral continuity. Further, some amount of the predictability would seem to be predicated on the relative continuity of the individual's environment. Even those strongly committed to the continuity position recognize that dramatic changes in an environment tend to produce significant changes in a child's behavior.

The continuity issue will no doubt remain a controversy for many years; however, for present purposes a reasonable resolution might be to accept the notion of contiguous continuity. That is, that current behavioral repertoires provide the foundation for the development of the next succeeding stage which, in turn, directly affects the next subsequent stage or level of development. This perspective was discussed in more detail in Chapter 2.

A child's current behavioral repertoire affects the acquisition of subsequent new response forms; therefore, rather than attempting to demonstration long term effects of early intervention, a more reasonable goal is to demonstrate successive impact over time. It is remarkable that investigations have been able to report long-term effects such as those described by Lazar et al. (1982). These outcomes suggest the importance of attempting to study the environments of the children to determine what aspects have maintained the original gain or what changes have occurred to reduce or dilute the initial experimental and control differences.

The collection of such information will no doubt reflect the interactive nature of development, as has been proposed by a number of major theorists (Piaget, 1970; Uzgiris, 1981; Sameroff & Chandler, 1975; Lewis & Rosenblum, 1974). Development is systematically shaped by the "transactions" between the organism and the environment. An intricate web of reciprocal transactions occur that lead to the transformation of the child's behavioral repertoire. Unless the child's biology and environment remain relatively constant, one would be correct to predict variable outcomes for individual children. When investigations report that experimental groups maintain their superiority over time, one might speculate that the early intervention has not only affected the child, but influenced other important environmental factors as well.

What, then, is a reasonable expectation for the longevity of program impact? A simple answer seems unlikely. Rather, longevity of program impact is most likely determined by a number of variables. The length, quality, and content of an early intervention effort will doubtless affect the longevity of the impact. In addition, the subsequent environments experienced by children and their families must be seen as the mediator of subsequent development and be responsible, in part, for subsequent outcomes regardless of program effects. Early intervention programs cannot protect children from the future. Such programs may be able to enhance the child's development, but these enhancements are surely not automatically retained. Rather, children's progress will depend upon their current repertoire and the transactions that occur with subsequent environment.

The Expectancy: Normal Behavior?

Another philosophical issue facing early interventionists and those concerned with the enterprise is the selection of outcome goals. Said another way, what is, or should be, the expectancies for children participating in early intervention programs? An immediate response is often to mention the paramount need for individualization of goals and objectives for children, thus requiring expectancies to be personalized as well. However, expectancies seem to acquire an added dimension when general program impact is examined. For groups of children, expectancies appear to drift towards normalcy. Readers may disagree that the expectation of normal functioning is a goal of early intervention programs focused on children who are handicapped. Nevertheless, the majority of early intervention programs previously reviewed employed measures that were standardized on normal children. Although such measures may be useful (Ramey, Campbell, & Wasik, 1982), their deployment suggests an implicit comparison to normal behavior. Establishing a target of normal functioning may be at times appropriate and sensible and may become troublesome only when programs which fail to reach that goal are devalued exclusively because of such comparisons.

Although decisions about program effectiveness tend to be based on whether the intervention produced statistically significant differences, a corollary step is to establish the educational significance or worth of such differences. For example, Clunies-Ross (1979) reported that the infants with Down syndrome who were enrolled earlier in an intervention program made the greater progress. The next question to ponder is the significance of such progress. Does an increase in the IQ render the quality of the child's or family's life better? I would venture to predict that if a program changed the enrolled children's IQ scores from 40 to 60, a less enthusiastic response by reviewers would be expected than if the IQ scores shifted from 70 to 90. The latter gain suggests the children are functioning within normal limits, while the gain from 40 to 60 does not. I do not believe that investigators, practitioners, and consumers consciously make such distinctions, but I strongly suspect that an inarticulated hope or expectancy for children who are handicapped is for functioning within the realm of normalcy. When programs fall short of this expectancy, their worth may be questioned (Piper & Pless, 1980; Ferry, 1981; Gibson & Fields, 1984).

Given current technology and knowledge, programs often assist children who are handicapped in making only modest gains (Bricker & Dow, 1980), giving rise to the question of whether the resource investment was "worth" the gain. Society appears to have agreed that assisting the handicapped individual to gain more independence is an acceptable goal toward which resources should be expended (e.g., P.L. 94-142 and P.L. 99-457). If so, then it seems important to tease from this commitment the often accompanying expectancy that intervention will render the child normal. Expectancies need to be tempered with the reality that less dramatic outcomes for children who are impaired are the rule rather than the exception. Although the goal of normal functioning may not be within reach of many children, this does not mean that efforts to assist children who are handicapped should be diluted or reduced. Rather, expectancies should be changed to accept consistent progress towards independent functioning, even if there is no associated evidence of change on more traditional standardized measures. Such changes in expectancy require that other reliable and valid indices of child progress be developed: a problem addressed in a later section of this book.

SUMMARY

This chapter has presented a review of a variety of early intervention programs designed to eliminate or attenuate deficits in handicapped populations or keep deficits from occurring in populations of biologically or environmentally at-risk children and to effect families in a positive manner. Although objective data on program impact was provided, the majority of these studies have serious methodological or design flaws which have lead to questioning the validity of such data in evaluating program effectiveness (see Dunst & Rheingrover, 1981; Odom & Fewell, 1983; Gibson & Fields, 1984; Guralnick & Bennett, 1987).

Many of the method and design flaws result from conducting research on intervention programs primarily designed to meet the needs of participating children and families. For example, of the reviewed studies, few had matched controls. Establishing nonintervention controls is difficult because of federal and state mandates, not to mention ethical and humanitarian concerns for the provision of services to children who are disabled. Comparing approaches or models is often difficult because participating children and families may not necessarily be similar in terms of critical variables such as age, SES, or developmental level. Except in large metropolitan areas, problems stemming from low incidence groups, attendance, and attrition cause serious problems for investigators attempting to examine change. Failure to specify the program philosophy, content, and treatment strategies also may render outcomes relatively uninterpretable. Without detailed knowledge of intervention content and approach, it is difficult to determine what reported gains by children and parents actually reflect in terms of programmatic input. Finally, there are few valid and reliable instruments that reflect a program's emphasis and measure functional change. These deficiencies present significant barriers to the intervention researcher.

Rather than to belittle past efforts at program evaluation, a more serviceable perspective is to use these investigations to provide guidance for developing a template for change. The analyses of available program evaluation data are an ideal base from which to develop future guidelines for investigators interested in documenting program effectiveness. In particular, more attention must be given to developing relevant and appropriate outcome measures for children and families. Finally, alternative nontraditional but acceptable control procedures must be found for comparing program outcomes.

References

Adelson, E., & Fraiberg, S. (1975). Gross motor development in infants blind from birth. In B. Friedlander, G. Sterritt, & G. Kirk (Eds.), *Exceptional infant* (Vol. 3). New York: Brunner/Mazel.

Adubato, S., Adams, M., & Budd, K. (1981). Teaching a parent to train a spouse in child management techniques. *Journal of Applied Behavior Analysis, 14*, 193-205.

Aronson, M., & Fallstrom, K. (1977). Immediate and long-term effects of developmental training in children with Down's syndrome. *Developmental Medicine and Child Neurology, 19*, 489-494.

Baer, D. (1981). The nature of intervention research. In R. Schiefelbusch & D. Bricker (Eds.), *Early language: Acquisition and intervention.* Baltimore, MD: University Park Press.

Bagnato, S., & Neisworth, J. (1980). The intervention efficiency index: An approach to preschool program accountability. *Exceptional Children, 46*, 264-269.

Bailey, E., & Bricker, D. (1984). The efficacy of early intervention for severely handicapped infants and young children. *Topics in Early Childhood Special Education, 4*(3), 30-51.

Bailey, E., & Bricker, D. (1985). Evaluation of a three-year early intervention demonstration project. *Topics in Early Childhood Special Education, 5*(2),52-65.

Baker, B. (1984). Intervention with families with young, severely handicapped children. In J. Blacher (Ed.), *Severely handicapped young children and their families.* New York: Academic Press.

Baker, B., & Heifetz, L. (1976). The Read Project: Teaching manuals for parents of retarded children. In T. Tjossem (Ed.), *Intervention strategies for high risk infants and young children.* Baltimore, MD: University Park Press.

Baker, B., Heifetz, L., & Murphy, D. (1980). Behavioral training for parents of mentally retarded children: One year follow-up. *American Journal of Mental Deficiency, 85,* 31-38.

Bayley, N. (1969). *Bayley Scales of Infant Development.* New York: The Psychological Corporation, 1969.

Beller, E. (1979). Early intervention programs. In J. Osofsky (Ed.), *Handbook of infant development.* New York: Wiley.

Bennett, F. (1987). The effectiveness of early intervention for infants at increased biologic risk. In M. Guralnick & F. Bennett (Eds.), *The effectiveness of early intervention for at-risk and handicapped children.* New York: Academic Press.

Berry, P., Gunn, V., & Andrews, R. (1984). Development of Down's syndrome children from birth to five years. *Perspectives and Progress in Mental Retardation, 1,* 167-177.

Bidder, R., Bryant, G., & Gray, O. (1975). Benefits of Down's syndrome children through training their mothers. *Archives of Disease in Childhood, 50,* 383-386.

Bricker, D. (1984). The effectiveness of early intervention with handicapped and medically at-risk infants. *Journal of Children in Contemporary Society, 17*(1), 51-65.

Bricker, D., Gentry, D., & Bailey, E. (1985). *Evaluation and Programming System: For Infants and Young Children.* Center on Human Development, University of Oregon, Eugene, Oregon.

Bricker, D., & Carlson, L. (1982). The relationship of object and prelinguistic social-communicative schemes to the acquisition of early linguistic skills in developmentally delayed infants. In G. Edgar, N. Haring, J. Jenkins, & C. Pious (Eds.), *Mentally handicapped children.* Baltimore, MD: University Park Press.

Bricker, D., Carlson, L., & Schwarz, R. (1981). A discussion of early intervention for infants with Down's syndrome. *Pediatrics, 67,* 45-46.

Bricker, D., & Dow, M. (1980). Early intervention with the young severely handicapped child. *Journal of the Association for the Severely Handicapped, 5,* 130-142.

Bricker, D., & Gumerlock, S. (1988). Application of a three-level evaluation plan for monitoring child progress and program effects. *Journal of Special Education, 22*(1), 66-81.

Bricker, D., & Sheehan, R. (1981). Effectiveness of an early intervention program as indexed by child change. *Journal of the Division for Early Childhood, 4,* 11-27.

Bromwich, R., & Parmelee, A. (1979). An intervention program for preterm infants. In T. Field, A. Sostek, S. Goldberg, & H. Shuman (Eds.), *Infants born at risk.* Jamaica, NY: Spectrum Publications.

Bronfenbrenner, U. (1975). Is early intervention effective? In B. Friedlander, G. Sterritt, & G. Kirk (Eds.), *Exceptional infant: Assessment and intervention* (Vol. III). New York: Brunner/Mazel.

Bryant, D., & Ramey, C. (1987). An analysis of the effectiveness of early intervention programs for environmentally at-risk children. In M. Guralnick & F. Bennett (Eds.), *The effectiveness of early intervention for at-risk and handicapped children.* New York: Academic Press.

Caldwell, B. (1978). *Home observation for measurement of the environment.* Syracuse, NY: Syracuse University Press.

Campbell, P., Leib, S., Vollman, J., & Gibson, M. (1989). Interaction pattern and developmental outcome of infants with severe asphyxia: A longitudinal study of the first years of life. *Topics in Early Childhood Special Education, 9*(1), 48-71.

Casto, G., & Mastropieri, M. (1986). The efficacy of early intervention programs: A meta-analysis. *Exceptional Children, 52*(5),417-424.

Cheseldine, S., & McConkey, R. (1979). Parental speech to young Down's syndrome children: An intervention study. *American Journal of Mental Deficiency, 83,* 612-620.

Christophersen, E., & Sykes, B. (1979). An intensive, home based family training program for developmentally delayed children. In L. Hamerlynck (Ed.), *Behavioral systems for the developmentally disabled: (I). School and family environments.* New York: Brunner/Mazel.

Cicchetti, D., & Sroufe, A. (1976). The relationship between affective and cognitive development in Down's syndrome infants. *Child Development, 47,* 920-929.

Clarke, A., & Clarke, A. (1976). *Early experience: Myth and evidence.* New York: The Free Press.

Clarke, A., & Clarke, A. (1977). Prospects for prevention and amelioration of mental retardation: A guest editorial. *American Journal of Mental Deficiency, 81,* 523-533.

Clarke-Stewart, K. (1981). Parent education in the 1970's. *Educational Evaluation and Policy Analysis, 3,* 47-58.

Clunies-Ross, G. (1979). Accelerating the development of Down's syndrome infants and young children. *The Journal of Special Education, 13,* 169-177.

Connolly, B., Morgan, S., Russell, F., & Richardson, B. (1980). Early intervention with Down syndrome children. *Physical Therapy, 60,* 1405-1408.

Cornell, E., & Gottfried, A. (1976). Intervention with premature human infants. *Child Development, 47,* 32-39.

Dmitriev, V. (1979). Infant learning program for Down's syndrome. In B. Darby & M. May (Eds.), *Infant assessment: Issues and applications.* Seattle, WA: WESTAR.

Dunst, C., & Rheingrover, R. (1981). An analysis of the efficacy of infant intervention programs with organically handicapped children. *Evaluation and Program Planning, 4,* 287-323.

Ferry, P. (1981). On growing new neurons: Are early intervention programs effective? *Pediatrics, 67,* 38-41.

Field, T. (1981). Intervention for high-risk infants and their parents. *Educational Evaluation and Policy Analysis, 3,* 69-78.

Field, T., Widmayer, S., Stringer, S., & Ignaloff, E. (1980). Teenage, lower-class black mothers and their pre-term infants: An intervention and developmental follow up. *Child Development, 51,* 426-436.

Filler, J., & Kasari, C. (1981). Acquisition, maintenance and generalization of parent-taught skills with two severely handicapped infants. *The Journal of the Association for the Severely Handicapped, 6,* 30-38.

Folio, R., & DuBose, R. (1974). *Peabody developmental motor scales* (IMRID Behavioral Science Monograph, No. 25). Nashville, TN: Peabody College.

Fowler, W. (1975). A developmental learning approach to infant care in a group setting. In B. Friedlander, G. Sterritt, & G. Kirk (Eds.), *Exceptional infant* (Vol. 3). New York: Brunner/Mazel.

Fraiberg, S. (1975). Intervention in infancy: A program for blind infants. In B. Friedlander, G. Sterritt & G. Kirk (Eds.), *Exceptional infant* (Vol. 3). New York: Brunner/Mazel.

Friedman, S., & Sigman, M. (Eds.). (1981). *Pre-term birth and psychological development.* New York: Academic Press.

Garber, H., & Heber, R. (1977). The Milwaukee project. In P. Mittler (Ed.), *Research to practice in mental retardation: Vol. I. Care and intervention.* Baltimore, MD: University Park Press.

Garber, H., & Heber, R. (1981). The efficacy of early intervention with family rehabilitation. In M. Begab, H. Haywood & H. Garber (Eds.), *Psychosocial influences in retarded performance.* Baltimore, MD: University Park Press.

Gibson, D., & Fields, D. (1984). Early stimulation programs for Down's syndrome: An effectiveness inventory. *Advances in Developmental and Behavioral Pediatrics* (Vol. V). Greenwich, CN: JAI Press.

Gordon, N., & Kogan, K. (1975). A mother instruction program: Behavior changes with and without therapeutic intervention. *Child Psychiatry and Human Development, 6,* 89-105.

Gray, S., Ramsey, B., & Klaus, R. (1982). *From 3 to 20: The early training project.* Baltimore, MD: University Park Press.

Guralnick, M. (1988). Efficacy research in early childhood intervention programs. In S. Odom & M. Karnes (Eds.), *Early intervention for infants and children with handicaps.* Baltimore, MD: Paul Brookes.

Guralnick, M., & Bennett F. (Eds.) (1987). *The effectiveness of early intervention for at-risk and handicapped children.* New York: Academic Press.

Guralnick, M., & Bricker, D. (1987). The effectiveness of early intervention for children with cognitive and general developmental delays. In M. Guralnick & F. Bennett (Eds.), *The effectiveness of early intervention.* New York: Academic Press.

Hanson, M. (1976). Evaluation of training procedures used in a parent-implemented intervention program for Down's syndrome infants. *AAESPH Review, 1,* 36-52.

Hanson, M. (1977). *Teaching your Down's syndrome infant: A guide for parents.* Baltimore, MD: University Park Press.

Hanson, M. (1987). Early intervention with children with Down syndrome. In S. Pueschel, C. Tingey, J. Rynders, A. Crocker & D. Crutcher(Eds.), *New perspectives on Down syndrome.* Baltimore, MD: Paul Brookes.

Hanson, M., & Schwarz, R. (1978). Results of a longitudinal intervention program for Down's syndrome infants and their families. *Education and Training of the Mentally Retarded, 13,* 403-407.

Harris, S. (1981). Effects of neurodevelopmental therapy on motor performance of infants with Down's syndrome. *Developmental Medicine and Child Neurology, 23,* 477-483.

Harris, S. (1987). Early intervention for children with motor handicaps. In M. Guralnick & F. Bennett (Eds.), *The effectiveness of early intervention for at-risk and handicapped children.* New York: Academic Press.

Hayden, A., & Beck, G. (1982). The epidemiology of high-risk and handicapped infants. In C. Ramey & P. Trohanis (Eds.), *Finding and educating high-risk and handicapped infants.* Baltimore, MD: University Park Press.

Hayden, A., & Dmitriev, V. (1975). The multidisciplinary preschool program for Down's syndrome children at the University of Washington model preschool center. In B. Friedlander, G. Sterritt, & G. Kirk (Eds.), *Exceptional infant* (Vol. 3). New York: Brunner/Mazel.

Hayden, A., & Haring, N. (1976). Programs for Down's syndrome children at the University of Washington. In T. Tjossem (Ed.), *Intervention strategies for high-risk infants and young children.* Baltimore, MD: University Park Press.

Hayden, A., & Haring, N. (1977). The acceleration and maintenance of developmental gains in Down's syndrome school-age children. In P. Mittler (Ed.), *Research to practice in mental retardation: Vol I. Care and intervention.* Baltimore, MD: University Park Press.

Hayden, A., & McGinness, G. (1977). Bases for early intervention. In E. Sontag, J. Smith, & N. Certo (Eds.), *Educational programming for the severely and profoundly handicapped.* Reston, VA: Council for Exceptional Children.

Hetherington, R., Suttill, J., Holmlund, C., & Frey, D. (1979). Evaluation of a regional resource center of multiply handicapped retarded children. *American Journal of Mental Deficiency, 83,* 367-379.

Holmes, D., Reich, J., & Pasternak, J. (1984). *The development of infants born at risk.* Hillsdale, NJ: Lawrence Erlbaum.

Hunt, J. (1980). Implications of plasticity and hierarchical achievements for the assessment of development and risk of mental retardation. In D. Sawin, R. Hawkins, L. Walker & R. Penticuff (Eds.), *Exceptional infant: Vol. 4. Psychosocial risks in infant-environment transactions.* New York: Brunner/Mazel.

Johnson, D. (1975). The development of a program for parent-child education among Mexican-Americans in Texas. In B. Friedlander, G. Sterritt, & G. Kirk (Eds.), *Exceptional infant: Assessment and intervention* (Vol. 3). New York: Brunner/Mazel.

Johnson, D., Breckenridge, J., & McGowan, R. (1984). Home environment and early cognitive development in Mexican-American children. In A. Gottfried (Ed.), *Home environment and early cognitive development.* New York: Academic Press.

Kagan, J., Kearsley, R., & Zelazo, P. (1978). *Infancy: Its place in human development.* Cambridge, MA: Harvard University Press.

Karnes, M., Schwedel, A., Lewis, G., Ratts, D., & Esry, D. (1981). Impact of early programming for the handicapped: A follow-up study into the elementary school. *Journal of the Division for Early Childhood, 4,* 62-79.

Kysela, G., Hillyard, A., McDonald, L., & Taylor, J. (1981). Early intervention, design and evaluation. In R. Schiefelbusch & D. Bricker (Eds.), *Early language: Acquisition and intervention.* Baltimore, MD: University Park Press.

LaVeck, B., & Brehm, S. (1978). Individual variability among children with Down's syndrome. *Mental Retardation, 16,* 135-137.

Lazar, I., Darlington, R., Murray, H., Royce, J., & Snipper, A. (1982). Lasting effects of early education: A report from the consortium for longitudinal studies. *Monographs of the Society for Research in Child Development, 47*(Serial No. 195).

Leib, S., Benfield, G., & Guidabaldi, J. (1980). Effects of early intervention and stimulation on the preterm infant. *Pediatrics, 66,* 83-90.

Lewis, M., & Rosenblum, L. (1974). *The effect of the infant on the caregiver.* New York: Wiley.

Lewis, M., & Starr, M. (1979). Developmental continuity. In J. Osofsky (Ed.), *Handbook of infant development.* New York: John Wiley & Sons.

Littlejohn Associates, Inc. (1982). *An analysis of the impact of the Handicapped Children's Early Education Program.* Prepared for Special Education Programs, U.S. Department of Education.

Ludlow, J., & Allen, L. (1979). The effect of early intervention and preschool stimulus on the development of the Down's syndrome child. *Journal of Mental Deficiency Research, 23,* 29-44.

McCall, R. (1979). The development of intellectual functioning in infancy and the prediction of later IQ. In J. Osofsky (Ed.), *Handbook of infant development.* New York: Wiley.

McCarthy, D. (1972). *McCarthy Scales of Children's Abilities.* New York: Psychological Corporation.

Meadow-Orlans, K. (1987). An analysis of the effectiveness of early intervention programs for hearing-impaired children. In M. Guralnick & F. Bennett (Eds.), *The effectiveness of early intervention for at-risk and handicapped children.* New York: Academic Press.

Minde, K., Shosenberg, N., Marton, P., Thompson, J., Ripley, J., & Burns, S. (1980). Self help groups in a premature nursery - A controlled evaluation. *The Journal of Pediatrics, 96,* 933-940.

Moore, M., Fredericks, H., & Baldwin, V. (1981). The long-range effects of early childhood education on a trainable mentally retarded population. *Journal of the Division for Early Childhood, 4,* 93-110.

Odom, S., & Fewell, R. (1983). Program evaluation in early childhood special education: A meta-evaluation. *Educational Evaluation and Policy Analysis, 5,* 445-460.

Olson, M. (1987). Early intervention for children with visual impairments. In M. Guralnick & F. Bennett (Eds.), *The effectiveness of early intervention for at-risk and handicapped children.* New York: Academic Press.

Oregon State Mental Health Division. (1977). *The Student Progress Record.* Salem, OR.

Petrie, P., Kratochwill, T., Bergan, J., & Nicholson, G. (1981). Teaching parents to teach their children: Applications in the pediatric setting. *Journal of Pediatric Psychology, 6,* 275-292.

Piaget, J. (1970). Piaget's theory. In P. Mussen (Ed.), *Carmichael's manual of child psychology* (Vol. I). New York: Wiley & Sons.

Piper, M., & Pless, I. (1980). Early intervention for infants with Down's syndrome: A controlled trial. *Pediatrics, 65,* 463-468.

Pueschel, S. (1984). The study population. In S. Pueschel (Ed.), *The young child with Down syndrome.* New York: Human Sciences Press.

Ramey, C., & Bryant, D. (1982). Evidence for prevention of developmental retardation during infancy. *Journal of the Division for Early Childhood, 5,* 73-78.

Ramey, C., Bryant, D., Sparling, J., & Wasik, B. (1985). Educational interventions to enhance intellectual development: Comprehensive day care versus family education. In S. Harel & N.

Anastasiow (Eds.), *The at-risk infant.* Baltimore, MD: Paul Brookes.

Ramey, C., & Campbell, F. (1979). Supplemental preschool education for disadvantaged children. *School Review, 82,* 171-189.

Ramey, C., Campbell, F., & Wasik, B. (1982). Use of standardized tests to evaluate early childhood special education programs. *Topics in Early Childhood Special Education, 1,* 51-60.

Ramey, C., Farran, D., & Campbell, F. (1979). Early intervention: From research to practice. In B. Darby & M. May, *Infant assessment: Issues and applications.* Seattle, WA: WESTAR.

Ramey, C., MacPhee, D., & Yeates, K. (1983). Preventing developmental retardation: A general systems model. In L. Bond & J. Joffe (Eds.), *Facilitating infant and early childhood development.* Hanover, NH: University Press of New England.

Rescorla, L., & Zigler, E. (1981). The Yale child welfare research program: Implications for social policy. *Education Evaluation and Policy Analysis, 3,* 5-14.

Revill, S., & Blunden, R. (1979). A home training service for preschool developmentally handicapped children. *Behavior Research and Therapy, 17,* 207-214.

Rogers, S., D'Eugenio, D., Brown, S., Donovan, C., & Lynch, E. (1977). *Early intervention developmental profile.* Ann Arbor, MI: University of Michigan Press.

Rosen-Morris, D., & Sitkei, E. (1981). Strategies for teaching severely/profoundly handicapped infants and young children. *Journal of the Division for Early Childhood, 4,* 79-93.

Rosenberg, S., & Robinson, C. (1988). Interactions of parents with their young handicapped children. In S. Odom & M. Karnes (Eds.), *Early intervention for infants and children with handicaps.* Baltimore, MD: Paul Brookes.

Rynders, J., & Horrobin, M. (1975). Project Edge: The University of Minnesota's communication stimulation program for Down's syndrome infants. In B. Friedlander, G. Sterritt, & G. Kirk (Eds.), *Exceptional infant* (Vol. 3). New York: Brunner/Mazel.

Rynders, J., & Horrobin, M. (1980). Educational provisions for young children with Down's syndrome. In J. Gottlieb (Ed.), *Educating mentally retarded persons in the mainstream.* Baltimore, MD: University Park Press.

Sameroff, A. (1981). Longitudinal studies of preterm infants: A review of chapters 17-20. In S. Friedman & M. Sigman (Eds.), *Preterm birth and psychological development.* New York: Academic Press.

Sameroff, A., & Chandler, M. (1975). Reproductive risk and the continuum of caretaking casualty. In F. Horowitz, M. Hetherington, S. Scarr-Salapatek, & G. Siegel (Eds.), *Review of child development research* (Vol. 4). Chicago: University of Chicago Press.

Scarr-Salapatek, S., & Williams, M. (1973). The effects of early stimulation on low-birth-weight infants. *Child Development, 44,* 94-101.

Shearer, D., & Shearer, M. (1976). The Portage Project: A model for early childhood intervention. In T. Tjossem (Ed.), *Intervention strategies for high risk infants and young children.* Baltimore, MD: University Park Press.

Shearer, M., & Shearer, D. (1972). The Portage Project: A model for early childhood education. *Exceptional Children, 39,* 210-217.

Shonkoff, J., & Hauser-Cram, P. (1987). Early intervention for disabled infants and their families: A quantitative analysis. *Pediatrics,80* (5), 650-658.

Shonkoff, J., Hauser-Cram, P., Krauss, M., & Upshur, C. (1988). Early intervention efficacy research: What have we learned and where do we go from here? *Topics in Early Childhood Special Education, 8* (1), 81-93.

Simeonsson, R., Cooper, D., & Scheiner, A. (1982). A review and analysis of the effectiveness of early intervention programs. *Pediatrics, 69,* 635-641.

Simmons-Martin, A. (1981). Efficacy report: Early education project. *Journal of the Division for Early Childhood, 4,* 5-10.

Soboloff, H. (1981). Early intervention - Fact or fiction? *Developmental Medicine and Child Neurology, 23,* 261-266.

Spiker, D. (1982). Parent involvement in early intervention activities with their young children with Down's syndrome. *Education and Training of the Mentally Retarded, 17,* 24-29.

Stock, J., Wnek, L., Newborg, E., Schenck, J., Gabel, J., Spurgeon, M., & Ray, H. (1976). *Evaluation of handicapped children's early education program (HCEEP).* Final report to Bureau of Education for the Handicapped, U.S. Department of Education. Columbus, OH: Battelle.

Strain, P., & Smith, B. (1986). A counter-interpretation of early intervention effects: A response to Casto and Mastropieri. *Exceptional Children, 53*(3),260-265.

Tyler, N., & Kogan, K. (1977). Reduction of stress between mothers and their handicapped children. *The American Journal of Occupational Therapy, 31,* 151-155.

Uzgiris, I. (1981). Experience in the social context. In R. Schiefelbusch & D. Bricker (Eds.), *Early language: Acquisition and intervention.* Baltimore, MD: University Park Press.

Uzgiris, I., & Hunt, J. McV. (1975). *Assessment in infancy: Ordinal scales of psychological development.* Urbana, IL: University of Illinois Press.

Walker, B., Slentz, K., & Bricker, D. (1985). *Parent involvement in early intervention.* Washington,D.C.: Rehabilitation Research Review, National Rehabilitation Information Center, The Catholic University of America.

Warner, E. (1986). A longitudinal study of perinatal risk. In D. Farran & J. McKinney (Eds.), *Risk in intellectual and psychosocial development.* New York: Academic Press.

Weiss, R. (1981). INREAL intervention for language handicapped and bilingual children. *Journal of the Division for Early Childhood, 4,* 40-51.

White, O., Edgar, E., Haring, N., Affleck, J., Hayden, A., & Bendersky, M. (1980). UPAS: *Uniform performance assessment system.* Columbus, OH: Charles Merrill.

White, K., Mastropieri, M., & Casto, G. (1984). An analysis of special education early childhood projects approved by the Joint Dissemination Review Panel. *Journal of the Division of Early Childhood, 9* (1), 11-26.

Zeitlin, S. (1981). Learning through coping: An effective preschool program. *Journal of the Division for Early Childhood, 4,* 53-61.

5.
Legal and Legislative Decisions Affecting Early Intervention

Although numerous legal decisions and legislative enactments have affected education policy and services in the United States, the focus of this chapter will be restricted to those decisions and enactments that have had impact on the area of early intervention. Further, no attempt will be made to provide extensive detail on particular cases or legislative enactments. Rather, the goal is to provide a general sense of the history that has led to contemporary perspectives, which will, in turn, serve as indicators for future decisions and policy.

This chapter begins with a discussion of the evolution of rights for minority and handicapped persons. This legal and legislative foundation has been essential to the development of programs and services for infants and young children. Information on the federal scene is complemented by information that governs state and local policy. A discussion of selected legal issues of particular pertinence to the birth-to-five population is then offered. Finally, issues which face parents and professionals in the future are highlighted.

EVOLUTION OF RIGHTS FOR THE HANDICAPPED

Understanding current laws and policy that affect the infant and young child who is at-risk or handicapped can be enhanced by a cursory examination of the historical development of rights for the handicapped in general.

Civil Rights Movement

Many authorities believe that the development of the civil rights movement for minority groups was the major impetus underlying the gradual acquisition of rights for the handicapped person. Handicapped populations constitute a minority group whose rights have been historically violated in ways similar to those experienced by other minority groups. Whether a person is discriminated against because of his or her race or because of a physical disability makes little difference in the outcome— that is, that the person's rights have been violated or restricted. The civil rights movement of the early 1950s required that the nation face the active discriminatory acts perpetuated in training, hiring, housing, and the public schools for racial minorities, the poor, and the handicapped (Allen, 1984). The civil rights movement brought into sharp focus the rights of the individual and, in particular, the "rights of children not to be labeled, right of due process, and the right of a child to challenge a system that purports to be operating in his interest" (Cohen & DeYoung, 1973, p. 262).

Early Court Cases

Perhaps the most influential case for establishing rights for minority groups in the realm of public education was *Brown v. Board of Education* (1954). As most people know, this case addressed the separate-but-equal stance of the public schools. Previous to this supreme court decision, many local public school districts operated one school or schools for white children and separate schools for black children. Public school officials who maintained separate facilities argued that, although the schools were separate, they were equal. The supreme court disagreed and ruled that separate is inherently unequal. The intent of the supreme court decision was to assure an equal educational opportunity for all children attending public schools. Although *Brown v. Board of Education* provided the basis for the federal government to become enmeshed in the development of educational policy (Noel, Burke, & Valdivieso, 1985), many years elapsed before an equal education was assured for all minority groups. This has been particularly true for the children who are handicapped and who are often still excluded from the "mainstream" of American education (Wang, 1989).

A second important early case was *Hobsen v. Hansen* (1967), in which the procedure of placing children in educational tracks based on test scores was challenged. The evidence indicated that children from poverty and minority circumstances were being labeled and assigned to "special education" tracks more frequently that nonminority children. The court ruled that the tracking system be abolished because the system represented "wrongful vestiges of the District's past history of segregation" (Burt, 1975, p. 315).

Two additional cases have had a significant impact on public school practice in relation to the testing and labeling of children. In both *Diana v. Board of Education* (1970) and *Larry P. v. Riles* (1972), the inappropriate or incorrect labeling of children from minority groups was addressed. The decisions rendered by the courts in both cases radically changed public school policy by requiring that:

- children be tested in their primary language

- children from minority groups (e.g., black, Mexican, and Chinese) currently in classes for the mentally retarded be re-evaluated

- children be assessed with measures appropriate to their culture (Abeson & Zettel, 1977).

Litigation Directly Related to the Handicapped Individual

In the early 1970s, advocacy efforts of parents of children who were handicapped began to reap outcomes. Parents who had grown weary of battling public school teaching and administrative personnel took their grievances to court in an attempt to achieve educational equity for their children who were handicapped. In a series of landmark decisions, the court affirmed or reaffirmed a child's rights to:

- a free and appropriate education

- due process for grievances
- special education services without regard to arguments about lack of funds
- not be labeled handicapped or placed in a special education program without an adequate diagnosis (Gallagher, 1984).

Four important cases assisted in establishing these rights for children who are handicapped and their families: *PARC v. Commonwealth of Pennsylvania* (1971), *Mills v. Board of Education of Washington, D.C.* (1972), *Wyatt v. Stickney* (1971), and *New York ARC v. Rockefeller* (1972).

In *PARC v. Commonwealth of Pennsylvania*, the plaintiffs charged that because they were retarded they had been excluded or excused from attendance in public schools, had their admissions postponed, or in other ways been denied free access to public education (Cohen & DeYoung, 1973). After the arguments had been presented, the plaintiffs and the Commonwealth of Pennsylvania agreed to a consent decree, which specified that the state could not invoke any policy that would postpone, terminate, or deny children diagnosed as mentally retarded access to a publicly supported education. Further, the court decreed that the Commonwealth was to provide all children who are retarded between ages six to twenty-one with a publicly supported education by 1972 (Abeson & Zettel, 1977). For the first time, any school-aged child, no matter how impaired, was eligible to receive a free, appropriate public education.

The parents of seven children residing in the District of Columbia brought a class action suit on behalf of all school-age handicapped children not currently being served in the District's public schools. In action similar to the PARC case, the court ruled that all school-age children, regardless of the severity of their handicap, were entitled to an appropriate, free education (Abeson & Zettel, 1977). Further, the public schools' arguments that adequate funds were unavailable for compliance with the court's ruling was explicitly addressed:

> If you have no special education funds, Judge Waddy (the presiding judge in the Mills case) replied, then reduce your expenditures on other educational programs, so that all children at least share equally in inadequate schooling (Burt, 1975, p. 296).

Finally, both the PARC and Mills decisions required access to education in the most normalized environment and assured procedural due process when problems or disagreements with school officials were encountered (Gilhool & Stutman, 1978). For a more detailed discussion of the PARC and Mills cases see Kirp, Kuriloff, and Buss (1975).

The PARC and Mills cases were focused on exclusion of children who were handicapped from the public schools. *Wyatt v. Stickney* and *New York ARC v. Rockefeller*, known as the Willowbrook case, addressed grievances brought by handicapped people incarcerated in large state residential facilities. In both cases, the plaintiffs argued that placement in such facilities required offering adequate treatment that is appropriate to their needs. In the Wyatt case, Judge Johnson ruled that institutionalized individuals have a constitutional right to appropriate treatment and that it be conducted in the least restrictive setting. While in the

Willowbrook case, the court ruled that institutionalized people who are retarded had the constitutional right to be protected from harm.

These early court cases have affected the provision of educational services for children who are handicapped. However, the nature of the impact has not always been clear nor necessarily produced the most desired outcomes for two reasons. First, as pointed out by Burt (1975), the courts have not always focused on the more critical issues. For example, Burt (1975) argues that the Wyatt court should have spent more effort in determining the community resources necessary to afford equal opportunities for institutionalized people rather than establishing detailed regulations for institutional living. In the PARC ruling, greater progress may have occurred if more effort had been directed toward emphasizing placement in least restrictive environments, rather than some of the other areas chosen for attention.

The second reason for unclear or undesired outcomes on the handicapped population of these and other related court decisions has been the court's inability to monitor or enforce implementation of judicial rulings. Kirp, Kuriloff, and Buss (1975) suggest five implementation difficulties faced by courts:

1. Changes in legal rulings do not automatically change behavior of school personnel.

2. Some changes are extremely difficult to implement despite court rulings.

3. Some mandated changes are not pragmatically possible.

4. Some change may require the undertaking of prerequisite tasks not specified by the courts.

5. Mandated legal change is not always congruent with variations in children, settings, and other factors (e.g., parents may not want their child placed in a mainstream classroom; communities may not want group homes for retarded people located in residential areas).

These realities often produce unexpected or unwanted outcomes following legal rulings; however, taken as a whole, these early court cases have provided, in part, the basis for current rulings as well as the basis for federal and state policy concerning education of children who are handicapped.

FEDERAL POLICY

Before discussing the specific federal policy which provides today's guidelines for education and treatment of handicapped populations, an understanding of the development of policy may be useful. Most often, federal policy is determined by legislation passed by the United States Congress. However, the interpretation of the legislation and, thus, the policy, often falls to the courts and federal agency personnel. In addition, the executive branch of government is largely responsible for the implementation of law passed by the Congress. Finally, concerned constituencies (e.g., public reaction, whether in general or from specific lobby or advocacy groups) can be instrumental in the determination of federal policy. Thus, the content of legislation from which federal policy derives is determined by the slowly evolving political process of compromise and negotiation between legislative bodies, executive agencies, and concerned constituencies (Garwood, 1984; Noel, Burke, & Valdivieso, 1985). The schematic contained in Figure 5-1 reflects the impact of legislation and public reaction on the development of federal, state, and local policy.

As shown in Figure 5-1, the agencies primarily responsible for the development of federal policy for the handicapped are the Office of Special Education and Rehabilitative Services, Administration on Children, Youth and Families, Bureau of Maternal and Child Health and Resource Development, and the Administration on Developmental Disabilities. These agencies are directed by relevant legislation passed by the U.S. Congress and are also responsive to public reaction. The policy evolved by federal agencies, in turn, affects the development of state policy for state departments of education, human services, mental health and public health. Personnel working in these state departments are responsible for the development of state policy emanating from laws

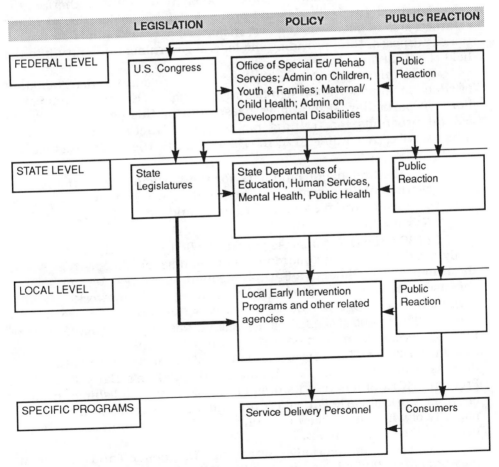

FIGURE 5-1. *A schematic of the relationship of legislative bodies and public reaction to federal, state, and local administrative bodies responsible for policy development.*

enacted by state legislatures. Local early intervention programs and other relevant public agencies develop their policy based on laws passed by their state legislature and policy developed by relevant state agencies. Service delivery personnel are the ultimate recipients of the federal and state policy that should provide the guidelines for their specific program. As indicated in Figure 5-1, public reaction can affect policy development and its implementation at the federal, state, and local levels (Martin, 1989).

FEDERAL LEGISLATION

Early Legislation

In the late 1950s, a rapid expansion in the development of federal policy for the handicapped began. According to Noel, Burke, and Valdivieso (1985), "The development of the federal policy base for special education is generally tied to the passage of two pieces of legislation"; these are P.L. 85-926 and the National Defense Education Act (NDEA). P.L. 85-926 provided support to institutions of higher education for training teachers to work with the mentally retarded population. NDEA authorized the use of federal funds to develop educational media for the mentally retarded and as such was the first major use of federal funds for educational purposes, thus providing the federal government an entry into the field of education of the handicapped.

From this modest beginning, the federal role in the determination of educational policy grew significantly during the Kennedy administration. In particular, several laws passed during this period established federal programs for training facilities construction, research, and direct service. According to Allen (1984), P.L. 88-164, which was passed in 1964 was:

> . . . the first major landmark for the participation of the federal government in service, training, and research activities focused specifically on mental retardation and related developmental problems. (p. 11)

In 1968, the U.S. Congress passed the first federal legislation specifically directed at young children who are handicapped. P.L. 90-538, or the Handicapped Children's Early Education Assistance Act, authorized the use of federal funds to establish a nationwide network of model demonstration programs designed to serve children who are handicapped. The intent of the federal legislation was to provide "seed" money for the development of model programs whose operation was to be assumed by the state or local district after thirty-six months. As discussed in Chapter 3, the Handicapped Children's Early Education Program (HCEEP) has met its original mission by establishing an influential network of early education programs throughout the nation—the majority of which have been maintained by local efforts upon the termination of the federal support (Swan, 1980).

The Early and Periodic Screening, Diagnostic, and Treatment Program or P.L. 90-248, was enacted in 1967 and was designed to promote early detection and prevention of developmental problems in young children. According to Allen (1984), passage of this law reflected congressional concern about variations in state law and policy focused on children who are handicapped and chronically ill. In 1972, P.L. 92-924, an amendment to the Economic Opportunity Act, required that the Head Start Program serve children with handicaps. A further amendment, P.L. 93-644, passed in 1974, redefined the term *handicapped* to include children with more severe impairments. In spite of the many federal enactments previously described, many persons with handicaps continued to be excluded from public education programs or placed in programs of questionable value (Wang, 1989). This reality, heightened by parent advocacy, served to goad the U.S. Congress into passage of P.L. 93-112, P.L. 94-142, P.L. 98-199 and most recently, P.L. 99-457.

Section 504 of the Rehabilitation Act of 1973 (P.L. 93-112) was enacted to prevent discrimination on the basis of an individual's disability. Discrimination of a qualified person with handicaps through architectural barriers and non-access to educational programs or services is explicitly prohibited by Section 504. Specifically for the young child, if a state offers programs to nonhandicapped children, these services must also be available to children who are handicapped. Failure to comply could result in withholding from the offending state all federal funds from the Department of Health and Human Services and the Department of Education (Ballard, 1977).

P.L. 94-142

Most authorities agree that the Education for All Handicapped Children Act (P.L. 94-142) is the single most important piece of legislation enacted to date for children who are handicapped. According to Allen (1984):

> A free, appropriate education in the least restrictive environment became, at long last, the right of every handicapped child.

P.L. 94-142 was developed by the United States Congress to ensure that children with handicaps had the right to:

- education—all school-age children with handicaps are to be provided with free appropriate public education

- nondiscriminatory evaluation

- an IEP—clear statement of objectives for each child along with documentation of child's current and expected performance

- education in least restrictive environment

- due process

- parental participation (Gallagher, 1984).

Although problems with the quality of services and where services are delivered remain, data indicate the law is working well for school-age children (Garwood, Fewell, & Neisworth, 1988; Garwood & Sheehan, 1989). However, unless explicitly mandated by state law, P.L. 94-142 does not require the provision of educational programs for preschool-age children; although Part B of the Act does offer small incentive grants to encourage states to develop programs for children three to five years of age. P.L. 94-142 does not address the birth to two population.

To address the need to extend services to the preschool-age handicapped population, Congress amended P.L. 94-142 in 1986. These amendments establish a national policy on early intervention in the form of P.L. 99-457, which mandates services for children three to five years of age, and offers incentives to provide services for birth to two year olds.

P.L. 99-457

As Trohanis (1989) indicates, P.L. 99-457 does more than extend existing programs to young children; it actually charts new policy. According to Trohanis, Title I, or Part H of the law:

> . . . creates a discretionary program to assist states in planning, developing, and implementing a statewide system of comprehensive, coordinated, multidisciplinary, interagency programs for all young handicapped children, from birth up to 3 years of age. (p.2)

According to the Part H regulations, services must be designed to meet needs of child and family, selected in "collaboration with parents", provided under public supervision, and be offered in settings with nonhandicapped infants by qualified personnel. Services must be specified in the Individual Family Service Plan, and can include, but are not limited to audiology, case management, family training and counseling, health, medical, nursing, nutritional, occupational therapy, physical therapy, psychological, social work, special instruction, speech/language pathology and transportation (Federal Register, June 22, 1989).

The Individual Family Service Plan (IFSP) is a concept introduced in P.L. 99-457 to guide and direct the services offered infants. The content of an IFSP should include:

- a statement of the child's level of development
- a statement of families' strengths and needs in relation to the child
- statement of major expected outcomes
- specific intervention services required
- projected dates for initiation and duration of services
- casemanager designation
- transition plan to Part B programs.

This law also specifies the 14 components necessary for a statewide comprehensive system of early intervention services for the birth to two population. These components include:

1. Designation of a lead agency with a single line of authority to carry out the administration of the program.

2. Determination of a definition of "developmentally delayed".

3. Establishment of timetables to ensure full service to all eligible infants and toddlers and their families by year 5.

4. Development of procedures to ensure the provision of timely, comprehensive, multidisciplinary evaluations of the functioning of eligible infants and toddlers, and the needs and strengths of the family.

5. Development of an IFSP and provision of case management.

6. Establishment of a comprehensive child-find system.

7. Development of a public awareness program.

8. Creation of a central directory of resources, experts, and research and demonstration projects in the state.

9. Development of a comprehensive system of personnel preparation.

10. Development of a policy governing contractual arrangements with local service providers.

11. Establishment of acceptable due process procedures.

12. Enactment of a state policy that incorporates all components of the statewide early intervention system described in P.L. 99-457.

13. Development of procedures for securing timely reimbursement of Part H funds.

14. Establishment of a comprehensive early intervention data collection system (Garwood & Sheehan, 1989, p. 65).

Title II or Part B ". . . creates enhanced incentives for states to provide a free, appropriate, public education to all eligible handicapped children who will be between three and six years of age by school year 1990-1991" (Trohanis, 1989, p. 5).

Money is appropriated by Congress and disbursed to state departments of education for delivery of services. States must have approved Part B plans in order to participate in this program. Failure to provide services to eligible children will result in the state's loss of new Preschool Grants, monies generated for three to five year olds under P.L. 94-142, and designated Education of the Handicapped Act discretionary programs (Ballard, Ramirez & Zantal-Wiener, 1987).

P.L. 99-457 is the most important legislation to be enacted for young children who are handicapped or at-risk and their families. The development of appropriate services and state policy specified by this law faces many obstacles which will take wisdom and perseverance to overcome. Yet there are already indications that progress is being made (Silverstein, 1989). Whatever barriers exist to the full implementation of P.L. 99-457, it is clear that efforts to remove and overcome such barriers will be worth the cost to do so.

FEDERAL AGENCIES

The federal agency most directly concerned with the implementation of P.L. 94-142 and P.L. 99-457 is the Office of Special Education and Rehabilitative Services (OSERS) in the U.S. Department of Education. This agency is primarily responsible for the development of programs for persons with handicaps, and is composed of three programs as shown in Figure 5-2. The Office of Special Education Programs (OSEP) is the principal agency for developing federal policy, programs, and projects

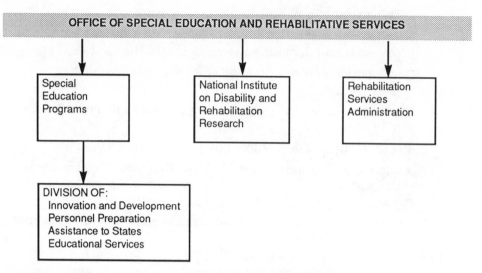

FIGURE 5-2. Organizational structure for the Office of Special Education and Rehabilitative Services.

relating to the education and training of the handicapped.[1] This agency deals primarily with state agencies and with training institutions which receive grants for research, and model program development. In addition, OSEP provides funds and technical assistance for the development of more effective methods and materials and to dissemination this information. OSEP has four divisions:

1. The Division of Innovation and Development which supports research, demonstration, and evaluation activities. This Division supports the HCEEP network.

2. The Division of Personnel Preparation which supports training programs for special education teachers, administrators, parents, and volunteers.

3. The Division of Assistance to States which provides aid to state special education programs and to implement P.L. 94-142 and P.L. 99-457.

4. The Division of Educational Services which develops and disseminates educational media.

The National Institute on Disability and Rehabilitation Research (previously called the National Institute of Handicapped Research) was established in November, 1978. The mission of this agency is to provide a comprehensive and coordinated federal approach to all government-funded research projects addressing handicapped populations. The Rehabilitation Services Administration provides services to disabled persons to assist them in becoming employable.

---

[1] This information was taken from DHEW publications entitled Directory of National Information Sources on Handicapping Conditions and Related Services, August, 1982.

The area of early intervention has historically been influenced most by the policy and program support coming from the Office of Special Education Programs: specifically, the Division of Innovation and Development, which is responsible for the Handicapped Children's Early Education Program, and the Division of Personnel Preparation, which has been instrumental in supporting colleges and universities in training interventionists, supervisors, and administrators to operate early intervention programs.

STATE POLICY

One might assume that state educational policies closely reflect federal policy; however, Noel, Burke, and Valdivieso (1985) argue that state and local procedures often compromise the intent of federal policy. The implementation of federal policy at the state level is determined, in part, by the availability of necessary resources and public opinion and interpretation of nonspecific federal mandates. Thus, different interpretations and implementation of federal policy does occur across states.

The U.S. Congress has never appropriated the necessary funds for states to completely implement the mandates of P.L. 94-142, and P.L. 99-457; thus, states have been required to provide much of the financial support for implementation. So, as Noel, Burke, and Valdivieso (1985) note, "Differences in state educational policies largely reflect the general wealth of an individual state, the strength of its commitment to the handicapped, and its available resources" (p. 27). As note previously, the federal government has gradually extended national policy to cover all children who are handicapped; however, state policy has not kept pace.

States that passed laws or instituted regulations for the preschool-age child with handicaps have generally employed two strategies. Some states have chosen to lower the school age for its children who are handicapped, making preschool children eligible to receive services. The rules and regulations governing school-age children have been expanded to include the younger children. Other states have chosen to establish a new authority with rules and regulations specific to preschool-aged handicapped populations (Smith, 1980).

Currently, state legislation addressing the birth-to-five population is in flux and will likely remain so until state policies are developed to accommodate the requirements of P.L. 99-457. State standards and regulations for certifying teachers of preschool children who are handicapped also vary. Bricker and Slentz (1988) surveyed the literature on certification standards and practices for early childhood/special education personnel and found that the number of states requiring certification appears to be increasing. However, they also found extreme variations in certification policy and procedures.

The lack of certification or consistent standards for personnel in this area can lead to two unfortunate outcomes. First, personnel may be poorly prepared in terms of content and strategies required to work effectively with infants or preschool children with handicaps. Second, personnel prepared to work with school-age children may be inappropriately assigned to programs that serve preschool populations. The uniqueness of infants and young children who are handicapped and the necessary focus on the family as the intervention target require that personnel working with this group receive specialized training if intervention programs are to be effective (Bricker & Slentz, 1988).

Even with the passage of P.L. 99-457, it seems apparent that many states lack a consistent and comprehensive policy to provide guidance in establishing a consistent definition of eligibility and in establishing training and certification guidelines for personnel to work with the birth-to-five population.

LOCAL POLICY

The lack of resources at state levels to implement programs for young children with handicaps has affected service delivery at the local or community level. Several serious barriers exist to the implementation of programs for the birth-to-five population.

First, either because states are generally still struggling to develop guidelines or to interpret federal regulations, programs may be faced with considerable ambiguity concerning mandates. On the state level, there may be disagreement about which agency is responsible for providing services, or two agencies may overlap in the provision of services causing conflict or other problems at the local level. Interagency collaboration continues to be a serious problem for early intervention programs and the families they serve.

Second, local programs are chronically underfunded if they depend entirely on state or local support, or both. This problem becomes particularly acute when local programs are not receiving adequate funds to even meet established state guidelines.

Third, often adequately trained personnel and instructional resources are not available (Burke, McLaughlin & Valdivieso, 1988). Programs may be staffed by individuals poorly prepared or trained to work with other age groups. In addition, resources for assisting in selecting evaluation and curricular materials may be unavailable at the local level, and states often cannot or do not provide adequate technical assistance.

Finally, programs for infants and young children with handicaps are developed and maintained through a variety of agencies: (1) public schools with local district and state support; (2) other state-supported agencies such as mental health, human services; (3) national nonprofit organizations such as United Cerebral Palsy; and (4) federally-supported programs such as Head Start and the Handicapped Children's Early Education Program. Support and regulations for these programs can vary considerably along many dimensions, introducing one more source of inconsistency.

In spite of the problems facing early intervention, programs for infants and young children continue to grow. A network of programs has been established and personnel are beginning to recognize the need for consistency in services and the need for adequate communication at the local, state, and federal level.

Summary

This discussion of federal, state and local policy should emphasize the need for further clarification and coordination of policy for the birth-to-five population. Many authorities believe that early intervention programs are severely hampered because of:

1. Conflicting or ambiguous legislation and regulations

2. Poor or nonexistent interagency coordination

3. Variation in definitions and eligibility requirements

4. Lack of adequately and appropriately trained intervention and leadership personnel

Recognition of such difficulties is a first step to their solution. The ensuing years will generate solutions to many of these current problems, resulting in a service delivery system that can effectively respond to the needs of all identified infants and young children who are at-risk and handicapped.

LEGAL ISSUES

. . .Supreme Court interpretations of federal law governing educational rights of handicapped students make clear that school districts have significant procedural and substantive legal responsibilities to handicapped children. (Laski, 1985, p. 37)

This statement emphasizes the importance of past and future litigation for children with handicaps. The purpose of this section is to highlight four major legal issues that have had and will continue to have significant implications for children with handicaps. These issues include the right to appropriate education, due process, appropriate placement, and right to treatment.

Right to an Appropriate Education

Through earlier court action (e.g., *PARC v. Commonwealth of Pennsylvania, Mills v. District of Columbia*) and subsequent federal legislation, the foundation for access to public education was assured to students with even the most severe handicaps. Although access to public education was granted, the quality of that education remains questionable. The result has been that the quality and appropriateness of the provided education has been a frequent issue in the courts.

Beginning with the PARC consent agreement, the courts have attempted to specify parameters of appropriate education for the student who is handicapped. The PARC decree stipulated the parameters of an appropriate program of education, including specification of hours of instruction, pupil-teacher ratios, curriculum, and teacher qualification (Laski, 1985). However, subsequent scrutiny by the courts determined that the PARC decree did not result in many students with severe handicaps receiving an "appropriate" education. Even with the advent of P.L. 94-142, which addresses the issue of an appropriate education through the mechanism of the IEP and multidisciplinary evaluation, many youngsters continued to be educated under regimes that were not designed to meet their educational needs.

In 1977, a petition for contempt and enforcement of the PARC decree was brought to the U.S. District Court. In this action, the parents of two boys with severe retardation alleged that the education their youngsters were receiving under the PARC decree was not appropriate. In 1982 the court ruled the Philadelphia public schools must provide an appropriate education for their students with severe retardation, and the court has attempted to ensure this through detailed specification of the school district's obligations.

In *Board of Education of Hendrick Hudson Central School District v. Rowley*, a deaf child's parents had requested the child be provided a sign language interpreter. This request was denied by school officials. Through appeal, this case provided the Supreme Court its first opportunity to interpret the provisions of P.L. 94-142. In 1982, the Supreme Court ruled that local schools must provide the necessary education and related services to permit the child to benefit from the instruction; however, "The majority further reasoned that it is not the role of courts to give substance to the term appropriate education" (McCarthy, 1983, p. 520). Thus, according to McCarthy (1983), the Supreme Court argued that the legal obligations imposed on states by P.L. 94-142 are primarily procedural and that determination of educational level or methods is the domain of state and local school officials.

A related court ruling occurred in *Campbell v. Talladega County Board of Education*. The court found the instructional program provided the plaintiff was inappropriate and ruled that the school district redesign the student's program to focus upon the acquisition of functional skills in four curricular areas: daily living activities, vocational activities, recreational activities, and social and community adjustment (Laski, 1985).

This brief review of selected legal action that has addressed the handicapped student's rights to an appropriate education leads to two observations. First, issues surrounding the determination of an appropriate education have been addressed by the courts, and thus, legal involvement specifying the parameters of an appropriate education is occurring. Second, the issue is far from resolved. Thus, the future should see continued legal activity directed towards further clarification of what constitutes an appropriate education for the handicapped population.

Appropriate Placement

The major issue surrounding the appropriate placement of students with handicaps is their access to least restrictive environments. The clear intent of P.L. 94-142 and P.L. 99-457 is to place children with handicaps in environments that provide them maximal opportunity to interact with nonhandicapped children.

Gilhool and Stutman (1978) have argued that Section 504 and P.L. 94-142 were formed by the Congress to eliminate the historic segregation of handicapped individuals into institutions or isolated programs. Through this legislation, the congressional intent was to integrate children with handicaps when possible into regular education programs and community settings. Gilhool and Stutman (1978) contend that "The integration imperative is thus crucial to all the purposes of the Acts [504 and P.L. 94-142]."

Many of the court decisions occurring in the 1970s are reflected in the Section 504 and P.L. 94-142 legislative intent for equal access and integration of the handicapped person into society. In particular, Gilhool and Stutman (1978) point out that the PARC decree states that placement in a regular class is preferred to placement in a special class and that placement in a special education class is preferable to placement in more isolated programs (e.g., special school, institutions). The Mills case encouraged placement in the most normalized settings, while the Wyatt ruling determined that even institutionalized persons have the right to be placed in the least restrictive setting necessary for effective training or education.

The integration of infants, toddlers and preschool-age children presents particularly difficult challenges because programs for non-handicapped young children do not always exist in the public domain. Public schools often do not offer programs for nonhandicapped three and four year old children; thus, reducing the options for least restrictive placement. Nonhandicapped infants and toddlers are likely to be found in day care programs that are operated by personnel who know little about the treatment of infants and toddlers with handicaps. These realities offer serious barriers to the integration of infants and young children into programs which included nonhandicapped peers.

Although the courts clearly appear to support the integration of the handicapped person into the "mainstream" of life, these rulings have, to date, provided little guidance in how to assess the adequacy of specific placements. Establishing the criteria to be used to gauge a successful placement most appropriately falls to the group of professionals designing, implementing, and evaluating programs and *not* to the courts. The legal decisions and federal legislation have made the intent clear. The challenge remains to develop functional methods for placing and maintaining handicapped people in least restrictive environments.

Right to Due Process

In years past, prior to clarification of the due process obligations of public schools, thousands of children were arbitrarily suspended, excluded, pushed out of school, or prevented from enrolling (Abeson, Bolick, & Hass, 1975, p. 1).

After years of exclusion from schools and appropriate programming, parents of students with handicaps began to seek assistance from the courts. In particular, the PARC and Mills cases provided court rulings pertinent to the establishment of due process procedures. According to Abeson, Bolick, and Hass (1975), the PARC decree set out a twenty-three step process for guaranteeing due process to parents or guardians of students who are mentally retarded. The Mills decision broadened the court ruling to include all students with handicaps.

Federal legislation and pertinent court rulings have also ensured due process for concerns other than exclusion from the public schools.

Inappropriate labeling and placement of children into special classes have been addressed in the courts (see e.g., *Hobsen v. Hansen*) as have inappropriate evaluations (e.g., *Diana v. State Board of Education*) and inappropriate instructional programs (e.g., *Fialkowski v. Shapp*).

As a result of litigation and legislation, parents or guardians are assured the right of due process over a range of areas that concern their child's evaluation, placement and education. P.L. 99-457 lists a series of procedural safeguards to ensure the rights of children and their families are protected (Garwood & Sheehan, 1989).

Smith (1981) reported a survey of state special education departments to determine the status of due process hearings. Data were obtained from forty-two states, although not all states responded to all questions. All respondents indicated that hearing officers were available, the majority being lawyers or representatives from higher education. The number of due process hearings held was reported to be 3,691, with significant variability in numbers occurring across states. Children with mentally retardation were the most frequent classification seeking a due process hearing, and the most prevalent issue raised by parents was their child's placement. Interestingly, although parents sought the hearing 96 percent of the time, rulings have occurred more often in favor of the schools.

The information obtained in this survey suggests that some parents are exercising their right to due process when they disagree with action taken by schools; however, this survey does not permit drawing conclusions about the number of parents, if any, who are not choosing to exercise their due process rights. Nevertheless, the legal and legislative base for due process has been laid. The remaining challenges are to educate parents to their rights and to develop procedures that benefit both schools and children.

Right to Medical Treatment

This intensely dramatic issue concerning the right of the handicapped to medical treatment looms on the legal horizon. The focus has been primarily on infants with handicaps who have been born with life-threatening conditions that normally can be corrected through some form of medical intervention. The controversy has occurred because some parents have chosen to forego treatment and thus allow their infant to die. Two major considerations are associated with this controversy. The first is ethical, while the second is practical (Taft, 1983). The ethical issue concerns the rights of infants with handicaps to be accorded the same treatment as nonhandicapped infants. The practical issue concerns ensuring compliance and cost of treatment.

In 1982, a Down syndrome infant with an incomplete esophagus was born. The parents of this infant, who became known as "Baby Doe," refused to permit the necessary corrective surgery, and before timely legal action could be taken, the baby died of starvation. The public, and the Reagan administration reacted, and in May, 1982, the Secretary of Health and Human Services issued a statement that informed hospitals that were recipients of federal support that it was unlawful to withhold appropriate nutrition or medical treatment from infants who are handicapped (Nice, 1983).

In 1983, a rule was published in the Federal Register that required all hospitals to post a notice to read: "Discriminatory failure to feed and care for handicapped infants in this facility is prohibited by federal law." The notice also invited reporting of any questionable practice to the Department of Health and Human Services. The posting of this notice was challenged by several professional organizations and brought to court. The presiding judge struck down the rule as "arbitrary and capricious" (Nice, 1983). Subsequently, the Reagan administration rewrote the rule.

This controversy was again brought to the public's attention when parents of an infant with serious handicaps refused to permit corrective surgery of an open spinal lesion. In consultation with medical, legal, and religious advisers, the parents of "Baby Jane Doe" decided against corrective surgery. Citing violation of Section 504, the government brought the case to court. In this instance, the court ruled in favor of the parents and did not require the surgery be completed; nevertheless, the issue remains unsettled.

In addition to the ethical issues involved in withholding medical treatment from persons with handicaps, are practical matters, particularly in the area of enforcement and cost. The American Academy of Pediatrics has been opposed to government regulation in this area and recommends that decisions concerning medical treatment be made by a bioethics committee (Taft, 1983). For some, such a recommendation is appealing for it permits consideration of individual cases rather than forcing physicians and parents to adhere to a set of inflexible regulations.

A factor that often escapes attention is the significant cost associated with the maintenance of some infants with severe handicaps. Medical costs continue to escalate, and families may be faced with financial ruin if an array of elaborate medical procedures are undertaken. If the family cannot shoulder the financial burden, then society becomes responsible. The question then becomes, As a society are we willing to spend considerable resources in the treatment of infants who are severely or profoundly impaired and who may not survive, or if they do, will most likely not become contributing members to society? (Lyon, 1985).

In a document prepared by The Association for Persons with Severe Handicap's Critical Issues Subcommittee on Infant Concerns (Guess, Dussault, Brown, Mulligan, Orelove, Comegys, & Rues, 1984), the argument is put forth that when operating from a philosophy that values all life, determining who lives and who dies using a cost analysis is inappropriate and unethical. This report discusses in detail the legal, economic, psychological, and ethical variables that need consideration before decisions are made to withhold treatment, withdraw treatment, or withhold sustenance from an infant because the infant is severely handicapped. This report concludes with a policy statement issued by the Executive Board of this organization which:

. . . reaffirms the right to equal medical treatment for all infants in accordance with the dignity and worth of these individuals, as protected by the Constitution and Bill of Rights of the United States of America. (Guess, et al., 1984, p. 30)

The legal issues raised by the right to treatment are complex and emotion laden; however, these issues need to be faced. As Powell and Hecimovic (1985) emphasize, both the professional and lay community should begin working toward solutions that at least attempt to acknowledge the inherent complexities surrounding medical treatment of infants who are severely disabled. Society must face the dilemma posed by withholding medical or other treatment from infants, and it is clear that the courts will play a fundamental role in the policy that evolves.

SUMMARY

The intent of this chapter has been to review federal, state, and local policy and legal action as it relates directly or indirectly to early intervention. The evaluation of mandates and regulations make clear the general movement to provide more protection to the handicapped population and to ensure, where possible, equal rights. Progress toward these goals has been substantial; however, the least satisfactory progress has generally occurred for the young child because often rulings and mandates have not extended to include the infant and preschool population. With the implementation of P.L. 99-457 the picture is changing. Within the next decade significant changes will occur permitting the development of quality services to all eligible children and their families.

References

Abeson, A., Bolick, N., & Hass, J. (1975). *A primer on due process.* Reston, VA: The Council for Exceptional Children.

Abeson, A., & Zettel, J. (1977). The end of the quiet revolution: The education for all handicapped children act of 1975. *Exceptional Children, 44*(2), 114-128.

Allen, K. (1984). Federal legislation and young handicapped children. *Topics in Early Childhood Special Education, 4*(1), 9-18.

Ballard, J. (1977). *Public Law 94-142 and Section 504 - Understanding what they are and are not.* Governmental Relations Unit, The Council for Exceptional Children.

Ballard, J., Ramirez, B., & Zantal-Wiener, K. (1987). *Public Law 94-142, Section 504, and Public Law 99-457: Understanding what they are and are not.* Reston, VA: Council for Exceptional Children.

Bricker, D., & Slentz, K. (1988). Personnel preparation: Handicapped infants. In M. Wang, M. Reynolds & H. Walberg (Eds.), *Handbook of special education: Research and practice, Vol. 3.* New York: Pergamon Press.

Burke, P., McLaughlin, M., & Valdivieso, C. (1988). Preparing professionals to educate handicapped infants and young children: Some policy considerations. *Topics in Early Childhood Special Education, 8*,(1), 73-80.

Burt, R. (1975). Judicial action to aid the retarded. In N. Hobbs (Ed.), *Issues in the classification of children* (Vol. 2). San Francisco: Jossey-Bass.

Cohen, J., & DeYoung, H. (1973). The role of litigation in the improvement of programming for the handicapped. In L. Mann & D. Sabatino (Eds.), *The first review of special education.* Philadelphia: JSE Press.

Federal Register.(June 22, 1989). Early intervention program for infants and toddlers with handicaps; *Final regulations, Vol.54*, No.119.

Gallagher, J. (1984). Policy analysis and program implementation / P.L. 94-142. *Topics in Early Childhood Special Education, 4*(1), 43-53.

Garwood, S. (1984). Social policy and young handicapped children. *Topics in Early Childhood Special Education, 4*(1), 1-8.

Garwood, S., Fewell, R., & Neisworth, J. (1988). Public law 94-142: You can get there from here! *Topics in Early Childhood Special Education, 8* (1), 1-11.

Garwood, S., & Sheehan, R. (1989). *Designing a comprehensive early intervention system.* Austin, TX: Pro-Ed.

Gilhool, T., & Stutman, E. (1978). Integration of severely handicapped students: Toward criteria for implementing and enforcing the integration imperative of P.L. 94-142 and Section 504. *Developing criteria for the evaluation of the least restrictive environment provision.* Washington, DC: U.S. Office of Education.

Guess, D., Dussault, B., Brown, F., Mulligan, M., Orelove, F., Comegys, A., & Rues, J. (1984). *Legal, economic, psychological, and moral considerations on the practice of withholding medical treatment from infants with congenital defects.* A report prepared by the Critical Issues Subcommittee on Infant Concerns. Seattle, WA: The Association for Persons with Severe Handicaps.

Kirp, D., Kuriloff, P., & Buss, W. (1975). Legal mandates and organizational change. In N. Hobbs (Ed.), *Issues in the classification of children* (Vol. two). San Francisco: Jossey-Bass.

Laski, F. (1985). Judicial address of education for students with severe mental handicaps: From access to schools to state-of-the-art. In D. Bricker & J. Filler (Eds.), *The severely mentally retarded: Research to practice.* Reston, VA: The Council for Exceptional Children.

Lyon, J. (1985). *Playing god in the nursery.* New York: Norton.

McCarthy, M. (1983). The Pennhurst and Rowley decisions: Issues and implications. *Exceptional Children, 49*, 517-52.

Martin, E. (1989). Lessons from implementing PL 94-142. In J. Gallagher, P. Trohanis & R. Clifford (Eds.), *Policy implementation and PL 99-457.* Baltimore, MD: Paul Brookes

Nice, G. (1983). Federal government, state legislature respond to "Baby Doe" controversy. *Interface, Vol. 8*(No. 4 & 5).

Noel, M., Burke, P., & Valdivieso, C. (1985). Educational policy for the severely mentally retarded. In D. Bricker & J. Filler (Eds.), *The severely mentally retarded: Research to practice.* Reston, VA: The Council for Exceptional Children.

Powell, T., & Hecimovic, A. (1985). Baby Doe and the search for quality of life. *Exceptional Children, 51,* 315-323.

Silverstein, R. (1989). A window of opportunity. *The intent and spirit of P.L. 99-457.* Washington, DC: National Center for Clinical Infant Programs.

Smith, B. (1980, October). *Policy options related to the provisions of appropriate early intervention services for very young exceptional children and their families.* (Policy Options Project). The Council for Exceptional Children.

Smith, T. (1981). Status of due process hearings. *Exceptional Children, 48*(3), 232-236.

Swan, W. (1980). The handicapped children's early education program. *Exceptional Children, 47,* 12-16.

Taft, L. (1983). A doctor's view . . . *Interface, Vol. 8* (No. 4 & 5).

Trohanis, P. (1989). An introduction to P.L. 99-457 and the national policy agenda for serving young children with special needs and their families. In J. Gallagher, P. Trohanis & R. Clifford (Eds.), *Policy implementation and P.L. 99-457.* Baltimore, MD: Paul Brookes.

Wang, M. (1989). Implementing the state of the art and integration mandates of PL 94-142. In J. Gallagher, P. Trohanis & R. Clifford (Eds.), *Policy implementation and PL 99-457.* Baltimore, MD: Paul Brookes.

6.
Population Description

Labeling and the classifying of children with special needs have been continuing problems for professionals and parents. During the late 1960s to the early 1970s, the concern intensified and became a paramount issue in special education and other associated fields. To bring clarification to the labeling and classification of exceptional children, a project headed by Nicholas Hobbs to study the salient issues associated with labeling children was commissioned by Elliot Richardson, Secretary of the U.S. Department of Health, Education and Welfare (currently the Department of Education). An array of professionals representing a variety of disciplines (e.g., law, education, medicine, sociology) were asked to address aspects of labeling and classification and each was asked to write a chapter based on their study and analysis. These chapters were compiled into two volumes and published in 1975. A third companion volume presented a synthesis of the information and opinion contained in Volumes 1 and 2 and offered a set of recommendations concerning the labeling and classification of children. These three volumes entitled, *Issues in the Classification of Children, Vol. 1* (Hobbs, 1975a), *Issues in the Classification of Children, Vol. 2* (Hobbs, 1975b), and *The Futures of Children* (Hobbs, 1975c), provide a rich source of information as well as comprehensive and useful perspectives about the need for labels and subsequent classification.

Although a message of concern about the misuse of labels and labeling is a prominent theme through the three volumes, a consensus about the need for effective classification systems exists. Hobbs (1975c) argues that persons who insist that labeling and classification of children is not required are not attending to the many demands of funding eligibility and practical management considerations. Methods for determining whether children are eligible for special services and methods for effectively grouping and managing children are essential elements for therapeutic and educational intervention. This position is reflected in P.L. 99-457, which requires that states identify and serve eligible populations. Part H of the law permits noncategorical identification, but requires states to define the term "developmentally delayed" (Garwood & Sheehan, 1989).

Effective intervention programs require valid and reliable strategies for classifying children and acquiring the kind of resources that will maximize their chances for growth and development. Conversely, care should always be taken to assure that the labeling and classification of children does not serve to harm or hinder rather than assist.

The younger the child, the more concern professionals and parents have about assigning labels. Considerable caution should be exercised when labeling an infant or young child because, historically our ability to predict subsequent outcomes based on earlier behavior has been poor, except for children with severe disabilities or who have a multiplicity of problems (McCall, 1979; Werner, 1986; Sameroff, Seifer, Barocas, Zax & Greenspan, 1987). The eventual impact of early biological insults and environmental variables are often unknown and thus render the development of many infants questionable. Such realities require that infants not be prematurely labeled.

Having made this brief introduction to labeling and classification, this chapter presents:

1. A description of early development as a basis for understanding deviations or atypical development

2. A discussion of factors that can interfere with normal development

3. A description of the population of infants and young children who are at-risk and handicapped

4. A discussion of problems associated with early diagnosis, labeling, and classification

EARLY DEVELOPMENT

Developmental Models

Many descriptions of early development begin by emphasizing the need to understand that normal or typical development can vary significantly. The study of developmental norms for most milestone behavior (e.g., see Cohen & Gross, 1979) emphasizes that skills can be acquired within a range of several months and youngsters still be considered normal. All children do not fear strangers at eight months, walk by twelve months, or talk by fifteen months. Rather, one infant may talk at ten months, while another may not utter his first words until sixteen months. Both infants may be developing appropriately. Nor do such discrepant onsets of specific behaviors mean that the earlier talker will retain his or, more likely, her headstart over the later talker. By age six years the late talker may be significantly more verbal than the early talker.

A number of models have been proposed to account for variations in children's development. Lewis (1984) has characterized these models as the status or medical model, the environmental model, and the transactional or interactional model. The medical model argues that the relative status of the child remains more or less stable over time because the environment can do little to impact the basic biological integrity of the organism. The environmental model asserts that development is controlled primarily by environmental influences except where extremely damaged children are concerned. Finally, the transactional model posits that a child's development is continually affected by the interaction between the environment and the child's biological status. In the transactional model, change occurs in children's status through variations in environment which may affect the child or changes in the child that may affect the environment.

Each of these models has generated a number of theories to explain deviation in development; however, one of the more satisfactory, in terms of explaining the range of development, is the theory proposed by

Fischer (1980). Fischer suggests that cognitive and other domains of behavior are a composite of individual skills. Skill acquisition follows a developmental hierarchy that moves from the simple concrete level to the representational level to the level of abstraction. Initially, skill sequences develop relatively independently. However, once a certain level is attained, coordination between skills or clusters of skills occurs. The skills that develop and the speed with which they are acquired is dependent upon environmental emphasis and input. This position would predict differences in skill acquisition across children and variability in individual children's mastery of different skills.

Determining how much a child can deviate from the norms and still be considered developmentally appropriate remains a challenge. Clearly, the repertoire of some infants and young children are so developmentally deviant that labeling the child as atypical is not a problem; however, many young children show deviations which makes their development suspect but not clearly atypical. Only with the passage of time can an appropriate diagnosis be made. This reality argues for caution in labeling infants and young children, for understanding that normal development tolerates significant deviations, and for awareness that the status of a youngster can vary significantly over time. With these caveats made, a brief discussion of early development follows.

Developmental Principles

Development can be conveniently divided into three major periods: prenatal, perinatal, and postnatal. Prenatal refers to the period from conception to the infant's birth, usually nine months in length. Because interventionists do not typically deal with parents during this period, prenatal development will not be discussed here. Perinatal refers to the period from birth to three to four weeks of extrauterine life. Although always considered important from a biological perspective, this period has become increasingly important in terms of the infant's social-emotional behavior (Klaus & Kennell, 1976; Sroufe, 1983). The postnatal period refers to the child's development past the perinatal period and is often divided into infancy, early childhood, and later childhood.

Because many books address development in detail, this chapter will only highlight the molar changes that index developmental change. As a foundation for this discussion, a set of critical developmental principles are reviewed.

Lewis (1984. p.3) has suggested there are five principles that can be derived from the important tenets associated with early development:

1. The infant as a competent organism

2. The infant as a social organism

3. The infant as an active organism

4. The infant's development as proceeding from undifferentiated to differentiated abilities

5. The infant's development as an interactive process between the infant's status at any point in time and the environment in which the infant is immersed

An important change during the past decade has been the perception of the infant. A contemporary research thrust has focused on demonstrating the competence of the infant, in stark contrast to an earlier prevailing view of the infant as having limited perceptual, memory, and discrimination abilities (Kagan, Kearsley, & Zelazo, 1978). A number of studies done over the past decade have emphasized the competencies of infants and young children. Many investigators have demonstrated that even neonates are capable of sophisticated visual and auditory discriminations (Trehub, Bull & Schneider, 1981; Fagan & Shepherd, 1982). These findings have demonstrated the infant's ability to search for and process a variety of environmental information shortly following birth and most likely before birth. This reality requires reexamination of the early developmental periods as a learning time for infants and would seem to have particular relevance for those infants experiencing some problem or difficulty.

Increasing emphasis is being placed on recognition of the infant's social responsiveness. The infant who smiles, coos, babbles, and subsequently produces words not only is practicing a number of skills but also is initiating and eliciting social feedback. The almost singular concern with the development of intellectual abilities is being displaced by growing attention to the sociocultural context for the child's learning. Meaning is not derived exclusively from manipulation of physical entities, but is also garnered by the infant from observing the caregiver's interpretation and actions. Thus, infants appear to need considerable social stimulation and feedback to become adequately adjusted as well as to learn about the social and physical world in which they live.

Major theorists concerned with human learning have emphasized the need for the learner to be actively involved if new information and responses are to be required. Bruner (1966), Piaget (1970), and Skinner (1961) have all advanced the notion that the learner needs to be actively involved if efficient learning is to occur. Infants and young children appear to be highly motivated to explore their social and physical environment. Active exploration permits children to acquire details about the physical properties of their tangible world. One can see the young child shake, bang, mouth, manipulate, and visually explore objects that are new or even to discover new "means" to use familiar toys through active exploration. The infant appears equally active in the social realm by responding to and initiating vocal interactions, by watching, listening, and touching other humans in the environment. Infants who are lethargic, or unresponsive, are of concern to parents and interventionists. Children who are difficult to move into action may continue to learn slowly and inefficiently presumably because they are not actively involved in the process of acquiring new information and skills.

As many books on early development note, the young child's response patterns move from undifferentiated to differentiated and become more complex. In fact, an important aspect of Piaget's theory of development is the view that the infant gradually learns to discriminate between environmental conditions first through accident, then trial and error, followed by purposeful exploration, and finally through mental manipulations. This process directs infants from using a few basic motor responses indiscriminately with all encountered stimuli to gradually learning to match their responses to the object or situation. Thus, the infant gradually requires an array of responses and learns to apply those responses in differentiated ways. At four months, an infant may bang a ball, doll, hammer, and book; but through experience and differential feedback the infant learns to bang the hammer, roll the ball, look at the book, and pat the doll. The infant also learns to gradually differentiate social responses. For example, the child learns to behave differentially with familiar and unfamiliar adults and learns to respond differently to "no" versus "good."

Viewing the development of children as a series of stages shown in Figure 6-1 may be useful. The initial stage represents the basic reflexive responses that the infant exercises during the first weeks of life. Through systematic interaction with the environment, the infant learns to use a few poorly controlled motor responses, such as visually tracking objects, waving arms, and kicking legs. Once acquired, these primitive responses become more controlled and differentiated so that infants learn to watch their hands, roll the body, vocalize when content or upon hearing an adult. Subsequently, these responses are expanded, modified, and combined to produce increasingly more differentiated behavior to move the infant to the next stage of development. For example, infants learn to coordinate their eyes and limbs to reach, grasp, and return an object to the mouth; to balance the head and trunk in order to sit; and to babble speech-like sounds. Figure 6-1 reflects the successive stages of development followed by most children.

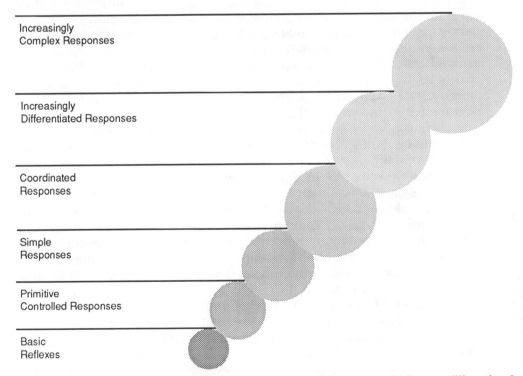

Increasingly
Complex Responses

Increasingly
Differentiated Responses

Coordinated
Responses

Simple
Responses

Primitive
Controlled Responses

Basic
Reflexes

FIGURE 6-1. Developmental change from basic reflexive responses to gradually more differentiated and complex responses.

The final developmental principle discussed by Lewis (1984) is that development is determined by the continual interactions between the child and the environment. The transactional model was discussed earlier in Chapter 3 and consequently will be only briefly reviewed here. Neither maturational nor environmental variables alone can account for development; rather, one must look to the interaction between children and their environment. The healthy young infant comes equipped with organized reflexes, such as sucking, grasping, vocalizing and looking. By interacting with the environment, the infant modifies these basic reflexive responses. Gradually shifting from involuntary to voluntary activation, the infant becomes capable of active exploration of the physical features of the environment. Such modifications result in more complex behavior. Environmental interactions allow infants to gradually build a more sophisticated knowledge of the world by selecting information and fitting it to their current organizational structure.

A similar interactive system exists between the child and the social environment. The interactional process between children and their caregivers accounts for the shaping of socially acceptable affective response forms into their repertoires. Without appropriate feedback, the child may not develop socially appropriate smiling, eye contact, and gazing; or establish joint reference and joint actions, which appear to provide the basis for more advanced communicative exchanges. The importance of interactional or transactional processes for appropriate development should be underscored.

In addition to the five principles of Lewis (1984), one further concept is required to complete the list. The principle of disequilibrium suggests development is predicated, in part, on the occurrence of events that require children to modify (i.e., accommodate or assimilate) their responses or their conceptual understandings. An important Piagetian principle of "moderate novelty," or just tolerable disequilibrium, is critical in the process of development or adaptation (Kagan, Kearsley, & Zelazo, 1978). Adaptation occurs as a function of the assimilation of new environmental inputs which, in turn, permit accommodation of these inputs to existing schemes or structures. The effectiveness of learning appears to be influenced by the amount of discrepancy between the novel or more difficult information to be acquired and the current schemes available to the child. If the discrepancy is too great, adaptation does not occur, possibly due to a paucity of external or internal cues pointing to a common linkage between the new circumstances and the existing schemes (Hunt, 1961). Similarly, if the discrepancy is too small, the child's interest is not maintained and no change in the repertoire occurs.

Development is probably optimal if environmental demands create a balance between asking too much or asking too little from the child. Arranging the environment to create a just manageable discrepancy between the child's current skill level and the next level of acquisition involves the arousal of conflict or disequilibrium by the presentation of a problem just beyond the child's current developmental level.

Birth to Six Months

According to Piaget, infants arrive in the world with a set of reflexive behaviors that are automatically triggered by either internal states or environmental stimuli (1970). As infants exercise these reflexes, their form changes to simple controlled responses that are maintained by the environmental changes they produce. Through subsequent interaction with both people and objects, these simple responses or action schemes (i.e., tracking, reaching, mouthing) become modified and elaborated into more complex and coordinated schemes (i.e., eye-hand coordination).

The basis for development is described by Piaget (1970) as the inevitable succession of states of disequilibrium which are produced as a natural consequence of encountering new environmental objects and events (both physical and social) for which no repertoire is available. During the first few months of life, adjustments toward equilibrium form the basis for expanding the reflexive behavior of newborns in terms of the number and the characteristics of events that evoke reflexes. When a particular reflexive behavior produces a consequence that is interesting to infants, the rate of that behavior will increase. Infants develop a number of different action schemes but do not use these schemes in a particularly differentiated manner. For example, an infant may attempt to suck any object placed in the mouth.

As a result of environmental interactions, infants begin to learn which objects (e.g., mobile) produce which consequences (e.g., moving) in response to specific forms of behavior (e. g., kicking). Thus, infants learn to discriminate among objects and events. The beginning of differential responding based on feedback from the environment forms the basis for infants' primitive knowledge about the social and physical environment.

Infants' first affective responses are rooted in attention to the human face and voice. Such responses can take many forms, such as quieting, becoming alert or attempting to keep the face or voice in the visual field. In the early stages of development, infants may smile when presented with a pleasant situation (e.g., a caregiver's attention, observation of an interesting object) and may indicate stress through crying when exposed to an aversive or excessively novel stimulus (e.g., a loud toy unfamiliar to the infant).

As infants develop, they begin to discriminate social smiling and show affective anticipation of common events. Once they become facile at discriminating mother and familiar persons from others, wariness and fear of strangers or different situations may emerge. The range of social responses and emotions that infants can produce are expanded; infants also become more adept at discriminating different social contexts. As infants learn both to discriminate and to produce a variety of social-emotional responses that depend upon both internal states and external conditions, they are also acquiring other social-affective behaviors of potential importance to the subsequent development of language (Tronick, 1981).

During the first few months of life, the vocal behavior produced is not like speech but is composed primarily of vowel-like sounds (Oller,

1981).   Infants seem to be learning to operate the sound-production mechanism and at this stage can produce noises and sounds that adults have difficulty imitating.   Early sound production indicate infants have learned to differentiate vocal activity into pleasurable (i.e., cooing) and distressful (i.e., crying) sounds.   At this early age, infants can discriminate or perceive differences between certain speech sounds and a number of nonspeech variables such as duration, intensity and pitch (Trehub, Bull & Schneider, 1981).

Infants learn to attend to objects in the environment, and gaze at them for long periods of time.   They learn to shift their gaze from object to object and turn their heads to locate an object.   Around the fourth month, infants begin to vocalize when hearing sounds produced by the caregiver.   Infants also learn to locate sound sources at this stage.   An indication that infants are becoming aware of their social-communicative environment is their apparent attempt to synchronize their activities or engage in actions similar to the adults (Tronick, 1981).   For example, if an adult waves an arm, infants, if watching, will often move their arms.

In the first few months of life, infants learn to attend to speech and, in time, to wait before responding to utterances.   By following mother's gaze, the infant is able to discover the mother's focus of attention and establish the same reference point.   Likewise, the infant learns to direct the adult's gaze by visually focusing on objects to which the adult subsequently attends.   Mothers often interpret their infant's intent by assigning meaning to the child's actions and vocal patterns.

During this period, infants are also gaining control of their motor system.   Newborns' motor responses are jerky and uncoordinated. Moving or making contact appears to be accidental occurrences over which infants have little or no control.   Continual use of arms, legs, trunk, head, fingers and other body parts produces increasing control, moving from the head to the extremities.   Thus, infants first learn to move the eyes in a controlled manner, then stabilize and turn the head. Trunk control is evident when infants begin to roll and squirm.   Sitting requires infants be able to balance the head and trunk, initially with support, then independently.   Infants become increasingly more adept at using their hands and feet to explore the environment, and by six months, they can retrieve a variety of objects within reach.

Six to Twelve Months

Between seven to ten months, most infants become facile at vocalizing the same speech-like sounds repeatedly.   This form of vocal behavior is termed *babbling*.   Around the tenth to eleventh month, infants' babbling has acquired many features of adult inflection.   The force, quality and pitch characteristics of vocal behavior are called prosodic features, and acquisition of early forms of prosodic features coincides developmentally with the acquisition of speech sounds.

Prior to nine months, infant vocalizations and primitive gestures appear as unconventionalized schemes, i.e., generally their form and purpose (or intent) are not mutually agreed upon by familiar persons. During this period, infants' communicative signals often seem oriented more toward direct goal attainment than primary social purposes. When the seven-month-old child plays with objects, action patterns tend to be directed solely toward the objects themselves (e.g., banging two blocks together and then dropping them into a container) or solely toward a person (e.g., vocalizing and reaching toward the adult). Instances in which a person and an object are involved in a social exchange are rare (Bricker & Carlson, 1982).

Around nine months, however, significant shifts are seen in infants' behavior as they start to coordinate actions with persons and objects. As their behavior becomes coordinated, infants are essentially demonstrating the capacity for social tool use, as in employing a person as a means for obtaining an unreachable desired object and using an object as a means for gaining adult attention. Infants can coordinate schemes to look and point to a favorite toy beyond reach, shift their gaze to the mother, vocalize, and look back to the goal. If further social bidding is necessary, infants can tug at mother's clothing and then mark the toy with a vocal or hand gesture. Coordination is also apparent in the behavior of infants who hold toys up to their mothers, look at her, gesture, and vocalize. At the same time that coordination of objects and persons develops, important changes in the infants' communicative signals may be observed. Existing sound/gesture schemes gradually undergo conventionalization. The meaning previously conveyed through signals is made more explicit and takes a form that is more easily interpretable by others (e.g., pointing to desired objects; calling for attention). Thus, by the end of the first year, infants become increasingly capable of integrating social interactions with object schemes, using conventional gestures, and showing an interest in social interaction (Tronick, 1981).

Affective behavior seems to be interrelated with cognitive systems. Kagan, Kearsley, and Zelazo (1978) have described the growth function of one aspect of affective behavior, separation distress. Studies of this phenomenon show that crying or inhibition of play following maternal departure is infrequent prior to eight months of age. From nine to eighteen months, infants characteristically show distress, and beginning soon after eighteen months such behavior declines. Kagan et al. (1978) suggest that the upswing in distress observed between nine and eighteen months may be due to the infant's improved memory capacity. When mothers depart, ten-month-olds are capable of detecting the incongruence between the scheme for their mother and the now empty environment. The third trend of the growth function, in which distress accompanying maternal departure diminishes, seems to coincide with infants' enhanced ability to retain structures of past experiences (e.g., mother will return) and concurrently generate anticipations of the future (e.g., wait for mother to return).

From six to twelve months infants gain considerable control over their motor system. They learn to sit, first with support, then independently. Many infants can shift from sitting to other positions, such as prone, being on the knees, or pulling to stand with support. Crawling, creeping, or some form of forward motion is generally acquired, permitting infants to access a considerably greater portion of their environment. The development of a precise pincer grasp occurs as does excellent control of hand and feet movement. The pinnacle of motor development during this period is the onset of independent walking or, at least, the acquisition of precursors to walking.

As the description of the acquisition of these responses suggests, there is a gradual sophistication of the motor system which culminates in the infant's ability to walk. In addition, infants have become adept at using their hands to acquire objects, hang on to adults, and manipulate most toys in some way. By the first birthday, most children have acquired a vast array of skills that moves them from early infancy to beginning the toddler stage.

One to Two Years

During the second year, the development of more complex and coordinated systems occurs. For example, children may learn to push a chair around the room as one coordinated response and to climb up and down from the chair as another coordinated response. Thus, when a toddler pushes the chair to the table and then climbs on it to get a cookie, the child has coordinated two schemes and is thereby beginning to separate means from goals.

The separation of means and goals also generally coincides with a differentiation of self from others. This stage occurs from about twelve to eighteen months of age. As children increase the number of differentiated responses in their repertoires and coordination among such organization increases, they may tire of known events and may actively search for the unknown in order to test existing repertoires.

Children's receptive language skills become more overt toward the end of the first year. Children will stop and turn when their names are called, will cease activity when an adult says no, and will produce meaningful gestures upon a familiar request, such as "Wave bye-bye." Although most children are able to produce a variety of sounds during their first year of life, it is during the second year that conventional words are produced. Studies of initial word acquisition suggest these words serve two broad functions for the child: social-communicative and referential. Social-communicative functions incorporate requests, demands, greetings, and so forth, while referential language is used to name, classify and comment on the world (Nelson, 1979).

The production of early words clearly show the interrelated nature of early communicative processes. That is, when the child says "car," the function as well as the referential meaning must be interpreted by the listener. The sequence of early-word production suggest that young children tend to focus their linguistic attention on those aspects of the environment that hold the greatest saliency for them—that is, young children talk about what they want, see and do. In the early productions of young children, both overextension and underextension of word meaning have been reported (Bowerman, 1976). However, few consistent patterns have been noted, suggesting that word-meaning acquisition may begin as a rather idiosyncratic undertaking by young children.

Between eighteen and twenty-four months, most toddlers begin sequencing words (Chapman, 1981). Producing two-word utterances is generally considered to be the initial stage of grammatical or syntactic development. Sequencing words assumes that the child has developed a rudimentary organizational system that functions by using rules. These rules enable a child to convey intentions and be understood by members of the language community. Many of the two-word utterances produced by young children can be classified as representing a variety of semantic relations. Brown (1973) reports that for children whose mean length of utterance is between 1.0 and 2.0 words, the following semantic relations describe the majority of their utterances:

Semantic Relation	Example
Agent-action	Boy sit; kitty run
Action-object	Hit block; go car
Agent-object	Baby rattle; Mama chair
Action-locative	Go there; eat here
Entity-locative	Ball there; dog here
Entity-attributive	Ball red; baby cold
Demonstrative-entity	That bed; this girl
Possessor-possession	Daddy pipe; Dog bowl

During this period, most children learn to walk with ease, and some learn to move with surprising speed and coordination. Children have learned many sophisticated motor responses, but these responses are used less on a trial-and-error basis and more often with obvious internal problem solving occurring (e.g., mental manipulations). The final state of the sensorimotor period is often called *invention of new means through mental combinations*. This stage is exemplified by the ability of eighteen to twenty-four month old children to deal with practical "here and now" problems through the use of various schemes that have become differentiated as means to a variety of ends. Toddlers have developed a repertoire of movements and discriminated relationships that allows them to overcome barriers, to use sticks and strings to obtain objects that are out of reach, to open new containers through exploratory manipulations, and to use chairs in order to reach desired objects. The hallmark of this period is children's ability to anticipate events based on environmental cues and regulate and organize their behavior based on predictions of successive happenings (Uzgiris, 1976). For example, if this happens, then that will occur. The baby crying for a drink sees mother open the refrigerator and stops crying because he or she knows a drink is coming.

Two to Three Years

At this stage, the period of infancy is completed and the repertoire has become more organized, differentiated, and complex in terms of both motor and cognitive-linguistic skills. Children are capable of mental manipulations (e.g., they do not have to directly manipulate an object to understand what the object can do) and can solve problems through the use of primitive logic (e.g., if I pull this string, I can get the toy attached to it). During this age span, children move from the sensorimotor stage to the preoperational or preconceptual stage (Flavell, 1977).

A hallmark of this age is children's increased facility with understanding and using language not only with family members but with other persons encountered in the environment. Specifically, children expand their knowledge and use of semantic relations to three- and four-unit (word) constructions. Children also learn to use articles, indicate possession, and use selected verb markings, such as attaching the "ing" suffix. Children can answer yes/no questions and pose questions through changes in intonation. The nonconventional (e.g., child will say "no want milk") use of negatives occurs as well. In addition to the verbal skills, children learn to construct models using blocks or similar toys, to complete puzzles or form boards. At this age, children can point to named pictures of known objects, events and people.

In the area of socialization, children are now able to recognize themselves and can provide their name upon request. Play is readily initiated, and they may be content to play alone or join with other children. Important self-help milestones are reached by most children during age two to three. Children acquire the skills to wash their hands and self-feed with both spoons and forks. Simple zippering and buttoning is done, and toilet training is accomplished by most children during this period. Finally, children at this age understand common dangers.

Three to Five Years

Children in this age range are capable of semilogical thinking. They use reasoning processes that are not always valid, but nonetheless show that they understand that the world operates in a predictable fashion. What is important, youngsters give evidence that they recognize invariants of identities (e.g., objects) even though the conditions of size, shape, placement and other dimensions may change considerably. For example, a glass, though dropped and broken, is still the glass. They also recognize invariants of functions—when placed on an incline, a ball will roll, and the steeper the incline, the faster the ball rolls. Understanding such invariants and regularities makes the world more understandable and predictable for children.

Language can now be used to manipulate information, and children at this age can learn from the communication of others. Extensive dialogues and discussion of topics that are not immediately happening or present can be managed. Linguistic productions become more elaborate as children's grammar expands and becomes more refined. Corrective feedback is sought by questioning or restatements, and children can comply with complex requests. Most four- and five-year-olds know their name and address.

During this age period, self-regulation, or self-control improves. Children have moved from a stage of immediate responding, to wait or even inhibit certain responses. The process of developing control appears to entail shifts in two dimensions. First, the regulation or inhibition shifts from others to the child; and second, regulation shifts from verbal to nonverbal, and eventually most children are able to completely internalize the control.

Mastery of several preacademic skills occurs during the three-to-five age. Children acquire the concepts of matching and reproducing shapes, understand relative size, and are able to sequence, arrange, or classify using logical rules. Several basic premath concepts, such as simple counting and discrimination of groups of objects with more or less are also acquired.

Children become well coordinated during this time, so that they can avoid barriers while running, climb ladders and trees, and ride wheeled toys without problem. A number of self-help skills are learned. Children are able to brush their teeth, wash and dry face and hands, brush their hair, use a knife, fix simple snacks, and independently use the toilet. Although children can successfully complete such tasks, some supervision is still necessary. Most children during this stage learn to work and play independently, but they are also able to cooperate with other children and adults.

Summary

The early-childhood stage encompassing the birth-to-five age range is marked by enormous growth and change. Neonates' behavior is restricted, disorganized, uncoordinated, and undifferentiated. As infants use their simple actions schemes, the environment provides corrective feedback and information. The assimilation of new information provides infants the basis for elaboration of current schemes and the replacement of familiar responses with many more effective modes for interacting with the environment. As infants interact with their social and physical world, they construct more coordinated, differentiated response patterns. One can observe the infant's successive levels of cognitive organization leading from accidental interactions to undirected exploration to trial and error to systematic testing of strategies to finally being able to mentally manipulate images in order to solve problems or accomplish desired goals. Similar growth patterns occur in the areas of motor, communication, social, and self-help areas. Children's early responses are often ambiguous and require significant interpretation and help from caregivers. Gradually, children demonstrate increasing skill and assume increasing independence. By the end of the early-childhood period, a remarkable metamorphosis has been completed, and now children's behavior is characterized by organized strategies to deal with environmental demands and self-initiated responses to acquire the elements necessary to meet the child's daily needs and desires.

This section has presented a brief overview of early development as a basis for understanding development that is either slowed or has gone astray, producing significant problems for the children and their families. More detailed description of early development can be found in the following sources: Charlesworth, 1982; Mussen, Conger & Kagan, 1980; Clarke-Stewart & Koch, 1983).

Factors That Disrupt or Interfere with Development

The overview of development that was provided should serve to set the general parameters of typical development. Most children follow—more or less—the general outlined sequences. Unfortunately, some children's development strays from the typical pattern enough to be of mild to profound concern.

The onset of a problem can occur any time during the three major developmental periods: prenatal, perinatal, and postnatal (Hayden & Beck, 1982). During the prenatal period, problems can arise because of mutant genes, radiation, toxic chemicals, harmful drugs, fetal malnutrition, maternal infection, blood incompatibility, placental insufficiency, and environmental factors such as maternal age, socioeconomic status and family size. In the perinatal period, problems can arise as the result of difficulties or trauma during labor or delivery, neonatal medications, prematurity, anoxia, or low birth weight. Problems may occur in the postnatal period for a wide variety of reasons, including illness, chronic disease, accidents, late onset of central nervous system disorders, environmental toxins, and other environmental factors, such as poverty, abuse, and family dysfunction (Ramey, Trohanis, & Hostler, 1982).

The traditional categories used for exceptional children can be related to nine separate causes:

1. Infections (e.g., encephalitis)

2. Intoxication (e.g., poisoning)

3. Trauma (e.g., blow to the head)

4. Metabolic disorder (e.g., PKU)

5. Central nervous system disorders (e.g., tumors in the CNS)

6. Chromosomal disorders (e.g., Down syndrome)

7. Gestational disorders (e.g., prematurity)

8. Psychosocial disorders (e.g., environmental deprivation)

9. Unknown (e.g., no overt causal factor)

These factors are discussed in more detail and as they specifically relate to the various subgroups of the target population in the following section.

TARGET POPULATION

For school-age populations, the estimate of children requiring some special service generally ranges from 12 to 15 percent. For infants and young children who are handicapped, determining such percentages is more difficult because of variations in definitions, eligibility guidelines, and services available across states.

Approximately 10 percent of the infants born in the United States are classified as at-risk because they spend time in a Newborn Intensive Care Unit (Holmes, Reich & Pasternak, 1984). However, as the number of risk factors increases, so does the percentage of children found to be at-risk or to have subsequent problems(Sameroff, 1985).

P.L. 99-457 asks that state departments of education determine disability categories or eligibility criteria for the three-to-five year olds, and Interagency Coordination Councils are required to do the same for the birth-to-two population, with the option of including at-risk infants (Smith & Strain, 1988). How states choose to define their handicapped population and if at-risk groups are included will affect the percentage of children requiring services. It may be helpful to think of populations of children as making up a linear continuum. The largest proportion of children on the continuum develop without problems and require no form of intervention. The next largest proportion have at some time been exposed to a factor(s) that places their development at-risk. Finally, successively smaller proportions of children are found to be mildly, moderately, and severely handicapped. The notion of a continuum also reflects the reality that children whose repertoires place them on the borders of categories (e.g., the slow child who manages well socially, but cannot read at grade level), can and do shift from one category to the other. The onset or termination of pathology or inappropriate environmental conditions may shift the child to the adjacent category.

It is helpful to dismiss from one's thinking the idea that uncontaminated categories of children exist. Rather, classification systems should be viewed as a convenient professional shorthand. Classification or categorical systems are necessary and can be helpful; however, the imprecision of such systems requires that they be used with flexibility and good sense.

At-Risk Infants and Young Children

Infants or children can be assigned to the at-risk category for either biological or environmental factors; although considerable overlap exists between these two groups. The concept of risk as applied to the classification of children indicates that presently the infant or child is either functioning normally or is expected to catch up (e.g., premature infant) or is likely to recover (e.g., infant with respiratory distress syndrome), *but* the concept indicates that these factors or conditions place the child in greater jeopardy for failing to attain or maintain a subsequent normal rate or pattern of development than children who had not experienced such conditions.

The classification of biological risk is assigned to infants or children with a history during the prenatal, perinatal, neonatal or early developmental period of a biological insult to the central nervous system or of a diagnosed medical disorder (Tjossem, 1976). Prematurity is the most frequent condition leading to the classification of biological risk. The more premature the infant, the greater the risk. Other biological risk factors include: birth weight under 1500 grams—a condition often associated with prematurity; infection; seizures; the need for resuscitation; and maternal disorders (Denhoff, 1983).

Though infants suffering some biological or medical insult have a higher percentage of neurological and developmental problems than full-term infants, the field has been continually frustrated in attempts to accurately predict subsequent developmental outcomes based on the biological/medical status of infants during the early developmental periods. As Sameroff (1981) has argued, the current best predictors are social factors such as maternal education and family income. Indeed, it should be remembered that the largest number (not percentages) of children who will require intervention services are term babies who are not labeled as at-risk. Nevertheless, studies have repeatedly found that 30 percent of the infants identified as biologically at-risk will require some form of intervention by age six (Scott & Masi, 1979). These findings suggest many of the babies identified as at-risk are likely to have problems, and therefore, this group continues to be of concern to early interventionists. A remaining challenge is to discover more cost-efficient and more accurate methods for determining which at-risk infants will need assistance and which will not (Bricker, Squires, Kaminski & Mounts, 1988).

Environmentally at-risk infants and children are those for whom some factor(s) or condition(s) in the social or physical milieu, or both, has a high probability of interfering with the youngster's normal development. These children most often live in poor or abusive homes. Often infants who are at environmental risk may have experienced other biologically threatening conditions as well. For example, women who live in poverty often do not have access to or seek consistent prenatal care, or teenagers who become pregnant may have a diet sufficiently poor to affect fetal development. The conditions of poverty often place the infant at-risk for biological and environmental reasons.

Infants and Young Children with Handicaps

An enormous array of handicapping conditions and causes exist. For example, there are estimates of 500 different anomalies associated with mental retardation, over 4,000 separate causes of severely handicapping conditions, and over 220 recognizable patterns of malformations (Hayden & Beck, 1982). This multitude of conditions can be caused by biological, psycho-social factors or combinations of both. The classification of handicapped differs from that of at-risk because the infant or child shows significant structural or behavioral deviation that requires medical or educational intervention, or both. As with the classification of at-risk, handicapping conditions can be divided into those that result from biological or environmental factors. Causes of biological handicaps can be conveniently divided into genetic factors, neurological/physical factors, infections, teratogens, sensory factors, and developmental delays.

Biological Factors

Genetic and Chromosomal Disorders. According to Crain (1984), 25 percent of the birth defects are due to gene disorders, and another 12 percent are due to chromosomal disorders. Genetic disorders occur because a gene or genes of one or both parents is abnormal, affecting the offspring. Chromosomal disorders occur when chromosomes are rearranged or when part of a chromosome detaches from its normal location and reattaches to another chromosome pair (Crain, 1984).

The most common chromosomal disorder is Down syndrome, and is most often the result of an abnormal arrangement of the twenty-first chromosome. Estimates of the disorder range in the neighborhood of 1.5 per 1,000 live births (Hayden & Beck, 1982); however, this rate is affected by maternal age. Characteristics of these children generally include poor muscle tone, slanting eyes, folds of skin at the corners of the eyes, low-set ears, short necks, small oral cavity, small hands, feet, and stature. In addition, heart defects are present in 40 percent of the children, hearing impairments are frequent, and intellectual impairment ranges from mild to severe (Garwood, 1983).

Other genetic disorders include:

- Turner's syndrome resulting from a female infant having only one X chromosome

- Klinefelter's syndrome resulting from the male infant having two X chromosomes

- Cri du chat syndrome resulting from an incomplete fifth chromosome pair

A variety of genetic disorders produce serious metabolic disturbances in infants. These disorders produce biochemical imbalances that can have devastating effects on the infant. Perhaps the best known metabolic disorder is phenylketonuria (PKU). Infants with PKU have an enzyme deficiency which permits the build up of phenylalanine to toxic levels that affect the brain. If not treated, the result can be severe retardation. Another deficiency is known as Tay Sach's disease. The onset occurs during the first year and results from an enzymatic defect in the metabolism of certain lipids essential to brain development. This condition is fatal to the affected child. Galactosemia is a metabolic disorder in which the infant is unable to digest milk. If this disorder goes uncorrected, the child will fail to thrive and develop progressive psychomotor retardation (Crain, 1984).

Many other genetic and chromosomal disorders have been identified, but their incidence is extremely low. For readers interested in more detail about chromosomal and genetic disorders, see Crain, 1984; Blackman, 1983; Hayden and Beck, 1982.

Neurological and Physical Impairments. The large number of central nervous system (CNS) abnormalities that have been identified are generally associated with a prenatal onset. Hayden and Beck (1982) indicate that most CNS abnormalities are recognized at birth or shortly thereafter. However, in instances of mildly to moderately involved cerebral palsy infants, early accurate identification does not always occur. Within this category, the following more common disorders will be briefly discussed: cerebral palsy, spina bifida, hydrocephalus, epilepsy, physical impairments, and other frequent health impairments.

Cerebral Palsy is caused by damage to the brain's motor control system. It is estimated that three of every one thousand children born in the United States are affected by cerebral palsy. Cerebral palsy is generally characterized by paralysis, weakness, and poor coordination (Garwood, 1983). Involvement can range from slight, which causes the child few problems, to major, in which all muscle systems are involved. In this latter group, voluntary control of muscle movements may be almost impossible—even the acts of breathing and swallowing may cause the child serious difficulty. As noted above, some infants with cerebral palsy may be difficult to diagnose before six to nine months; however, early diagnostic signs include difficulty in sucking and feeding, weak cry, abnormal muscle tone, and continuation of reflexes past the time when they should become integrated into other response systems

(Langley, 1983). Cerebral palsy is frequently accompanied by retardation, speech difficulties, and emotional problems (Garwood, 1983).

The onset of spina bifida occurs during the fetal development period and can take two forms, meningocele and myelomeningocele. During the development of the nervous system, some disruption interferes with the fusion of the vertebrae, producing an open lesion in the spinal column. The higher the lesion occurs on the spinal column, the more serious the child's impairments. Characteristics of spina bifida include mild to severe visual and perceptual-motor disorders, mild to moderate tone, strength, and muscle movement problems, and disorganized language and thought processes (Langley, 1983). A frequently encountered problem associated with myelomeningocele is bladder and bowel control, which can lead to physical as well as emotional problems (Lozes, 1988). It is estimated that one child in three-hundred to four-hundred births in the United States is born with spina bifida.

Hydrocephalus often occurs in conjunction with myelomeningocele. Generally a structural defect obstructs the flow of cerebrospinal fluid and produces a build up of fluid that produces progressive cranial distention and resulting damage (Langley, 1983). Characteristics include an enlarged head, thin scalp, upward retraction of the face skin, and in the more severe cases, generalized spasticity and poor motor control (Langley, 1983). Disorders in language and retardation often accompany hydrocephalus.

Epilepsy is caused from disturbances in electrical discharges of the brain, resulting in loss of control over specific muscle groups and observable seizures. There are three major types of epilepsy. Grand mal seizures are characterized by the child becoming unconscious and losing postural control. Muscles become rigid and then jerking reactions take over lasting from one to ten minutes. Petit mal seizures can occur as a variety of minimal muscle reactions and last only a few seconds. The number of seizures can vary with some children having as many as one hundred seizures per day (Garwood, 1983). This form of epilepsy is generally accompanied by mental retardation. Psychomotor epilepsy is characterized by a sudden loss of muscle tone and involuntary contraction of limb and trunk muscles (Langley, 1983).

Physical impairments encompass neurologic, orthopedic or health-related conditions that adversely affect the child's development and performance. Such conditions can include muscular dystrophy, osteogenesis imperfecta, rheumatoid arthritis, and spinal and bone deformities (for a discussion of these problems see Langley, 1983, pp. 105-113). The extent of the impairment produced by these and other disorders varies and determines whether the child is mildly, moderately, or severely disabled.

Health impairments that affect the child's development or ability to cope with environmental demands can be acute (e.g., hepatitis, mononucleosis) or chronic (e.g., congenital heart defect, cystic fibrosis, diabetes, nephrosis). The severity of the condition often determines the impact on the child.

Infections.   In utero infections of the fetus with syphilis, rubella, cytomegalovirus, toxoplasmosis, or herpes may result in spontaneous abortion or a variety of manifestations depending upon the severity of infection and the gestational age when infection occurs (Crain, 1984, p. 34). A relative newcomer to this list is AIDS. Currently it is estimated that only 1 to 2 percent of the AIDS patients are children; however, increases are expected because the number of HIV-infected women of childbearing age is increasing (Andersen, 1988). Prevention of maternal infection is preferred because no effective treatment is yet available for many of these viral infections (for further discussion of prenatal infection see Crain, 1984 and Andersen, 1988).

Teratogens.   Environmental substances implicated in producing malformations in developing organisms are called teratogens. Well-known teratogens include certain drugs such as Thalidomide and alcohol, chemicals such as PCB and mercury, radiation and lead. The effect on the child is determined, in part, by the quantity of the substance ingested and the developmental period in which the substance is ingested. For example, the drug Thalidomide appears to be teratogenic only during the first trimester of pregnancy (see Crain, 1984 or Blackman, 1983 for further information).

Sensory Impairments.   Hearing impairments can range from mild to severe. Forty to sixty percent of hearing impairments result from genetic or chromosomal abnormalities, while the remaining causes are disease related. Children whose hearing disability precludes auditory processing of spoken language are considered deaf, while children who can successfully understand speech, with or without an aid, are considered hard-of-hearing (Fewell, 1983). The severity and the age at which children become hearing impaired affect their facility with language. Congenital impairments tend to have the greatest impact.

Visual impairments can be divided into blind and partially sighted. Functionally, children who must read using Braille are classified as blind, while children who can read print using magnifying devices or large print are classified as partially sighted (Hallahan & Kauffman, 1978). Frequent causes of visual impairment are infectious disease, trauma, or exposure to harmful substances (e.g., an excess of oxygen during the perinatal period producing retolental fibroplasia). Although marked delays may occur in early motor development, given adequate environmental compensation, most visually impaired children function within normal limits in important domains of behavior by age six.

Developmental Delays.   Some children show a developmental delay or disorder in communication, cognition, motor, or social areas which appear to have no specific etiology or in which the cause is unclear. Many children exhibiting general delays are eventually labeled as mentally retarded. Within this classification, one can be severely, moderately, or mildly retarded. Psychosocial (environmental) and unknown factors account for the cause of approximately 75 percent of the mentally retarded population; however, causes of more severe retardation can often be pinpointed as genetic, teratogenic, infectious, or neurologic. Characteristics of children who are retarded vary depending on the level of retardation and the effectiveness of the environmental intervention.

Language-delayed or disordered children are a second large group of children found under the classification of developmental delays. Some children in this group show abnormal patterns of speech and language development (e.g., disorders), while other children show typical patterns but that are significantly delayed in their emergence (e.g., delayed). Often language delays or disorders are associated with difficulty in problem solving and other academic functioning (Cole & Garwood, 1983).

Environmental Factors

Although the causal factors for many handicapping conditions are biological, there are significant numbers of children whose behavioral repertoires are deficient but for whom there is no obvious biological cause. However, the absence of a clearly specifiable biological factor does not necessarily rule out such factors. There are, without doubt, genetic and neurological deficits or dysfunctions that have yet to be identified. In the future, certain handicaps of currently unknown origin may become identified as a specific syndrome or the result of a certain biological problem.

The more severely handicapped the child, the more probable the cause can be identified as biological as opposed to environmental. As indicated above, the causes for 75 percent of the mentally retarded population are attributed to unknown or environmental factors. Many of the children served in Head Start programs or in classes for the educable mentally retarded come from poor homes that often fail to provide adequate stimulation or nutrition. Some are even abusive. Such conditions may adversely affect the child's rate or quality of learning. Without adequate early intervention, many children living in circumstances of poverty fall progressively behind their age mates (Bryant & Ramey, 1987).

PROBLEMS IN IDENTIFYING AND LABELING THE TARGET POPULATION

The previous discussion has defined the population of infants and young children who are at-risk or handicapped. These groups are the focus for the conceptual and practical intervention framework described in this book. The previous discussions of the major prenatal, perinatal, and postnatal factors resulting in development that is at-risk or deviant should not be construed to mean that professionals are able to accurately identify and correctly label most infants and young children during the early developmental period who will eventually require intervention.

· Throughout this chapter, problems in appropriately identifying infants and young children in need of assistance have been mentioned. For a variety of reasons, our ability to accurately identify those infants and young children who would benefit from some form of intervention is imperfect. A small percentage of infants can be identified as handicapped at birth; but for the majority of children, problems do not become clearly manifest until later in their life. Further, some infants and young children have problems that are transitory. In particular, as many as 70 percent of the infants labeled as at-risk eventually are functioning within the normal range of development (Scott & Masi, 1979). There are two major problems associated with the appropriate diagnosing, labeling, and classification of infants and young children: the range of acceptable variations in development and longitudinal prediction based on early repertoires.

Variations in Development

In spite of the abundance of information on developmental norms and growth, abnormal development in infants and young children is often difficult to identify with certainty for several reasons. Developmental norms are derived from large groups of children, and thus, application of such norms to the individual child must be done with caution. That is, the central tendency is reported and often little indication of the variation around it is provided. Also, if one compares the reported onsets of specific skills, considerable variations can be found. These variations are probably the result of differences in the definitions, criteria for the normative performance, and legitimate variations in developmental rates and patterns.

Some children appear to stray significantly from the more typical path of development and yet eventually are found to function within normal limits. For example, many premature infants show considerable delays in the acquisition of developmental milestones; but by age two, most are developing without problem. Other children may show atypical patterns, for example, failure to crawl prior to walking, and yet learn to perform more advanced gross motor skills without difficulty. These deviations suggest that the human organism is capable of wide variations in development and still acquire a normal behavioral repertoire. Some children's development deviates enough so that intervention in some form is required to assist the child in adapting to environmental expectations. The problem is how to determine or specify when a child's developmental deviations are within the range of acceptability and will self-correct, versus deviations that will not self-correct and which will move the child beyond the range of appropriate and expected functioning.

Prognosis

The previous discussion provides insight into some of the problems associated with the prognosis of development in young populations. As the discussion in Chapter 2 indicates, in spite of the lack of empirical support, most of us are comfortable with the idea that there is continuity in development. The most frequent strategy employed to study the relationship between early performance and later development has been through the use of intelligence tests. Infants are tested during the early years and then tested again as children or adults. The relationship between the individual's IQ scores are then examined. As reported by a number of investigators (see e.g., Lewis, 1976; Honzik, 1976; McCall, 1979), infant intelligence scores attained before age two have little relationship with later IQ scores. Although these findings call into question the notion of continuity in development, they should not be unexpected.

Attempting to establish a prognosis for many infants and young children is hampered by many factors. First, as already described, significant deviations exist in developmental rates and patterns. Second, a number of investigators have suggested that qualitative changes in mental functioning occur between infancy and childhood (Zelazo & Kearsley, 1980). If qualitative changes do occur, this would argue for discontinuity between infancy and early childhood and explain the inability to predict later performances from earlier performances. Third, it seems that a prognosis made on an infant's current level of performance does not take into account the impact of the environment. As discussed in Chapter 3, the transactional perspective argues that the quality of the child's repertoire is determined by the continuing interaction between children and their environment. Attempting to predict a child's future performance based on the current repertoire does not recognize the potential impact of the environment. Fourth, the accuracy and quality of information generated by infant assessment instruments is suspect (Bricker, 1978). Although significant advancements in testing the perceptual and mental process of infants has occurred (see e.g., Minifie & Lloyd, 1978), considerable concern still exists as to the validity of the information obtained from early infant testing for future prediction. Each of these reasons can hamper the field's ability to examine early developmental repertoires and establish an accurate prognosis of children's subsequent development.

Difficulties in Diagnosis, Labeling, and Classification

Reflection upon the problems in establishing the parameters of abnormal development and accurate prognosis make obvious many of the difficulties associated with diagnosing, labeling, and classifying children based on their performances during the early developmental periods. Infants and young children exhibit a wide range of behaviors and patterns of development which do not fit neatly into single diagnostic categories. Without accurate diagnostic procedures, establishing appropriate labels and subsequent classifications becomes guesswork. Dangers in misidentifying normal children and missing children with problems exist. Given this state of affairs, one might reasonably ask, Why label or classify? As indicated earlier in this chapter, the field must have systems for placement and obtaining support for children who require additional services, thus the need for labeling and classification. If infants and children who are at-risk or handicapped are to receive appropriate intervention services, they must be identified and at the very least, labeled as needing some form of support services.

SUMMARY

A general overview of early development was offered to assist in establishing the parameters and definitions of at-risk and handicapped populations. Based on these definitions, the major factors or causes associated with these two populations were presented. Volumes have been written about early development and the factors which interfere with the acquisition of normal repertoires; the present discussions were only able to highlight selected critical pieces of information. The purpose was not to assist the reader in becoming fluent in these areas but to provide exposure to the general guidelines about at-risk and handicapped populations and what major factors might contribute to the infant or child being labeled and classified as either at-risk or handicapped.

References

Andersen, R. (1988). Management of developmentally disabled children with chronic infections. *Infants and Young Children, 1* (1),1-9.

Blackman, J. (1983). *Medical aspects of developmental disabilities in children birth to three.* Iowa City, Iowa: Division of Developmental Disabilities.

Bowerman, M. (1976). Semantic factors in the acquisition of rules for word use and sentence construction. In D. Morehead & A. Morehead (Eds.), *Normal and deficient child language.* Baltimore, MD: University Park Press.

Bricker, D. (1978). Early intervention: The criteria of success. *Allied Health and Behavioral Sciences Journal, 1,* 567-582.

Bricker, D., & Carlson, L. (1982). The relationship of object and prelinguistic social-communicative schemes to the acquisition of early linguistic skills in developmentally delayed infants. In E. Edgar, N. Haring, J. Jenkins, & C. Pious (Eds.), *Mentally handicapped children: Education and training.* Baltimore, MD: University Park Press.

Bricker, D., Squires, J., Kaminski, R., & Mounts, L. (1988). The validity, reliability, and cost of a parent-completed questionnaire to evaluate their at-risk infants. *Journal of Pediatric Psychology, 13,* 5-68.

Brown, R. (1973). *A first language: The early stages.* Cambridge, MA: Harvard University Press.

Bruner, J.S. (1966). *Toward a theory of instruction.* Cambridge, MA: Harvard University Press.

Bryant, D., & Ramey, C. (1987). An analysis of the effectiveness of early intervention programs for environmentally at-risk children. In M. Guralnick & F. Bennett (Eds.), *The effectiveness of early intervention for at-risk and handicapped children.* New York: Academic Press.

Chapman, R. (1981). Mother-child interaction in the second year of life. In R. Schiefelbusch & D. Bricker (Eds.), *Early language: Acquisition and intervention.* Baltimore, MD: University Park Press.

Charlesworth, R. (1982). *Understanding child development.* Albany, NY: Delmar.

Clarke-Stewart, A., & Koch, J. (1983). *Children: Development through adolescence.* New York: John Wiley.

Cohen, M., & Gross, P. (1979). *The developmental resource: Behavioral sequences for assessment and program planning.* New York: Grune & Stratton.

Cole, K., & Garwood, S. (1983). Language development and language disorders in young children. In S. Garwood (Ed.), *Educating young handicapped children: A developmental approach.* Rockville, MD: Aspen Systems Corp.

Crain, L. (1984). Prenatal causes of atypical development. In M. Hanson (Ed.), *Atypical infant development.* Baltimore, MD: University Park Press.

Denhoff, E. (1983). Intervention practices for developmentally disabled and high risk infants: Rationale and management. *The exceptional child, 30*(1), 67-75.

Fagan, J., & Shepherd, P. (1982). Theoretical issues in the early development of visual perception. In M. Lewis & L. Taft (Eds.), *Developmental disabilities theory, assessment, and intervention.* New York: SP Medical and Scientific Books.

Fewell, R. (1983). Working with sensorily impaired children. In S. Garwood (Ed.), *Educating young handicapped children: A developmental approach.* Rockville, MD: Aspen Systems Corp.

Fischer, K. (1980). A theory of cognitive development: The control and construction of hierarchies of skills. *Psychological Review, 87,* 477-531.

Flavell, J. (1977). *Cognitive development.* Englewood Cliffs, NJ: Prentice-Hall.

Garwood, S. (1983). Physical bases of handicapping conditions. In. S. Garwood (Ed.), *Educating young handicapped children: A developmental approach.* Rockville, MD: Aspen Systems Corp.

Garwood, S., Sheehan, R. (1989). *Designing a comprehensive early intervention system.* Austin TX: Pro-Ed.

Hallahan, D.P., & Kauffman, J.M. (1978). *Exceptional children: Introduction to special education.* Englewood Cliffs, NJ: Prentice-Hall

Hayden, A., & Beck, G. (1982). The epidemiology of high-risk and handicapped infants. In C. Ramey & P. Trohanis, *Finding and educating high-risk and handicapped infants.* Baltimore, MD: University Park Press.

Hobbs, N. (Ed.). (1975a). *Issues in the classification of children* (Vol. 1). San Francisco: Jossey-Bass.

Hobbs, N. (Ed.). (1975b). *Issues in the classification of children* (Vol. 2). San Francisco: Jossey-Bass.

Hobbs, N. (1975c). *The futures of children.* San Francisco: Jossey-Bass.

Holmes, D., Reich, J., & Pasternak, J. (1984). *The development of infants born at risk.* Hillsdale, NJ: Lawrence Erlbaum.

Honzik, M. (1976). Value and limitations of infant tests: An overview. In M. Lewis (Ed.), *Origins of Intelligence.* New York: Plenum Press.

Hunt, J. McV. (1961). *Intelligence and experience.* New York: Ronald Press.

Kagan, J., Kearsley, R., & Zelazo, P. (1978). *Infancy: Its place in human development.* Cambridge, MA: Harvard University Press.

Klaus, M., & Kennell, J. (Eds.). (1976). *Maternal-infant bonding.* St. Louis: Mosby.

Langley, M. (1983). The implications of physical impairments for early intervention strategies. In S. Garwood (Ed.), *Educating young handicapped children: A developmental approach.* Rockville, MD: Aspen Systems Corp.

Lewis, M. (1976). What do we mean when we say "infant intelligence scores?" A sociopolitical question. In M. Lewis (Ed.), *Origins of intelligence.* New York: Plenum Press.

Lewis, M. (1984). Developmental principles and their implications for at-risk and handicapped infants. In M. Hanson (Ed.), *Atypical infant development.* Baltimore, MD: University Park Press.

Lozes, M. (1988). Bladder and bowel management for children with myelomeningocele. *Infants and Young Children, 1* (1), 52-62.

McCall, R. (1979). The development of intellectual functioning in infancy and the prediction of later IQ. In J. Osofsky (Ed.), *Handbook of infant development.* New York: Wiley & Sons.

Minifie, F., & Lloyd, L. (1978). *Communicative and cognitive abilities-early behavior assessment.* Baltimore, MD: University Park Press.

Mussen, P., Conger, J., & Kagan, J. (1980). *Essentials of child development and personality.* Hagerstown, MD: Harper-Row.

Nelson, K. (1979). The role of language in infant development. In M. Bornstein & W. Kessen (Eds.), *Psychological development from infancy: Image to intention.* Hillsdale, NJ: Lawrence Erlbaum Associates.

Oller, D. (1981). Infant vocalizations: Exploration and reflexivity. In R. Stark (Ed.), *Language behavior in infancy and early childhood.* New York: Elsevier.

Piaget, J. (1970). Piaget's theory. In P. Mussen (Ed.), *Carmichael's manual of child psychology* (Vol. 1). New York: Wiley.

Ramey, C., Trohanis, P., & Hostler, S. (1982). An introduction. In C. Ramey & P. Trohanis (Eds.), *Finding and educating high-risk and handicapped infants.* Baltimore, MD: University Park Press.

Sameroff, A. (1981). Longitudinal studies of preterm infants: A review of chapters 17-20. In S. Friedman & M. Sigman (Eds.), *Preterm birth and psychological development.* New York: Academic Press.

Sameroff, A. (1985). Environmental factors in the early screening of children at risk. In W. Frankenburg, R. Emde, & J. Sullivan (Eds.), *Early identification of children at risk.* New York: Plenum Press.

Sameroff, A., Seifer, R., Barocas, R., Zax, M., & Greenspan, S. (1987). *Pediatrics, 79*(3), 343-350.

Scott, K., & Masi, W. (1979). The outcome from the utility of registers of risk. In T. Field, A. Sostek, S. Goldberg, & H. Schuman (Eds.), *Infants born at risk.* Jamaica, NY: Spectrum Publications.

Skinner, B. (1961, November). Teaching machines. *Scientific American* (reprint), 1-13.

Smith, B., & Strain, P. (1988). Early childhood special education in the next decade: Implementing and expanding P.L. 99-457. *Topics in Early Childhood Special Education, 8* (1), 37-47.

Sroufe, A. (1983). Infant-caregiver attachment and patterns of adaptation in preschool: The roots of maladaptation and competence. In M. Perlmutter (Ed.), *Development and policy concerning children with special needs.* Hillsdale, NJ: Lawrence Erlbaum.

Tjossem, T. (1976). Early intervention: Issues and approaches. In T. Tjossem (Ed.), *Intervention strategies for high risk infants and young children.* Baltimore, MD: University Park Press.

Trehub, S., Bull, D., & Schneider, B. (1981). Infant speech and nonspeech perception. In R. Schiefelbusch & D. Bricker (Eds.), *Early language: Acquisition and intervention.* Baltimore, MD: University Park Press.

Tronick, E. (1981). Infant communicative intent: The infant's reference to social interaction. In R. Stark (Ed.), *Language behavior in infancy and early childhood.* New York: Elsevier/North-Holland.

Uzgiris, I. (1976). Organization of sensorimotor intelligence. In M. Lewis (Ed.), *Origins of intelligence: Infancy and early childhood.* New York: Plenum Press.

Werner, E. (1986). A longitudinal study of perinatal risk. In D. Farran & J. McKinney (Eds.), *Risk in intellectual and psychosocial development.* New York: Academic Press.

Zelazo, P., & Kearsley, R. (1980). The emergence of functional play in infants: Evidence for a major cognitive transition. *Journal of Applied Developmental Psychology, 1,* 95-117.

7.
Caregivers and Families

Being an effective caregiver[1] is an arduous endeavor demanding a commitment and understanding few recognize prior to coming face to face with an infant shortly after birth. As babies grow and their repertoires and needs become increasingly more complex, the realities of parental and caregiving roles and responsibilities become apparent. Equally important are the concomitant expansion of parental expectations and ever increasing demands on the child to keep pace with peers by acquiring more complex behavior and becoming socialized. The foundation for a varied, intricate interaction has been established. Caregivers and children use a variety of mechanisms to balance the demands of their complex interactive system; however, when the balance of this interactive system is upset, disruption in the child-caregiver relationship can occur. The birth of an infant who is handicapped often can be the beginning of a serious and long-term disruption in family functioning. It is essential that professionals working or preparing to work with children who are at-risk or handicapped and their families acquire information about families, how they function, how their functioning can be affected, and how to assist families in reaching their desired outcomes.

To disregard or to underestimate the potential effect of a child who is at-risk or handicapped on the family may interfere with all aspects of the prescribed plan and delivery of services to that child. As Phil Roos (1978) suggests, a productive caregiver-professional partnership is constructed on mutual respect and understanding. One of the first steps in the professional's gaining respect and understanding is to attempt to grasp what many parents feel upon learning their child is handicapped.

> Most parents make it, given time. But they are generally ill prepared for the trauma, and the familiar ways of relieving grief are not available. It is not like having a death in the family, when people come together to grieve and draw comfort from the presence of friends and family. Learning that one's child is "not normal" is a lonely experience; having such a child tends to thrust the parents outside the mainstream of help, comfort, and advice. Uncommon problems cannot be shared with next-door neighbors. Friends and relatives feel, and often are, ill qualified to advise or assist. The usual sources of professional help, like one's physician, may seem inappropriate. The parent himself may feel some alienation from the "normal" world around him. (Gorham, DesJardins, Page, Pettis, & Scheiber, 1975, p. 156)

---

[1] The term caregiver has been chosen to indicate that the content of this chapter is applicable not only to a child's parents but other persons who provide care and stimulation on a regular basis.

The fact of life for parents of handicapped children which is least understood by others is this: It is difficult and exhausting to live normally, and yet we must. To decide on the other route, to admit that having a disabled child makes us disabled persons, to say no to the ordinary requirements of daily living is to meet the second enemy—loneliness. It means drifting slowly out of the mainstream of adult life. In a very real sense, we are damned if we do make the extraordinary effort required to live normally, and damned if we don't. (Morton, 1978, pp. 144-145)

These parental words are offered to assist in creating a heightened sensitivity to the realities and responsibilities facing families who have a handicapped member. Our effectiveness with families may be dependent, in part, upon our expertise in recognizing and respecting the variety of feelings and concerns found in the families seeking our help.

The purpose of this chapter is to provide information covering a broad range of topics related to family functioning when a child who is at-risk or disabled is present. In particular, the discussion will focus on: (1) the relationship between the young child and his or her family; (2) interactive effects of early experiences on infants; (3) potential disruptions of the family-child relationship; and (4) some general intervention strategies for involving families in their child's treatment program. However, before these topics are addressed, a brief discussion of the historical evolution of parent involvement in early intervention programs will be presented.

PARENT INVOLVEMENT: PHILOSOPHICAL CHANGES

Parental participation in programs for young children who are handicapped or at-risk seems commonplace today and is the expectation that most professionals hold. Reminding ourselves that parental involvement in early intervention previously was the exception rather than the rule may be useful. During the decade of the 1970s, there has been a dramatic and radical shift in the philosophy surrounding the involvement of parents in their child's intervention program.

Although in the early 1970s parent participation was encouraged in a few exemplary or model programs (see Tjossem, 1976), most programs and professionals did not seriously consider the inclusion of the parent until the advent of P.L. 94-142 in 1975. Turnbull, Turnbull, and Wheat (1982) argue that the United States Congress revolutionized special education by enacting P.L. 94-142 because this law mandated parental involvement.

Although passage of Section 504 of the Rehabilitation Act in 1973 ensured a legal basis for nondiscriminatory practice against the handicapped as well as other minority groups, this legislative act did not assure parent involvement in the handicapped child's education as discussed in Chapter 5. The passage of P.L. 94-142 stipulated parental participation and thus established a legal basis for the inclusion of the parent in the handicapped child's educational program. Since the passage of P.L. 94-142, a struggle to develop a reasonable and productive rapprochement between parents and the professional community has been underway.

Before the advent of P.L. 94-142 and, more recently, P.L. 99-457, parental participation was largely restricted to attending meetings during which the professional would explain the child's problems or progress. Occasionally, parents might be asked to attempt to reinforce the occurrence of specific behaviors within the home once those behaviors had been acquired under the tutelage of professional interventionists. During the early 1970s, and more obviously after the passage of P.L. 94-142, some parents developed into vocal advocates for their children's rights. Often, school personnel felt beleaguered by forced compliance with a set of regulations they felt poorly prepared to actualize, compounded by the demands of angry, combative parents.

In hindsight, the legitimate implementation of P.L. 94-142 may have been seriously hindered by rash and defensive reactions by some parents and some members of the professional community. Neither group was probably entirely objective nor balanced in implementing the spirit of the law. Some due process hearings may have served a useful purpose, but many did not yield results productive for the parent, child, or the professional (Strickland, 1982). Angry and emotional attacks by parents, which may or may not have been justified, have served to drive some effective, dedicated interventionists from the field and to entrench less responsible professionals into positions that hinder effective communication and action. Then too, continued inappropriate actions and attitudes on the part of program personnel have served to further embitter parents and build substantial obstacles to constructive parental involvement. Reactions from both parents and the professional community have served to seriously impede the participation of many parents in their child's intervention program.

A second problem that has contributed to limiting parents in becoming partners has been misguided professional philosophy or belief about the manner in which caregivers should be involved in their child's program (Dunst, Trivette & Deal, 1988). Often well-meaning professionals fail to see the barriers they erect to effective parental involvement because they presume to specify for the parent the nature of their involvement in the child's program. For example, the teacher who developed a child's educational plan *prior* to the IEP meeting surely must have conveyed to the attending parents that their input in the development of goals and objectives for their child is not necessary. Early intervention personnel who require that all parents perform the same function must be suspect in terms of their genuine interest and ability in determining the needs and values of individual parents. Morgan's (1982) analysis of IEP meeting data tends to indicate that while attendance is high for parents, contributions to the IEP for their child has been low. That is, parents attend, but assume the role of listener during the meeting. As professionals, we need to ask ourselves why parents are reluctant to speak up and why we have been so unsuccessful in involving parents who tend to be less well educated and poor.

Since the inception of early intervention programs, the philosophy of parent involvement in their child's treatment program has evolved through three stages. The first stage could be termed <u>Professionally Controlled</u>. In the early programs, professionals conducted the assessments of the children, constructed the treatment plans, conducted the intervention, and evaluated the outcomes with minimal participation from parents. The second stage could be called Family Involvement. In this stage, parents and professionals recognized the wisdom of involving family members in intervention efforts with their children. However, in large measure, professionals conducted the assessment and evaluation procedures, and designed intervention content and procedures. Parents were asked to sign off on the Individual Education Plan (IEP) and were expected to conduct treatment activities specified by professionals. The third stage could be called Family-Focused. This stage reflects another major shift from a child-centered approach to a child-family-centered approach. Understanding the family, its needs and resources, is seen as fundamental to designing appropriate treatment and intervention programs for the child.

The changes reflected in these stages are optimistic. A trend towards professional awareness of the parent and other family members as legitimate members of the early intervention team is occurring. These changes are providing the foundation for a fourth philosophical stage which can be termed Family-Guided and which moves a step beyond Family-Focused. Family-Guided, a term suggested by Kristine Slentz (personal communication), suggests that most families are able to discern their strengths and needs, and are able to determine their important family goals and outcomes. Early intervention personnel assume the role of assisting families in articulating their interests in locating the necessary resources to reach their chosen child goals and family outcomes. This change is philosophical important, for it removes the professional from the role of assessing the family and determining their needs, to the role of supporting the family in setting and reaching their desired goals and objectives.

This new perspective lays the foundation for two major changes. The first is a reconceptualization by early intervention program personnel of their approach to, and role with, family members in the child's program. The second is the recognition that the family dictates the child's goals and family outcomes.

Changing Caregiver Roles

Changing philosophies about family involvement have produced associated changes in caregivers' roles. The enthusiasm and manner in which caregivers have been involved in early intervention programs is, however, undergoing a steady and remarkable shift. Initially, during the Professionally Controlled stage, caregivers were not encouraged to participate in their child's treatment. During the Parental Involvement stage, caregivers were permitted to participated in the treatment activities designed by professionals. Reading previously published program descriptions give the impression that professionals conceived of caregivers as a homogeneous group who were able to contribute little to the understanding of their child's current behavioral repertoire as well as being in need of firm guidance from professionals. This guidance was most often offered in intervention activities developed by the interventionists without assistance from caregivers.

Many programs described in the literature have suggested that their parent programs have been successful in terms of both attendance and short-term changes in behavior (see e.g., Baker & Heifetz, 1976). However, other analysis tends to suggest that programs for caregivers are often successful with only a select group of parents (Baker,1984). Most programs are able to successfully engage a certain percentage of caregivers, are partially successful with another group, and are unsuccessful with a third group. The percentage of caregivers that falls into each of these categories is probably largely dependent upon three intersecting sets of variables: characteristics of family members, program personnel expertise, and logistics, such as transportation that may affect the ability of the program to successfully reach all of the participating families.

Given the general approach adopted by many programs, the lack of success with specific groups of caregivers should not surprise us. The most prevalent approach appears to have been the devising of a caregiver involvement program composed of a combination of large group meetings and individual meetings as the need arose (Bricker, 1986). In the past, programs rarely reported systematic attempts to elicit interest or needs assessments from caregivers prior to the development of a treatment program. Implicit in this approach is the attitude that the professional worker knows what the family needs and how to best present that information. Slowly, we are coming to recognize the fallacy of such thinking. If this attitude has been pervasive, it is perhaps not surprising that our programs have often missed the mark of meaningful family involvement across a range of diverse cultural, educational, and economic populations.

Programs at the <u>Family-Focused</u> stage (see e.g., Vadasy, Fewell, Meyer, Schell, & Greenberg, 1984; Bailey & Bricker, 1984; Bailey, 1987), reflect a different attitude toward involving family members in their child's program in two areas: the growing professional interest in eliciting from caregivers statements of needs and preferences for their child and themselves prior to the development of a treatment plan; and the professional's willingness to expand the caregiver's role.

Parents can accurately identify problems in their children, assess the general nature of those problems, and intervene effectively when provided assistance by the professional community (Walker, Slentz, & Bricker, 1985). For example, Brooks-Gunn and Lewis (1979) report that parents often are the first to suspect their child has a problem and may actually have informally diagnosed the problem months before a professional does so. In a large study that examined the ability of parents to monitor the development of their at-risk infant at four-month intervals using a simple question format, parents were found to be in agreement with the results obtained by professional examiners using the Gesell approximately 80 percent of the time (Bricker, Squires, Kaminski & Mounts, 1988; Bricker & Squires, 1989). Finally, there is a rich literature on the ability of caregivers to acquire effective instructional strategies (Baker, 1984). These data indicate that many of the roles and functions previously thought to be the exclusive domain of the professional need not be so.

In addition to caregiver roles which are directly related to the child that Stoneman and Brody (1984) have characterized as "manager" and "teacher" roles, caregivers can fill a variety of other roles that may enhance their feelings of self value, satisfaction, and knowledge that they have much to contribute to their child's welfare. The key to moving to the fourth stage, Family Guided, is the professional's willingness to acknowledge that caregivers often know most accurately and adequately what their needs and interests are. We, as professionals, can no longer afford to presume that we can determine the goals and objectives for the child, as well as the role the caregiver should assume in their child's education and treatment. Rather, we should be working toward the development of communicative exchanges that convey the importance we attach to the caregivers' own desires for themselves and their child. The development of the child's IFSP or IEP and the caregiver's participation in a program should ideally be jointly determined.

As the label Family Guided implies, the caregivers' role should shift so that they decide what should be priority goals for the child and the primary interests of the family. The role of the professional is to assist the caregivers in clarifying their objectives, finding the resources to meet these objectives and assist in evaluation of the outcomes.

Family Context

In addition to shifts in caregiver roles, changes in philosophy of parent involvement have also resulted in the acknowledgement of the importance of examining the ecological context of the child who is at-risk or handicapped when formulating an intervention plan. Historically, the field has moved its focus from the child to the child-caregiver dyad to the child within the family and the family within the community. Increasingly, early interventionists are recognizing that for treatment plans to be effective, they must be developed with a consideration of the many subsystems that impact the child and the parents (Parke & Tinsley, 1982; Barber, Turnbull, Behr & Kerns, 1988).

Robinson, Rosenberg and Beckman (1988) review four models of family functioning which acknowledge the importance of the family as a context for the growing child. These models include: family systems, ABCX, family life cycle and transactional.

Family system theorists such as Minuchin (1974) postulate four major types of subsystems within the nuclear family. These subsystems are: parent-child (parental); parent-parent (executive); child-child (sibling); and family-extra family, which includes extended family, friends, neighbors, and the larger community. There are several important features to remember about the roles that family members play in these subsystems. First, the roles of individuals within the different subsystems may vary considerably across families. There are no static definitions of how family members behave within a subsystem. Second, roles differ for family members dependent upon the subsystem within which they are functioning. A third way in which roles may vary occurs as conditions warrant change. As children mature, roles within the parent-child subsystem are expected to change along a developmental dimension to allow the child to assume more independence and terminate the parent's role as caregiver.

Finally, roles that individual family members take within each subsystem are dependent upon how functional or dysfunctional each family member is in a given role. According to family system theory, the interventionist's effectiveness should be greatly enhanced if he or she understands the varying roles that family members play within each of the subsystems and the dynamic nature of these roles over time and with changing conditions (Turnbull, Summers & Brotherson, 1983).

The ABCX model has four components. "The stressor event (A) interacts with family's resources (B) and the family's definition of the event (C) to determine the extent to which the event becomes a crisis for the family (X)" (Robinson, Rosenberg, & Beckman, 1988, p 113).

According to Robinson et al. (1988), the ABCX model is useful in explaining variability of reaction across families. For example, a stressor event (A) could be the birth of a child with handicaps. According to this model, the family's ability to cope with the stressor event is determined by the number and type of resources available (B). A large extended network of friends who are able to provide social support and respite care may permit the family to perceive the birth of the infant as not an overwhelming negative event (C). Thus, in this case, the stressor event does not become a serious crisis (X) for this family. In another family, the same stressor event might be perceived differently because the family lacks personal (e.g.,father is ill) or community resources (e.g., few friends, non-supportive grandparents), and thus, the birth of an infant with handicaps does become a crisis for this family.

The **Life Cycle Model** is based on the premise that families evolve in a manner not unlike the individual; moving through a series of developmental stages. Stages occur as families mature and include: the establishment stage, first parenthood, family with preschoolers, family with school-age children, family with adolescents, family as a launching center, family in middle years and family in retirement. As family members move through the various stages, their roles may shift and the functions of the family may change as well. The Life Cycle Model provides an interesting perspective from which to view families as they currently exist and as they change over time; however, as Robinson et al. caution, families with a handicapped member may not enter each of these stages. For example, the child with severe handicaps may not enter the stage of adolescence in which social independence from the family is achieved. In addition, the generalizability of the stages of this model to nontraditional families (e.g., single parent) is questionable.

The fourth model described by Robinson et al. (1988) and the one most compatible with the themes offered in this book is the **transactional approach**. The family is influenced by each of the members who are, in turn, shaped by the continuing interplay between biological and environmental factors. As discussed earlier in this chapter, the interaction between child and caregiver is affected by each participant and by their respective histories. In addition, the interactions that occur between families member is influenced by other social agents (Stoneman & Brody, 1984).

The transactional model offers three important features. First, it provides a framework to better understand the child in the family context. Second, it offers the most flexible and generalizable explanation of family dynamics. Third, it is useful for the development of intervention approaches. If one is comfortable with the assumption that the social context in which young children reside has a major impact on their development, then the adoption of a model to explain family functioning holds great appeal. Intervention plans should be based on relevant goals and objectives for children, but these goals and objectives should be filtered through the family context.

THE RELATIONSHIP BETWEEN THE CHILD AND THE FAMILY: AN INTERACTIVE MODEL

Before understanding the impact of children who are at-risk or handicapped on their environment, it is necessary to have an idea about the evolution of the feedback system or the developing relationship between children and their caregivers.

Not too many years ago, the predominant theoretical position concerning caregiver-child interaction appeared to be unidirectional. That is, investigators looked primarily at the effect the caregiver or the environment had on the infant or young child and did not appear to concern themselves with the child's effect on his caregiver. For example, in a series of influential investigations (e.g., Bowlby, 1973; Spitz, 1946), findings were reported that suggested the dramatically depressing effect of institutional environments on young children. The focus of this important body of research was unilateral because the investigators focused primarily on what they thought were the effects of inconsistent caregiving or mothering on the young child.[2] These investigators did not, however, look at the effect of the child on her environment. Of equal interest were another group of investigations that concerned themselves with more specific infant responses that could be controlled or manipulated by the caregiver. For example, Rheingold, Gewirtz, and Ross (1959) found that responses such as vocalizing are affected by social consequences provided by caregivers. These investigators found that providing pleasurable social consequences to babies increased the frequency of vocalization while neutral consequences reduced the frequency. Although such investigations were important in demonstrating that environmental manipulations can control affective behavior, again the focus of these investigations was unilateral because the investigators examined only the effect of the caregiver's behavior on the child's behavior.

Although an interactionist model has been a feature of many theories of cognitive development, Piaget perhaps being the most notable of interaction theorists, an interactive position did not appear to have

---

[2] A number of investigators (e.g., White & Held, 1967; Dennis & Najarian, 1963) have suggested that the reactions of infants that Bowlby and his colleagues observed could have been attributed to the lack of appropriate environmental stimulation rather than caused primarily by maternal deprivation.

much influence on aspects of the child-parent relationship until the early 1970s. A number of investigators (see e.g., Lewis & Rosenblum, 1974) were beginning to explore the child-caregiver relationship as one in which both participants affected the behavior of the other. That is, there appeared to be a reciprocal exchange governed by each participant's response to the other. The caregiver responds to a baby's crying by comforting the infant who, in turn, quiets and may coo to the adult, who, in turn, may smile at the infant, the smiling, in turn, eliciting a smile from the baby. One can begin to see a pattern of interaction which appears, in many instances, to be governed by the participants' responses to each other.

This circular feedback system could be viewed as a simple interaction model; however, a number of investigators have pointed out the need for a more complex model in which both the child and caregiver are actively influencing and being influenced by an array of factors (Ramey & MacPhee,1986).

Complex interactional or transactional models suggest the interactions that occur between the infant and caregiver at time one (e.g., feeding the infant at the hospital), can affect the infant (e.g.,hunger was satisfied), the caregiver (e.g., stopped the infant's crying, felt useful) and their subsequent interactions (e.g., next feeding time). If interactions are pleasant and satisfying, the infant and caregiver are affected one way, but if the interactions are unpleasant or difficult, less positive outcomes may occur.

In another example, a mother takes her young child to the grocery store and seats the child in the cart. The child sees a box of cookies and indicates to the mother "want cookie," which is the initiation of this interactive exchange. Mother says, "no cookies now, but you can have one later at home." This response produces a reaction in the child (e.g., denial of child's request produces anger) and a reaction in the mother (e.g., pleasure at being firm with the child for an inappropriate request), which leads to a second exchange. The child begins to cry and scream for a cookie. The mother responds to the child by ignoring the child's crying and pointing to another child in the store, leading to the third interaction in the sequence. The child responds by looking toward the child and stops crying followed by the mother smiling and talking to the child.

At each interaction point, the behavior of both the child and mother have the potential of being different based on their reactions to each other and their past experience in similar situations. For example, if the child had a history of obtaining cookies in the store by crying, the mother may have been unsuccessful at her attempts to distract the youngster, and the third interaction might have been one of more crying by the child, thus producing an angry response from the mother. Yet another scenario is possible. Had the mother responded affirmatively to the child's initial request for a cookie, the probabilities are high that the subsequent exchanges between the mother and child would have followed a different course of action.

Clearly, chains of interactions between the child and the caregiver are governed by multiple factors that must be appreciated if we are to develop mechanisms for influencing caregiver-child interactions.

THE INTERACTIVE EFFECTS OF EARLY EXPERIENCE ON THE CHILD

There seems to be a consensus that both cognitive and affective developments are the result of an interactive system (DeCaire, 1978; Saarni, 1978). The environment affects the child and, of equal importance, the child affects the environment. Having established the interactive nature between the child and the environment, we can next examine early factors that tend to influence the child-caregiver relationship. However, as a foundation for evaluating these factors, let us briefly discuss the nature of early affective development.

According to Piaget, the infant arrives in the world with a set of reflexive behaviors that are automatically triggered by either internal states or environment stimuli (1970). As the infant exercises these reflexes, the form changes to simple volitional responses that are maintained by the environmental changes they produce. Through subsequent interaction with both people and objects, these simple responses, or action schemes (i.e., tracking, reaching, mouthing), become modified and elaborated into more complex and coordinated schemes (i.e., hand-eye coordination). During the sensorimotor period, the behavior repertoire of the infant continues to expand as the infant looks, touches, listens, and acts on the environment. Although the acquisition of cognitive or problem-solving behavior is of critical importance, so, too, is the infant's affective development.

For any number of reasons, studying affective behavior and its development has been a more elusive, difficult task than exploring the genesis of more cognitive forms of behavior (Lewis & Michalson, 1983). The affective domain of behavior refers to those responses that have to do with feelings or emotions which produce psychological change in the organism. In general, there are two basic models found in the literature to explain the development of affective behavior: the biological model and the socialization model (Lewis & Rosenblum, 1978). The biological model suggests that certain conditions produce specific emotional responses that are unlearned. That is, the approach of an unfamiliar adult may automatically trigger "fear" in an infant. Contrarily, the socialization model suggests that the relationship between internal states (e.g., increased heart rate) and surface behavior (e.g., look of fear on the face) are learned behaviors. "Thus, the emotional state or experience is a consequence of the social environments' responses to the child's behavior in a specific context" (Lewis & Rosenblum, 1978, p. 8). It is likely that the development of affective behavior results from learned *and* unlearned behavior. There may be some basic unlearned, biologically based emotional responses (e.g., rocking, crying) to specific conditions (Harlow & Mears, 1978), but it is equally probable that more complex meaning-laden affective behavior is learned through interaction with the social environment. Figure 7-1 presents a schematic representation of these elements.

Although some investigators feel that affective and cognitive behaviors are separate areas of development, attempts at separation are

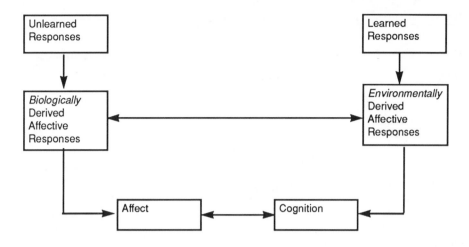

FIGURE 7-1. Hypothesized parallel and interactive development of the affective and cognitive systems.

often futile and unsatisfactory—particularly in the case of the young child (Lewis & Michalson, 1983).

> From an ontogenetic standpoint, it appears impossible to study cognitive development in the absence of affective development. This follows because the behavioral performance that we observe and infer as being the result of cognitive functioning is equally a result of affective functioning (i.e., motivation, interest, expectancy). As Piaget contends (and I concur), without affect, there would be no intelligence, from either a competence or a performance point of view. (Saarni, 1978, p. 362)

If one accepts this position, then as DeCarie (1978) suggests, it makes little sense to ask whether cognitive or affective behavior occurs first or which causes which. Rather, there is a reciprocal, interactive, ongoing relationship between cognitive and affective behavior.

Emde, Kligman, Reich, and Wade (1978) have proposed a model to explain the development of affective expressions in the infant. In their developmental model they suggest:

> . . . that the organization of the central nervous system is such that soon after three months of age, the three dimensions of emotional expression are apparent. In contrast, categories of emotional expression, characterized by discrete messages, undergo an epigenesis continuing through the first postnatal year and beyond. Cognitive development plays an increasingly important role in this epigenesis, and the study of its integration with ongoing motoric components of expression offer an exciting challenge. (Emde, Kligman, Reich, & Wade, 1978, p. 145)

Using the elements of the Emde et al. model and the levels of cognitive organization suggested by Uzgiris (1976), a speculative account of the parallel development of the affective and cognitive systems and how they may reciprocally affect each other has been constructed. This hypothetical model of parallel development is shown in Table 7-1.

Levels of Developmental Organization	Age	Affective System*	Sensorimotor System†
I	Neonate	Biologically based affective expressions of: pleasant–unpleasant high activation–low activation internal–external	Reflexes: e.g., rooting, sucking, startle
II	4–9 months	Regulation of categorical responses (fear, surprise, anger)	Simple undifferentiated actions (mouthing, looking, banging)
III	8–12 months		Differentiated actions (throw balls, pound with hammer)
IV	12–18 months		Regulation by differential feedback
V	18–24 months	Affective response in anticipation of event	Anticipatory regulation

*Emde et al. (1978), pp. 141–145.
†Uzgiris (1976), pp. 150–155.

TABLE 7-1. Hypothetical Sequence of Affective and Sensorimotor Development.

The purpose of the present section has been to provide a brief overview of how young children acquire cognitive and affective forms of behavior. The difficulty of attempting to separate the development of the cognitive from the affective system in the young child has been emphasized. The parallel, yet intertwined nature of these two systems argues that early experience of a young child, no matter what its nature, will likely have a significant effect on both cognitive and affective development. It is important to view environmental input to the young child with handicaps from this perspective; therefore, a healthy, productive caregiver-child interaction is essential to all aspects of growth and development.

THE IMPORTANCE OF THE CAREGIVER-CHILD RELATIONSHIP

The quality of the interactive system of the caregiver-child relationship seems to be affected by two major variables: the timing and the nature of the responses made to the partner. The back-and-forth nature of caregiver-child interactions assumes an underlying time-sequence frame. That is, one partner's response generally precedes the other's. The timing of the caregiver's response to the baby appears to have the potential of seriously affecting the quality of their relationship even during the very early phases of development (Field, 1983). Especially in the case of caregiver-child interactions, synchrony of responding refers to the caregiver's ability (and to a lesser extent the child's capacity) to monitor the state, mood, or needs of the child and respond in a facilitating manner according to the child's needs. For example, if a baby is thrashing and crying vigorously, an appropriate move on the part of the caregiver might be to respond with behaviors that would be soothing to the infant; therefore, the caregiver might lift the child, rock him and talk quietly in his ear. If the baby were in an awake, alert state, an appropriate response might be to offer some form of stimulation the baby might find interesting, for example, showing the baby a bright colored toy, tickling her toes, or returning her coos and gurgles.

Such in-tune responding to infants would seem to take the form of "doing what comes naturally" to most caregivers. Fortunately, most babies and their caregivers do arrive at reasonably effective interactions. However, as noted by a number of investigators (Brazelton, Koslowski, & Main, 1974; Denenberg & Thoman, 1976), the needs of some babies apparently exceed the ability of their caregivers to cope or respond in a healthy, productive manner. The development of an unsatisfying relationship may result from having a difficult-to-manage child (e.g., an autistic child) or a caregiver with little sensitivity to the state or needs of the child. Child abuse or neglect, either psychological or physical, may result when the unfortunate combination of a difficult-to-manage child with an insensitive parent occurs. As Meier (1985) suggests, the causal factors for abuse are probably multiple and complex. In examining caregivers' sensitivity, Brazelton et al. (1974) report the differential effects produced by mothers on two similarly tense, overreactive infants. The mother who was able to modulate her behavior to the infant apparently assisted the baby in becoming more responsive, while in the other case, the infant appeared to learn to escape his mother's increased stimulation by tuning her out.

These two parallel cases demonstrate that a mother's behavior "must not only be reinforcing and contingent upon the infant's behavior, but that it must meet more basic 'needs' of the infant in being aware of his capacity to receive and utilize stimuli" (Brazelton et al., 1974, p. 60).

Although the quality of the early caregiver-child interaction is probably more dependent upon the sensitivity of the adult, disruptions in the relationship can be produced by the infant as well. Denenberg and Thoman (1976) discuss a case in which the infant's irritable and unresponsive behavior made it extremely difficult for a mother to respond appropriately. An investigation of the state or mood changes of this infant were revealing because this baby was found to shift states significantly more often than other infants of comparable age. Apparently this baby's erratic behavior made it difficult for the mother to modulate her responses accordingly, and the amount of time this mother spent with her infant was observed to gradually decrease over time. Decreasing the amount of interaction between the child and caregiver may lead to a progressively ineffectual relationship. Other investigators (e.g., Mahoney & Robenalt, 1986) have reported less satisfying communicative exchanges between mothers and their infants with handicaps.

DISRUPTIONS IN THE CAREGIVER-CHILD RELATIONSHIP

With the birth of a child who is at-risk or handicapped, at least two unusual events tend to occur: extended physical separation between parent and child and the psychological impact of being told the infant is ill or handicapped. The birth of a child who is handicapped or medically fragile may necessitate a number of unusual and often dramatic maneuvers. In many cases, the hospital staff may have to perform lifesaving medical procedures. The premature or sick infant is often placed in an isolette, and the parents' first view of their baby may be with the infant attached to a threatening array of tubes, wires, and machines. Seeing their child under such conditions must be frightening for parents, and their feelings of concern and apprehension may be heightened by being unable to hold or be close to the infant. The physical separateness may interfere dramatically with the development of bonding and attachment between parents and child (Blacher, 1984). The parent may not have the opportunity to touch, hold, or care for the infant for days, weeks, and in some cases, months. Such extended separation may produce significant barriers to the development of positive early interactions between the infant and the parents.

A second possible disruption is the shock of being told one's child is seriously ill or handicapped. Interviews with parents give credence to the emotional upheaval produced by the birth of a child who is handicapped (Klaus & Kennel, 1976).

The birth of a child who is handicapped tends to shatter not only the psychological but also physical expectations of the parent. In many instances the infant or child who is handicapped looks significantly different. The child may have a physical anomaly (e.g., open spine), motor impairment (e.g., cerebral palsy), sensory deficit (e.g., blind), or atypical features (e.g., Down syndrome) that are clearly visible to the parent as well as the rest of the world. Such overt physical difference may affect the parent's ability to interact with the child.

The general appearance alone of an infant who is handicapped or premature may elicit unusual responses from parents. Seeing an infant that is obviously distressed, ill, or both no doubt colors the parent's perception of the baby and his or her needs. Much of the "over-protection" demonstrated by caregivers of children who are at-risk or handicapped may stem from their initial contact with the infant. Caregivers who have experienced periods during which the survival of the child was in question may acquire feelings about and reactions to the child that are counter to the development of independent, adaptive behaviors in the child (Gable, McDowell, & Cerreto, 1983).

Behavioral as well as physical differences may impact the nature of caregiver-child interactions. Caregivers seem to endow even the neonate with behavioral intentionality, and when the infant's behaviors are discrepant or do not meet the caregiver's expectations, then disruptions in the relationship may occur. For example, in comparing the smiling behavior of Down syndrome babies with normally developing babies, Emde, Katz, and Thorpe (1978) report observable differences. Although the onset of social smiling was somewhat delayed in the Down babies in the investigators' sample, the more significant differences seem to be qualitative in nature; the corners of the mouth turned up less, less eye contact was made, the eyes were less bright, and there was less motoric activity.   The end result is that the Down baby "seems less engaging" when smiling and therefore does not meet the general expectancy of the onlooker.   In effect, the adults are disappointed because the baby does not meet their expectations for a smiling baby (Emde, Katz, & Thorpe, 1978). Cicchetti and Sroufe (1976) also report finding affective differences in the responding of infants with Down syndrome when compared to non-handicapped babies.   Fraiberg (1975), too, has discussed the problems parents face when their baby does not meet their expectations.   In partic-ular, she notes the impact of smiling at a blind baby who does not return the smile "feels curiously like a snub."   Each of us has certain expectan-cies in terms of others' behavior toward us, and those infants or children that cannot or do not meet the behavioral expectations of their care-givers run the risk of developing a less than satisfactory caregiver-child relationship.

In summary, unsatisfying interactions between caregivers and children are likely to occur for a number of reasons.   The advent of a "different" infant demands that family members either expand existing skills or acquire new ones to cope with the disequilibrium produced by the atypical infant.   Thus, a major objective for most program personnel dealing with children who are at-risk or handicapped is to assist family members in their adjustment to and subsequent ability to effectively cope with their atypical infant.

FAMILY-GUIDED INTERVENTION

The beginning sections of this chapter have been devoted to a description of the interactive system which exists between caregiver-child and between family members.   The most important aspect of the caregiver-child and child-family relationships is that the family members' behav-ior affects the child and, equally important, the child's behavior affects the family members.   In such an interactive system, the quality and timing of each partner's response contributes substantially to the over-all relationship.   The birth of an infant who is at-risk or disabled can interfere with or disrupt the development and maintenance of satisfying relationships between family members.

The potential jeopardy of the child-family relationship in concert with a number of other variables often associated with children who are at-risk or handicapped argues for providing intervention services to families.   In addition, these services should be available when the family determines a need for them.

Rationale for Family-Guided Intervention Programs

Intervention services for families have been labeled Family-Guided Programs for a very specific reason.   Intervention offered to families should not be prescriptions of what to do designed by professionals; nor should the professional be conducting all of the procedures or making all the decisions in terms of the child's program.   Rather, a Family-Guided approach requires the involvement of caregivers and other interested family members in planning, executing and evaluating activities. A number of points form the rationale for family-guided approaches and these are discussed below.

Perhaps one of the strongest arguments for family-guided approaches has to do with time and contact. Except in unusual circumstances, caregivers spend more time with their infant or young child than do professionals or even paraprofessionals. It is hard to conceive of an effective intervention program without including those individuals who spend the most time with the child. For example, the initiation of a toilet training program without the inclusion of the home environment will be, at best, only partially successful. Without extending training into the home, it is doubtful that the toilet training success achieved elsewhere will transfer. In fact, it would, in most instances, make more sense to initiate a toilet training program in the home or day care center since that is the environment where young children are apt to use the bathroom most often. Other important behaviors, such as expressive language, will, no doubt, be acquired more rapidly if training is implemented where the child generally spends more time. Work on any important intervention target should include participation of those caregivers who spend considerable portions of the day with the child, for reasons of consistency as well as increased learning opportunities.

The second point in the rationale concerns economics and personnel factors. The trend in public health, education, mental health, and welfare agencies concerned with at-risk and handicapped populations seems to be the provision of extended services to more clients with fewer resources. Such demands are now and will continue to tax the ability of public agencies to provide quality services (Trohanis, 1988). Clearly, more efficient, economical strategies will be necessary to meet these demands. In addition, the field of early intervention has a serious personnel shortage (Meisels, Harbin, Modigliani & Olson, 1988). Given these realities, it is doubtful that adequate numbers of qualified professionals in the area of early intervention will keep pace with demand.

One obvious solution to the discrepancy between the number of children needing intervention and the number of available trained personnel is to enlist the primary caregiver and other family members. Most families have a healthy investment (psychological as well as economic) in their children. They have more to lose and more to gain than anyone else associated with the intervention process. With the support and assistance of the professional staff, caregivers can become effective change agents with their children. The use of caregivers either as the primary change agent or working in conjunction with an interventionist is an economically sound strategy for dealing with young children who are at-risk and handicapped.

A third reason for involving families rests with legal and legislative mandates. For three-to-five year old children, Part B of P.L. 99-457 specifies that parents are to be integrally involved in the development of their child's Individual Education Plan (IEP). The IEP is a document that states the long-term and short-term goals for the child. The plan or behavioral objectives are to be selected by the interventionist, necessary support staff, parents, and the child, if possible. Part H of P.L. 99-457 is directed to the birth to two population and requires the development of an Individualized Family Service Plan (IFSP). "The purpose of the IFSP is to identify and organize formal and informal resources to facilitate families' goals for their children and themselves" (Johnson, McGonigel & Kaufmann, 1989, p1). If family members are active, involved intervention team partners, then their participation in the IEP or IFSP process not only makes sense but will be productive.

A number of court cases have been initiated by parents on behalf of their handicapped children, such as *PARC vs. the Commonwealth of Pennsylvania* (see also Chapter 5). In many of these cases, parents are seeking appropriate treatment or education for their children. In general, the court rulings are in favor of handicapped individuals and their parents as advocates. In the due process procedures established by P.L. 94-142, parents may question the placement and appropriateness of their child's education. Such hearings, not to mention more formal litigation, are costly.

The federal government has established some stringent mandates concerning informed consent. That is, before children may participate in a wide variety of activities (e.g., research, or the dissemination of materials), parents or guardians must give written approval. Prior to the agreement, the activity must be explained in detail to the parents. Also, parents must be apprised of any potential risk to their child. The parents are free to decide if they will allow their child to participate in the activity. Active involvement of the caregivers should mean that they are knowledgeable about the program's daily operation and their child's individual treatment goals and special events such as field trips, research, or evaluation activities. Informing parents or guardians becomes an integral, ongoing responsibility of the program. The inclusion of caregivers in the intervention program responds to federal mandates and should reduce possible conflicts between program personnel and the home.

Another source of information arguing for the inclusion of caregivers in the intervention process is more empirical. A number of investigators have reported that early intervention programs which actively focus on the parent or include the parent as an important part of the intervention program, produce significantly greater effect on the children than programs that did not have strong parent involvement (Bronfenbrenner, 1975; Shonkoff & Hauser-Cram, 1987).

The final point in our rationale for family-guided intervention is parental rights. Underlying the above arguments is the assumption that parents have the basic right to be included in the intervention process and the planning-decision making process (Turnbull, Turnbull, & Wheat, 1982). As suggested earlier, no one has more to gain or more to lose in designing effective intervention procedures for children than their parents. Responsibility for the child lies with the family, and therefore, the family should take an active role in determining the goals of intervention. Without substantial family guidance, it will be difficult, if not impossible, to establish intervention targets that are relevant for the child and satisfactory to the family. To be effective, professionals must understand, acknowledge, and respect individual family values, and design intervention programs that are consistent with these values (Kaiser & Hemmeter, 1989).

Principles Underlying Family-Guided Intervention

The first underlying principle of family-guided intervention is to begin intervention when the family indicates a need. Forcing families to receive assistance before they are prepared, except in extreme situations such as neglect and abuse, may not produce the desired outcomes. Families can be assisted in evaluating their circumstances and encouraged to explore options, but they should never be forced or feel pressured to participate in a program. Hopefully, most families will choose to seek help when it becomes apparent that their child will benefit from some form of intervention or the family requires assistance in developing strategies for coping with the child.

A second principle of family-guided intervention focuses on the need for an ecological approach to intervention to ensure maximum behavioral development in the young child who is at-risk or handicapped. As Bronfenbrenner (1975) has suggested, all elements of a child's environment need to be working in concert if maximum benefits from intervention are to be obtained. To provide an exceptionally fine preschool program can probably only partially offset the effects of a nonstimulating, inappropriate home environment. Gains made during the day at school may be neutralized by the hours spent with parents and family who do not respond appropriately to the child. There is a need to coordinate home and school expectations, which demands designing an intervention program that includes as many facets of the child's life as possible.

The need for individualization of approach is the third principle that should guide intervention efforts with families. Carefully designed individualized programs are necessary if interventionists hope to be effective with participating families. Implementing general approaches that fail to recognize the individuality of each family constellation is doomed to be as ineffective as general nondiscriminating approaches have been with children who have varying needs (Slentz, Walker & Bricker, 1989). Program personnel need to devise strategies for determining individual families' functioning patterns and for determining parental goals and desires for themselves and their children (Bailey, 1987). These strategies need to take into account individual differences in parental interest, motivation, and abilities as factors which influence participation in programs. Individualization of intervention targets and strategies for family members is as important as individualization for children.

The fourth principle underlying family-guided intervention concerns the delineation of caregiver and professional roles in the intervention process. Variations of the parental role are to be expected depending upon the child's problem and the type of intervention provided. Slentz, Walker and Bricker (1989) suggest caregivers can fill roles as advocates, interventionists, recipient of specialized services, and decision makers, while Dunst, Trivette, Gordon and Pletcher (1989) indicate professional staff can fill the roles of empathetic listener, resource, consultant, mobilizer, enabler, and mediator.   As the listing of these roles indicates, professionals should avoid becoming "the expert" and telling the parent what to do and how to do it.   Rather, it is more facilitative if the partners work toward a cooperative relationship in which each has valuable information and skills to contribute (Turnbull, 1983).   A major responsibility of professionals should be, then, to assist parents in learning to become working partners.   Becoming a member of the team has associated responsibility which should be taken seriously by every parent.

Family-Guided Intervention: The IFSP

Fundamental to family-guided intervention is the development of an IFSP for infants and young children as specified in P.L. 99-457.   The law indicates that a multidisciplinary assessment should be conducted, followed by the development of a written IFSP.   The IFSP is to be reviewed at 6 month intervals and is to contain the following information:

1. Description of the child's present level of development
2. Statement of the family's needs and strengths as they relate to the child's problem
3. Description of major outcomes to be achieved by child and family
4. Statement of specific services required to meet the stated outcomes
5. Projected dates for beginning services and the duration
6. The case manager's name (Garwood & Sheehan, 1989)

The satisfactory development of an IFSP requires participation by the family and the conduct of relevant assessment.

The National Early Childhood Technical Assistance System has prepared a book on recommended guidelines for developing and implementing IFSPs (Johnson, McGonigel & Kaufmann, 1989).

Step One is the initial contact between the family and the early intervention program. The purpose is to share basic information and determine the child's and family's eligibility for the services.

Step Two is assessment planning. The purpose of this step is for professionals and parents to exchange information for the appropriate selection of assessment procedures.

Step Three entails assessment of the child. The IFSP requires statements about the child's level of physical, cognitive, language, speech, psychosocial and self-help development.

Step Four requires determining family strengths and interests that are related to the child's needs and goals. The purpose of this step is to acquire information that will permit formulating outcomes that are consistent with the families goals and values.

Step Five is the stage at which child and family outcomes are formulated. "An outcome must be functionally stated in terms of what is to occur and what is expected as a result of these actions" (Johnson et al. 1989).

Step Six focuses on implementation of the IFSP, during which the necessary activities are undertaken to reached the outcomes listed at Step Five.

Step Seven requires evaluation of the child's and family's progress toward acquisition of the agreed upon outcomes. The purpose of this step is to measure the success of the intervention for the child and family.

In many ways the IFSP development and implementation parallel that of an IEP. The basic differences are that IEP goals and objectives are broadened to become outcome statements on the IFSP, and that targets may include family as well as child outcomes. The basic sequence of steps is similar for the IEP and the IFSP if done properly, and both require the genuine participation of the family in planning, implementing and evaluating the services.

With the advent of the concept of the IFSP and increased pressure for family involvement, there has been a rush to develop a range of instrument to assess family needs and strengths (see for example Bailey & Simeonsson, 1988a; Dunst, Trivette & Deal, 1988). Although the availability of new tools and procedures may be helpful, the nature of some of these instruments raise a concern. Specifically, instruments used to obtain information from families about their relationships with friends, martial harmony, ego strength and so on send a message that these are legitimate areas for involvement by early interventionist. However, since most personnel working in early intervention programs have little formal training or experience as family therapists or counselors, it is not appropriate for them to assess adults in these areas or to devise intervention plans to deal with problems that may require considerable clinical skill.

Great care and caution should be exercised when assessing families, and unless the early intervention program has access to trained counselors, measures that probe into areas of personal dynamics should be avoided. It should also be emphasized that P.L. 99-457 requires that family's needs and strengths be assessed in relationship to the target child. The law does not advocate full-scale assessment of family dynamics. Clearly, there is important information that early interventionists need about families, but indiscriminant testing of families in all areas will not be beneficial and may be harmful.

Family-Guide intervention is dedicated to the full participation of the family in the development of the IEP and IFSP. Using this approach, the family is not given a broad range of assessments, but rather, is asked to complete a simple questionnaire that permits them to indicate their interests and the priority they assign those interests. Such an approach is simple and straightforward and delivers the appropriate message to the family and to the professional staff.

Intervention Strategies

Initial approaches to include or involve caregivers in early intervention programs tended to focus on teaching caregivers specific intervention skills to assist them in becoming more effective change agents with their child. Although this still is a paramount goal, interventionists have learned that other family needs must often be met before caregivers are able to learn to apply intervention strategies to assist their child. As the major theme of this chapter suggests, family involvement should be comprehensive in nature. For example, a mother's feeling of protective-ness may prevent her from dealing effectively with a problem of compli-ance in self-feeding. In other cases, it is necessary to appreciate that a family's need for food stamps and financial assistance may supersede the implementation of a home training program for their child.

The family situation itself dictates where, when, how, and in what areas to begin intervention. As in child programming, one must assess the family situation, select outcomes, intervene and then evaluate progress. Intervention targets should be based primarily on a family's needs and secondarily on information and skills that professionals believe a caregiver should have.

It also seems necessary that family involvement programs accom-modate the significant need for individualization. As mentioned before, intervention goals should be based on an individual family's needs. Families participating in programs often have widely disparate cultural, socioeconomic and educational backgrounds. Such divergence mandates program flexibility and individualization in the IFSP, content of inter-vention, and in the method used to attain specified outcomes (McGonigel & Garland, 1988).

Service Delivery Approaches

Filler (1983) has categorized approaches to parent training as home-based, center-based, and a combination of both. Cartwright (1981) adds the category of media-based programs for those few programs which have employed the use of written materials in lieu of human instruction (e.g., Baker & Heifetz, 1976). Each of these approaches has some similari-ties and differences. The goals of most family programs, regardless of the service delivery model, can be generally categorized as: (1) to assist caregivers in becoming more effective teachers or managers with their children; and (2) to assist the family in meeting other needs that will enhance family-child interaction. Although the goals are similar, the strategies adopted by program personnel to reach these goals are varied. For example, some programs use a group format to teach parents management and handling techniques, while others employ an individ-ual approach, and some programs use both. Some programs have trained parents to act as interventionists with other parents; others have used spouses or family members as teachers. Some programs employ sophis-ticated video equipment while others rely on feedback from human observers.

Home-based programs require access to the home on a regular basis. The professional, usually called a home visitor or parent trainer, visits the child at home and assists the primary caregiver in implementing treatment strategies with the infant or child. Most home visitors have a regular routine designed to maximize their impact with the caregiver and child. The specific approach employed is determined by the visitor and the family. That is, the home visitor attempts to approach the parent or caregiver in a manner that will build rapport and accomplish the intervention goals established for the child and the family. Most home visitors spend the first few minutes catching up on the family's happenings and feeling the caregiver out in terms of problems. The second phase usually focuses on a specific discussion of the child's progress. Using feedback from the caregiver and available objective information, the home visitor encourages further work in an area or suggests an alternative. During the final phase, the home visitor may demonstrate or discuss the suggested changes.

There are many reasons to adopt a home-based approach (Bailey & Simeonsson, 1988b). For example, parent participation is required, the home visitor has many opportunities to observe the caregiver-child interactions, and generalization of new skills may be enhanced. Conversely, drawbacks have been noted. Parents may feel isolated and lack opportunity to talk with other parents or receive respite from the child. In addition, special services such as physical therapy may be more difficult to access on a regular basis. An obvious solution to these difficulties is to offer a combination approach in which training occurs in the home but in which parents have regular opportunities to participate in programs outside the home.

Programs that serve the birth-to-three population often use a home-based approach while programs serving the three-to-five group often employ a center-based model. Most center-based models offer a structured classroom program for participating children usually three to five times per week. These programs tend to have a set format that combines large-group, small-group, and individual training activities (Bricker & Veltman, in press). The instructional strategies and curricular focus is largely determined by the program personnel's philosophy and can range from experiential to direct instruction approaches (Harbin, 1979). Most programs have small child-to-staff ratios, and staff may be required to have some form of teacher certification. Many programs begin with a large-group activity in which all the children are expected to participate in some way. After the large-group exercise, children may be assigned to small-group or individual training activities. Many programs attempt to assist children in all essential developmental areas: social, self-help, communication, cognitive, gross motor, fine motor, and preacademic. To do this, the interventionists develop IEPs for each child and then have some procedures for monitoring each child's progress towards individual training targets.

Although caregivers may be encouraged to participate in a center-based program, some may never become involved, and some may decrease their involvement over time. Often, center-based approaches have relatively structured parent training programs that center on regular group meetings. A variety of topics may be covered during these meetings, and generally, topics that are of interest to parents are selected. In addition, the classroom personnel are available to parents at specific times should parents wish to discuss their child's progress or other issues. Some programs encourage caregivers to participate in the classroom activities with their child; however, such participation is generally restricted to a few highly motivated parents that have available time.

The major drawback attributed to center-based approaches is the lack of consistent communication between home and school. Often, interventionists do not have adequate time to make regular home visits; thus, caregivers must shoulder the responsibility of transferring the child's newly acquired skills into other environments. Caregivers may be poorly equipped to assist the child in generalization of skills, and consequently, progress in the application of useful skills by the child may occur less efficiently and effectively.

The positive aspects of center-based approaches are: they provide the child with more professional input which can be effectively coordinated if professionals communicate with one another; they provide the child with the opportunity to interact with a variety of other children and to experience other environments; and they provide caregiver respite and the opportunity to meet each other.

As suggested for the home-based approaches, a home- and center-based combination seems to answer the major criticisms of the center-based approaches. As family involvement takes on importance, it is likely that more programs will adopt models that combine elements of the home- and center-based approaches. The problem with such omnibus programs will most likely be the cost associated with operating a center-based program while offering extensive home visitation.

SUMMARY

Professionals' attitudes about caregivers have changed dramatically over the years and fortunately, changing attitudes often are accompanied by performance changes. Early interventionists have given lip service to the involvement of families for many years, and yet, the outcomes of our efforts have been limited, indeed. However, the confluence of legal decisions, legislative enactments, advocacy by parents, and genuine change by many in the professional community has led to three important new perspectives. First, professionals are beginning to recognize that parents and other family members can assume many roles in the habilitation of their children. Second, the objectives and goals selected for the child as well as the family must be determined in concert with the parents. Third, for intervention efforts to be effective, they should be formulated from the family's perspective.

References

Bailey, D. (1987). Collaborative goal-setting with families: Resolving differences in values and priorities for services. *Topics in Early Childhood Special Education, 7*(2), 59-71.

Bailey, D., & Simeonsson, R. (1988a). *Family assessment in early intervention.* Cols.,OH: Merrill.

Bailey, D., & Simeonsson, R. (1988b). Home-based early intervention. In S. Odom & M. Karnes (Eds.), *Early intervention for infants and children with handicaps*. Baltimore, MD: Paul Brookes.

Bailey, E., & Bricker, D. (1984). The efficacy of early intervention for severely handicapped infants and young children. *Topics in Early Childhood Special Education, 4*(3), 30-51.

Baker, B. (1984). Intervention with families with young, severely handicapped children. In J. Blacher (Ed.), *Severely handicapped young children and their families*. New York: Academic Press.

Baker, B., & Heifetz, L. (1976). The Read Project: Teaching manuals for parents of retarded children. In T. Tjossem (Ed.), *Intervention strategies for high risk infants and young children*. Baltimore, MD: University Park Press.

Barber, P., Turnbull, A., Behr, S., & Kerns, G. (1988). A family systems perspective on early childhood special education. In S. Odom & M. Karnes (Eds.), *Early intervention for infants and children with handicaps*. Baltimore, MD: Paul Brookes.

Blacher, J. (1984). A dynamic perspective on the impact of a severely handicapped child on the family. In J. Blacher (Ed.), *Severely handicapped young children and their families*. New York: Academic Press.

Bowlby, J. (1973). *Attachment and loss: Separation, anxiety, and anger*. New York: Basic Books.

Brazelton, B., Koslowski, B., & Main, M. (1974). The origins of reciprocity: The early mother-infant interaction. In M. Lewis & L. Rosenblum (Eds.), *The effect of the infant on its caregiver*. New York: Wiley & Sons.

Bricker, D. (1986). An analysis of early intervention programs: Attendant issues and future directions. In R. Morris & B. Blatt (Eds.), *Special education: Research and trends*. New York: Pergamon Press.

Bricker, D., & Squires, J. (1989). Low cost system using parents to monitor the development of at-risk infants. *Journal of Early Intervention, 13*(1), 50-60.

Bricker, D., Squires, J., Kaminski, R., & Mounts, L. (1988). The validity, reliability, and cost of a parent-completed questionnaire to evaluate their at-risk infants. *Journal of Pediatric Psychology, 13*, 56-68.

Bricker, D., & Veltman, M. (in press). *Early intervention programs: Child focused approaches*. In S. Meisels & J. Shonkoff (Eds.), Cambridge, MA: Cambridge University Press.

Bronfenbrenner, U. (1975). Is early intervention effective? In B. Friedlander, G. Sterritt, & G. Kirk (Eds.), *Exceptional infant: Assessment and intervention* (Vol. III). New York: Brunner/Mazel.

Brooks-Gunn, J., & Lewis, M. (June, 1979). *Parents of handicapped infants: Their role in identification, assessment, and intervention*.

Paper presented at the Ira Gordon Memorial Conference, Chapel Hill, NC.

Cartwright, C. (1981). Effective programs for parents of young handicapped children. *Topics in Early Childhood Special Education, 1*(3), 1-9.

Cicchetti, D., & Sroufe, A. (1976). The relationship between affective and cognitive development in Down's syndrome infants. *Child Development, 47,* 920-929.

Decarie, T. (1978). Affect development and cognition in a Piagetian context. In M. Lewis & L. Rosenblum (Eds.), *The development of affect.* New York: Plenum Press.

Denenberg, V., & Thoman, E. (1976). From animal to infant research. In T. Tjossem (Ed.), *Intervention strategies for high risk infants and young children.* Baltimore, MD: University Park Press.

Dennis, W., & Najarian, P. (1963). Development under environmental handicap. In W. Dennis (Ed.), *Readings in child psychology.* Englewood Cliffs, NJ: Prentice-Hall.

Dunst, C., Trivette, C., & Deal, A. (1988). *Enabling and empowering families.* Cambridge, MA: Brookline Books.

Dunst, C., Trivette, C., Gordon, N., & Pletcher, L. (1989). Building and mobilizing informal family support networks. In G. Singer & L. Irwin (Eds.), *Support for caregiving families.* Baltimore, MD: Paul Brookes.

Emde, R., Katz, E., & Thorpe, J. (1978). Emotional expression in infancy: II. Early deviations in Down's syndrome. In M. Lewis & L. Rosenblum (Eds.), *The development of affect.* New York: Plenum Press.

Emde, R., Kligman, D., Reich, J., & Wade, T. (1978). Emotional expression in infancy: I. Initial studies of social signaling and an emergent model. In M. Lewis & L. Rosenblum (Eds.), *Development of affect.* New York: Plenum Press.

Field, T., (1983). Early interactions and interaction coaching of high-risk infants and parents. In M. Perlmutter (Ed.), *Development and policy concerning children with special needs, Vol. 16.* Hillsdale, NJ: Lawrence Erlbaum.

Filler, J. (1983). Service models for handicapped infants. In G. Garwood & R. Fewell (Eds.), *Educating handicapped infants.* Rockville, MD: Aspen Publications.

Fraiberg, S. (1975). Intervention in infancy: A program for blind infants. In B. Friedlander, G. Sterritt, G. Kirk (Eds.), *Exceptional infant* (Vol. 3). New York: Brunner/Mazel.

Gabel, H., McDowell, J., & Cerreto, M. (1983). Family adaptation to the handicapped infant. In G. Garwood & R. Fewell (Eds.), *Educating handicapped infants.* Rockville, MD: Aspen Publications.

Garwood, S., & Sheehan, R. (1989). *Designing a comprehensive early intervention system.* Austin, TX: Pro-Ed.

Gorham, K., Jardins, C., Page, R., Rettis, E., & Scheiber, B. (1975). Effect on parents. In N. Hobbs (Ed.), *Issues in the classification of children* (Vol 2). San Francisco: Jossey-Bass.

Harbin, G. (1979). Mildly to moderately handicapped preschoolers: How do you select child assessment instruments? In T. Black (Ed.), *Perspectives on measurement: A collection of readings for educators of young handicapped children.* Chapel Hill, NC: TADS.

Harlow, H., & Mears, C. (1978). The nature of complex, unlearned responses. In M. Lewis & L. Rosenblum (Eds.), *Development of affect.* New York: Plenum Press.

Johnson, B., McGonigel, M., & Kaufmann, R. (1989). *Guidelines and recommended practices for the individualized family service plan.* Chapel Hill, NC: NEC*TAS.

Klaus, M., & Kennell, J. (Eds.). (1976). *Maternal-infant bonding.* St. Louis: Mosby.

Kaiser, A., & Hemmeter, M. (1989). Value-based approaches to family intervention. *Topics in Early Childhood Special Education, 8*(4), 72-86.

Lewis, M., & Michalson, L. (1983). *Children's emotions and moods.* New York: Plenum Press.

Lewis, M., & Rosenblum , L. (Eds.). (1974). *The effect of the infant on its caregiver.* New York: Wiley & Sons.

Lewis, M., & Rosenblum, L. (1978). Introduction: Issues in affect development. In M. Lewis & L. Rosenblum (Eds.), *The development of affect.* New York: Plenum Press.

McGonigel, M., & Garland, C. (1988). The individualized family service plan and the early intervention team: Team and family issues and recommended practices. *Infants and Young Children, 1*(1),10-21.

Mahoney, G., & Robenalt, K. (1986). A comparison of conversational patterns between mothers and their Down syndrome and normal infants. *Journal of the Division for Early Childhood, 10* (2), 172-180.

Meier, J. (1985). Definition, dynamics and prevalence of assault against children: A multifactorial model. In J. Meier (Ed.), *Assault against children.* San Diego: College-Hill Press.

Meisels, S., Harbin, G., Modigliani, K., & Olson, K. (1988). Formulating optimal state early childhood intervention policies. *Exceptional Children, 55*(2), 159-165.

Minuchin, S. (1974). *Families and family therapy.* Cambridge, MA: Harvard University Press.

Morgan, D. (1982). Parent participation in the IEP process: Does it enhance appropriate education? *Exceptional Education Quarterly, 3,* 33-40.

Morton, K. (1978). Identifying the enemy - A parent's complaint. In A. Turnbull & H. Turnbull (Eds.), *Parents speak out.* Columbus, OH: Charles E. Merrill.

Parke, R., & Tinsley, B. (1982). The early environment of the at-risk infant. In D. Bricker (Ed.), *Intervention with at-risk and handicapped infants.* Baltimore, MD: University Park Press.

Piaget, J. (1970). Piaget's theory. In P. Mussen (Ed.), *Carmichael's manual of child psychology* (Vol. 1). New York: Wiley & Sons.

Ramey, C., & MacPhee, D. (1986). Developmental retardation: A systems theory perspective on risk and preventive intervention. In D. Farran & J. McKinney (Eds.), *Risk in intellectual and psychosocial development.* New York: Academic Press.

Rheingold, H., Gewirtz, J., & Ross, H. (1959). Social conditioning of vocalizations in the infant. Journal of Comparative Physiological Psychology, 52, 68-73.

Robinson, C., Rosenberg, S., & Beckman, P. (1988). Parent involvement in early childhood special education. In J. Jordan, J. Gallagher, P. Hutinger & M. Karnes (Eds.), *Early childhood special education: Birth to three.* Reston, VA: Council for Exceptional Children.

Roos, P. (1978). Parents of mentally retarded children - Misunderstood and mistreated. In A. Turnbull & H. Turnbull (Eds.), *Parents speak out.* Columbus, OH: Charles E. Merrill.

Saarni, C. (1978). Cognitive and communicative features of emotional experience, or do you show what you think you feel? In M. Lewis & L. Rosenblum (Eds.), *The development of affect.* New York: Plenum Press.

Shonkoff, J., & Hauser-Cram, P. (1987). Early intervention for disabled infants and their families: A quantitative analysis. *Pediatrics, 80*(5), 650-658.

Slentz, K., Walker, B., & Bricker, D. (1989). Supporting parent involvement in early intervention: A role taking model. In G. Singer & L. Irwin (Eds.), *Support for caregiving families.* Baltimore, MD: Paul Brookes.

Spitz, R. (1946). Hospitalism: A follow-up report. *Psychoanalytic Study of the Child, 2,* 313-342.

Stoneman, Z., & Brody, G. (1984). Research with families of severely handicapped children: Theoretical and methodological considerations. In J. Blacher (Ed.), *Severely handicapped young children and their families: Research in review.* New York: Academic Press.

Strickland, B. (1982). Parental participation, school accountability, and due process. *Exceptional Education Quarterly, 3,* 41-49.

Tjossem, T. (1976). *Intervention strategies for high risk infants and young children.* Baltimore, MD: University Park Press.

Trohanis, P. (1988). Preparing for change: The implementation of Public Law 99-457. In J. Jordan, J. Gallagher, P. Hutinger & M. Karnes (Eds.), *Early childhood special education: Birth to three.* Reston, VA: Council for Exceptional Children.

Turnbull, A. (1983). Parent professional interactions. In M. Snell (Ed.), *Systematic instruction of the moderately and severely handicapped.* Columbus, OH: Charles E. Merrill.

Turnbull, A., Summers, J., & Brotherson, M. (1983). *Working with families with disabled members: A family systems approach.* Lawrence, KS: University of Kansas Research and Training Center.

Turnbull, H., Turnbull, A., & Wheat, M. (1982). Assumptions about parental participation: A legislative history. *Exceptional Education Quarterly, 3,* 1-8.

Uzgiris, I. (1976). Organization of sensorimotor intelligence. In M. Lewis (Ed.), *Origins of intelligence: Infancy and early childhood.* New York: Plenum Press.

Vadasy, P., Fewell, R., Meyer, D., Schell, G., & Greenberg, M. (1984). Involved parents: Characteristics and resources of fathers and mothers of young handicapped children. *Journal of the Division for Early Childhood, 8,* 13-25.

Walker, B., Slentz, K., & Bricker, D. (1985). *Parent involvement in early intervention.* Rehabilitation Research Review, National Rehabilitation Information Center, The Catholic University of America, Washington, DC.

White, B., & Held, R. (1967). Experience in early human development: II. Plasticity of sensorimotor development in the human infant. In J. Hellmuth (Ed.), *Exceptional infant: Vol. I. The normal infant.* Seattle, WA: Strauband Hellmuth.

8.
Approaches to Early Intervention

Before the 1960s, genetics and physiology were considered crucial for predicting a child's future success. With the advent of the sixties came a resurgence of the environmental position. In particular, beliefs supported by evidence accumulated by investigators such as Hunt (1961) reinforced the idea of the importance of early experience. As discussed in Chapter 2, these beliefs were responsible, in part, for the development of compensatory education in this country and the gradual growth of intervention programs for young children who are at-risk or handicapped.

Today, early intervention programs can be found throughout this nation and in many other countries (Journal of the Division for Early Childhood, 1985). Since 1968, the federal government has supported a network of projects developed under the aegis of the Handicapped Children's Early Education Program (Karnes & Stayton, 1988). The passage of P.L. 99-457 requires states to provide services for preschool children who are handicapped, and offers incentives to develop programs for the birth-to-two population. In large measure, federal legislation has been responsible for the development of a network of publicly supported early intervention programs at state and local levels. In addition, early intervention programs have been established by private non-profit organizations such as Easter Seal and United Cerebral Palsy.

The purpose of this chapter is to provide an overview of contemporary approaches to early intervention. In addition, the elements or components common to most programs will be discussed. Before describing the various approaches to and elements of early intervention programs for children who are at-risk and handicapped, it may be useful to note briefly why a single generic description of early intervention programs is not adequate. Programs serve children with a variety of ages, etiologies, behavioral repertoires, and family backgrounds. Thus a uniform approach, given such population variability, seems unwarranted. Second, program personnel come from an array of disciplines and training backgrounds which produce variations in approaches and program emphases. Third, pragmatic and logistic concerns (e.g., availability of appropriate space, transportation) may produce substantial differences in program approaches. These factors have generated a range of approaches that share some commonalities but that also are significantly different. The ensuing discussion attempts to highlight both the consistencies and variations in approaches.

CONTEMPORARY EARLY INTERVENTION APPROACHES

Early intervention programs serve children from birth through five years, and some programs may serve children who are older and more severely impaired. In addition, children ranging from those designated as at-risk to those who are profoundly impaired can be found participating in early intervention programs. The backgrounds of the enrolled children vary as well. For example, some programs may be especially designed for teenagers with infants (McDonough, 1984), while others may serve a range of families with different economic and educational backgrounds (Bricker & Veltman, in press).

Program Rationales

Rationales for contemporary early intervention programs can be conveniently divided into direct impact, indirect impact and societal benefits. Direct impact refers to program goals and objectives designed to alter the behavior of the child and family members. Most programs see child change and family support as their primary objectives, and rationales are developed to reflect these foci. Indirect impact refers to changes in the child and family members that permit maintenance of the child in the least restrictive educational or care setting. A second important indirect impact is the family's or community's willingness to maintain the child in the home and community.

Finally, many programs suggest that their impact on the child and family produce benefits for society. According to a United States House of Representatives Report that accompanied P.L. 99-457, societal benefits accrued from early intervention programs include:

1. Enhancement of intelligence in some children

2. Substantial gains in physical development, cognitive development, language and speech development, psycho-social development and self-help skills

3. Prevention of secondary handicapping conditions

4. Reduction in family stress

5. Reduction in societal dependency and institutionalization

6. Reduction in the need for special class placement in special education programs once the children reach school

7. Substantial cost savings to society and schools (U.S. House of Representative Report to accompany H.R. 5520, 1986, p.5).

Service Delivery Approaches

According to Filler (1983), there are three service delivery approaches used by early intervention programs: home-based, center-based and a combination of home- and center-based. Cartwright (1981) has suggested a fourth approach, which she has labeled media-based programs.

Programs for infants often deliver services in the home (Bailey & Simeonsson, 1988). The target in the home-based approach may be the parent or caregiver who is helped to acquire effective intervention skills to use with the child. As implied in the name, the center-based model requires that the infant or child be brought to an educational or treatment setting on a regular basis. The setting might be a classroom or a more informal arrangement. The focal target in center-based models is usually the child; however, many center-based programs stress parental involvement and may even provide structured training for the parent (Bricker & Veltman, in press).

Some programs have adopted a combined approach in one of two ways. First, there are programs that stress training occur both in the classroom and in the home (Bailey & Bricker, 1985). Second, there are programs that serve the child initially in the home. After the child reaches a certain age or develops targeted skills, he or she is transferred to the center-based component of the program (Wolery & Dyk, 1985).

Media-based approaches employ methods which do not require face-to-face instruction. Approaches such as videotapes or self-instruction manuals are examples (Cartwright, 1981).

The home-based, center-based and combination approaches that make up the bulk of early intervention programs are composed of a set of fundamental elements or components. Although the composition of most programs includes these fundamental elements, they vary in the ways they are operationalized.

PROGRAM ELEMENTS

A number of writers (Guralnick & Bricker, 1987; Gentry & Olson, 1985) have suggested that successful programs contain certain elements. Those elements approved by the Joint Dissemination and Review Panel of the U.S. Department of Education and National Institute of Education include: (1) a philosophical basis on which a program is developed; (2) a clearly specified curriculum; (3) an appropriately trained staff; (4) parent and family involvement; and (5) a comprehensive program evaluation plan. In the present chapter intervention strategies are discussed as an element separate from curriculum, while the philosophical orientation and curricular approach have been combined. Each of these five elements are discussed below.

Philosophical/Curricular Focus

Essential to the functioning of an effective early intervention program is a clearly articulated philosophy. This philosophy provides the necessary structure for selection of program goals, curricular content, and individual education plans for the enrolled children and families. In addition, this structure provides the guidelines for selection of appropriate assessment and evaluation tools. Without a clearly articulated orientation, the program is apt to be inconsistent, overlook important intervention targets, and generally lack the cohesiveness of a smoothly operating system.

Perhaps one of the more important functions of a program's philosophical orientation is to provide guidelines for the selection of a curricular approach and the content to be targeted in the program. Two theoretical perspectives have influenced the major curricular efforts for children who are at-risk and handicapped. These perspectives are: (1) developmental and (2) functional.

The developmental approach is based on the assumption that important developmental changes are both hierarchical and sequential. That is, developmental progress involves the integration and reorganization of earlier acquired behavioral schemes, and development occurs in a generally consistent sequential order. Age-related developmental milestones such as those identified by Arnold Gesell (Gesell & Armatruda, 1962) often make up the curricular content for this approach.

One frequently employed developmental approach is based on the work of Piaget (Piaget, 1970). With this approach, curricula for children who are at-risk or handicapped center on sensorimotor and initial pre-operational skills. Personnel that use this approach work on assisting children in the acquisition of developmental processes and concepts, such as problem solving, object permanence and means-ends.

The basic premise of the functional model is that development should be viewed as the acquisition of those skills that will immediately or in the future improve a child's ability to interact with the environment and to become more self-sufficient and independent. The content of such a curriculum consists of those skills which are or will be "functional" for the child.

According to Le Blanc, Etzel and Domash (1978), the essential aspect of a functional curricular approach is establishing relevant curricular goals. The goals should then be analyzed in terms of their observable behaviors and the environmental conditions necessary to teach these behaviors. Thus, the intervention staff's primary roles are to assess the child's current behavioral repertoire, to operationalize the target responses, and to arrange the environment to assist the child in acquiring these responses. For a detailed description of a functional curricular approach see Le Blanc, Etzel and Domash (1978).

Although programs can and do operate using a variety of orientations, our preference is for the adoption of a flexible combination of the developmental and functional approaches. A developmental orientation assumes several underlying constructs about the nature and cause of growth and change. As mentioned before, this position assumes that important developmental changes are both hierarchical and sequential. Current developmental progress by a child involves the integration and reorganization of earlier acquired behavior, and development occurs in a generally consistent sequential order. In addition, this position assumes that many important developmental changes result from the resolution of disequilibrium between the child's current level of development and the demands of the environment. The problem posed by the environment must be neither too simple nor too difficult for the child's developmental level in order for change to result (Hunt, 1961). The task of the interventionist is to structure the environment in such a way as to place increasing demands on the child's current level of functioning. By requiring the child to actively adapt to greater environmental demands, growth and change occur. The type and nature of the environmental demands should be tempered, in part, by knowledge of those skills that will assist the child in adapting to his or her present and future environments. Finally, the approach assumes that what is critical to development in some cases may be specific behaviors, and in other cases, broad conceptual targets tied to a class of behaviors rather than one specific behavior. These broad conceptual targets index changes in underlying structural organization as well as change in the behavioral topography.

The majority of programs providing services to children who are at-risk or handicapped tend to offer a comprehensive menu of educational and treatment targets. The comprehensive nature of these programs is appropriate because by definition, infants and young children who are at-risk or handicapped tend to show deficits in many critical areas of functioning. There is often need to assist the child in gaining cognitive, communication, social, self-help, and motor skills, thus making mandatory a comprehensive curricular approach.

Chapter 13 provides a more detailed discussion of curricular issues and controversies. In addition, a general curricular approach is suggested.

Intervention Strategies

Intervention strategies adopted to present the curricular content rely on some form of environmental engineering. That is, the intervention staff arrange antecedent events to elicit and reinforce the occurrence of targeted behaviors by the children. However, the rigor and rigidity with which the behavioral technology is employed varies considerably across programs.

Harbin (1979) suggested using a continuum that classifies curricula as experiential, Montessori, Piagetian, information processing, diagnostic-prescriptive or behavioral. A fair generalization might be that those programs reflecting the more adult-directed approaches are the programs that tend to begin intervention focused on specific targets using highly controlled presentation formats. As the child shows progress in the acquisition of the target response, the presentation shifts to encourage generalization of the response to other settings and appropriate conditions. Those programs that are more child-directed tend to employ a more flexible application of behavioral principles. The child is encouraged to use a targeted response in a variety of settings and conditions with the primary goal of making the response functional. Once the response becomes functional, the use of artificial contingencies can be eliminated. Effective intervention requires that staff be skilled behavior managers and programmers if children are to make adequate progress.

The application of behavioral learning principles has provided the most effective and useful set of intervention principles currently available. Initially, using these principles to manage behavior and to teach were often applied using extremely structured formats. Children were tutored one-on-one, and frequently treatment targets were narrowly focused (e.g., teaching children specific imitative responses). Often, interventionists failed to extend the training to assure generalization of responses across settings, people, and events. The early use of behavioral learning principles tended to minimize flexibility and adaptability because children were primarily reinforced for adherence to adult-imposed tasks.

As experience has been gained in the application of instructional and management strategies, important changes have occurred (Warren &

Rogers-Warren, 1985). These changes reflect the need to assist children in developing more generalized and adaptive behavioral repertoires—for example, from teaching discrete responses under the control of a specific cue to developing a variety of responses for problem solving or obtaining information from the social environment. Interest continues to grow in how to apply sound and empirically verifiable behavioral teaching principles to aid children in acquiring more functional and independent repertoires (Hart, 1985), and concern increases for assisting disabled individuals in learning to initiate and make choices based on self-determined needs (Guess & Siegel-Causey, 1985).

Contemporary views held by interventionists tend to favor approaches that specify the goals and objectives for the child and outcomes for families, but leave the implementation to be decided, in part, according to events occurring in the environment and the interests of the child and family. For example, a treatment goal might be to assist the child in using more agent-action-object phrases. Rather than using a specific drill on a set number of predetermined phrases, the interventionist uses opportunities that arise during the day to target this activity (Koegel & Johnson, 1989). Looking at a book chosen by the child might provide the interventionist many opportunities to teach agent-action-object sequences. Using such an approach requires careful attention to the daily activities to assure that each child is receiving adequate training on selected objectives. Often, it is difficult to monitor the training of each objective, and successful employment of such a system requires systematic collection of data on the child's progress toward specified objectives.

Some programs focus on reinforcement of the desired response using some form of tangible or verbal feedback. Often this feedback is in the form of verbal comments such as "good boy," "that's right," "you did that well," and so on. If tasks are primarily selected by the adult, motivating children may be a problem and therefore require the use of artificial contingencies. When children have more freedom to determine the activities in which the training exercises will be embedded, reinforcement is often inherent in the activity and thus is preferable (Mahoney & Weller, 1980). For example, searching for a desired toy promotes the concept of object permanence, and finding the toy provides the reinforcement and subsequent motivation for further searches. It is probably not necessary or useful to tell the child, "good looking" when the child discovers the toy. Pouring juice into a cup provides practice in wrist rotation and self-help skills, and getting to drink the juice may be reward enough to continue to practice the behaviors. This same analysis may hold for families. Interventionists may find families lack motivation to work on outcomes chosen by professionals; however, motivation may improve when family goals are chosen by family members.

The goal then is to employ strategies that embed treatment objectives in daily and functional activities that are of interest to children and their families. Designing an environment that elicits and reinforces appropriate responses should lead to the children's efficient acquisition of independent coping behaviors.

Family Involvement

As argued in Chapter 7, there is an increasing awareness that intervention plans for children must be designed and implemented within the family context. From the development of the IEP or IFSP to their implementation, family members need to be consulted, involved in decision making and the treatment effort. Increasingly, programs are recognizing the legal requirements as well as the training benefits to be accrued through active family involvement.

Family involvement in a program should begin as soon as caregivers feel benefit for their child and themselves will occur. For different families, the period of time needed to adjust to the birth of a child who is handicapped or even at-risk is variable. Some families appear to want immediate involvement in an intervention effort and to benefit from it, while other families need time to work out their feelings prior to beginning active involvement (Calhoun, Calhoun & Rose, 1989). Nevertheless, a goal should be to involve families before inappropriate caregiver-child and child-family relationships develop. To intervene after the development of punishing interactions for the caregiver or child, or more likely both, means substantial amounts of time and energy must be devoted to changing these patterns. Time and energy could be more productively used to assist caregivers in helping their child gain new appropriate social and cognitive behaviors.

A second principle of family involvement focuses on the need for an ecological approach to intervention (i.e., include family members in the intervention effort) in order to assure maximum behavioral development in the infant and young child. As Bronfenbrenner (1975) has suggested, elements of a child's environment need to be working cooperatively if maximum benefit from intervention is to occur. The provision of an exceptional preschool program can probably only partially offset the effects of a non-stimulating, inappropriate home environment. Gains made during the day at school may be neutralized by the hours spent with caregivers and family who do not respond appropriately to the child. There is a need to coordinate family and professional expectations, which demands designing an intervention program that includes as many facets of the child's life as possible.

The family situation itself should dictate where, when, how and in what areas to begin intervention. As in child programming, the family situation should be assessed, outcomes selected, intervention conducted, and then progress evaluated. A family-guided philosophy holds that intervention targets should be selected primarily by families with support and guidance by professionals.

It is essential that the family involvement program accommodate the significant need for individualization. Families included in programs often have widely disparate cultural, socioeconomic and educational backgrounds, as well as different strengths, needs and interests. Such divergence mandates program flexibility and individualization both in the content of intervention targets and in the method of reaching those targets.

Finally, we have found the need to approach family involvement in a comprehensive manner. Isolated skill training with caregivers is not always effective. For example, assisting a mother in working on the development of labeling skills without assisting her in developing strategies to manage the child may be counterproductive. In other cases, it may be necessary to appreciate that a family's need for recreation should, at times, supplant the implementation of a home training program for their child. Often, it is essential to see that families are accessing necessary social service assistance and counseling as well as educational information and skill training.

If professionals establish themselves as "the experts" telling the caregiver how to behave, change in parents may occur slowly or not at all. Rather, the goal should be the development of a cooperative relationship in which both the caregiver and professional have valuable information and skills to contribute. Becoming a member of the team has associated responsibility that should be taken seriously by every caregiver and by every professional.

Staff Training and Management

Early intervention program staff members are responsible for the shape and flavor of a program. The way in which the staff operate the program is influenced by at least two important variables: the quality of their training, and the fidelity with which they adhere to established program goals and objectives. No doubt, other factors could be specified, but these two seem of overriding importance.

Many early intervention programs are operated by staff members who have had minimal formal training in the area of early intervention (Meisels, Harbin, Modigliani & Olson, 1988). Teachers "left over" because student enrollment has decreased in other areas are reassigned to become the teacher in the early intervention program. Communication specialists without formal training or experience in infancy or caregiver-child interactions find themselves working in early intervention programs. Although this may be a political reality, the underlying assumption that a teacher who worked effectively with fourth-grade learning disabled children can work effectively with preschoolers who are handicapped is unwarranted. Expecting communication specialists to be effective with infants and their caregivers when their training and experience has focused on school-age populations is equally unrealistic. Although overlap may exist in some educational or therapeutic strategies employed, obvious differences exist. Working effectively with infants and young children is dependent upon understanding the process and content of early childhood development. With infants and children experiencing problems, what is the appropriate intervention content and the sequence of that content? What intervention techniques are effective? What type of data collection and measurement strategies are suited to the population? What of managing family involvement and parent education and counseling? Where is the available literature that suggests the ideas and methods that have been shown to be effective with young children who are disabled? What are the new and important directions being explored? One does not often hear of an electrical engineer being assigned to design a bridge, nor an industrial psychologist assigned to conduct clinical intervention with psychotic individuals; it is perhaps no more reasonable to expect teachers and therapists trained to work with elementary-age children to be able to effectively cope with younger populations without additional training. Thus the acquisition of staff with appropriate preservice or inservice training is essential. To keep staff members current, on-going training should be provided.

Personnel working in early intervention programs can be divided into two categories: direct service and support service. Direct-service personnel are those interventionists, teaching aides, parents, or others who interact with the child in a regular and consistent manner; for example, the early interventionist in a center-based program or a parent trainer in a home-based approach. Early interventionists and other direct-service personnel are called on to fill a number of roles as developmental specialist, behavior manager, synthesizer, and evaluator. These roles are discussed in detail in Chapter 10.

Support personnel include specialists, such as a physical therapist, occupational therapists, medical personnel, nutritionists, psychologists, social workers or communication specialist, who have been trained in a specific discipline. In addition, bus drivers, administrative personnel and others who provide intervention staff with services that are necessary for the operation of an effective program fall into the category of support personnel.

Prior to the initiation of a program, P.L. 94-142 and P.L. 99-457 require an appropriate assessment be conducted on the child. To be appropriate, the participation of a physical therapist, occupational therapist, communication specialist, psychologist, medical personnel, and possibly other professionals may be required. These personnel, along with the direct interventionist and family members, form a team that must develop the IEP or IFSP and then monitor progress (McGonigel & Garland, 1988). Once the IEP or IFSP is developed, if special services such as physical therapy are included, a specialist should be available periodically to evaluate the child's progress, help to formulate the daily intervention plan, and teach and supervise the direct-intervention personnel in the delivery of the necessary therapeutic routines.

Because most programs cannot support a cadre of needed specialists on a full-time basis, these professionals may only be available to serve on the assessment team or as consultants. In this approach, termed a consulting model, the specialist functions primarily as an assessor-evaluator and teacher-supervisor. The primary hands-on training of the child is provided by the direct-service personnel rather than by specialists.

The success of the consulting model is predicated on the willingness of the direct interventionists and the specialists to interact. In particular, there is an ongoing need to share information about children and families. In effect, the interventionist's attempt to acquire relevant information will be futile if the specialist is not willing to provide the information. The specialist must be willing to explain and share assessment information and assist in implementation of appropriate programs. This willingness is based on the specialist's belief that the interventionist is capable of using specific input properly and that allowing the interventionist to function in such a role is an efficient, effective approach for helping the child and family.

The use of specialists in consulting roles has been adopted by many programs, in part because of financial exigencies; however, many staff, parents, and specialists have become convinced that, generally speaking, this approach is more effective in producing desired change in children. Established training or therapeutic regimes can be employed throughout the day rather than for only brief periods when the specialist is available to work directly with the child. Employing a consulting model increases the training time as well as enhances generalization across settings, people, and events (McCormick, 1984).

When first introduced, the consulting model met considerable resistance; however, observation of its use over time has convinced many direct-service and support-service personnel of its value. As the demands for services from early intervention programs increase, a parallel growth in the popularity of the consulting model will occur. More detail on the consulting model is provided in Chapter 10.

Assessment and Evaluation

Evaluation of early intervention programs has been generally focused on measuring child change (Bricker, Bailey, & Bruder, 1984). A few programs have measured training impact on parents, and even fewer have collected information on other relevant variables, such as changes in attitude, cost factors or longitudinal effects (Ramey, MacPhee, & Yeates, 1983). Perhaps even more disturbing is that many programs described in the literature do not provide any objective evaluation information on program impact on child, family or any other variables.

Development of an assessment-evaluation plan and its implementation is essential for effective intervention. The assessment of individual change and programmatic impact requires that intervention methods and systems be undergirded with procedures that are appropriate for evaluating their efficacy. Evaluation should determine the program format and success of intervention for individual children and assess the impact of programs on groups of children and families. Thus, assessment and evaluation serve three distinct but complementary functions: guidance for the development of IEPs or IFSPs, feedback about success of child and family interventions, and information for program evaluation purposes (Bricker & Gumerlock, 1988).

The need for a comprehensive evaluation of the child requires that the assessment measures be carefully selected. The measures should tap the child's abilities across a wide range of domains, since the IEP or IFSP will be constructed on the basis of the initial assessment information. Second, assessment instruments should be geared to the developmental age of the child. A test which is above or below the level of the child will provide practically no useful information for evaluation of either the individual child's progress or of the program's impact on the child. Third, the instrument or format should be useable by available program personnel. Selection of a sophisticated instrument that cannot be administered appropriately by program personnel is of little value. Finally, at least some of the assessment-evaluation tools should yield information that can be used directly to formulate the child's IEP or IFSP and specific program plans.

Assessment of the family should be guided by the family's interests and priorities. Use of a simple questionnaire or interview with parents to determine their interests and priorities should preclude the use of a broad range of measures that may be inappropriate and offensive to families. Bailey (1987), has pointed out the importance of collaborative goal setting with families if interventionists hope to be successful with their efforts.

In addition to the more global assessments-evaluations that tend to be conducted episodically, programs should develop procedures for the collection of weekly probe data that indicate a child's progress toward established short-term treatment objectives as well as family progress toward outcomes, if appropriate. Thus, staff should collect systematic objective information on child change and family progress on a regular basis.

A useful assessment-evaluation system is essential to monitor the impact of program input. Without comprehensive evaluation plans, early interventionists can only guess at their impact. Chapter 15 provides an extensive description of a linked assessment-intervention-evaluation approach.

SUMMARY

The goal of this chapter has been to assist the reader in gaining some general knowledge about the nature of early intervention programs. A review of early intervention programs reveals considerable variability in the way in which intervention for this population is conceived, implemented, and evaluated. However, some consistencies do exist among programs. Most programs, for example, appear to operate from a rationale that argues change can be made in the target children and families and that such change, in turn, may produce other, indirect positive outcomes. Although staffing patterns, family involvement, curricular content, intervention strategies, and assessment-evaluation systems differ along many dimensions, there exists a commonality of effort to enhance the repertoire of the child and family members.

Progress has been made in serving infants and young children, yet significant needs remain. Future activities should be directed toward more complete descriptions of programs and enhanced evaluation efforts. Through the identification of critical program elements, progress toward the development of more cost-accountable programs can be made as well as the development of more effective programs.

Future Trends

Most likely, future trends in early intervention will be a continuation of the changes and advances in current practice which have evolved from the need to increase the quality of services. There exists a general trend in educational and therapeutic intervention toward cost-benefit accountability. This move for programs to become more accountable should lead to improvements in the areas of assessment, curricula, and intervention strategies. Because of the shortage of adequate, relevant program assessment-evaluation measures, there will be an increase in the development and use of assessment instruments specifically for the infant and young child. In the area of curriculum, Brinker (1985) suggests there will be a greater synthesis between behavioral, developmental, and ecological perspectives. Gentry and Olson (1985) further suggest that the new curricula and intervention strategies which are a result of the synthesis between these perspectives will be incorporated into more "naturalistic," less structured, models of intervention. There is a growing trend in early intervention toward greater parent and family involvement; this trend will continue to develop (Walker, Slentz, & Bricker, 1985). Another trend is the growing recognition of the need for personnel working in early intervention programs to have received specialized training. Increasingly, disciplines will develop special licensures or certificates for those wishing to work with infants and young children and their families.

A final future trend that seems certain is increased activity in determining the impact of early intervention programs on infants and children and their families. In particular, we believe an emphasis will be on research designed to determine what approaches produce the more significant outcomes, what program elements contribute substantially to child and family growth, and what is the comparative cost-outcome of specific intervention procedures.

References

Bailey, D., (1987). Collaborative goal-setting with families: Resolving differences in values and priorities for services. *Topics in Early Childhood Special Education, 7*(2), 59-71.

Bailey, D., & Simeonsson, R. (1988). Home-based early intervention. In S. Odom & M. Karnes (Eds.), *Early intervention for infants and children with handicaps.* Baltimore, MD: Paul Brookes.

Bailey, E., & Bricker, D. (1985). Evaluation of a three-year early intervention demonstration project. *Topics in Early Childhood Special Education, 5*(2), 52-65.

Bricker, D., Bailey, E., & Bruder, M. (1984). The efficacy of early intervention and the handicapped infant: A wise or wasted resource? *Advances in Developmental and Behavioral Pediatrics (Vol. V).* Greenwich, CT: JAI Press.

Bricker, D., & Gumerlock, S. (1988). Application of a three-level evaluation plan for monitoring child progress and program effects. *The Journal of Special Education, 22*(1), 66-81.

Bricker, D., & Veltman, M. (in press). Early intervention programs: Child focused approaches. In S. Meisels & J. Shonkoff (Eds.), *Early intervention : A handbook of theory, practice and analysis.* Cambridge, MA: Cambridge University Press.

Brinker, R. (1985). Curricula without recipes: A challenge to teachers and a promise to severely mentally retarded students. In D. Bricker & J. Filler (Eds.), *The severely mentally retarded: From research to practice.* Reston, VA: The Council for Exceptional Children.

Bronfenbrenner, U. (1975). Is early intervention effective? In B. Friedlander, G. Sterritt, & G. Kirk (Eds.), *Exceptional infant (Vol. 3)*. New York: Brunner/Mazel.

Calhoun, M., Calhoun, L., & Rose, T. (1989). Parents of babies with severe handicaps: Concerns about early intervention. *Journal of Early Intervention, 13*(2), 146-152.

Cartwright, C. (1981). Effective programs for parents of young handicapped children. *Topics in Early Childhood Special Education, 1*, 1-9.

Filler, J. (1983). Service models for handicapped infants. In S. Garwood & R. Fewell (Eds.), *Educating handicapped infants*. Rockville, MD: Aspen Publishers.

Gentry, D., & Olson, J. (1985). Severely mentally retarded young children. In D. Bricker & J. Filler (Eds.), *The severely mentally retarded: From research to practice*. Reston, VA: The Council for Exceptional Children.

Gesell, A., & Armatruda, C. S. (1962). *Developmental diagnosis*. New York: Paul B. Hoeber.

Guess, D., & Siegel-Causey, E. (1985). Behavioral control and education of severely handicapped students: Who's doing what to whom? And why? In D. Bricker & J. Filler (Eds.), *Severe mental retardation: From theory to practice*. Reston, VA: The Council for Exceptional Children.

Guralnick, M., & Bricker, D. (1987). The effectiveness of early intervention for children with cognitive and general developmental delays. In M. Guralnick & F. Bennett (Eds.), *The effectiveness of early intervention*. New York: Academic Press.

Harbin, G. (1979). Mildly to moderately handicapped preschoolers: How do you select child assessment instruments? In T. Black (Ed.), *Perspectives on measurement: A collection of readings for educators of young handicapped children*. Chapel Hill, NC: TADS.

Hart, B. (1985). Naturalistic language training techniques. In S. Warren & A. Rogers-Warren (Eds.), *Teaching functional language*. Baltimore, MD: University Park Press.

Hunt, J. McV. (1961). *Intelligence and experience*. New York: Ronald Press.

Journal of the Division for Early Childhood. (1985). *International perspectives on early childhood handicapped programs: Western Europe, 9*(3), 195-283.

Karnes, M., & Stayton, V. (1988). Model programs for infants and toddlers with handicaps. In J. Jordan, J. Gallagher, P. Hutinger & M. Karnes (Eds.), *Early childhood special education: Birth to three*. Reston, VA: Council for Exceptional Children.

Koegel, R., & Johnson, J. (1989). Motivating language use in autistic children. In G. Dawson (Ed.), *Autism*. New York: Guilford Press.

Le Blanc, J., Etzel, B., & Domash, M. (1978). A functional curriculum for early intervention. In K. Allen, V. Holmes, & R. Schiefelbusch

(Eds.), *Early intervention—A team approach.* Baltimore, MD: University Park Press.

McCormick, L. (1984). Extracurricular roles and relationships. In L. McCormick & R. Schiefelbusch (Eds.), *Early language intervention.* Cols., OH: Merrill.

McDonough, S. (1984). Intervention programs for adolescent mothers and their offspring. *Journal of Children in Contemporary Society, 17*(1), 67-78.

McGonigel, M., & Garland, C. (1988). The individualized family service plan and the early intervention team: Team and family issues and recommended practices. *Infants and Young Children, 1*(1),10-21.

Mahoney, G., & Weller, E. (1980). An ecological approach to language intervention. In D. Bricker (Ed.), *A resource book on language intervention with children.* San Francisco: Jossey-Bass.

Meisels, S., Harbin, G., Modigliani, K., & Olson, K. (1988). Formulating optimal state early childhood intervention policies. *Exceptional Children, 55*(2), 159-165.

Piaget, J. (1970). Piaget's theory. In P. Mussen (Ed.), *Carmichael's manual of child psychology* (Vol. I). New York: Wiley.

Ramey, C., MacPhee, D., & Yeates, K. (1983). Preventing developmental retardation: A general systems model. In L. Bond & J. Joffe (Eds.), *Facilitating infant and early childhood development.* Hanover, NH: University Press of New England.

U.S. House of Representatives Report accompanying H.R. 5520. (1986). Washington,DC.

Walker, B., Slentz, K., & Bricker, D. (1985). *Parent involvement in early intervention.* Rehabilitation Research Review, National Rehabilitation Information Center. Washington, DC: The Catholic University of America.

Warren, S., & Rogers-Warren, A. (1985). Teaching functional language. In S. Warren & A. Rogers-Warren (Eds.), *Teaching functional language.* Baltimore, MD: University Park Press.

Wolery, M., & Dyk, L. (1985). The evaluation of two levels of a center based early intervention project. *Topics in Early Childhood Special Education, 5*(2), 66-77.

Part Two

Practical Application

9.
Linking Program Components

The intent of the first section of this book is to acquaint the reader with the theory and conceptual framework that underlies the practice contained in Part Two of this book. Thus, based on the major perspectives currently evident in early intervention and the previously presented rationale for providing services to infants and young children who are at-risk and handicapped and their families, the following chapter describes the necessity for linking program components and for having program philosophy and goals undergird program operation.

PROGRAM PHILOSOPHY

A sound and effective early intervention program needs to be governed or regulated by a program philosophy or framework. Such a framework should provide cohesiveness and consistency to the program by directing the decision-making process at a number of levels, which include: (1) the determination of program goals and objectives; (2) the selection of assessment targets and strategies; (3) the determination of individual child goals and family outcomes, and the selection of curricular content and intervention strategies for facilitating acquisition of the selected goals and outcomes; and (4) the selection of appropriate evaluation instruments to monitor change and modify intervention programs. Figure 9-1 presents a schematic of how a program philosophy links to goal setting and decision-making at the four specified levels.

The program philosophy presented here is based on a developmental model in which the implementation of curricular content is governed by behavioral learning principles. Stated differently, the developmental literature provides the source for the content of intervention for children, while the behavioral learning literature provides information for selecting the intervention strategies to be used. Finally, the transactional model provides the perspective from which to view the developing child within the environment. As indicated before, a program philosophy should guide and direct the decision-making of the program personnel. The program philosophy and the four implementation levels presented in Figure 9-1 that evolve from the program philosophy are described in the following sections.

Orientation: Transactional Perspective

Piagetian theory has been instrumental in the growth of intervention programs for infants and young children. In early programs for children who are handicapped, attempts to interpret and incorporate the basic premises of Piagetian theory to guide intervention efforts were undertaken (Bricker, Seibert, & Casuso, 1980). Early intervention efforts

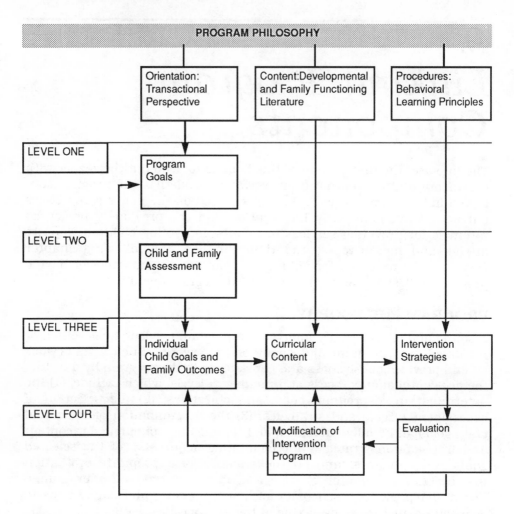

FIGURE 9-1. A schematic of how a program philosophy directs, selects and guides decision making for program goals, assessment, child and family goals and evaluation.

using Piagetian theory and a rich literature on early development (see Schaffer, 1977; Osofsky, 1979) have led to expansion and reinterpretation of developmental theory which may render intervention efforts more effective. In particular, more emphasis is being placed on the reciprocal nature of the child-environment interaction and the social context in which these interactions occur. This emphasis focuses attention on the families, in addition to the children themselves.

The Piagetian position suggests that development is the result of a complex interactional process between the growing child and environmental input. Interaction between early cognitive and motor schemes and environment produces progressive and continuous adaptations that the infant must make to develop into a mature organism. Neither maturational nor environmental variables alone can account for development. Rather, one must look to the interaction between the child and the environment. The healthy neonate's repertoire consists of organized reflexes such as sucking, grasping, vocalizing, and looking. By interacting with a demanding environment, the infant modifies this basic reflex structure and gradually shifts from involuntary to voluntary action. Such modifications result in more flexible and generalizable responses that in time are reorganized into more complex structures.

The child-environmental interactions allow infants to gradually build a sophisticated knowledge of the physical and social world by selecting information and fitting it to their current repertoire. These two processes, the modification of structures or schemes, and the acquisition of information, Piaget has called accommodation and assimilation, respectively. This position tends to place the emphasis on the child as explorer of the physical environment and tends to underrate the social aspects of the environment (Uzgiris, 1981). That is, Piaget's focus was on the child and what the child is able to glean from first watching events occur, then exploring for the source of actions, and finally learning to efficiently produce a consequence. How the environment might aid or deter that progress was given little attention.

Environmental responsiveness may be of minimal concern for the child who is biologically intact but takes on increased importance for those infants or children who have significant impairments. Uzgiris (1981) has also pointed out that Piagetian theory tends to minimize the importance of the social context in a child's development. Uzgiris (1981) favors, as do we, the increased recognition of the importance of the sociocultural context for the child's interpretation of incoming social and nonsocial stimuli. Meaning is not derived singularly from manipulation of physical entities (e.g., objects), but is also garnered from the caregivers' interpretations and actions.

The transactional (Sameroff & Chandler, 1975) or interactional (Lewis & Lee-Painter, 1974) model is focused upon the social responsiveness of the environment and interactive nature of the child-environment exchange. The child's growth and development are the sum of the actions to and reactions from the environment over time (Sameroff, 1981). Consequently, concern must extend to environments and their impacts on children as well as the reverse. The transactional perspective is represented in the simple schematic below, which was designed to indicate the cyclical and reciprocal nature of the child-environment interaction.

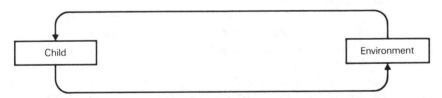

In addition to an emphasis on the reciprocity between the child and environment, the transactional model reinforces the importance of the child's social environment. The infant's earliest experiences with the physical environment is largely mediated by the primary caregivers. This social mediation is of significant importance and should be a focal point for interventionists interested in facilitating the development of infants and young children who are at-risk or handicapped.

The importance of the transactional perspective as the primary orientation from which to derive an intervention context is emphasized by four additional points. First, infants possess a wealth of organized behaviors. Infants have the ability to discriminate and to show preferences among stimuli (Fagan & Shepherd, 1982), to take the roles of initiators and responders in social interaction, and to actively organize, integrate and adapt to experiences (Bruner, 1975; Sugarman, 1984). Infants' characteristics and behaviors elicit and influence the quality of caregiving they receive (Massie, 1980). Second, problems arising from prenatal and perinatal difficulties may be attenuated or intensified by the conditions of the environment. Third, increased understanding of mutual adaptations made by infants and families would make professional intervention more effective. Fourth, critically important social-communicative behaviors evolve during the period of infancy from reciprocal exchanges between caregivers and infants. For example, analyses of "communicative" interaction between mothers and infants show it to be based on a turn-taking structure. Turn-taking seems to be both a force and a result of early socialization. The alternating interchange allows the mother or caregiver to model or provide corrective feedback at a time when the child's attention is focused. These early vocal interactions seem to lay the groundwork for later communicative interactions (Bricker & Carlson, 1981).

Intervention personnel should be trained to facilitate activities that will enhance transactions between the child and the environment (Bricker & Schiefelbusch, 1984). Mutual stimulation should be arranged for the caregiver and infant in a recurring daily context (usually during caretaking and play). A context of shared experiences increases the likelihood that each partner stimulates the responses of the other and should develop patterns that are frequent and sustained. Adults should respond directly to infants' initiations so that infants may learn the direct effects of their social-communicative behavior. Adults should model and prompt responses to sustain and accelerate infants' social-communication activities. The initial goal for intervention should not be to teach infants specific responses but to enhance the infants' reciprocal social-communication acts that are fundamental to the development of more complex skills.

The basis for social-communicative exchanges is the partners' responsiveness to one another. Strategies for molding these exchanges may differ greatly if the child is handicapped. For infants who are impaired, programs of visual, tactile, kinesthetic, and auditory stimulation should be undertaken as soon as the caregiver is able to comfortably interact with the infant. Both the child's expressive and receptive capabilities should be enhanced by these transactional experiences. Early and continuous stimulation may do much to remediate developmental delays and maximize an infant's possibilities of acquiring a functional behavioral repertoire.

Not only are transactions between the infant and the primary caregivers vital but the field is becoming increasingly aware of the importance of the transactions between all family members. The quality of intervention for the target child seems directly related to the comfort and support provided to family members and garnered by each other and by external support systems (Dunst, Leet, & Trivette, 1988). A mother may be unable to effectively initiate and maintain a home intervention routine with her infant who is handicapped if the father is hostile to the procedure or if other children make excessive demands on her time. Without consideration of the transactions that occur between parents, siblings, family and community agents, the usefulness and effectiveness of proposed intervention regimes may be seriously compromised.

Too often, the transactional perspective has been restricted to examining and formulating interventions for infants and their mothers. In the present approach, the transactional perspective is applied to the entire family constellation. Consequently, the formulation of intervention plans must be guided by family members and must attend to priorities expressed by parents, siblings and significant others (e.g., grandparents) as opposed to an exclusive focus on the needs of the target child. However, early interventionists should remember the family has sought help from them for their child, and therefore, a complete refocus on family outcomes that excludes targets for the child is also inappropriate.

Content: Developmental and Family-Functioning Theory and Literature

The developmental and the family-functioning literature has served as a major source for creating a framework from which to formulate program content. Developmental theory and, in particular, Piagetian theory, provides a useful description of normal development during infancy and early childhood, while the family-functioning literature provides helpful information for designing approaches to families (Robinson, Rosenberg & Beckman, 1988).

A critical premise of Piagetian theory that provides an appropriate theoretical basis for child-focused intervention is its assertion that development is the result of a complex interactional process between children and environmental input. This interactional process between the child's sensorimotor and social-communicative repertoire and environment requires continual adaptations that the infant must make to develop into a mature organism. Neither maturational nor environmental variables alone can account for that development; rather, one must look to the interaction between children and their environment.

A second critical premise of Piaget's theory asserts that the general sequence of development is both universal and invariant; although, contrary to common misconceptions, the theory is not maturational. Rather, it asserts that the hierarchy and sequence of development is determined by the logic of the interactional process, i.e., that certain levels of understanding and therefore, action, must logically precede higher, more complex levels of understanding. Piaget's assertion that the general sequence of development is both universal and invariant has resulted in criticism of adopting Piagetian theory for use with populations of infants who are handicapped (Brinker & Bricker, 1980). Often the interventionist working with handicapped populations finds that the children do not appear to follow the predicted patterns either in terms of content or sequence. That is, the premise underlying stage theory is not met (Brown & DesForges, 1977). This criticism is indeed accurate and has caused us difficulty, both from a programming perspective and at a conceptual level.

An answer to the criticisms of the Piagetian approach has been developed by Fischer (1980) who has proposed an approach termed *skill theory*. Fischer suggests that cognitive and other domains of behavior are a composite of individual skills. Skill acquisition follows a developmental hierarchy that moves from the simple concrete level to the representation level to the level of abstraction. A skill sequence initially develops relatively independently, then coordinations between skills or clusters of skills occur. The skills that develop and the speed with which they are acquired is dependent upon environmental emphasis and input. This position would predict differences in skill acquisition across children and variability in the individual child's mastering of different skills. A home that encouraged running and ball playing might well produce a child with running and ball throwing skills that, for a time, exceed reading and writing skills. This picture represents more closely the reality of observed behavior, particularly with handicapped populations as opposed to children moving consistently and uniformly forward in the mastery of all skills.

We believe the application of general developmental theory is enhanced by the skills theory perspective. Developmental theory provides general maps of emerging behavior. These maps are based on data that suggest typical patterns of development for the young child in the motor, sensorimotor, social-communication, social, and self-help domains. The resultant developmental hierarchies should be viewed as composites of sequentially acquired skills that constitute the most appropriate focus of most early intervention. Such a framework specifies long range goals, intermediate objectives, and also suggests programming sequences. However, these sequences only provide *general* guidelines, and interventionists must expect that many children who are at-risk or handicapped will *deviate* from the typical pattern as well as show variation in acquisition rates across skill areas.

Attention to developmental prerequisites can also suggest what the immediate intervention priorities should be. Sensitivity to relationships among domains of behavior can help the interventionist select targets that are both appropriate within and across domains. For example, many early social and self-help skills require a level of understanding of objects in terms of their social functions (e.g., a spoon is for eating, shoes are to wear). To understand these functions, children must have passed the stage at which objects are only sucked, banged, or dropped. Children must have begun to attend to the unique physical properties of objects before they can begin to understand their social significance. Likewise, children must have an understanding of means-ends relationships in order to use a spoon as a tool to bring food to their mouths. Self-feeding, of course, may be a good context in which to stimulate development of the understanding of such means-ends relationships. Nevertheless, ultimate success in training self-feeding with a spoon will depend on the infant's understanding of the spoon as a tool or means to the end of getting food to the mouth.

In the area of gross motor development, observations of blind infants have demonstrated the role of sensorimotor development in the emergence of crawling. Fraiberg and her colleagues (Fraiberg, 1975; Adelson & Fraiberg, 1975) observed that blind infants do not begin to crawl until they learn that sounds signal the presence of objects or persons to crawl toward. Apparently, crawling must be considered not only as a gross motor development but as a goal-directed behavior within the context of sensorimotor development (e.g., to retrieve an object or seek proximity to the caregiver).

The developmental framework indicates strategies of intervention to foster development toward the chosen program goals and objectives. Beyond suggesting a task analysis, the information available from the developmental-interactive framework suggests strategies which should, if applied correctly, produce more functional and generalizable response forms. For example, the interventionist operating within this framework will not focus exclusively on verbal expression when working on communication but will also target important sensorimotor and conceptual skills that research suggests are associated with the development of communication (Rice, 1984). The interventionist operating from this framework will also make use of strategies that provide experiences that conflict with children's current level of understanding or development. Such conflicts produce disequilibrium that should assist children in acquiring increasingly more functional and independent skills.

The developmental framework provides a basis for selecting assessment and evaluation instruments. Appropriate instruments specify developmental sequences that provide a framework for selecting goals and objectives in important areas. In addition, these instruments can assist interventionists in seeing the interrelationships between developmental areas. The developmental sequences, once translated into valid and reliable procedures, also provide the means for the evaluation of progress towards the acquisition of both long-range goals and training objectives. Perhaps equally important for assessment and evaluation, the developmental-interactive framework assists the interventionist in classifying responses into those that are critical intervention targets themselves (e.g., head control, sitting) and those that serve only as indices of underlying structures or understanding (e.g., pulling covers off hidden objects or using sticks as tools). Generally, traditional measures such as frequency counts can be used to monitor the acquisition of critical targets, while monitoring responses that serve as indices of understanding or general concepts may necessitate the adoption of assessment and evaluation measures that focus on generalizability of the response across settings, conditions, and people.

Finally, the developmental framework can direct the modifications and adaptations of curricular materials for individual children as well as guide the construction of new materials. For example, in attempting to train a child with cerebral palsy in the concept of object permanence, the teacher may find it necessary to substitute rigid cardboard screens for the more traditionally used soft clothes. The stiffness of the screens allows the child with only gross motor movements to push or move them from the hidden object. Programs focusing on young children who are severely to profoundly handicapped should be prepared to make many modifications in intervention strategies and training content. Interventionists should have an adequate grasp of the major outcome desired in order to successfully modify the child's response or specific training activities to accommodate the varying deficits of the child.

Family-functioning theory and literature has provided a helpful perspective when formulating the intervention content for families. This literature has assisted in broadening the approach to families in several ways. First, this literature suggests that families may go through developmental stages. It may be important for interventionists to acknowledge the family's level or stage of development or how families deviate from expected patterns. Second, family-functioning theory suggests that early intervention should not be focused exclusively on the child but family interests and priorities be recognized. Third, the selection of child goals and family outcomes should be guided by the family as opposed to the professional staff.

The job of early interventionists can be facilitated by the adoption of a consistent theoretical framework that can serve to guide the selection of intervention content for children and their families.

Procedures: Behavioral Learning Principles

Developmental theory and skill theory provide the content and general structure for the systematic selection of curricula content and its most likely sequence of presentation. However, these theories provide little assistance in the delivery of that content to children. Currently, the most effective intervention strategies available rely on the behavioral learning principles. These principles have been described in detail elsewhere (see e.g., Alberto & Troutman, 1982; Bailey & Wolery, 1984; Tawney & Gast, 1984; Sulzer-Azaroff & Mayer, 1977).

Whenever possible, training should be woven into the child's ongoing activities. For example, rather than establishing special sessions for teaching specific responses, intervention should be conducted in the context of a relevant activity. In this way, training is most likely to become salient for the child. In addition, such integration of training targets into the child's daily activities eliminates motivational problems often found when the infant or young child is forced to engage in a tutorial session. When embedding training in child-selected activities, contingent events often are naturally reinforcing. For example, when the child requests a toy, the payoff is receiving the requested object, and it should not be necessary to introduce an artificial reward, such as saying, "good asking." Further, this approach assists in keeping intervention objectives functional and relevant for the child. Each acquired skill should be useful and aid the child in adjusting to and coping with environmental demands. Although monitoring child change is more difficult with ecologically relevant intervention strategies, the outcomes warrant the additional effort.

Training that is embedded in the child's daily routines and activities is called Activity-Based Intervention. Effectively meeting a child's educational and therapeutic objectives using such an approach requires considerable understanding and finesse by interventionists. A formal structure to guide the selection of daily training activities is essential to ensure the right types and quality of activities for enhancing the acquisition and maintenance of targeted behaviors. The interventionist needs to be able to operationalize behavioral learning principles across a variety of settings and within a range of activities. For example, consequences should be designed to co-occur with the activity or be introduced in a manner that enhances rather than detracts from the child's participation. Finally, interventionists should be tuned to capitalize upon the many daily unplanned opportunities that can be used to assist the child in acquiring targeted skills and using those skills in functional and more independent ways. Activity-Based Intervention is described in detail in Chapter 12.

Level One: Program Goals

As can be seen in Figure 9-1, the first level at which the program's philosophy guides and directs a program is establishing the overall goals. Early intervention programs should have a set of formal goals that assist the staff in planning, organizing, and implementing an intervention program with the target population. The program's goals evolve directly from the program philosophy that has also dictated the orientation, content, and procedures. For example, if the orientation chosen is the transactional perspective, this approach should be reflected in the program goals by the inclusion of the parents or other caregivers in intervention efforts. A set of program goals generated by the program philosophy previously discussed is as follows:

1. To maximize the child's progress toward independent functioning in the areas of self-help, social, cognitive, gross motor, fine motor, and social-communication. Developmental literature is used to select individual child goals and objectives and the sequence in which those targets *might* be taught.

2. To maintain the child in the family context by assisting the family in gaining information and developing skills to maximize their adjustment to the child and to each other. To intervene, when possible, with the focus being child-family transactions.

3. To employ intervention strategies based on behavioral learning principles and to do so in a way that takes into account the child and family ecological context.

Level Two: Child and Family Assessment

Initial assessments should be conducted on the child and with other family members consistent with the program's orientation. Further, the program's goals of, for example, maximizing the child's progress in the areas of motor, cognitive, social, social-communication, and self-help, should dictate the general parameters of the child assessment. The second goal of assisting the family in gaining information and acquiring skills should dictate the general parameters of the assessments to be conducted with the family so long as it meets their priorities and approval. Finally, the reliance on behavioral learning principles requires that the instruments or procedures chosen should be restricted to collecting data on behaviors that can be objectively observed and reliably measured.

Assessment of the child's behavioral repertoire should be comprehensive to reflect program goals and to provide interventionists with information on how the child functions in cognitive, social-communicative, motor, social, and self-help areas. Consequently, instruments or procedures that cover these areas are needed. Comprehensive curriculum-based assessment measures are most appropriate for this purpose (Neisworth & Bagnato, 1988).

Assessment of families addresses two interrelated areas. First, an effort should be made to determine the family's interests and concerns and what they wish to obtain from participation in the program. Second, strategies to determine the family's understanding of the child's problems and appropriate intervention strategies to address these problems are necessary. The intervention staff may be required to select several different assessment tools or strategies to obtain the information necessary to formulate sound intervention plans for caregivers and families.

Level Three: Individual Child Goals and Family Outcomes

The selection of goals for individual children and families is guided by the program goals and more specifically by the information collected on the child and family during the initial assessment period. The program goals set the general guidelines for the selection process, and the data collected during the initial assessment procedures provide the specific information that permits the establishment of appropriate goals for the child and outcomes for the family. At least three types of long-range goals should be considered.

The first type of long-range goals includes those that address the child's deficits or behavioral areas that need attention. For example, a child with cerebral palsy may need assistance in developing better control of the motor system and work on cognitive and social-communication skills. The second type of long-range goals or outcomes focuses on the caregiver and family. For example, an overburdened mother might need some respite from caregiving activities. The third type of goals addresses the interactions or transactions between the child and other family members. For example, parents might request assistance in learning how to manage the child's negative and uncooperative behavior.

Once the long-range goals are selected by the intervention staff in concert with the family, the curricular content is determined. Again, there is a direct relationship between the individual child goals and family outcomes, and the content of intervention. If the child's ability to communicate is poor and work on this area is selected as an individual goal, then a communicative intervention program needs to be developed that is appropriate both for the child and for reaching the established goal. After a specific goal has been selected, as shown in Figure 9-1, the curricular content is determined in large part by examining information provided by the developmental literature—although as indicated before, significant deviations are often necessary, especially for children with more serious problems.

The final component of level three is the determination of the intervention strategies to be used to present curricular materials in such a way that they meet the individual child goals. Selection of intervention strategies, as indicated in Figure 9-1, is guided by the program philosophy and by the individual goals established for the child and the family. For example, if it has been determined that the communicative exchanges between parents and a hearing impaired infant are too infrequent, the parents could be assisted in increasing the frequency by using a variety of strategies based on behavioral learning principles. When the infant vocalizes, the parent could imitate the child's vocalization in return and nuzzle the infant. The parent could hold the infant and vocalize in front of a mirror. The parent could show the infant a desired object and wait for the baby to reach and vocalize before giving the object to the baby.

Level Four: Evaluation and Modification

The fourth level at which a program philosophy has impact is the selection of evaluation strategies. Program goals and individual child goals and family outcomes exert a direct influence on the selection of evaluation strategies. These strategies include measurement of general program impact by examining group progress toward the established program goals and measurement of progress by children and families toward specific individual goals. The selection of instruments should reflect the program philosophy, program goals, and the individual child goals and family outcomes.

In addition, as shown in Figure 9-1, the evaluation procedures provide the necessary feedback for modification of individual child and family goals, curricular content, and intervention strategies. Evaluation of a child's progress toward developmental objectives assists the staff and caregivers in determining if the intervention plan is being effective or if some modification in the goal, content, or intervention is required. The same form of feedback is provided at the level of program goals. More detail on program assessment and evaluation is provided in Chapter 15.

Summary

The approach to intervention advocated in this book directly links the program philosophy to the goals and operational procedures of the program. Such a linked system enhances the organization and cohesiveness of the program (Hutinger, 1988). Program staff, parents, and others can discern the common threads that provide the substance and structure of the program.

A clearly articulated philosophy provides the basis for developing program goals and individual child goals and family outcomes. The determination of goals, in turn, influences the selection of curricular content and intervention strategies. Further, the selection of curricular content and intervention strategies is dictated by the program's philosophy. In effect, a matrix exists which emphasizes the need for coordination and consistency between the various levels of program operation. The linkage between these levels specified in Figure 9-1 is essential to the delivery of effective services to young children who are at-risk and handicapped and their families.

PROGRAM COMPONENTS

The program approach being advocated is composed of an intervention component for infants and children and a second, interdependent family-involvement component. Unless located in a large metropolitan area, most early intervention programs must face the reality of providing adequate services to children and their families who vary widely across a number of important variables and characteristics. Thus, programs should be formulated to permit flexibility in service delivery to accommodate, when possible, the variability found in children and families.

Because most programs will serve a wide range of children and families, programs are advised to offer flexibility in their service-delivery format so that families can select from a continuum of minimum to maximum services. Maximum involvement might include participation in the center-based unit with associated home visits and regular attendance at parent meetings. Minimum involvement might be participation in the intake interview, attendance at the IEP of IFSP meetings, and periodic home visits. The extent of child and family involvement is dependent upon several variables including the nature of the child's problem, the child's age, family interest or need, family resources in terms of time, transportation, child care and program parameters. Child and family involvement is determined by weighing these and other relevant factors to determine the type and extent of participation. As child and family needs change, different arrangements for children and family members may need to be negotiated.

Child Intervention Component

Ideally, early intervention programs should offer families a continuum of services including home-based, center-based, and other options such as combined home-and-center services, and day care placements. Based on the information acquired during the initial intake and assessment, the family should be permitted to select the option that most closely matches the child and family needs.

Home-Based Services. Although variations exist, most home-based services are designed to see the child and family on a periodic basis (e.g., weekly). Home visits are generally divided into four phases. Upon arrival, the home interventionist spends time talking with the caregiver about the success of the home programming undertaken the previous week. During the second phase, the home visitor observes the caregiver and child working on current training objectives. The home interventionist provides feedback and encouragement to the caregiver as well as suggests and models other alternative teaching strategies. During the third phase, new training objectives are introduced if the child and caregiver have demonstrated adequate competence on previous targets. At this time, other activities or concerns of the caregiver can be discussed. The final phase is a wrap-up when the home interventionist reviews the session with the caregiver.

Variations on the above format are frequent in order to address individual child and family needs. If the home visitor arrives and finds the infant ill, the session can be used to discuss management problems the mother may be having with the older siblings. If on another occasion the caregiver is particularly disturbed by a recent incident, then part or all of the session may be beneficially used to discuss the incident. Periodic variations in the home interventionist's plans are tolerated and even encouraged. Only when sessions routinely stray from the child goals and family outcomes should the interventionist suggest a formal review of the IEP or IFSP.

The majority of children served in home-based units fall into four categories: infants less than fifteen months of age; infants or children whose conditions (e.g., children on respirators) suggest home treatment over traveling to a center; families who live significant distances from the center; and families and programs who do not have the resources to transport the child to and from the center.

Center-Based Services. Most center-based services are composed of classrooms for children assigned on the basis of their developmental functioning level. Often classes are designed for infants whose developmental range may include six to fifteen months, toddlers whose developmental range may include sixteen to thirty months, and preschoolers whose developmental range may include thirty-one to sixty months. Ideally, classrooms will include several nonhandicapped children. Center-based services generally operate on a regular schedule and the older the children, the greater the duration of services. For example, an infant group may meet once or twice a week for two hours, toddlers might attend a program three half-days per week, and preschoolers might attend from 9:00 to 12:00, five days a week. Parents are generally encouraged to become involved in center-based services in a variety of ways. For example, parents are encouraged to observe their child in class, help with field trips, participate in parent meetings, or serve as program advocates.

In center-based approaches the curricular focus tends to be comprehensive and includes activities designed to teach information and skill acquisition in the fine motor, gross motor, self-help, social, cognitive, and social-communication domains. Center-based services tend to be structured and follow pre-arranged schedules, although infant groups tend to be less so. The following schedule is representative of center-based programs for toddlers and preschoolers. Upon arrival, children and parents are greeted and may engage in self-selected activities until all children arrive. Parents often take this opportunity to talk with the interventionist or chat with each other. The first formal activity is generally a large group time directed to assist children in generalizing learned skills, developing social skills, using acquired information and having fun. The next portion of the day is divided into a variety of small group activities. The children participate in several successive group activities designed to provide opportunities to acquire their individual intervention objectives. Snack time usually occurs next followed by outside activities. When the children return to the classroom the small group activity sessions are repeated. The day concludes with another large group activity.

Home-Center Service Combinations. Combination services offers the family the advantage of receiving assistance within the home setting while permitting the child and caregiver to attend a center-based activity group. Although variation exists, in general, the caregiver brings the child to the center for one or two sessions per week and receives a home visit every one or two weeks. This schedule is often preferred by families with infants between the ages of eight to eighteen months. Often infants can benefit from limited exposure to other settings and children provided by the less formal activity group. Typically, these so-called "baby groups" begin with a large group activity followed by small group and individual work. Each child's caregiver usually attends to help arrange and execute the specified intervention regimes with their child. During the sessions, caregivers have an opportunity to talk with each other about their children and related concerns.

The combined home-center option is particularly appealing to caregivers who want assistance in the home but feel isolated if not provided the opportunity to participate in activities outside the home. Many parents apparently benefit significantly from the chance to meet other parents and to share and discuss common concerns and problems about their children and families.

Day Care Services. There is a growing number of families who have children with special needs who cannot participate in home- or center-based services (Klein & Sheehan, 1987). The service option needed by these families is some form of day care. Bagnato, Kontos and Neisworth (1987) indicate that data on the availability of day care for children with handicaps is scarce but it may be safe to assume that adequate placements are not available to most families. In addition, most day care facilitates, when available to families, may not have personnel with the necessary training to work effectively with children who have special needs.

No particular approach to the placement of children with handicaps in day care appears to be prevalent. Some families are able to arrange for the placement of their child in both an early intervention program and a day care program. Other children are placed only in a day care program. Ideally, when children with handicaps are placed in day care programs, early intervention personnel will work cooperatively with day care personnel and parents to assure the child receives appropriate help.

Family-Involvement Services

Family-involvement services should cover a range of areas such as educational and social service. Participation in offered services is guided by the families' interest and priorities. During the development of the IEP or IFSP, the family in conjunction with program personnel, make decisions about interests, needs and strategies for accomplishing the desired outcomes.

Educational services generally covers three types of activities: individual work, small-group participation, and large-group participation. Individual work is generally provided to family members by the early intervention staff. The type of individual instruction or support and the appropriate provider is determined by the nature of the caregiver's need. The major thrust of home-intervention components follow this individual instruction-to-caregiver approach, but caregivers of children in center-based services also request individual attention.

In addition to individual work, small-group meetings are often held on a regular basis by specific staff members. The topics for small group meetings are determined by caregiver's need. The objective of the small group meetings is to assist caregivers in acquiring more effective child management and intervention skills. Large-group meetings are often conducted in early intervention programs. Caregivers meet to discuss mutual concerns and problems, to make announcements, and to share their feelings about their children. Often, counselors or family specialists serve as the facilitator for these meetings. A wide variety of individuals (e.g., educators, physicians, legislators) are invited to address the group on selected topics. Spin-off parent groups may also meet on a regular basis with advocacy efforts frequently their central concern.

The social service areas encompass a broad range of activities to assist families in addressing environmental or interpersonal problems. The social service needs of families can range from transportation to marital counseling. Parents with the latter problem, or other serious interpersonal or psychological problems, should be referred to appropriate community mental health professionals unless the program has such professional on staff.

PROGRAM OPERATION

The organizational and administrative structure of a program can facilitate or undermine the effectiveness of intervention efforts. Advanced planning and the development of procedural guidelines assist the staff in using their time more efficiently and ensure consistency among interventionists. A variety of organizational and management issues confront intervention programs. Table 9-1 provides an overview of some of the more prominent activities that benefit from attention to their organizational and management aspects. These activities have been divided into several somewhat arbitrary categories including: scheduling,

Scheduling	Personnel	Physical Environment	Intervention Program	Intake Assessment Evaluation	Administration	Operational Policies
1. Home Program: Appointments Activities	1. Intervention Staff Responsibilities and Roles	1. Home: Remove Obstacles Encourage Exploration	1. Curricular Content	1. Schedule Activities: Daily Weekly Yearly	1. Budget	1. Absenteeism
2. Center Program: Daily/weekly/ Yearly Activities Routine Activities Transition	2. Support Staff Responsibilities and Roles	2. Center: Arrange Furniture and Equipment Repair and Replace	2. Intervention Strategies	2. Data Collection and Display Procedures	2. Feedback to Parent Agency	2. Consent Forms
3. Meetings	3. Staff Training		3. Behavior Management Strategies	3. Tests: Order Maintain	3. Personnel: Hiring Firing Vacation Evaluation	3. Emergencies
	4. Staff Coordination		4. Materials: Order Repair			
	5. Family Members Responsibilities and Roles					

TABLE 9-1. Activities requiring organization and management.

personnel, physical environment, intervention program, intake-assessment-evaluation, administration, and operational policies.

Scheduling

The smooth functioning of an intervention program is somewhat dependent upon the efficiency with which personnel and other resources are deployed. Appropriate scheduling of activities can help attain the goal of efficient program operation.

For home programming, scheduling is developed in conjunction with the caregiver and therefore tends to be idiosyncratic to each family's specific needs. The determined schedule of activities is followed by the home interventionist to ensure objectives are met during each visit.

The center-based services requires more formal and systematic scheduling. General schedules are developed for daily, weekly, and yearly activities. In addition, schedules for routine activities, such as arrival, departure, and snack time are formulated. Transitions between activities are also scheduled, to eliminate wasted time in moving the children to new activities and locations.

A management problem of some significance is the scheduling of staff meetings and parent conferences. Again, effective scheduling can reduce wasted effort. IFSP or IEP conferences are scheduled when families enter the program and then at the required follow up interval (e.g., 6 months for the IFSP). In addition, times should be made available for parent meetings that are needed in the interim. Regular times should be set for weekly staff meetings. A consistently scheduled time for staff meetings and family conferences enhances the chances of people attending and being prepared.

Personnel

A number of organizational and management issues surround the responsibilities and roles of the intervention and support staff. Using the intervention and support staff effectively is dependent, in part, upon how their available time is scheduled. Each staff member should be responsible for designing daily activities to maximize the probability of meeting the goals and outcomes selected for participating children and families. Coordination of staff members' various schedules is required as well.

Scheduling inservice training efforts should be designed to coincide with program and personnel needs. It is probably useful to conduct a survey of staff and program needs each year. These needs should be compiled and prioritized. Inservice training sessions should be scheduled in response to the established priorities.

Physical Environment

Effective organization of the physical environment and management of physical resources is essential to ensuring maximum impact by intervention personnel. Although interventionists have little control over a child's home environment, caregivers are often responsive to suggestions that do not require major rearrangements of their home. For example, parents can be encouraged to remove dangerous or breakable objects to allow their child more freedom to explore.

Within center-based programs, staff should try to arrange inside and outside activity areas, furniture, and equipment to best meet program goals. Areas should be made inviting and accessible to the children. Management strategies for purchasing, repairing, and periodically rearranging furniture, play apparatus, and smaller toys are necessary.

Intervention Program

The curricular content and delivery of that content requires organization. Training or treatment targets should be sequenced from easy to more difficult. Thus, interventionists should begin working on those behaviors that appear to be the most appropriate next target for the child. Instructional strategies can be organized from least to most intrusive. For example, the interventionist should begin with the strategy, usually verbal cues, which requires the most independent response from the child. If the child is unable to perform the target response, then a more controlling, structured strategy is invoked.

General policies for managing child behavior should be designed by staff and shared with caregivers. Again these strategies should be arranged in order of invasiveness. Initially, the least invasive strategy should be selected. If this procedure does not yield the desired outcome, then more controlling procedures are employed.

The ordering and purchasing of appropriate curricular materials requires planning and organization. The materials selected should be determined through careful consideration of program goals, the needs of participating children and families, and the staff's background. Once materials are available, management of their use is required. Replacement and repair need consideration as well.

Intake, Assessment, and Evaluation

As indicated in Table 9-1, a number of activities in this category require organization and management. Scheduling of intake, assessment, and evaluation activities should be done by the staff. Organization of the initial and final assessment and evaluation procedures is particularly essential if information on children and families is to be gathered within a specified time frame.

Organized procedures for collecting weekly, quarterly and annual data are necessary to permit timely gathering of the appropriate information. Systems for obtaining raw data, compiling and displaying data should be designed and then employed by the staff. The same general procedures should be employed across enrolled children and families.

Management of the test materials is generally required. If the program's standardized and criterion-referenced tests are used by several staff members, a system for scheduling the use of these tests is necessary as well as strategies to indicate when test materials need repair or replacement.

Administration

A number of activities are assigned to the administration category. Budgets should be organized to indicate what expenditures have been made and what fiscal resources remain for the year. Untimely feedback on the program's fiscal status may lead to premature expenditure of funds or having a significant surplus.

Most programs must provide reports and feedback to their parent or funding agency; for example, information often sought is the number and type of children served by programs during the year. Without adequate recordkeeping, the staff will be unable to provide such information.

All but the smallest of programs will have need for personnel policies to cover staff evaluation, hiring, firing, vacations, and other similar areas which require established policy.

Operational Policies

Most programs have a number of areas that require the development of specific policies if the situations are to be handled efficiently and fairly, for example, child absenteeism from the program. Policies for similar issues need to be developed and disseminated to staff and families. Consent forms are necessary and need to be developed to be in compliance with federal policy on the protection of human subjects. Development of policies for emergencies is also necessary. To minimize the disruption an emergency situation produces, procedures for handling accidents should be posted for immediate referral by staff. Procedures should be specified for handling the child as well as procedures for covering for missing staff.

Many other areas or situations exist which can benefit from systematic organization and management. The areas and examples presented in Table 9-1 are more illustrative than comprehensive. Attention to the development of efficient organization and management systems yields consistent rewards for staff, children, and families.

SUMMARY

The development of a program's philosophy provides a cohesive framework from which should evolve the program orientation, components, and general operational framework. The program's philosophy should guide the determination of program goals, individual child goals, and family outcomes. These goals, in turn, govern the selection of assessment and evaluation tools, curricular focus, and intervention strategies.

The program philosophy adopted for the present approach emphasizes the link between assessment-intervention-evaluation. The service delivery format should be flexible to meet a range of child and family needs. Finally, attention to the organizational and management aspects of program elements leads to more efficient and effective use of program resources.

References

Adelson, E., & Fraiberg, S. (1975). Gross motor development in infants blind from birth. In B. Friedlander, G. Sterritt, & G. Kirk (Eds.), *Exceptional infant* (Vol. 3). New York: Brunner/Mazel.

Alberto, P., & Troutman, A. (1982). *Applied behavior analysis for teachers.* Columbus, OH: Charles E. Merrill.

Bagnato, S., Kontos, S., & Neisworth, J. (1987). Integrated day care as special education: Profiles of programs and children. *Topics in Early Childhood Special Education, 7*(1), 28-47.

Bailey, D., & Wolery, M. (1984). Teaching infants and preschoolers with handicaps. Cols., OH: Merrill.

Bricker, D., & Carlson, L. (1981). Issues in early language intervention. In R. Schiefelbusch & D. Bricker (Eds.), *Early language: Acquisition and development.* Baltimore, MD: University Park Press.

Bricker, D., & Schiefelbusch, R. (1984). Infants at risk. In L. McCormick & R. Schiefelbusch (Eds.), *Early language intervention.* Cols., OH: Merrill.

Bricker, D., Seibert, J., & Casuso, V. (1980). Early intervention. In J. Hogg & P. Mittler (Eds.), *Advances in mental handicap research.* London: Wiley & Sons.

Brinker, R., & Bricker, D. (1980). Teaching a first language: Building complex structures from simpler components. In J. Hogg & P. Mittler (Eds.), *Advances in mental handicap research.* London: Wiley & Sons.

Brown, G., & DesForges, C. (1977). Piagetian psychology and education: Time for revision. *British Journal of Educational Psychology, 47,* 7-17.

Bruner, J. (1975). The ontogenesis of speech acts. *Journal of Child Language, 2,* 1-19.

Dunst, C., Leet, H., & Trivette, C. (1988). Family resources, personal well-being, and early intervention. *The Journal of Special Education, 22*(1), 108-116.

Fagan, J., & Shepherd, P. (1982). Theoretical issues in the early development of visual perception. In M. Lewis & L. Taft (Eds.), *Developmental disabilities: Theory, assessment, and intervention.* New York: SP Medical & Scientific Books.

Fischer, K. (1980). A theory of cognitive development: The control and construction of hierarchies of skills. *Psychological Review, 87*(6), 477-531.

Fraiberg, S. (1975). Intervention in infancy: A program for blind infants. In B. Friedlander, G. Sterritt, & G. Kirk (Eds.), *Exceptional infant* (Vol. 3). New York: Brunner/Mazel.

Hutinger, P. (1988). Linking screening, identification, and assessment with curriculum. In J. Jordan, J. Gallagher, P. Hutinger & M. Karnes (Eds.), *Early childhood special education: Birth to three.* Reston, VA: Council for Exceptional Children.

Klein, N., & Sheehan, R. (1987). Staff development: A key issue in meeting the needs of young handicapped children in day care settings. *Topics in Early Childhood Special Education, 7*(1), 13-27.

Lewis, M., & Lee-Painter, S. (1974). An interactional approach to the mother-infant dyad. In M. Lewis & L. Rosenblum (Eds.), *The effect of the infant on its caregiver.* New York: Wiley & Sons.

Massie, H. (1980). Pathological interactions in infancy. In T. Field (Ed.), *High-risk infants and children.* New York: Academic Press.

Neisworth, J., & Bagnato, S. (1988). Assessment in early childhood special education: A typology of dependent measures. In S. Odom & M. Karnes (Eds.), *Early intervention for infants and children with handicaps.* Baltimore, MD: Paul Brookes.

Osofsky, J. (1979). *Handbook of infant development.* New York: John Wiley.

Rice, M. (1984). Cognitive aspects of communicative development. In R. Schiefelbusch & J. Pickar (Eds.), *The acquisition of communicative competence.* Baltimore, MD: University Park Press.

Robinson, C., Rosenberg, S., & Beckman, P. (1988). Parent involvement in early childhood special education. In J. Jordan, J. Gallagher, P. Hutinger & M. Karnes (Eds.), *Early childhood special education: Birth to three.* Reston, VA: Council for Exceptional Children.

Sameroff, A. (1981). Longitudinal studies of preterm infants: A review of chapters 17-20. In S. Friedman & M. Sigman (Eds.), *Preterm birth and psychological development.* New York: Academic Press.

Sameroff, A., & Chandler, M. (1975). Reproductive risk and the continuum of caretaking casualty. In F. Horowitz, M. Hetherington, S. Scarr-Salapatek & G. Siegel (Eds.), *Review of child development research* (Vol. 4). Chicago: University of Chicago Press.

Schaffer, H. (Ed). (1977). *Studies in mother-infant interaction.* New York: Academic Press.

Sugarman, S. (1984). The development of preverbal communication: Its contribution and limits in promoting the development of language. In R. Schiefelbusch & J. Pickar (Eds.), *The acquisition of communicative competence.* Baltimore, MD: University Park Press.

Sulzer-Azaroff, B., & Mayer, R. (1977). *Applying behavior-analysis procedures with children and youth.* New York: Holt, Rinehart & Winston.

Tawney, J., & Gast, D. (1984). *Single-case research in special education.* Cols., OH: Merrill.

Uzgiris, I. (1981). Experience in the social context. In R. Schiefelbusch & D. Bricker (Eds.), *Early language: Acquisition and intervention.* Baltimore, MD: University Park Press.

10.
Early Intervention Personnel

Although a number of factors contribute to the quality of a program, one of the more important elements is the personnel who compose the inter-disciplinary teams, deliver services, supervise, and provide the program administration. The best designed curricula, intervention strategies, and evaluation plans, are effective only when executed properly. Conversely, the effectiveness of even the most qualified personnel may be severely curtailed if a program lacks cohesiveness, structure, and organization. This chapter begins by discussing the major personnel issues facing early intervention. In addition, the roles and responsibilities of direct interventionists, allied health personnel, and family members are described. Finally, strategies for state-wide training as well as local training efforts are discussed.

Issues

The passage of P.L. 99-457 has had a significant effect on the delivery of early intervention services to children and their families through the appropriations of federal funds for developing and expanding programs. In addition, this law is affecting state policies and regulations (Trohanis, 1988). The effect in the area of personnel will occur within two areas. First, states are required to develop a comprehensive system of personnel development as one component of a state-wide system. The personnel development system must provide interdisciplinary preservice and inservice training, and provide training to a variety of personnel (Garwood & Sheehan, 1989). Second, states are required to develop standards that will ensure that early intervention personnel will be adequately prepared. In addition, the established standards must be consistent with other approved state certification or licensing (Federal Register, 1989). This means that the licensing and certification standards set for other populations (e.g, school age children) cannot be different for infants and toddlers who are handicapped. If state licensure requires communication specialists to have a master's degree, then that requirement is the same for personnel working in early intervention programs.

The personnel standards set by P.L. 99-457 are clearly appropriate and should be met; however, there are two serious barriers. First, several surveys have reported serious shortages of early intervention personnel (Burke, McLaughlin & Valdivieso, 1988; Meisels, Harbin, Modigliani & Olson, 1988). These shortages include teachers and interventionists and allied health personnel, such as communication and motor specialists. In addition, high percentages of personnel working in early intervention programs have had little or no formal training in the area. The quality of services offered to children and families is likely to be affected. There is a national need for more early interventionists and allied health professionals specifically trained to deliver services to young children and their families.

An associated problem is the variability in state personnel standards. Bricker and Slentz (1988) report that there is little consistency across states in terms of certification for early intervention personnel; however, many states appear to be moving toward the adoption of an endorsement or certification for personnel working with infants and young children who are handicapped. The Division of Early Childhood of the Council for Exceptional Children has recommended the adoption of a two level certification plan for early childhood special educators (McCollum, McCartan, McLean, Odom & Kaiser, 1989). Other allied health disciplines are recommending specialized training for their area (Hanft & Humphry, 1989). Concerned groups, such as the University Affiliated Program's Early Intervention Training Initiative, have issued position statements recommending specialized training for personnel working with early intervention populations.

A final personnel issue concerns the roles and responsibilities of early intervention professionals. The varying facets of this issue become particularly problematic for the infancy specialist. Should there be specialists or generalists, who should train these personnel and what competencies should they be expected to acquire? It seems likely that variability in training and in perspective will be the rule; however, there is some agreement on the core competencies that early intervention personnel should have (Bricker & Slentz, 1988; Throp & McCollum, 1988). These competencies include: knowledge of typical and atypical child development; family involvement strategies; program administration and management skills; assessment and evaluation skills; intervention skills; and, interdisciplinary team collaboration skills. Translation of these competencies into personnel roles and responsibilities follows.

The personnel issues facing early intervention are serious. The manner in which these issues are resolved will greatly affect the future of early intervention and the quality of services offered children and families.

PERSONNEL RESPONSIBILITIES

Staff roles and responsibilities in an early intervention program should reflect the program's philosophy and structure. In order to facilitate the program's effectiveness, competencies as defined by staff roles, and responsibilities should be defined and understood by the staff, parents, and volunteers.

The program's coordinator responsibilities generally include monitoring the quality of intervention and ensuring that procedures for intake, assessment and evaluation, IEP or IFSP development, daily programming, and data collection be systematically implemented. Additional responsibilities include: providing feedback to the staff; organizing and providing inservice training for staff; serving as a resource person for parent education groups; coordinating evaluation efforts; serving as a liaison with outside agencies; and conducting general administrative tasks.

Interventionist responsibilities encompass: the training and supervision of paraprofessional personnel; conducting initial assessment procedures; the development and implementation of IEP or IFSP goals and objectives for enrolled children and families; the monitoring of appropriate data collection procedures; implementation of quarterly and annual evaluation procedures; and the provision of systematic feedback to caregivers of enrolled children.

Paraprofessional assistants are generally responsible for ensuring that the intervention activities occur smoothly and as scheduled. The assistant also assumes the responsibilities of the interventionist when the need arises (e.g., if the interventionist is absent or meeting with parents).

Responsibilities of the allied health professionals (e.g., physical therapists, occupational therapists, communication specialists, psychologist, social workers, physicians and nurses) generally entail participation on an interdisciplinary assessment team. Members of the team are responsible for administering their specific assessments, assisting in developing the IEP or IFSP, monitoring implementation of the specified interventions, and evaluating progress.

Family members, most often parents or other primary caregivers (e.g., grandparents, foster parents, baby sitters), have four major areas of responsibility. First, they should participate in the assessment process and development of the IEP or IFSP. Second, they should ensure that the services specified in the IEP or IFSP are delivered. This entails becoming *genuine* partners in the intervention and evaluation process. The third area of responsibility entails following through on agreed upon intervention strategies for the child or themselves. In the case of the home-based program, caregivers are responsible for setting appointments at convenient and appropriate times (e.g., not during the child's nap period). For center-based services, the caregiver may be responsible for ensuring that the child is transported to and from the center. The final area of responsibility is to follow through on other agreed upon program relevant activities. Thus, if a mother has agreed to assist in the classroom three days per week, she is expected to fulfill that responsibility. If another parent has accepted a liaison role with a community agency, it is his or her obligation to act in this capacity.

EARLY INTERVENTIONIST'S ROLES

Early interventionists should be able to fill five major roles: conceptualizer, synthesizer, instructor, evaluator, and listener. A conceptualizer approaches intervention from a broad conceptual base. A synthesizer seeks and coordinates input from a variety of professionals. An instructor provides information and models intervention approaches for caregivers and paraprofessionals. An evaluator designs and implements strategies for determining program impact. A listeners gathers verbal and other forms of information and provides feedback to family members as appropriate. Each of these roles is described in more detail below.

Conceptualizer

The multiplicity of conditions and their presenting manifestations and the variability of functioning levels both within and across children are too great to expect any single procedure, any single material, or any single prescribed curriculum to be applicable across the many children found in intervention programs. Interventionists who are trained to use "cookbook" approaches that emphasize the acquisition of situation-specific responses by following "frozen" curricular sequences are limited in their effectiveness. Rather, interventionists are well-advised to approach the problems of the young at-risk and handicapped population from a broad conceptual base. A conceptual base should provide the basis for selection of optimal content and the sequence of that content within any given domain. It should also permit flexibility in presentation of training opportunities required by individual differences in children.

Only if interventionists have an adequate grasp of the content covered by a particular developmental domain and the probable sequence of acquisition can they effectively develop a program of creative activities relevant for a specific child in a particular learning situation. For example, an interventionist might develop a training sequence to teach a child the concept of tool use (e.g., using sticks to get objects, chairs to reach food, strings to pull toys). Awareness of how tool-use skills fit into an overall developmental progression for a child (e.g., as a component of more complex means-end sensorimotor tasks) should be the first concern. This awareness provides a perspective on how the development of tool use fits into the large scheme of general development. In addition, the interventionist needs to become familiar with the content and the sequence of that content for the development of tool-use skills. Having knowledge of the parameters of tool-use skills should allow for greater flexibility in generating learning activities and routines that are child-appropriate throughout the day. Rather than having only specific training times when the child is presented with activities that necessitate using "reaching" to gain a desired goal, the interventionist would remain alert to using activities that occur naturally throughout the day, and which can be used to engineer the shaping or practice of more sophisticated skills. For example, when the child is attempting to gain a desired toy which is out of reach, the interventionist should use this opportunity to help the child problem solve by obtaining a stick to push the toy into reach. Using such opportunities maximizes the child's own motivation—the child wants the toy and so may actively use his or her skills to find a tool to solve the problem.

The integration of training activities into the child's daily routine should also facilitate the generalization of the target responses across people, settings, and stimuli. With an adequate understanding of the behavioral targets and some idea of effective sequences (e.g.,developmental hierarchies or task analysis), interventionists can generate, both on a preplanned and a spontaneous basis, specific activities which have a high probability of being effective in assisting children acquire and use targeted skills.

At least two bodies of information are important in helping an interventionist build a knowledge base for the development of conceptual skills: knowledge of developmental processes, both typical and atypical, and familiarity with the broad content of curricular domains. For too long we have made the mistake in early intervention of creating relatively sophisticated pathologists who can talk at length on various handicapping conditions, their manifestation and incidence but who are unable to describe the language of a typical two-year-old. If the interventionist is to fill the role of a normalization agent as specified by many of our current concepts of "least restrictive environment," then that interventionist needs to be conversant with the target—normal development. Background knowledge of normal development can serve as a prerequisite to the effective use of developmental assessments and curricula. Without knowledge of sequential skill development, it is difficult to assess a child's present functioning level and to determine the next appropriate developmental target.

An objection often raised to adopting a developmental approach concerns the validity of the assumption that children who are handicapped do progress through typical sequences of development (Sailor & Haring, 1977). Consistent alterations in developmental patterns associated with various handicapping conditions have not yet been determined. When a child who is handicapped is observed to deviate from typical developmental progressions, the modifications may be adaptations to topographically more convenient responses rather than basic alterations of underlying organizational structure. For example, a visually impaired infant obviously cannot display those behaviors relating to object constancy which require visual tracking or searching; such typical behaviors are simply not part of the possible repertoire. But to conclude that the child does not follow typical developmental progression may be inaccurate. Alternative behaviors, such as tactile or auditory tracking and searching, may be present and be substituted for gaining environmental input that would facilitate the more basic development of the object permanence (Fraiberg, 1975).

Other modifications in response form which are far less obvious may be the mechanism by which children who are handicapped progress through developmental sequences despite the handicap and greatly reduced rate of progress. For example, rather than learning to babble and then produce labels, a motorically impaired child may learn to scan the environment and then eye point. Until more definitive data become available, it would seem that the developmental approach can provide a theoretical framework from which to program long-range goals and intermediate objectives for children who are at-risk and handicapped even though major modifications in the topography of the response may be necessary.

The selection of appropriate developmental targets across domains lays the basis for an integrated and comprehensive approach to intervention. With a developmental orientation, an interventionist is less likely to devise a program for a child which unwittingly emphasizes motoric development at the expense of cognitive growth. Moreover, since intervention targets can be developmentally ordered, more information can be obtained on prerequisite behaviors that are often necessary for building toward important developmental goals. For example, attempting to teach more complex language skills to a child who does not demonstrate mastery of sensorimotor skills thought to be prerequisite for representational thought (Carlson & Bricker, 1982) is less likely to occur if the interventionist is aware of the connection between early cognitive and communicative development.

The second major focus of the interventionist as a conceptualizer is a knowledge of curricular domains. The effective interventionist must be opportunistic; that is, naturally occurring environmental situations should be seized to assist the child in practicing or building targeted skills (Brinker & Lewis, 1982). The interventionist working with children who are at-risk or handicapped may not have adequate curricular guides available to develop the necessary intervention programs for all enrolled children. Rather, the interventionist needs to have a working knowledge of curricular domains and the hierarchical sequences of major behaviors in order to effectively program for children and be able to use opportune environmental happenings, sometimes referred to as incidental teaching (Halle, Alpert, & Anderson, 1984).

Curricular content is important, but so is the process of curriculum development. Although new curricular materials are becoming increasingly available, many of these new materials have distinct problems. First, children who are at-risk and handicapped exhibit a wide variety of individual differences. A curricular activity might be completely appropriate for a child with a severe intellectual impairment, but totally irrelevant to a child with severe motoric impairments who is functioning cognitively within normal limits. Even curricula which have activities appropriate for specified developmental ages may be of little interest to children of differing chronological ages. Curricular materials and suggestions for their use may be different for a four-year-old child than for an eighteen-year-old child (both of whom could easily be developmentally at the same level). In order to deal with this type of curricula selection and implementation problem, interventionists should be prepared to modify existing curricula and to supplement published curricula with other materials and methods.

Synthesizer

The interactive effects of children's physical and mental health, nutrition, and social environment on their developmental progress make it imperative that program staff actively seek, evaluate, and use information from a wide range of professionals. In fact, P.L. 99-457 requires that children and families be given interdisciplinary team assessments prior to the development of an IEP or IFSP. To ensure that team assessment results and on-going input from involved professionals is well used, someone must coordinate and synthesize this information. This job often falls to the early interventionist. To act as a synthesizer, the interventionist must engage in three activities: (1) to seek input from allied health specialists as appropriate; (2) to coordinate input from the involved professionals into a cohesive program for the child and family; and (3) to devise an effective service delivery strategies.

During the IEP or IFSP meeting, the appropriate allied health professional should participate on the interdisciplinary assessment team. If the necessary support personnel are not on the team, then the interventionist must seek their input as appropriate for individual children and families. Increasing numbers of allied health specialists are alert to and supportive of the need to assess a child and family in specific areas in order to develop an appropriate intervention plan. In addition, their continued participation is vital once implementation of the IEP or IFSP has begun.

The second activity is the coordination of various specialized inputs into a consistent, comprehensive, and realistic treatment program. A nutritionist's advice on food types and textures should be coordinated with the occupational therapist's input on feeding techniques. Positioning recommendations from the physical therapist need to be translated into classroom activities in order to maximize cognitive stimulation as well as provide muscular strengthening practice. To maximize the impact of intervention efforts, the recommendations made by one professional should be consistent with suggestions made by another professional. Often the home or center-based interventionist is responsible for ensuring that recommendations made by allied health specialists do not conflict with but rather blend into a cohesive intervention approach.

Another task of the synthesizer involves encouraging allied health specialists to accept and utilize the valuable information which direct intervention personnel have acquired about the child. Unless the child and family is seen on a regular basis, every specialist runs the risk of diagnosing or recommending a program change based on insufficient data. Information derived from a brief assessment or evaluation session conducted in surroundings unfamiliar to a child may result in an inaccurate picture of the child's typical behavior. The program staff and caregivers, however, may be able to offer more reliable information on a child's typical performance. By recognizing the value of interventionist and caregiver observations, pediatricians could compile valuable medical information, physical therapists could compile more detailed information on range of motion in various settings and positions, and communication specialists could learn about vocalizations and alternative communication systems used daily. Careful documentation is essential to offering such information. Readiness with accurate, well-documented information may encourage specialists to continue to seek staff and parental input.

The final activity of the synthesizer is to determine how "special" interventions will be delivered to children. The more traditional model has been that the specialist provides the special therapy or recommended procedures. Except in unusually well-funded programs, this approach means the child receives the special treatment once or twice per week. If the remedial effect of these helping professions is to make a significant impact, specialists should be willing to actively share their expertise using a consulting model. Rather than always providing direct therapy to each child, specialists must adopt the role of a resource person or consultant using the program staff and parents as the primary implementers of the habilitative program (Sternat, Nietupski, Messina, Lyon, & Brown, 1977).

Professionals should be prepared to accept and use a consulting model. This can be done by ensuring that interventionists are provided with general background information upon which allied health specialists can rely for a basic level of understanding and communication. The level of information shared across various specialty areas is not sufficient to provide the skills to develop a program independently but could provide some common terminology and a basic framework that should facilitate understanding and correct implementation of programs discussed by the specialist. For example, a physical therapist may have a much easier time implementing a program to inhibit an asymmetrical tonic neck reflex in a child if she could communicate with an interventionist who had some general information on reflex development and positioning. Obviously there are some activities that will remain in the province of a highly trained clinician, but it is becoming apparent that many forms of therapeutic intervention may be effectively conducted by interventionists and caregivers.

Instructor

The first and most obvious instructional target for the interventionist is the children enrolled in the program. To be an effective instructor, a working knowledge and the ability to effectively apply behavioral learning principles are deemed essential since this technology functions as a basic tool for producing behavioral change. What is being advocated, however, is a sensitive and discriminating application of this technology both to the individual child and to a specific intervention task. Interventionists must wrestle with the difficult task of structuring environments to provide adequate cues to elicit the desired behavior (antecedent event manipulation), that facilitate the gradual approximation toward the desired target behavior (response event management), and that provide appropriate environmental feedback on the effect of such behaviors (consequence tactics). Several modifications in the more traditional application of this technology are recommended.

First, the use of appropriate forms of consequence is recommended. Gratefully, the heyday of M&M popping is past. What, unfortunately, may not be so archaic in typical practice (but which should be considered archaic) is the routine dispensing of socially positive feedback (e.g., "good walking," "good sitting"). These so-called reinforcers are rarely evaluated by the only appropriate test of a reinforcer: the impact on behavior. Evaluation of the use of tangible rewards and artificial contingencies is appropriate, given indications from studies that some potentially undesirable effects of using artificial consequence or prolonged programs of contingency management may be occurring (Guess & Siegel-Causey, 1985; Brinker & Bricker, 1980).

Interventionists need to create learning situations in which the production of the targeted behavior is functionally reinforcing for the child. Creating situations in which aspects of the training activity are designed to be inherently interesting to the child and which capitalize on that interest should be a goal. In some cases, this might be as simple as placing interesting toys on low tables for children who need practice in pulling to a standing position. In other cases, development of naturally occurring contingencies may require considerable thought and preparation.

The second instructional target group includes parents or other primary caregivers. Just as interventionists must actively solicit and receive informational from other professionals, they must, in turn, be willing to extend that type of partnership to parents (Turnbull & Turnbull, 1986). Inclusion of parents or other caregivers as partners in the intervention effort is important because federal policy specifies the right of parents to be informed of and participate in decision-making for their child at every level. P.L. 94-142 and P.L. 99-457 clearly indicate the necessity for professionals to consult and be guided by parental desires in program preparation.

The actual number of intervention hours required for most children with handicaps to make significant developmental gains exceeds the amount of time the child spends with the early intervention program staff. Consistent programming should be carried out across settings (not just home, but grocery stores, buses, restaurants, etc.) so that the effect of intervention efforts will not be greatly diminished or even neutralized. Implementing a toilet training program without follow-through in the home poses a difficult challenge, indeed.

In addition to increasing the amount and consistency of intervention time, inclusion of caregivers in the child's program makes sense for other pragmatic reasons. Caregivers often have valuable information about a child's ability to respond that might take many weeks for an interventionist to discover. In many cases, it will be more efficient to ask caregivers what they think the potential effect of a particular program, consequence, or situation may be for their child. Additionally, caregivers often are more effective than interventionists in providing consequences for their child. They often have both a greater number of and more powerful consequences available to them than does the interventionist: meal times, leisure activities, mild punishers. Parents and other family members also have had a longer time to become reinforcing agents for their children. Even the most skillful interventionist may never acquire as many reinforcing properties as relatively consistent caregivers. Program follow-through by caregivers also provides a crucially needed method for helping children generalize a skill. To assume that children will generalize learning across situations and personnel without specific training is often erroneous.

While the advantages of caregiver participation in the intervention process are real, it would be naive to expect that all caregivers will immediately adopt this new partnership role. The interventionist should develop skills to encourage and maintain appropriate and realistic parental involvement. This encouragement may take the form of sitting down with caregivers and indicating the advantages of their follow-through at home, or it may take the form of helping caregivers acquire specific skills that will be necessary for such follow-through. Many caregivers may not recognize their potential role in some specific area without careful instruction. If such caregiver-interventionist partnerships are going to be built and maintained, then strategies for including the caregivers in the implementation of the intervention plan must be used.

The third group requiring instruction by interventionists are others who may be working in the program; for example, aides, volunteers, or personnel such as bus drivers. Assisting these ancillary personnel in acquiring effective intervention skills may be beneficial to the children and their families as well as assisting in a more smoothly operating program.

Evaluator

The initial evaluation task is assessment of children's current functioning level and family's interests. The purpose of such assessment is the determination of appropriate intervention targets. Assessment activities that merely define a child as a member of a particular group or rank him in relation to other children or establish eligibility, while appropriate for other purposes, have little utility for developing IEPs or IFSPs. Generating appropriate IEP or IFSP goals and subsequent intervention targets is a more important purpose for the initial assessment effort. Once such targets are derived, there needs to be some system of prioritizing the targets. For many children, there may be more acceleration and deceleration targets than can be covered in daily programming. The systems used to set priorities (e.g., parent concerns, required curricula guides, prerequisites to other programming, life support, etc.) may vary, but, it is essential that some effort is exerted to assign weights to the various potential interventions. Once targets have been selected and prioritized, intervention strategies can be developed. An integral part of programming is having an objective system to monitor progress. Regardless of the strategy for monitoring change, to be worthwhile the data collected must be translated into useful information for making program decisions.

To adequately fulfill these evaluation requirements, the interventionist is faced with several tasks: developing evaluation objectives that are congruent with program goals; selecting measurement tools or procedures that reflect the evaluation objectives; establishing procedures for implementing the evaluation plan; and monitoring the specific evaluation activities. For successful completion of these tasks, the interventionist needs to have specific skills and information including: knowledge of appropriate tests or measurement procedures; skills to accurately administer or train others to administer the selected procedures; and finally, skills to interpret and use the outcomes to adjust the program.

Implementing a complete evaluation plan provides interventionists with direct and continuous indication of the effects (or lack of them) of their programs (Bricker & Gumerlock, 1988). A certain aspect of programming requires educated and creative guessing. Even knowing that some intervention strategies and materials are more likely to be effective does not mean they will be with a specific child. In a sense, any preplanned program is a hypothetical statement to be tested. Only by building an adequate evaluation system into the program will the feedback necessary to make decisions on the efficacy of the proposed strategy be ensured.

Another crucially important benefit from careful evaluation is feedback to program staff. Significant efforts are expended by interventionists and specialists to assist enrolled children and family members. In order to maintain the interventionists' motivation, some mechanism by which they can derive a sense of accomplishment is necessary. A sensitive, thorough evaluation system can demonstrate to the interventionist and caregivers the beneficial effects of their effort. Without such evidence of their successes, interventionists may not maintain enthusiasm for their jobs.

Listener

As our understanding of the importance of including parents and other family members in the intervention process has grown, a fifth role as listener and supporter has evolved for the interventionist. It is important to note that this role should not be construed as the interventionist engaging in psychotherapy but rather developing and using skills that enhance listening, question asking, and assisting caregivers in problem solving.

From time to time, most family members experience problems with one another. There are families with young children, handicapped or not, who experience a range of difficulties. When these difficulties are associated with the child, the interventionist may become involved in the family's concern.

To fill the listener role, the interventionist needs to develop three types of skills: listening and asking questions, evaluating and problem solving. Sensitive listening is essential for evaluating and problem solving. The interventionist needs to be able to listen nondefensively and separate fact from perception as well as to try to determine the nature of the problem. A young mother may say she is unable to manage the child at meal time. Such statements taken at face value may be misleading. It may be the mother is saying she cannot manage her other children or that she receives little help from her husband during meal time. Asking a few pertinent questions may assist in clarifying the problem.

A second important skill is to evaluate and determine whether the problem exceeds the bounds of the program or the expertise of the personnel. Parents may be having marital difficulties that affect the child; if so, the parents should be encouraged to seek assistance from other professionals particularly trained to handle interpersonal problems. Thus, the interventionist must learn to listen to the problem and then determine what type of assistance should be sought.

Finally, in the listener's role, the interventionist should be prepared to suggest problem-solving strategies. Although listening may be essential and helpful in and of itself, most problems of any consequence cannot be resolved without additional action. Interventionists should be able to assist caregivers in finding problem-solving strategies that produce desired outcomes. For example, if a family needs medical assistance for the child, the interventionist can assist the parents in locating several potential sources who could make appropriate referrals.

One problem often confronted by well-meaning interventionists is to assume too much responsibility in solving families' problems. Rather than help a family find an appropriate medical resource, the interventionist finds the resource. Assuming too much responsibility is inappropriate for two reasons. First, the parents or other family members do not learn to handle or solve their own problems. Instead, they become dependent upon others to derive solutions for them. Second, problem solving is time-consuming and interventionists may find too much of their professional or their personal time is being spent on problems of participating families.

Viewing the family as the context for the child makes every member integral to the success of the program. Family members may require assistance and feedback in numerous areas. Listening and providing appropriate constructive feedback are skills to be learned and used by interventionists; and interventionists need to learn to balance this role with the other many demands of their job.

ALLIED HEALTH SPECIALIST'S ROLES

Contributions from a variety of allied health professionals are essential to the delivery of quality services to infants and young children. Many programs have need for the services of physical therapists, occupational therapists, psychologists, communication specialists, nurses, physicians, nutritionists, and counselors.

Employing a consulting model requires that the specialist fill three roles: assessor, program consultant, and evaluator. Some children with extensive or particularly difficult problems may require direct intervention by a specialist; however, once the intervention for these children becomes specifiable, the specialist should relinquish the role of direct interventionist.

The interdisciplinary team assessment requires participation by appropriate professionals. The specialist should administer any specialized assessment deemed necessary. In this role, the specialist must select and administer the appropriate assessments to gather the necessary information to help develop an appropriate IEP or IFSP.

The second role for the specialist is that of program consultant. In this role, armed with the assessment results, the specialist can assist in developing an appropriate IEP or IFSP for the child. Those domains and subsequent long-range goals affected by the child's particular problem or disability should receive detailed input from the specialist. For example, a hearing impaired child should be assessed by a communication specialist who then assists in developing the long-range goals and training objectives for the communication domain. The second aspect of program consulting is to provide guidance to the interventionist staff and caregivers in the implementation of the intervention program. For the child with motoric disabilities, the motor specialist should instruct caregivers and staff in positioning, handling and other pertinent aspects relative to the motor program for the child.

The final role for the specialist is that of evaluator. The specialist is responsible for monitoring the fidelity with which specific procedures are used and the impact of those procedures on the child and family. For example, if signing is used with a child, do the staff and parents use it consistently, and, if so, is the child learning to communicate?

FAMILY MEMBERS' ROLES

Because of the need for individualization of the family's participation in early intervention, role specification for family members is more difficult. However, Slentz, Walker and Bricker (1989) have suggested that there are four general roles that caregivers can potentially fill: advocate, interventionists, recipients of special services, and decision-makers.

Caregivers and other family members can be important and effective advocates for their child, for the program, or for early intervention in general. In this role, family members need to effectively represent their constituency, their problem as well as offer solutions to the problem.

The role as interventionists is perhaps the role most often filled by caregivers. In this role, caregivers need to acquire effective intervention and management skills that they can use with their child. Many of the skills encompassed in this role are similar to the interventionist's instructor role.

The third role for family members is as recipient of special services. With philosophical and legislative change, family members have become legitimate clients of early intervention services. With parental approval, programs can include family goals in the IFSP, and families should expect to receive services designed to meet these goals. In this role parents must also exercise control. That is, they are recipients of services but they should determine which services they want and how those services are delivered.

The final general role that family members can fill is as decision-maker. This role for parents is generally consistent within the program and within the family. That is, parents tend to make numerous daily decisions about the family and the child; some of which relate to the early intervention program and some of which do not. To fill this role in the context of the program, professionals must provide caregivers information and the latitude to arrive at the decision which the parent believes is best for the child and the family. In addition, parents must exercise their right to chose and not leave decisions entirely to the program staff.

THE CONSULTING MODEL

Traditionally, physical therapy, occupational therapy and speech-language therapy have been offered using an "isolated therapy model" in which the designed intervention is provided in a treatment room apart from the living and working environment two or three times per week. The problems associated with the use of the isolated-therapy model have been discussed by Nietupski, Scheutz, and Ockwood (1980). These authors suggest that one problem is the episodic nature of the intervention when deploying an isolated-therapy model. Services provided for one-half hour, two or three times per week, have not generally been found to be effective. Episodic training is particularly ineffective and unappealing when the intervention target is the development of functional communication skills (Bricker & Schiefelbusch, 1984). For most disabled children, more frequent and long-term intervention is required.

A second problem often found in the application of the isolated-therapy model is the lack of systematic communication between the allied health specialist, the primary caregiver and the early interventionist. When the young child is removed from the home or intervention program in order to receive therapy, the "significant others" in those environments generally are not free to participate in or observe the therapy session. Given this situation, it becomes essential for the specialist to arrange a time to meet and discuss the therapy activities with caregivers, interventionists, and other specialists who interact on a regular basis with the child. Often because of heavy time demands and scheduling problems, adequate numbers of meetings are not arranged, are cancelled, or are limited to brief exchanges in passing. This limited exchange of information may result in nonsystematic intervention approaches, or worse, conflicting content and strategies in spite of IFSPs developed by interdisciplinary teams.

Thirdly, generalization becomes a concern when using an isolated-therapy model. Children with problems often do not spontaneously transfer skills from one learning environment to another or often from one task or activity to another. Generalization of behaviors can be facilitated by systematically varying the materials, persons, verbal cues, and training. For example, Bricker and Carlson (1980) and Mahoney and Weller (1980) suggest that providing training within the environments in which the child with handicaps must ultimately use newly acquired communication skills permits access to a variety of persons who can provide meaningful social interactions. In addition, the acquired communication skills can be used to identify salient objects and events as well as provide a means for discussing predictable routines and interesting topics that occur. Such meaningful experiences can stimulate active learning and more spontaneous use of communication skills.

When an isolated-therapy model is used to teach communication or language, a fourth problem arises. Communication is a social behavior; the desire to share information with another human being, or make your needs or desires known by responding with verbal or gestural signals, must be established if intentional communication is to occur (Warren & Kaiser, 1988). Labeling pictures of animals or household items, and practicing rote phrases or isolated words or gestures in simulated activities does not create the same level of interest or learning that "real life" situations appear to provide for children. The routine and familiarity of "real" conversations and "real" social activities allow children to anticipate the positive consequences of their behavior, and therefore, may functionally reward the development and use of more adequate communicative behaviors. The use of small groups or the inclusion of significant others in the isolated-therapy activities may increase the realism of the communicative drills, but the effort to organize such gatherings seems senseless when real social groups and situations already exist (Nietupski et al., 1980).

One final and important problem inherent in the isolated-therapy model requires attention. In most states, personnel and resources for providing services to all those handicapped persons needing services are limited. State and federal legislation backed by recent court decisions (Laski, 1985) mandates that all children who are disabled and who demonstrate a need for support services, such as physical therapy or speech-language therapy, must be provided those services as specified in their IEP or IFSP. The delivery of allied health services using a traditional isolated-therapy model in which the specialist delivers the direct service is extremely costly from two perspectives. First, the interventionist-to-client ratio (in this case, the specialist) must be high, requiring that programs either allocate significant amounts of money to hire specialists *or* do not provide all clients with adequate services. This latter alternative is, of course, no longer a legal option. Thus, programs must find ways to develop more cost-efficient strategies to provide interdisciplinary support services.

The second cost factor to be considered is the effectiveness of the isolated-therapy model. The problems discussed previously may lead to the conclusion that such an approach is inefficient in terms of assisting children in generalizing acquired skills from specific therapy settings to other environments. If therapy were conducted within the individual's daily environments, it would seem logical that generalization might occur more readily and thus intervention time significantly reduced. A reduction of therapy time would mean that finite resources were being used in more cost-effective ways.

The problems with the isolated-therapy model argue strongly for the use of a consulting model approach. This model requires change in the roles and responsibilities of the direct interventionist and the specialist.

Interventionist as Synthesizer—Specialist as Consultant

In the consulting model, the specialist functions primarily as an evaluator and consultant who subsequently monitors the implementation of the developed intervention program. In such a model, daily or weekly interactions with children and families occur between the program interventionist staff rather than the specialists. In this approach, the interventionist must organize the input from other disciplines into an integrated, developmentally sound approach.

The success of the consulting model is based on the willingness of the early interventionist and the specialist to interact. In particular, there is an ongoing need to share information about specific children and families. In effect, the interventionist's attempt to acquire relevant information will be futile if the specialist does not support such a model. The specialist must be willing to explain, share, and assist in implementation of appropriate programs. That willingness is based on the specialist's belief that the interventionist is capable of using specific input properly and that allowing the interventionist to function in such a role is an efficient, effective approach.

The consulting model approach is receiving support, in part, because of financial exigencies, but also because many early intervention staff, parents, and specialists have become convinced that, generally speaking, this model is more effective in producing desired change.

The interventionist or caregiver who seeks appropriate information or techniques from specialists in other disciplines, applies such information or techniques to develop effective intervention strategies, and implements such strategies in order to remediate problems, is functioning as a synthesizer. The synthesizer needs skills to organize input from professionals that either are not, or cannot, be included as daily, integral parts of an intervention program.

The synthesizer becomes the pivotal force in the overall intervention program by seeking and coordinating the necessary resources to produce growth and change in the child and family members. When the interventionist takes on the role as the synthesizer or case manager, the specialist operates in a consulting capacity rather than as a direct intervention agent. For this approach to succeed, both the specialist and the interventionist must be willing to modify their roles. For example, rather than providing a child with a brief period of therapy each week, the physical therapist assists the interventionist and caregiver regarding how to lift, carry, position and exercise the child. In this way, the child receives the benefit of continuous appropriate therapy, which should enhance the acquisition of motoric functioning and control.

The development of a consulting model demands that two basic goals be pursued. First, the interventionist must be helped to gain those skills necessary for the successful synthesis of material from other disciplines. Second, for successful implementation, the specialist's role must be reshaped. That is, the specialist needs to develop skills that will allow productive interactions with interventionist and caregivers. The interventionist needs to seek or encourage input from other disciplines, while the specialist needs to provide relevant information. Not only is it important to elicit and give information, but the form and content of such material becomes critical. For example, the physical therapist who tells the interventionist to exercise the child's deep tendon reflexes may be of little assistance unless the interventionist knows what deep tendon reflexes are and how to exercise them. Conveying useful information is not solely the responsibility of the specialist; interventionists must consider the development of a functional relationship their responsibility as well.

INTERDISCIPLINARY TEAM

In addition to the cooperation required between allied health professionals using a consulting model, early intervention personnel need to be able to function effectively as an interdisciplinary team member (Spencer & Coye,1988). P.L. 99-457 indicates that no single agency of discipline can meet the diverse and complex needs of infants and toddlers who are handicapped and their families (Johnson, McGonigel & Kaufmann,1989). The law requires that a "multidisciplinary assessment" be conducted and the IFSP be developed by a "multidisciplinary team" (Garwood & Sheehan, 1989).

According to McGonigel and Garland (1988), teams are interdependent and collaborative groups who function well only when there is a structure for interaction to occur. In addition to the need for an interactive structure, several other factors affect the functioning of a team. These factors include: attitude, accessibility, communication and transmittal of selected information.

Any on-going functional team interaction is probably dependent upon participants' willingness to interact; in this instance, a willingness to participate on a team by offering information and considering other input. Without such an attitude, professionals and parents may be reluctant or even unwilling to share information. Equally vital is the team members' attitude toward the inclusion of family members and other disciplines in making decisions and designing intervention strategies.

A second underlying principle to successful team functioning is accessibility. Family members and professionals must have regular and continuing access to each other if teams are to develop into efficient and effective information generators and decision-makers. Regular meeting times should be established in order to conduct initial assessments for the development of the IFSP, and then for systematic review at six-month intervals, or sooner, if requested by parents.

A third factor that may facilitate team functioning is the attempt to enhance communication by the reduction of professional jargon. Not only should nonessential jargon be reduced, but parents and other professionals should be willing to ask for explanations of unfamiliar language. The speech pathologist, in describing a child, can say the child has difficulty coordinating his tongue, lips, and mouth movements, rather than saying the child is dysarthric. Concurrently, all team members should feel some obligation to increase their vocabulary and understanding of other fields. A solution to communication problems can be developed by employing behavioral descriptions whenever possible, and using objective outcomes to support statements about children, families and program impact.

A final factor that may prove important to developing an effective team interaction is selective informational transferral. Specialists and interventionists have spent many years acquiring information pertinent to their particular area of expertise. In team meetings, professionals should not try to convey all the information they have gained during their professional life; rather they should pinpoint relevant and helpful information. Discussing material that is technical and specific to the specialist's discipline may have the potential of interfering with efficient decision-making and program implementation, particularly for family members. For instance, in planning a special diet for an allergic child, it may not be essential that the caregiver understand the body's reaction to certain substances. It may only be essential that the caregiver becomes aware that the child should not ingest foods containing, e.g., lactose, and which foods contain this substance.

Flynn and Harbin (1987) have listed five dynamic dimensions they believe affect human service delivery systems: climate, resources, policies, people and process. Each of these dimensions is posed as a continuum from positive to negative. The continuum for climate can range from supportive to nonsupportive. Resources can range from insufficient to plentiful, while policies can range from sparse and conflicting to sufficient and complementary. Factors surrounding people can range from insufficient numbers, poor attitudes, and inadequate training, to sufficient numbers, good attitudes and sufficient training. The process continuum can range from promoting conflict to ensuring cooperation (Flynn & Harbin, 1987). Where interdisciplinary teams function along these dimensions is likely to predicate their effectiveness.

PERSONNEL TRAINING

Two major personnel training problems will move with the field of early intervention from the 1980s into the 1990s. The first problem is significant shortages of early interventionists and allied health professionals formally prepared to work with populations of infants and young children and their families. The second problem is the information and skill deficits of personnel currently working in early intervention programs. These personnel training issues are addressed at the state level and at the individual program level.

State-Level Training

P.L. 99-457 requires that states develop a comprehensive system of personnel development. This system is to offer a coordinated program of preservice and inservice training designed to address the needs of all personnel working in early intervention programs. Further the training is to be conducted using an interdisciplinary focus if possible.

The regulations accompanying P.L. 99-457 indicate that all early intervention personnel are to be appropriately and adequately trained. In addition, certification and licensure requirements for early intervention personnel must meet the states highest level entry requirements (Federal Register, 1989). Grandfathering of personnel who have worked in programs previously, but who do not meet state personnel standards, will not be permitted.

To meet the training and personnel specification of P.L. 99-457, a state's comprehensive system of personnel development should be composed of three components: inservice, preservice and a coordinated technical assistance, demonstration and evaluation network. The coordinated network should include a central technical assistance and evaluation project, a series of regional demonstration and training centers, and the local early intervention programs. A schematic of this network is presented in Figure 10-1.

The central technical assistance and evaluation project should be linked directly to regional demonstration and training centers. The central project should work with the regional staff to provide them training and technical assistance. In turn, the staff of the regional center should work with personnel from intervention programs located in that region. This organized approach to providing training and technical assistance has several advantages. First, it permits the efficient use of resources. Second, coordination of training and technical assistance efforts are ensured. Third, training and technical assistance personnel are available to provide on-going assistance.

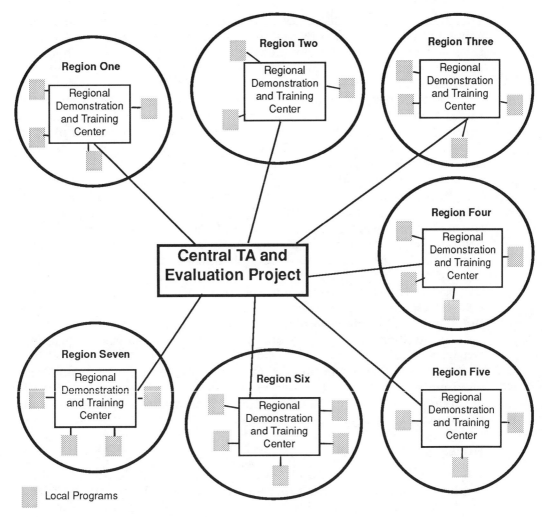

FIGURE 10-1. Technical assistance, demonstration and evaluation network designed to coordinate state-wide training and technical assistance efforts.

Training efforts associated with the inservice and preservice components should be coordinated with the central technical assistance, demonstration and evaluation network. Inservice training can be delivered through the regional network and can be designed to meet the regional training needs identified by the network.

Inservice training should be based on needs of local program personnel. The preservice training should also be coordinated with the network as well as with inservice training efforts when appropriate. The primary objective of the inservice training and network is to enhance the knowledge base and skills of personnel working in the field. The primary objective of preservice training is to increase the number of qualified early intervention personnel available to the field.

Local-Level Training

The interventionist working with children who are at-risk and handicapped must engage in activities that extend beyond traditional teaching roles. Therefore, staff development and continuing education should be viewed as a critical element in providing better services to children and their families.

Staff development and training can be divided into two phases: initial training and ongoing training. The purpose of the initial staff training is to familiarize the staff with aspects of the program philosophy, assessment strategies, IEP or IFSP process, program curriculum, data collecting procedures, and program organizational procedures.

If staff skills and knowledge are to grow, inservice training should remain a priority even after the program is underway. Topics for inservice training should be determined by conducting a needs assessment of the staff at the beginning and throughout the year. Based on the formal needs assessment and informal feedback, a series of staff development and training sessions should be scheduled. Mechanisms should be devised for ensuring that new information or skills that are acquired during the training sessions get put to use in the program. Ensuring transfer of skills and knowledge requires more thought, time, and effort than simply scheduling speakers.

In addition to providing formal inservice training sessions, proper supervision of intervention personnel can do much to enhance their skills. Strategies for periodic observation of personnel working with children and with family members should be developed. Goals for the observation should be set and systematic feedback provided following the observation period.

SUMMARY

The roles and responsibilities of personnel and family members involved in early intervention programs have been described. Although most programs will have idiosyncratic personnel needs, there appear to be three requisites for efficient functioning: establishment of responsibility, delineation of roles, and adequate training to ensure that roles are properly executed.

Roles and their associated activities have been specified for the interventionists, allied health professionals, and family members. The roles vary, and yet interdependence is the rule. In particular, the consulting model permits the use of specialists in an efficient and effective manner. The early interventionist acts as a "generalist" who coordinates and integrates the variety of information obtained from the "specialist" into a cohesive intervention program.

Philosophical changes toward family involvement have served as an impetus to reevaluate how caregivers are expected to function in programs. Rather than being passive recipients of information, family members are being encouraged to become members of the interdisciplinary team. As the attitudes of professionals and parents change, a foundation is being laid for more effective involvement of family members in their child's program.

Finally, organized training and technical assistance efforts are required if the skill level of early interventionists is to improve and if personnel shortages are to be reduced. These training efforts must be undertaken at the state and local level.

References

Bricker, D., & Carlson, L. (1980). An intervention approach for communicatively handicapped infants and young children. In D. Bricker (Ed.), *Language resource book*. New York: Jossey-Bass.

Bricker, D., & Gumerlock, S. (1988). Application of a three-level evaluation plan for monitoring child progress and program effects. *The Journal of Special Education, 22*(1), 66-81.

Bricker, D., & Schiefelbusch, R. (1984). Infants at risk. In L. McCormick & R. Schiefelbusch (Eds.), *Early language intervention*. Columbus, OH: Charles E. Merrill.

Bricker, D., & Slentz, K. (1988). Personnel preparation: Handicapped infants. In M. Wang, M. Reynolds & H. Walberg (Eds.), *Handbook of special education, Vol. 3*. New York: Pergamon Press.

Brinker, R., & Bricker, D. (1980). Teaching a first language: Building complex structures from simpler components. In J. Hogg & P. Mittler (Eds.), *Advances in mental handicap research*. London: John Wiley.

Brinker, R., & Lewis, M. (1982). Contingency intervention. In J. Anderson (Ed.), *Curricula for high-risk and handicapped infants*. Chapel Hill, NC: TADS.

Burke, P., McLaughlin, M., & Valdivieso, C. (1988). Preparing professionals to educate handicapped infants and young children: Some policy considerations. *Topics in Early Childhood Special Education, 8*(1), 73-80.

Carlson, L., & Bricker, D. (1982). Dyadic and contingent aspects of early communicative intervention. In D. Bricker, (Ed.), *Intervention with at-risk and handicapped infants*. Baltimore, MD: University Park Press.

Federal Register. (June 22, 1989). 34 CFR Part 303.

Flynn, C., & Harbin, G. (1987). Evaluating interagency coordination efforts using a multidimensional, interactional, developmental paradigm. *Remedial and Special Education, 8*(3), 35-44.

Fraiberg, S. (1975). Intervention in infancy: A program for blind infants. In B. Friedlander, G. Sterritt, & G. Kirk (Eds.), *Exceptional infant: Vol. 3. Assessment and intervention*. New York: Brunner/Mazel.

Garwood, S., & Sheehan, R. (1989). *Designing a comprehensive early intervention system*. Austin, TX: Pro-Ed.

Guess, D., & Siegel-Causey, E. (1985). Behavioral control and education of severely handicapped students: Who's doing what to whom? And why? In D. Bricker & J. Filler (Eds.), *The severely mentally retarded: From research to practice.* Reston, VA: The Council for Exceptional Children.

Halle, J., Alpert, C., & Anderson, S. (1984). Natural environment language assessment and intervention with severely impaired preschoolers. *Topics in Early Childhood Special Education, 4*(2), 36-56.

Hanft, B., & Humphry, R. (1989). Training occupational therapists in early intervention. *Infants and Young Children, 1*(4), 54-65.

Johnson, B., McGonigel, M., & Kaufmann, R. (1989). *Guidelines and recommended practice for the individualized family service plan.* Chapel Hill, NC: National Early Childhood Technical Assistance System.

Laski, F. (1985). Judicial address of education for students with severe mental handicaps: From access to schools to state-of-the-art. In D. Bricker & J. Filler (Eds.), *The severely mentally retarded: From research to practice.* Reston, VA: The Council for Exceptional Children.

McCollum J., McCartan, K., McLean, M., Odom, S., & Kaiser, C. (1989). Position Paper: *Recommendations for certification in early childhood special education.* Personnel Subcommittee, Division for Early Childhood, Council for Exceptional Children.

McGonigel, M., & Garland, C. (1988). The individualized family service plan and the early intervention team: Team and family issues and recommended practices. *Infants and Young Children, 1*(1), 10-21.

Mahoney, G., & Weller, E. (1980). An ecological approach to language intervention. In D. Bricker (Ed.), *A resource book on language intervention with children.* San Francisco: Jossey-Bass.

Meisels, S., Harbin, G., Modigliani, K., & Olson, K. (1988). Formulating optimal state early childhood intervention policies. *Exceptional Children, 55*(2), 159-165.

Nietupski, J., Scheutz, G., & Ockwood, L. (1980). The delivery of communication therapy services to severely handicapped students: A plan for change. *Journal of the Association for the Severely Handicapped, 5*(1), 13-23.

Sailor, W., & Haring, N. (1977). Some current directions in education of the severely/multiply handicapped. *AAESPH Review, 2,* 3-23.

Slentz, K., Walker, B., & Bricker, D. (1989). Supporting parent involvement in early intervention: A role-taking model. In G. Singer & L. Irvin (Eds.), *Support for caregiving families.* Baltimore, MD: Paul Brookes.

Spencer, P., & Coye, R. (1988). Project Bridge: A team approach to decision-making for early services. *Infants and Young Children, 1*(1), 82-92.

Sternat, J., Nietupski, J., Messina, R., Lyon, S., & Brown, L. (1977). Occupational and physical therapy services for severely handicapped students: Toward a naturalized public school service delivery model. In E. Sontag, J. Smith, N. Certo (Eds.), *Educational programming for the severely and profoundly handicapped.* Reston, VA: Division on Mental Retardation, The Council for Exceptional Children.

Thorp, E., & McCollum, J. (1988). Defining the infancy specialization in early childhood special education. In J. Jordan, J. Gallagher, P. Hutinger & M. Karnes (Eds.), *Early childhood special education: Birth to three.* Reston, VA: Council for Exceptional Children.

Trohanis, P. (1988). Preparing for change: The implementation of public law 99-457. In J. Jordan, J. Gallagher, P. Hutinger & M. Karnes (Eds.), *Early childhood special education: Birth to three.* Reston, VA: Council for Exceptional Children.

Turnbull, A., & Turnbull, H. (1986). *Families, professionals, and exceptionality: A special partnership.* Cols., OH: Merrill.

Warren, S., & Kaiser, A. (1988). Research in early language intervention. In S. Odom & M. Karnes (Eds.), *Early intervention for infants and children with handicaps.* Baltimore, MD: Paul Brookes.

11.
A Linked Assessment-Intervention-Evaluation Approach[1]

The approach to early intervention described in the remainder of this book captures the important developments in the field and reflects state-of-the-art knowledge. A systems approach to intervention is advocated. System is defined as a complex unity formed of many parts but designed to service a common purpose. In this approach, system refers to the active linking of assessment, intervention and evaluation activities in early intervention programs. In particular, a _linked system_ uses the information _acquired_ during the assessment phase to develop IEPs or IFSPs. The IEP or IFSP in turn, _guides_ the selection of intervention content and strategies. Evaluation of child and family progress is _focused_ on attainment of goals and outcomes and is _congruent_ with the assessment procedures.

In this approach, the program philosophy provides the basis for the selection of general program goals. These goals direct the type of assessment that is conducted. The information derived from assessment procedures serves to formulate the intervention plans. Figure 11-1 illustrates the links between the various program components. The arrows indicate the reciprocal nature of the feedback from evaluation outcomes to program components.

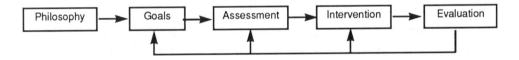

FIGURE 11-1. _A linked systems approach to early intervention._

As indicated in Figure 11-1, this system is composed of five major elements: philosophy, goals, assessment, intervention, and evaluation. As discussed in Chapter 9 the program philosophy should provide a cohesive framework for setting goals and making decisions. Goals refer to the overriding program outcomes and should provide guidance for the structure and operation of the program.

Assessment refers to the process of establishing a baseline or entry level measurement of the child's skills and desired family outcomes.

---

[1] Sections of this chapter were taken from a paper entitled, Evaluation and Programming System: For Infants and Young Children by D. Bricker, S. Janko, J. Cripe, E. Bailey, and R. Kaminski.

The assessment process should produce the necessary information to select appropriate and relevant intervention targets. Intervention refers to the process of arranging the physical and social environment to produce the desired growth and development specified in the formulated intervention plan for the child and family. Evaluation refers to the process of comparing the child's performance on selected intervention objectives before and after intervention, and to comparing the progress toward established family outcomes. In addition to depicting the relationship of these five elements, the vertical arrows in Figure 11-1 illustrate the feedback loop between the evaluation process and program goals, assessment and intervention.

This linked systems approach can be divided into the six phases described below:

Phase One: Intake

Phase Two: Initial assessment

Phase Three: Formulation of Individual Education Plans (IEP) or Individual Family Service Plans (IFSP)

Phase Four: Ongoing monitoring for immediate feedback on individual intervention procedures

Phase Five: Quarterly evaluation of children and families

Phase Six: Annual evaluation of individual child and family progress and program effectiveness for total group and subgroups of children such as those at-risk or mildly, moderately or severely handicapped

Phase One: Intake and Program Preliminaries

P.L. 94-142 and 99-457 require states to have child find systems. The development of an effective and comprehensive system for notifying appropriate medical and community agencies of available early intervention and family involvement services and for rapidly following up on incoming referral is important for effective service delivery systems. Interagency collaboration is an essential component for the operation of efficient child find and referral. Efficient procedures for referral of children and families between community agencies need to be established.

Early intervention programs have available an array of strategies for working with referral agencies. The strategy chosen is often dictated by state law and policy. For example, some states have interdisciplinary teams that assess children and families, develop IFSPs, and then refer the family to a specific program. Other states have systems which permit the inclusion of program personnel on the interdisciplinary team. The later option is clearly preferable.

Whatever option used, program personnel should work closely with referring agencies and should have procedures for determining if children and families are eligible for the services offered by their program. Procedures should also be developed for helping families who are not eligible for the program to find alternative resources.

Once a child and family are determined to be eligible for services, enrollment procedures designed to efficiently collect information should be undertaken. The number of forms required for program admission should be kept to a minimum. To make the process less cumbersome, family members can be given all forms in one packet. Consent forms for testing and acquiring confidential information from other educational or medical agencies should be included, as should medical authorization forms and immunization records.

Most programs will require that parents or guardians sign several form. Consent forms will likely be needed: to alert parents that they and their child may be tested at periodic intervals while participating in the program; to indicate that all test results are confidential; and to seek parental permission for the proposed testing. Consent forms to photograph, videotape and audiotape are needed to obtain permission for the conduct of these procedures.

A medical authorization form should be on file in the event of an emergency. A medical report and immunization record form provides health information about the child; specifically, a record of diseases or conditions, immunization summary, and the results of the child's most recent medical examination. Accurate information in this area is important to protect the safety of all participating children.

A demographic form should be used to obtain relevant information on the child and the family. An authorization to request confidential information will be necessary to obtain any information which might assist program personnel in developing more effective programs for enrolled children and their families.

Another important intake activity is to provide the family with an introduction to the program and the staff. Often it is useful to provide family members with a written description of the program. The description should be kept brief and focused on issues of concern to caregivers (e.g., times child is to attend program or home visits). During the introductory meeting with family members the stage should be set for the family becoming a member of the intervention team.

Parents should have a basic understanding of the program's philosophy and operational structure. While intervention programs should be flexible enough to accommodate a wide variety of family needs and beliefs, some common philosophical ground is likely to be necessary for effective family-staff cooperation. Frequently, a brief introductory explanation helps parents understand procedures which might otherwise be unclear or contradictory to recommendations they have read or received from other professionals.

Phase Two: Initial Assessment

The link between assessment, intervention, and evaluation begins with the entry of children and their family into a program. The major objective of the initial assessment phase is to formulate a realistic and appropriate IEP or IFSP with an accompanying evaluation plan.

Unfortunately, confusion exists about the purposes for initial assessment. In the present approach, the initial assessment procedures are predicated on previously established child diagnosis and program eligibility as shown in Figure 11-2.

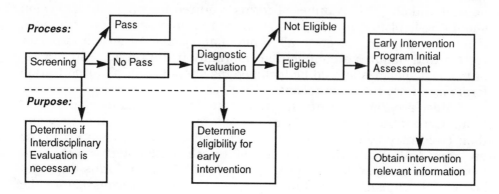

FIGURE 11-2.   *Three-step screening, diagnostic evaluation and initial program assessment indicating process and purpose.*

The objective for screening, which is by definition a quick, simple and economical procedure, is to determine if a child requires further, more comprehensive evaluation and is generally performed by a professional team (Frankenburg, Emde, & Sullivan, 1985). During diagnostic evaluation, standardized norm-referenced tests are often used to determine whether the child performs in a manner similar to age-mates. In addition, specialty tests that attempt to document specific deficiencies may be given. The objective of the diagnostic evaluation is to determine if a child is eligible to receive early intervention services, and when options exist, to make a referral to the most appropriate intervention program.

Once a child has been determined eligible for services, the final step in the initial assessment process is to administer program-relevant (e.g., curriculum-based) assessments to determine the content of the IEP or IFSP. The content of the IEP or IFSP provides the *road map* for moving children from their beginning skills repertoire to the acquisition of skills specified as annual goals in the IEP or IFSP. For the family, this initial assessment should help determine priority interests which can be developed into family outcomes.

The formulation of the IEP or IFSP is crucially dependent on an accurate assessment of the child's beginning skill level so that an intervention plan can be developed toward improving areas where the child has problems. In addition, the assessment strategies employed should yield information that precisely describes the child's behavior in the following ways:

- First, the assessment should include information about the child's performance of skills that are appropriate intervention targets. Norm-referenced and screening tests typically do not include items that are appropriate or useful for designing intervention programs.

- Second, the assessment should include a scoring system that is sensitive to how the child performed the skill and if the skill was performed independently, with different people, or in different settings. A standard binary scoring system provides only information on whether the child's response was correct or incorrect, and important information for developing treatment programs may be lost (Cole, Swisher, Thompson, & Fewell, 1985).

- Third, the assessment measure should be designed to be administered by intervention personnel in the child's usual environment. Individuals working with the child should be able to use the test in the home or other environments in an unobtrusive manner.

- Fourth, the assessment should have some procedure for the formal inclusion of input from parents or primary caregivers.

- Finally, the information generated by the test should be directly usable in the development of an IEP or IFSP. Instruments developed for purposes of screening and traditional norm-referenced tests do not generally meet these criteria and therefore are not useful for developing IEPs or IFSPs.

An assessment that measures functional skills and is sensitive to the conditions in which a child is most likely to perform the skill will facilitate the development of appropriate and realistic IEPs or IFSPs. Quality IEPs or IFSPs should lead to enhanced child progress and should permit more sensitive measures of child progress throughout the intervention process.

Formulation of an IFSP requires specification of family outcomes as well as child goals. Family assessment should yield program relevant information that will aid in developing functional outcome statements, but should not be seen as intrusive by family members. An effective approach is to use a parent-interest checklist, followed by a structured interview to assist families in developing outcomes they see as relevant and important for themselves and their child.

Phase Three: Formulation of the IEP or IFSP

The IEP or IFSP should be based primarily on information accumulated during the initial assessment period, though assessment is better viewed as an on-going process and results benefit from periodic updates. Relevant information should be obtained from parents' knowledge of their child as well as professional observation and testing. The initial information should be used to develop a plan of action for the interventionists and parents to identify the specific content areas that the IEP or IFSP will address. The child's portion of the IEP or IFSP should contain long-range goals, training objectives, behavior prescriptions, and a time-frame for meeting selected goals. The IEP or IFSP should be straightforward so that it can be used as a guide for interventionists and parents working with the child. The IEP or IFSP can also be used as a criterion against which the success of the intervention can be evaluated in quantitative terms.

The family portion of the IFSP should contain statements of family strengths and needs related to enhancing the child's development. These statements should be based on information obtained from the family's assessment of their interests and needs. Priorities can be collaboratively established during a focused or structured interview. From these priorities, a set of outcome statements should evolve, and activities and resources necessary for reaching outcomes, as well as a timeline, should be indicated.

Phase Four: Ongoing Monitoring

A useful IEP or IFSP specifies both the tasks to be conducted and the manner in which the success of the program will be evaluated. A variety of strategies may be used for daily or weekly monitoring of child progress (e.g., trial-by-trial data, brief probes during or after intervention activities). The strategies selected should be determined by specific treatment goals or objectives, program resources, and the need for daily or weekly monitoring as a source of feedback to keep intervention efforts on track. Weekly monitoring may enhance the prospects of demonstrating individual improvement and program efficacy at quarterly and annual evaluations by providing ongoing feedback that will allow caregivers and interventionists to detect and remedy ineffective program targets and strategies that impede child progress.

Ongoing monitoring also allows timely identification of child progress (e.g., reaching the specified criteria), so that children can proceed with subsequent treatment objectives in the most efficient manner. The IFSP requires specification of activities to be conducted for the family as well as the child and the associated evaluation procedures. Caregivers and staff must arrive at a mutually agreeable procedure for monitoring progress toward selected family outcomes. Ongoing monitoring is also important for family outcomes. Family interests are dynamic and must be reviewed and updated to ensure their continued appropriateness for the family.

Phase Five: Quarterly Evaluation

Quarterly evaluation should focus on determining the effect of intervention efforts on the child's quarterly objectives specified in the IEP of IFSP. This can be done by using the initial assessment measures in conjunction with the weekly data. Quarterly evaluation should be used to compare the child's progress with some standard or expectation. Without assigning an expected date of completion for objectives, interventionists may not be able to determine whether progress made by the child and family is acceptable.

For example, quarterly IEP or IFSP objectives should have accompanying timelines (e.g., the child is expected to reach criterion on quarterly objectives within three months). Through frequent plotting of the child's progress toward the established quarterly objectives, interventionists and caregivers can establish more realistic objectives. In addition, comparisons between expected and attained outcomes will generate information that may eventually allow the establishment of relevant norms for subgroups of children who are at-risk and handicapped.

Quarterly evaluations provide information for revising the IEP or IFSP program. If all children fail to reach their established quarterly objectives in the motor domain, program staff or caregivers may not be providing enough training time in this area, or the training may be ineffective. In either case, the quarterly evaluation may suggest that a modification of the program is in order. Information from the quarterly evaluations provides feedback about the child's progress and necessary modifications or revisions in the IEP or IFSP.

Similar procedures can be employed for monitoring family progress. Goal Attainment Scaling (GAS) is an effective strategy for helping families and professionals monitor progress toward established outcomes. Goal Attainment Scaling helps determine if progress is better than expected, as expected, or not up to expectations. Procedures for using GAS can be found in Bailey, Simeonsson, Winton, Huntington, Comfort, Isbell, O'Donnell and Helm (1986). Dunst, Trivette and Deal (1988) advocate the use of a six-point rating scale to evaluate progress or determine if family outcomes should be changed. The type of system employed should be useful for monitoring change and should also be nonjudgmental of the family's participation or progress.

Phase Six: Annual Evaluation

Although encouraged at the federal level through legislative policy and guidelines, implementation of appropriate evaluation efforts at the local or program level has fallen short. The generation of methods to produce objective evidence supporting program effectiveness has been a continuing problem for professionals who work with populations of infants and young children who are handicapped (Meisels, 1985; Guralnick & Bennett, 1987; Shonkoff, Hauser-Cram, Krauss & Upsur, 1988). Many conceptual and methodological problems exist, such as incongruence between program philosophy and intervention procedures, population variability, inadequate instrumentation, inappropriate statistical analyses, and the use of assessment and evaluation systems that do not reflect program emphases (Bricker, Bailey, & Bruder, 1984).

To appropriately determine the impact of intervention content and procedures, a method of comparison should be used that takes into account child behavior prior to the intervention. For meaningful comparison, it is essential that the content of intervention programs be reflected in their evaluation procedures, and this requires a strong and continuing link from assessment to IEP or IFSP development to curricular emphasis to evaluation.

Annual evaluations can be used to monitor the progress of individual children and families and the generic impact of the program (i.e., subgroup analysis). Without subgroup comparisons, it is difficult to know how to improve intervention strategies for subpopulations of children and families. Methodological design and measurement problems facing the field of early intervention make subgroup evaluations difficult; however, analyses of subgroups yield important findings on generalization of impact for certain constellations of children and families.

Summary

The six phases of the linked system exemplify the need to directly relate program philosophy and goals to the processes of assessment, intervention, and evaluation. To employ such systems allows for efficiency of effort and use of resources, accountability in terms of program impact over time, and individualization through the design of programs specific to the needs of children and their families.

ISSUES ASSOCIATED WITH USING A LINKED-SYSTEM APPROACH

Assessment-Evaluation Measures

Fundamental to the operation of a linked system is an assessment-evaluation tool that yields the information necessary to devise appropriate intervention plans. Personnel who work with young children who are at-risk or handicapped often use tests that were devised for screening or diagnostic purposes for program assessment and for measuring child progress. Frequently, outcomes from these measures are not reflective of a child's actual abilities or progress and are not helpful in selecting appropriate educational or therapeutic objectives. Further, the progress made by children with handicaps is often slow and gradual, and the increments between items on screening and norm-referenced instruments often do not reflect small changes in behavior seen in at-risk and handicapped populations. Additionally, standardized assessments often penalize children with sensory or motoric handicaps by allowing only a single correct response.

To counter these and other problems faced by personnel interested in assessing children who are at-risk or handicapped, interventionists should select program assessment and evaluation instruments that meet the following criteria:

- First, the instrument should measure functional skills, that is, skills thought to be essential for infants and young children to function independently and to cope with environmental demands. The focus on functional skills ensures that each test item is potentially an appropriate intervention target.

- Second, the instrument should be comprehensive in nature. The content should cover the major areas of fine motor, gross motor, cognition, self-care, social-communication, and social development.

- Third, the instrument should permit the collection of data through observation of the infant or child in familiar and usual environments. This provides the assessor critical information about what responses the infant or child uses in a functional manner and when and how they are used.

- Fourth, the instrument should permit the examiner to adapt or modify either the presentation format of items or the stated criteria that may interfere with the child's performance. This is particularly important for infants and children who are motorically or sensorially impaired.

- Fifth, the items should be written to reflect conceptual or response classes rather than as singular, specific responses. For example, an item should ask about hand-eye coordination rather than if the child can insert pegs in a pegboard.

- Sixth, a parallel parent assessment-evaluation form should be available for caregivers to assess their child. Completion of a parallel parent form assists the family in preparing to contribute to the IEP or IFSP meeting. In addition, asking parents to complete an assessment form on their child clearly conveys that the professional staff considers the parents' knowledge of their child to be an important contribution to the assessment and IEP or IFSP process.

Interventionists often indicate they need assessment and evaluation tools that can be administered quickly. Employing comprehensive program instruments that use an observational format requires a significant time investment. However, interventionists need to weigh the different outcomes. Use of quick-to-administer tools will yield information that may be inaccurate, narrow and not provide the necessary information to develop quality and useful IEPs or IFSPs. The investment of time to administer a comprehensive assessment through observation of the child under different conditions will yield outcomes that will be more accurate and useful.

In addition, assessment should not be viewed as a discrete activity that can be completed in a predetermined period of time. Rather, assessment should be viewed as a continuous process that occurs across time and situations and permits the development of a comprehensive behavioral and developmental profile of a child. Hastily completed assessments that do not include information about a child's performance of skills across materials, people, and settings, will yield results that are incomplete and often inaccurate. Comprehensive, detailed assessments are fundamental to the development of appropriate IEPs or IFSPs and to the quality of subsequent intervention.

Parent Involvement in Assessment and Evaluation

There is considerable interest in ensuring that parents and other family members become involved in the assessment and evaluation process (McGonigel & Garland, 1988). To ensure family participation, methods agreeable to both caregivers and professionals are needed. One useful strategy is to use program assessment and evaluation tools that have associated parent forms. The *Evaluation and Programming System: For Infants and Young Children* (Bricker, Gentry & Bailey, 1985) is one such tool that has an associated parent form. The parent form contains a comprehensive set of assessment-evaluation items developed to obtain information from parents about their infant's or child's behavioral repertoire. The parent form was designed to be used in conjunction with the professional form of the instrument.

A primary purpose for using parent forms is to obtain information from parents or other caregivers about their children's skills and abilities—across major areas of development—in situations outside the program. However, the use of parent forms can serve several other purposes. First, they can be used to check the agreement between caregiver's impressions of a child's skills and abilities and the professional assessment or evaluation of the child. Second, they can assist caregivers in selecting appropriate IEP or IFSP goals and intervention objectives. Third, they can be a helpful intervention tool for teaching caregiver about the developmental sequences or skills hierarchies important for their children's development. Fourth, use of parent forms may increase parental involvement in the IEP or IFSP process and may enhance parent-professional communication.

ASSESSMENT TO INTERVENTION

Since the passage of P.L. 99-457, the IEP and IFSP have become an integral part of early intervention. This section discusses the relationship between data gathered from the assessment phase and the development of the IEP or IFSP, and then the link between the IEP or IFSP and daily or weekly intervention plans.

IEP or IFSP Development

The relationship between the program assessment instrument and the development of the IEP and IFSP provides an important link between assessment and programming. Three features of program-relevant or curriculum-based assessment instruments can make this link between assessment and intervention direct and relevant. First, many of these instruments are comprehensive and cover all developmental areas for which one would program (i.e., gross motor, fine motor, social-communication, cognitive, self-care, and social). Second, each developmental area is composed of many items that are hierarchically arranged from simple to increasingly complex, which is helpful in determining the sequence of skills to be taught. Third, items on these measures tend to focus on functional skills, and are thus potentially relevant training objectives. Fourth, many of these instruments have associated curricular activities which facilitate program plan development and intervention efforts for individual children.

The importance of family involvement in a child's program, particularly for the infant and young child, cannot be overemphasized. Therefore, it is important to use an IEP or IFSP process that generates meaningful family involvement. Some ways of encouraging active family involvement are to provide caregivers with an understanding of the IEP or IFSP process before the IEP or IFSP meeting is actually conducted and to develop strategies to assist caregivers in selecting and prioritizing appropriate goals for their child. A strategy for enhancing active family involvement in the IEP or IFSP process is to provide information to help them select relevant treatment goals for their child. The use of associated parent forms is helpful in reaching this goal.

The first step in developing an IEP or IFSP should be summarization of the results from the curriculum-based assessment and the parent form. The focus should be on learned and unlearned skills rather than scores. Items taken from these assessments should be used by the interventionist and parent as a basis for developing IEP or IFSP Long Range Goals and Intermediate Training Objectives (or quarterly objectives or short-term objectives). The parents and interventionist should review the results from each developmental domain, and goals and objectives should be selected from test items that the child does not demonstrate or demonstrates inconsistently. Parent priorities should be given first consideration, with additional input from the interventionist or others attending the meeting. Attention should be given to selecting goals that can be organized into a comprehensive but manageable intervention program for the child.

By using this procedure, all Long Range Goals (LRGs) and Training or Treatment Objectives (TO)s selected for inclusion on the child's IEP or IFSP can be taken directly from the child's program-relevant assessment. This procedure provides a direct tie to assessment and a common base for the selection of IEP or IFSP goals by parents and interventionists.

Once the LRGs and their associated TOs are selected, the next step should be for program staff and parents to prioritize the LRGs. Often children have a variety of problems, and thus only the most important target areas to children and their families should be selected for training. The next step is to develop intervention plans for priority goals. These plans should specify the intervention setting, type of training activities, child progress procedures, and decision rules.

Development of Child Intervention Plan

Each objective on a child's IEP or IFSP should be developed into an intervention plan and written on a Child Intervention Plan Form such as the one contained in Table 11-1.
The intervention program plan includes the following items:

1. Identification information: child and interventionist

2. Dates for: initiation, expected completion, and completion

3. Domain: Fine Motor, Gross Motor, Self-Care, Cognitive, Social-Communication, and Social

4. Intervention setting: group, individual, home

5. Long Range Goal

6. Training Objective

7. Program Steps (as needed)

8. Antecedents-Responses-Consequences

9. Child progress procedures

10. Decision rules

When using curriculum-based assessment instruments, intervention suggestions are available from the associated curriculum. The curriculum items correspond directly to assessment items, making it easy to direct intervention activities to specific needs of the child. Once the program plans have been completed, intervention can begin. The approach

Table 11-1
Child Intervention Plan Form

Child: ___Sally Jones_____   **Interventionist:** ___Ms. Thomas_____

Initiated:___9 / 15 / 89___   **Expected Completion:**___1 / 30 / 90___   **Completed:**____ / ____ /____

Domain: Fine Motor [ ]   Gross Motor [ ]   SocCom. [ ]   Cognitive [ ]   Social [X]   Self-Care [ ]

Intervention Setting(s):   Small Group [X]   Large Group [ ]   Individual [ ]   Home [ ]

Long Range Goal: Initiates and maintains interaction with peer.

Training Objective: During free play periods, child will initiate and maintain interaction with peers for 2 minutes of a 10 minute sample, 1 time per day for 2/3 days. Based on child's rate of acquisition of skills the following program steps may need to be implemented.

Program Steps:

1) During free play, child will initiate and maintain interaction with peer with adult model and verbal prompts as per criterion in the treatment objective.

2) During free play, child will initiate and maintain interaction with peer with adult verbal prompts as per criterion in the treatment objective.

3) Same as Training Objective.

Antecedents	Responses	Consequences
1.0.1 Adult models and verbally prompts Sally to initiate and maintain interaction with peer (i.e., "Sally, throw the ball to Paul, like this." Adult models - Paul throws ball, "Throw it again.")	+ Sally initiates and maintains activity - Sally doesn't initiate and maintain activity	+ Peer responds by continuing play or game with Sally - Repeat step
1.0.2 Adult verbally prompts Sally to initiate and maintain interaction (i.e., "Sally throw the ball to Paul, throw it to him again.")	+ Sally initiates and maintains activity - Sally doesn't initiate and maintain activity	+ Peer responds by continuing play or game with Sally - Repeat step 1.0.1
1.0.3 Sally initiates and maintains interaction with peer during free play (i.e., ball, block building, etc.)	+ Sally initiates and maintains activity - Sally doesn't initiate and maintain activity	+ Peer responds by continuing play or game with Sally - Repeat step 1.0.2

Specify child progress procedure(s):
1. Data on progress will be collected 3 days per week during morning free play time.
2. Data collected will be recorded on data graph in Sally's folder.

Specify decision rules:
If data does not show an improvement within a 2-week period, review and/or modify program steps.

to intervention advocated here is called Activity-Based Intervention and is described in Chapter 12.

Development of Family Intervention Plan

A process similar to the one delineated for the development of the child goals and objectives can be used for completing the family outcomes and activities on the IFSP. Family strengths and interests should be identified directly from the assessment information collected on families. The use of a checklist to permit family's to indicate their interests is suggested.

A follow-up interview should be used to clarify the family's expectations. During the interview, the outcomes deemed appropriate and of interest to the family should be selected. Priorities should be established by the family. Some families will have few priorities while others will have interests and needs in many areas. The child goals and family outcomes should complement each other and enhance the family's ability to function independently.

Family outcomes are different from behavioral objectives written for child targets on the IEP or IFSP. An IFSP outcome is the statement of the changes family members wish to see for their child or themselves (Johnson, McGonigel & Kaufmann, 1989). It should be stated in straightforward language that identifies what is going to occur, who will participate in the activity, and what are the anticipated results.

As indicated previously, the family and the interventionist should determine the activities necessary to attain the desired outcomes through a focused or structured interview process. This must be *carefully* designed to acknowledge the possible differences in values and priorities between the family and the professionals, and to maximize the development of mutually acceptable outcomes and corresponding activities. Communication between families and professionals should be open, honest, and collaborative. Families (and professionals as well) may be new to the process and need to develop skills in evaluating service options, selecting strategies which match preferences and accommodate the family unit, and determining practical, nonintrusive evaluation measures.

As a check, Kaiser and Hemmeter (1989) have posed a series of questions that interventionists should ask to ensure they are employing an appropriate and family-guided approach to intervention.

1. Is the intervention based on a valid needs assessment?
2. Did the family indicate this as a priority area?
3. Is the intervention likely to be sufficient to meet the priority need?
4. Is the level of intervention appropriate for the problem?
5. Does the intervention plan include a comprehensive evaluation of its effects?
6. Is the ratio of benefits to costs acceptable to the family?
7. Are the family members willing and able to meet the costs?
8. Is the intervention consistent with the family's values?

9. Does the intervention fit with the family's context in the community and the prevailing social norms?

10. Is the amount of change, relative to the status quo, required of the family acceptable to them? (Kaiser & Hemmeter, 1989, p.84)

Developing the family portion of the IFSP is an important activity for staff and family members. Family members should be encouraged to participate in the IFSP process by guiding the selection of outcomes and determining the strategies for reaching those outcomes.

INTERVENTION TO EVALUATION

Child Progress Procedures

A critical component of the linked-systems approach is evaluation which should be tied directly to the intervention efforts as well as the initial assessment. Objective data collection and recording are necessary to accurately measure the effect of the intervention. The type of child progress monitoring that is chosen will depend largely on the background of the professional staff and on program resources. The better trained the staff and the more resources available, the more elaborate can be the evaluation procedures. Every program should collect at least two types of data: weekly probes and quarterly evaluations.

Weekly Probes.   At least once a week, brief probes of one or two trials should be administered to determine the child's progress toward meeting an IEP or IFSP objective. For example, if a child is working on pulling to stand, he can be placed before a suitable piece of furniture, and the interventionist can note his behavior (e.g., no attempt to stand, an unsuccessful or successful attempt) prior to introduction of an activity that targets this objective. These weekly data should be plotted on a graph, so that caregivers and interventionists have a visual display of the child's progress.

In a center-based program, the collection of data using probe techniques can be organized in a variety of formats to accommodate the program and individual child needs. The interventionist might choose to collect data on different children each day of the week as they participate in the center-based activities. For example, data could be collected on Carrie's and Bill's IFSP targets on Monday, data on Susie's and Sally's IFSP targets on Tuesday, and so on. Another option is to collect weekly data on each child during a limited number of activities designed to emphasize targets within a particular domain. Thus, gross motor data would be collected during outdoor play, and communication data would be collected during circle time for all children with IFSP targets in those domains. Data could be collected during a specified time within each activity, such as during the first or last ten minutes of the activity, or as the opportunity arose. Data on motor skills could be scheduled for collection as the children gathered the materials and set up the activity or on social skills as the children worked together at clean-up time. After skills are acquired, behaviors should be observed periodically to determine if target skills are used functionally and if skills are generalizing to other settings.

The Intervention Plan Form contained in Table 11-1 provides a space for indicating decision rules for each training objective. These rules are needed to indicate when the child's lack of progress should be reviewed. For example, if no progress is made on "pulling to stand" after two weeks, the training activities for the child might need to be reviewed. This will help ensure that program modifications are undertaken in a timely manner.

Quarterly Evaluation. Every three to six months, the curriculum-based assessment instrument should be readministered. This retest can be made efficient by observing only those items that have been targeted for training during the past quarter. Often this involves only a few items and makes quarterly assessments brief. Again, outcomes should be recorded on the proper forms, and child progress should be graphed for easy visual inspection by caregivers and interventionists.

Implementation of the linked systems approach described in this chapter will help ensure a direct tie between assessment and intervention, intervention and evaluation, and assessment and evaluation. These connections should make the program staff efforts more efficient and effective.

SUMMARY

A major barrier to sound intervention and evaluation efforts in early intervention has been the lack of appropriate approaches and instrumentation. This chapter has described a linked assessment-intervention-evaluation system. Fundamental to this system are assessment-evaluation tools that can accurately describe children's current repertoires, as well as provide specific content for subsequent intervention objectives. During the assessment phase, information for developing IEPs or IFSPs is gathered. The heart of any effective intervention program is the IEP or IFSP developed for participating children and families. Time spent on developing an accurate and useful IEP or IFSP is never wasted. More likely, hastily constructed IEPs or IFSPs will result in poorly conceived goals that will require reformulation. Strategies which ensure the development of comprehensive and appropriate IEPs or IFSPs will consistently pay off for the staff, the children, and their families. The IEP or IFSP provides the structure for the development of individual child and family program plans.

The evaluation of family and child progress should be tied directly the goals and outcomes specified on the IEP or IFSP. If relevant evaluation procedures reflecting program treatment emphasis are used on a systematic basis, valuable feedback on the success of intervention efforts will be forthcoming.

References

Bailey, D., Simeonsson, R., Winton, P., Huntington, G., Comfort, M., Isbell, P., O'Donnell, K., & Helm, J. (1986). Family-focused intervention: A functional model for planning, implementing, and evaluating individualized family services in early intervention. *Journal of the Division for Early Childhood, 10*(2), 156-171.

Bricker, D., Bailey, E., & Bruder, M. (1984). The efficacy of early intervention and the handicapped infant: A wise or wasted resource? In M. Wolraich & D. Routh (Eds.), *Advances in developmental and behavioral pediatrics:* A research annual, Vol 5. Greenwich, CT: JAI Press.

Bricker, D., Gentry, D., & Bailey, E. (1985). *Evaluation and programming system: For infants and young children - Assessment level I: Developmentally 1 month to 3 years.* Eugene, OR: University of Oregon.

Cole, K., Swisher, M., Thompson, M., & Fewell, R. (1985). Enhancing sensitivity of assessment instruments for children: Graded multidimensional scoring. *Journal of the Association for Persons with Severe Handicaps, 10*(4), 209-213.

Dunst, C., Trivette, C., & Deal, A. (1988). *Enabling and empowering families: Principles and guidelines for practice.* Cambridge, MA: Brookline Books.

Frankenburg, W., Emde, R., & Sullivan, J. (1985). *Early identification of children at risk.* New York: Plenum Press.

Guralnick, M., & Bennett, F. (1987). (Eds.). *The effectiveness of early intervention.* New York: Academic Press.

Johnson, B., McGonigel, M., & Kaufmann, R. (1989). *Guidelines and recommended practices for the individualized family service plan.* Chapel Hill, NC: National Early Childhood Technical Assistance System.

Kaiser, A., & Hemmeter, M. (1989). Value-based approaches to family intervention. *Topics in Early Childhood Special Education, 8*(4), 72-86.

McGonigel, M., & Garland, C. (1988). The individualized family service plan and the early intervention team: Team and family issues and recommended practices. *Infants and Young Children, 1*(1), 10-21.

Meisels, S. (1985). The efficacy of early intervention: Why are we still asking this question? *Topics in Early Childhood Special Education, 5*(2), 1-11.

Shonkoff, J., Hauser-Cram, P., Krauss, M., & Upsur, C. (1988). Early intervention efficacy research: What have we learned and where do we go from here? *Topics in Early Childhood Special Education, 8*(1),81-93.

12.
Activity-Based Intervention

by: Diane Bricker and Juliann Cripe

Development and Background

Early intervention programs for infants and young children have emerged as a synthesis of philosophies, curricular approaches and instructional methodologies of special education, regular early childhood education, applied behavior analysis, developmental psychology and speech-language pathology (Odom, 1988; Warren & Kaiser, 1988). While this convergence of disciplines has not occurred without debate (Brinker & Bricker, 1980), the results of the last twenty-five years of research from these diverse fields has resulted in the development of unified, transdisciplinary intervention approaches, i.e., activity-based intervention.

Visiting an early intervention classroom twenty-five years ago would have been a very different experience from a visit today. In those early programs, skills were generally taught in a "didactic" fashion which used one-to-one highly structured, adult-directed, massed trial training techniques. The initial intervention approaches were primarily downward extensions of programs used with school-aged children in special education classrooms. The content and instructional strategies appeared largely to be based on research conducted in the 1950s and 1960s with institutional populations.

The use of behavior analysis techniques has been effective in teaching infants and young children a variety of skills; however, as our experience with intervention programs has grown, there has been increased questioning about the manner in which some behavior analysis techniques have been applied (Brinker, 1985; Guess & Siegel-Causey, 1985). It is important to note that the principles used to assist children in acquiring new behaviors are not questioned; it is, rather, the application of those principles that has stimulated debate.

Beginning in the 1980s, growing numbers of investigators and clinicians described the use of behavior analytical techniques in approaches that permit the use of children's self-initiated activities and unplanned or routine environmental occurrences as primary vehicles for teaching new skills (McDonald, 1989; Snyder-McLean, Solomonson, McLean & Sack, 1984; Warren & Kaiser, 1988; Bricker & Veltman, in press).

Since 1978, the Early Intervention Program at the Center on Human Development, University of Oregon has been refining a systems approach that links assessment, intervention, and evaluation. This system has been described in the previous chapter. The intervention component of the linked system uses behavior analytic techniques to assist infants and young children in acquiring skills that will enhance their communication, problem solving, and independent functioning.

This intervention approach, termed *activity-based intervention*, is based on behavior analytic techniques of specifying antecedents, responses and consequences, but in ways that capitalize on the child's motivation and the social interactions in routine or planned daily activities. This chapter describes this intervention approach, its salient features, issues in its application, and a set of procedures for its implementation.

DESCRIPTION OF ACTIVITY-BASED INTERVENTION

A twelve month old is side-stepping down the length of the couch when he happens upon a favorite ball that is out of reach. The baby points to the ball and says, "Ba?" The father happens by, and the baby looks at him and then back to the ball; again pointing at the ball and saying, "Ba?" Father stops, leans over the infant and says, "Ball, you found a ball." The baby says, "Ba," and father says, "That's right, a ball, do you want to play ball?" The baby looks at the father, then at the ball and then back to the father saying "Ba." Father retrieves the ball and places it on the floor beside the infant. The infant stoops to pick up the ball. Father holds out his hands and says, "Throw the ball to me." The baby releases the ball, laughs and waves his arms. The father laughs and gets the ball and holds it out to the baby. "Do you want the ball? Come and get it." The baby says, "Ba" and takes several steps to the father. "Here's the ball. Such a big boy."

A five month old is in an infant seat on the kitchen counter while her mother is putting away the groceries. The baby waves her arms and coos. The mother leans toward the infant and imitates the cooing sound. The mother then picks up a paper bag to discard it. The crackling paper attracts the infant's attention. She looks intently at the paper and again waves her arms. The mother shakes the paper bag again for the infant who immediately quiets and stares at the paper bag. The mother then places the paper bag within easy reach of the infant. The infant reaches for the paper bag, grasps it, and moves it to her mouth. The mother says, "That's a noisy paper bag." She then guides the infant's hand from her mouth and prompts the baby to shake the paper bag. As the bag shakes, the crackling sound occurs and the infant stops her activity. After a few seconds, the mother gently shakes the infant's arm again making the paper produce the sound. The infant again pauses but shortly after, shakes her arm independently to produce the crackling noise.

Such transactions, which occur frequently for most children, appear to provide much of the information and feedback that is necessary for them to learn how to negotiate their social and physical environment. There are some extremely interesting features about the child-parent transactions described above that should be noted. First, the transactions were, at least, equally initiated and directed by the infant. The parents followed their children's lead and provided the information and feedback that appeared to meet their children's immediate need. Second, the transactions appear to be a set of reciprocal exchanges that followed a meaningful sequence for the infant with a beginning, middle and end. Contrast these parent-child transactions with the following episode.

A sixteen month old Down syndrome child is crawling toward a toy on the floor. The mother intercedes, picks up the child and seats her in a small chair at a table. The mother sits across the table and says, "Come on Lori, it's time for your lesson." The mother goes on to explain that today it's Lori's job to find hidden objects. To begin, the mother holds a small rattle for Lori to see. Lori looks at the rattle and then reaches for it. Without letting the child touch the rattle, the mother removes the rattle and while Lori is watching, places it under a small cloth saying, "Lori, find the rattle." Lori looks away and the mother prompts the response by shaking the cloth. Lori looks at the cloth and picks it up. The child shakes the cloth and places on her head to play "peek-a-boo." The mother says, "Lori, look at the rattle," and then removes the cloth from the child's head. Lori sweeps the rattle on the floor with her arm.

Probably few would question Lori's mother's motivation and concern for her daughter, or the concern and commitment of the early intervention personnel who prescribe such intervention activities. Nevertheless, repeated observation of such transactions generates questions about the effectiveness of intervention activities that do not appear to recognize the child's motivation or the relevance or meaningfulness of the activities for the child. The first interactional sequences, described above, between the infants and their parents, appear rich in comparison to the transaction that occurred between Lori and her mother. If the essence of the first two transactions can be captured into reliable training procedures that incorporate behavior analytic techniques, then it would appear that a more powerful intervention approach is available to early intervention personnel.

Definition

The activity-based intervention approach is designed to take advantage of the many aspects of "natural" instruction that many caregivers use with their young child, and to do so in a way that is objective and measurable. To begin, a definition is required.

Activity-based intervention is a child-directed, transactional approach, that embeds training on a child's individual goals and objectives in routine or planned activities and uses logically occurring antecedents and consequences to develop functional and generalizable skills.

This definition contains four major elements:

1. Child-directed transactional approach

    2. Embeds training on children's goals and objectives in routine or planned activities

    3. Uses logically occurring antecedents and consequences

    4. Develops functional and generalizable skills

A schematic of this approach is contained in Figure 12-1.

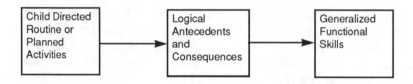

FIGURE 12-1. *Schematic of the activity-based intervention approach.*

    Two features of this approach require comment. First, multiple targets (e.g., motor, communication, social, cognitive, self-help) can be addressed in single activities. For example, a water activity in which children are washing baby dolls can be used to promote communication, (e.g., I need soap), social skills (e.g., taking turns with the soap), self-help (e.g., washing hands), motor (e.g., reaching and grasping), and problem solving (e.g., finding something with which to dry the baby). A second feature is the built-in reinforcement for children participating in fun and desired activities. If well-chosen, or chosen by the child, the activities provide ample motivation for children and the use of artificial contingencies can be eliminated.

Elements of Activity-Based Intervention

1. Child-Directed Transactions: The first major element of this intervention approach is its attention to the child's motivation, interests, and actions. This is done primarily by encouraging the child to *initiate* activity. The premise is that activity and actions initiated by children are more likely to engage and maintain their attention and involvement. Rather than the caregiver or interventionist selecting activities, the child's interests are identified. The adult joins the child and plays the game or with the toys selected by the child.

    In addition to encouraging child initiation, this intervention approach is designed to follow the child's lead in terms of directing the activities whenever possible. Using this strategy, Lori's mother would have shifted attention to the cloth since that is where the child's interest was focused and followed Lori's desire to play "peek-a-boo." Lori's mother could have taken turns playing "peek-a-boo" with the cloth and hiding the cloth (perhaps under the table, in back of Lori, or under her shirt) since that was the focus of the child's attention, rather than hiding the rattle which did not appear to interest the child. The goal of working on object constancy would still have been maintained, but the object and activities changed to match the child's interests.

In capitalizing on children's motivation, the need for using reinforcers apart from the activity is eliminated. Lori's attainment of an object of interest would likely be adequate reinforcement to maintain her searching behavior and thus, the need for delivering tangible or secondary rewards is unnecessary (e.g., adult saying "good looking").

The other important aspect of this first element is the transactional nature of the child's responses or actions. That is, as the child behaves, the social and physical environment respond in a reciprocal manner. If the child vocalizes, caregivers or interventionists vocalize in return. In general, they respond to the nature of the child's vocalization if it is interpretable. If not, they will request clarification. For example, if the child points at a picture and says, "Da?", with rising inflection, the caregiver may respond in several appropriate ways to maintain the interaction and encourage the child to continue responding. The caregiver might say, "Yes, that's your ball. Do you want to play ball?" or ask "What do you see?" or "That is a ball, can you say ball?" or "Do you want the ball?" Such exchanges or transaction provide the child feedback that is informational (e.g., labeling the object), that indicates the social environment's responsiveness (e.g., caregiver responds to the child's communicative attempts), and that assists the child in learning the communication game (e.g., speakers and listeners take turns).

Transactions such as the one described previously are likely very useful to children if they have initiated the action and the caregiver follows the child's lead. Such transactions take advantage of the child's motivation. Using children's motivation or interest has been shown to enhance learning in a variety of populations and settings; however, it is important to point out that this element of activity-based intervention can be used even when planned activities are introduced to children. For example, during opening-group time when the interventionists plan to sing songs, children can be encouraged to initiate actions in a variety of ways. Children can suggest which songs to sing, actions to accompany the songs, and variations on how the group responds. In addition, interventionists can introduce variations into planned activities that may encourage children to initiate different actions. The record player could suddenly not work and the interventionist might use this opportunity for the children to ask questions, suggest solutions to fix the problem or suggest alternative activities.

2. Embedding Training in Routine or Planned Activities: As a child's day unfolds, whether at a center-based program, day care arrangement or at home, a variety of daily or routine activities occur. The activity-based intervention approach is designed to use such activities for working on children's IEP or IFSP goals and objectives as frequently as possible. Enhancement of communication skills can occur when children need to communicate a need or message and as they negotiate these daily activities. For example, working on "requesting" can happen and is appropriate when children need coats to go outside, juice for their cups, hats for dress up play, containers for blocks, comfort when hurt. Using such natural and relevant occurrences makes the communication genuine in the sense of the child's need (e.g., getting a coat), and yet, still relates directly to the IEP or IFSP target of improving expressive language through verbal requesting. It seems likely that learning to express one's need under natural and relevant conditions leads to more effective and efficient learning by children.

Although we believe that many IEP or IFSP goals and objectives can be targeted during routine activities, there may be times when planned activities can be beneficially employed. Such activities should be viewed by infants and young children as fun and interesting compared to structured training endeavors. For example, if working on improving hand-eye coordination, problem solving, and communication, an interventionist might introduce a water-play activity. To begin, the children would have to assemble the necessary materials such as bowls, small toys that float and sink, aprons and papers. Assembly provides the opportunity to practice problems solving skills (determining what is needed for the activity), communication (asking questions and making statements about retrieving materials), motor skills (obtaining, carrying and arranging materials), and social skills (taking turns getting materials and sharing materials). Once set up, this activity provides children many opportunities to retrieve small toys that float and sink (hand-eye coordination). While retrieving toys and pouring water, many opportunities present themselves for working on communication skills (requests, labeling objects and actions, exclaims of delight) and problem solving (how to balance toys, how to retrieve toys without getting your shirt wet, or how to dry your shirt once it's wet). The activity ends by the children putting away toys and cleaning up spilled water. The clean up period also provides the children with practice in problem solving (putting materials back together, returning items to where they are stored), communication (practicing new words or word combinations), self-help and motor skills (drying, and rearranging items), and social skills (determining who will do what and talking about the activity). Including the children in the assembling and dismantling of the activity provides a clearly defined logical sequence, offers many opportunities for child initiation and training on targeted skills, and establishes a consistent framework which allows children to gain independence. Working on hand-eye coordination by sitting children around a table to pick up blocks provided by the interventionist and insert them in a form board provides a clear contrast. The water-play activity would appear to provide a much richer context from which children can learn a variety of functional skills.

The primary strategy of this intervention is to embed treatment goals into the activities. For clarity, it may be useful to define what is meant by an activity. An activity refers to a sequence of events that has a beginning, a logical outcome, and requires a variety of both initiated and reciprocal actions by the child. In the previous discussion, three types of activities have been discussed that can be used in this intervention approach : routine, planned, and child-initiated.

- Routine activities refer to events that occur on a predictable or regular basis such as meals, diapering or dressing. Often, with thought, these activities can be used or refocused to provide children opportunities to learn new skills or practice skills being acquired.

- Planned activities refer to designed events that ordinarily do not happen without adult intervention. Planned activities should interest children and should be developed in ways that children find appealing as opposed to being designed exclusively to practice a target skill.

- Child-initiated activities refer to those that are instigated by the child. It seems safe to assume that if children introduce and persist in an activity, the actions and events associated with it are appealing to them. Activities that are inherently interesting to children require little use of external support or reward systems.

It is possible that the three types of activities described above can be and often are combined. That is, children can initiate some action within a planned or routine activity. In fact, caregivers or interventionists should encourage child-initiation within activities. There should be no problem with a planned or routine activity being redirected by children if the subsequent activity provides children opportunities to develop and practice important skills targeted in their IEPs or IFSPs. This requires that caregivers or interventionists be flexible in their use of routine and planned activities.

Routine, planned, and child-directed activities share some important commonalities in this approach. First, activities should make sense to children. Labeling pictures from a photo file may not be as functional to a child as labeling objects that one is using to attain a certain outcome (e.g., assembling the necessary objects for water play). Asking children to perform behaviors apart from their usual context may be confusing and constitute inefficient training. Second, activities should be those that children find interesting to do. As described previously, this often reduces or precludes the use of artificial reinforcement systems. Third, activities should be gauged to children's developmental capabilities and require children to expand their repertoire to the next level of developmental sophistication.

3. Logically Occurring Antecedents and Consequences: Simply taking advantage of daily routines or planning interesting activities will not necessarily produce desired change in children. Such activities provide a rich and natural context for intervention, but additional safeguards are necessary to ensure that children are developing the behaviors targeted in their IEP or IFSP. In this approach, such assurance is provided through the systematic use of appropriate antecedents and consequences that can occur as logical outcomes of activities.

Permitting children to engage in water play may or may not result in changes in behavior depending upon the caregivers' or interventionists' use of the activity. Prior to initiation of an activity or use of a routine activity, the caregiver or interventionist must be aware of the participating childrens' goals and objectives. If improving pincer grasp, wrist rotation, and release of objects are objectives for participating children, then the interventionist must ensure that antecedents appropriate for eliciting these motor skills occur frequently during the activity; that children have adequate opportunity to practice the target responses, and that environmental feedback is adequate to acquire and maintain the responses.

Children's response repertoires will not expand and become more sophisticated by simply engaging in fun activities. The interventionist must provide the necessary materials, events, models, and assistance as needed. In activity-based intervention, the children are not just "left to play" with the hope that learning will occur. The caregiver or interventionist assumes an active partnership role, following and leading, arranging and waiting, asking and answering, showing and guiding. Antecedents (e.g., materials, questions, comments, models and physical assistance) need to be carefully analyzed to meet each child's individual needs to ensure learning occurs not through magic, but through careful use of antecedents and consequences.

During child-initiated routine or planned activities, it is essential to measure the number and type of antecedents offered, the type and frequency of children's responses, and the nature of the feedback. Only through careful documentation of antecedents, responses, and consequences can the impact of intervention be determined.

In this approach it should be emphasized that, for the most part, consequences are seen as an integral part of the system—that is, that consequences are generally inherent in the activity or as a logical outcome of the activity. For example, if a toddler sees a bottle of juice (antecedent) and requests a drink (response), the natural or inherent consequence is getting to drink the juice. If the child is learning to go up steps of a slide, the logical outcome is getting to slide down. If a child desires an adult's attention, the consequence for calling to the adult is securing his or her attention. Using this approach requires minimal use of artificial consequences for producing desired responses.

4. Functional and Generalizable Skills: Early intervention personnel should target skills for infants and young children that are functional and generalizable. By functional skills, we are referring to skills that permit children to negotiate their physical and social environment in an independent and satisfying manner. For example, it is more functional to assist children in learning how to open and close doors, turn on faucets, and flush toilets than to focus on helping them learn how to stack blocks or complete puzzles. It is more useful for children to learn to request needed items than to label pictures of zoo animals. Equally important is the need to help children acquire generalizable skills that will assist their independent functioning in a variety of settings. For example, learning to assign the label of car to all appropriate vehicles as opposed to only the family car, or learning to remove caps from all types of jars and bottles as opposed to only those used in training assists in acquiring independence. Activity-based intervention provides caregivers and interventionists many opportunities to target functional skills and to do so in a way that will encourage the generalization of the response to other appropriate conditions.

The primary goal of activity-based intervention is to assist infants and young children in acquiring functional and generalizable skills. This approach is not interested in teaching children to respond to specific cues under specific conditions, but rather, to develop generalized motor, social, self-help, communication, and problem solving skills that will permit independent functioning. Rather than beginning intervention with a tight correspondence between the antecedent and the response, this approach attempts to develop associations between classes of antecedents and classes of responses.   More traditional approaches might begin training on single words by showing a child a set of objects or pictures (e.g., spoon, car, ball). Often specific cues (antecedents) are used to elicit responses; for example, "Tell me what this is. This is a _____." As the child learns the association between the specific antecedents and responses, variations in the antecedents are introduced until the response generalizes across appropriate antecedents. Activity-based intervention uses a different approach. A variety of antecedents are associated with the response, and response variation is encouraged (Stremel-Campbell & Campbell, 1985). In this approach antecedents are seen as classes of events that should be associated with classes of responses as shown below:

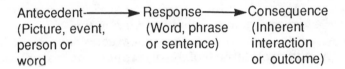

Antecedent⟶ Response⟶ Consequence
(Picture, event,   (Word, phrase   (Inherent
person or   or sentence)   interaction
word   or outcome)

If a child is learning to label objects, personnel using the activity-based approach would employ pictures of cars, varieties of toy cars, real cars, and symbols for cars (e.g., words) to help ensure that the child understands that the label "car" can and does stand for all these exemplars. This procedure helps ensure that the response "car" generalizes to all appropriate exemplars, making the word a functional part of the child's language repertoire.

Summary

The four elements of activity-based intervention blend together to create an approach that can be used in a variety of settings such as home, center, school, store or playground. This approach permits intervention to occur in almost any setting under a wide variety of conditions.

ISSUES ASSOCIATED WITH ACTIVITY-BASED INTERVENTION

A number of issues have been raised concerning the implementation of an activity-based approach. These issues include: adequacy of training in deficit areas, opportunities to practice skills, relevance for children who are severely handicapped, and monitoring change over time.

Adequacy of Training in Deficit Areas

While capitalizing on activities of interest to each particular child may help alleviate the need for extrinsic reinforcement, it raises the question as to whether children will direct themselves to all developmental areas in need of intervention. To expect children to select a broad range of activities that would naturally enhance or expand their current repertoire, especially when some of their identified needs are physically, mentally, or emotionally challenging, may be unrealistic. One of the basic elements of activity-based intervention is the use of child-initiated and directed activities while another element requires the embedding of targeted objectives into these activities. The balance of these elements ensures that while the children are encouraged to initiate and direct the activities, the activities incorporate the major training needs of children and not just those that children preferred.

The second aspect of this approach that helps to ensure that children cannot avoid focusing on important developmental areas is the attention given to the acquisition of functional and generalizable skills. Critical areas of development, which encourage children's growth toward independent functioning, are targets for all children. That does not mean that all children will learn to walk within an activity-based intervention approach, but it does mean that independent mobility is a goal for every child whether mobility is accomplished by foot, using a walker, wheel chair or other augmentative system. Thoughtful and innovative caregivers or interventionists should be able to ensure numerous opportunities for acquisition of critical skills, even for children who actively avoid practicing skills in certain areas.

Activity-based intervention should not be construed as a liaise faire approach in which children solely determine the nature of the activities in which they participate. Activity-based intervention will not produce efficient child change in important areas of development unless the intervention content is driven by children's IEP or IFSP long-range goals and short-term training or treatment objectives. If caregivers and interventionists are aware of the children's educational and therapeutic goals and objectives, then activities that are routine, planned or child-initiated can be directed towards acquisition of the skills specified in those goals and objectives. Using IEP or IFSP goals and objectives to establish intervention content ensures that this approach is not directed by the whims of children but rather by their developmental needs.

It should be acknowledged that when caregivers and interventionists employ activity-based intervention, they may need to be more creative than when using more traditional intervention approaches in order to capitalize on activities that are introduced by and that appeal to young children. For example, when confronted with a child who likes to blow bubbles but does not need practice in blowing, this activity can be used to target a variety of other important skills such as communication, (e.g., requesting bubbles, following directions, using words like blow, pop, more, all gone), social interaction (e.g., taking turns, sharing, playing with peers), and motor areas (e.g., visually tracking bubbles, chasing and popping bubbles, opening and closing the lid on the bubble jar). Most activities that children enjoy can be arranged to practice a wide range of developmental skills. Often using one activity to target many skill areas does not occur because the caregiver or interventionist has not carefully examined the activity to determine all the various training targets that could be woven into a single activity. Discussing the child's needs and designing activities as a team (e.g., caregivers, interventionists, allied health professionals) often results in richer and more diverse training opportunities. With only a little imagination, some trial and error, and the willingness to have fun, activities can be used to target a variety of different skills and skill levels.

Adequate Opportunities to Practice Skills

A second concern often voiced about activity-based intervention is closely associated with the issue of adequacy of training in deficit areas. This concern, again legitimate, speaks to the number of opportunities available to children to practice developing skills if activities are predominantly child-initiated and dispersed throughout the day.

Is the need to practice skills compatible with activity-based intervention? Many children appear to require considerable practice to develop new responses or modify existing responses. Thus during activities, whether child-initiated, routine or planned, thought must be given to the number of opportunities children need for learning target skills. Activity-based intervention can be implemented so that children have ample opportunity to learn and practice new skills. To do this, caregivers or interventionists must give thought to the type of activities needed for practice and, in particular, how to use routine and child-initiated activities for practicing target skills. Encouraging practice of new and learned skills under a variety of conditions and settings has the further advantage of building responses into generalizable skills.

Caregivers or interventionists can learn to weave many opportunities for practicing target skills into routine, planned and child-initiated activities. For example, if a child were learning the names of common objects, there are numerous times throughout the day that the child could work on labeling objects. The caregiver or interventionist would need to look at their daily schedules and determine the potential number of times the child would have to practice object names. If the number seemed insufficient, the caregiver or interventionist could add activities or incorporate additional opportunities that occur during routine activities. For example, at diapering time, which generally occurs several times a day, objects could be hidden behind the child's head. As the child reaches for and grasps the object, the caregiver could ask, "What did you find?" Three or four objects could be hidden several times at each diaper change to provide many opportunities for the child to label objects. This could result in forty-to-fifty responses in addition to other child-initiated or planned activities.

When using activity-based intervention it is essential to analyze child-initiated, routine or planned activities to ensure that children are being given adequate opportunity to practice targeted skills. Providing children the necessary opportunities for practicing emerging skills and maintaining learned skills is possible when employing activity-based intervention.

Severely Handicapped Children

Another important issue is the applicability of activity-based intervention with infants and young children who are severely handicapped. Children who are at-risk or mildly-to-moderately handicapped tend to engage in many more diverse activities than children with more severe handicaps. In addition, children who are less handicapped are often more easily engaged and their attention maintained longer than individuals who are more severely impaired. Finally, children who are less impaired tend to initiate action and respond more frequently than children who are more seriously disabled. In fact, one of the major characteristics of many persons with severe handicaps is their lack of self-initiated activity.

A number of investigators have asked whether the lack of initiation seen in individuals with severe handicaps is inherent in the population or whether behavioral initiations have been systematically extinguished (Guess & Siegel-Causey, 1985; MacDonald, 1989). Most likely the low frequency of initiations by people with severe handicaps is a combination of physiological functioning and training. It may be that changes in early-training approaches could do much to increase the frequency of initiated behavior by many children with severe handicaps.

Social and play interactions provide the foundation for normally developing children to gain more complex social, communication, and object manipulation skills. These interactions are also important for children with severe handicaps. Learning to interact with others provides opportunities to learn from others, to learn to have an effect on others, and more importantly, to learn to initiate interactions with others. Activity-based intervention supports this form of learning by emphasizing the importance of child-directed interactions within daily caregiving routines. Caregivers and interventionists need to carefully observe and respond to children's signals and actions (however minimal) as they happen, and to build on them using logically occurring antecedents and consequences.

Children who are severely handicapped often need structure and careful programming; however, increased attention to enhancing appropriate child-initiated and directed activity (not self-destructive behavior or stereotypes) may result in children with severe handicaps being able to show caregivers or interventionists what they like and what interests them. By capitalizing on activities that are appealing to individual children, the need for extrinsic reinforcers will be reduced as many activities have natural consequences.

Activity plans can be developed which embed targeted objectives in preferred activities and daily routines. The adequacy of training across all deficit areas and the provision of sufficient opportunities for learning to occur does require coordination and planning by all professionals, paraprofessionals, and family members involved in the child's intervention program. Such coordination and planning is especially beneficial for developing functional and generalizable skills for children with severe handicaps.

Monitoring Change Over Time

A final issue of concern is monitoring change in children's behavior over time when employing an activity-based intervention approach. There is no doubt that attempting to determine the systematic impact of training using activity-based intervention is more difficult than employing techniques that use primarily interventionist-directed activities and that present training activities in a massed trial format. Nevertheless, there are strategies for measuring treatment impact using activity-based intervention that can be managed by most caregivers or interventionists.

Given the nature of the intervention approach—that it uses child directed, routine, and planned activities—it is imperative that child progress toward established goals and objectives is monitored. The approach to measurement that we find most practical and yet provides adequate information for making sound treatment decisions is a probe system. When children's program plans are formulated, their long-range goals and associated training or treatment objectives are noted. Objectives are written in behavioral terms, (e.g., the child's response) to ensure progress can be monitored. Accompanying each objective is a list of antecedents that can be embedded in routine, planned, and child-initiated activities. In addition, a variety of activities are suggested that could be used to elicit or practice the skill or skills targeted in the objective. Finally, a data collection plan is specified. In most cases, the data collection entails administering short probe tests to children once or twice per week. To do this, certain times or activities are designated for collecting probe data for each objective. For example, recording two or three trials at the end of an activity in which the child is engaged.

Summary

This section has discussed the major issues or concerns associated with activity-based intervention. It is likely that other problems may be identified as other interventionists employ activity-based intervention; however, it seems equally likely that solutions will be found.

APPLICATION OF ACTIVITY-BASED INTERVENTION

As indicated in Chapter 11, a first step in the intervention process is the determination of IEP or IFSP goals and objectives for children and outcomes for families participating in a program. Once goals and objectives are selected for individual children, activity-based intervention employs three types of activities for meeting established goals and objectives: child-initiated, routine and planned activities.

For most children, caregivers or interventionists will use a combination of these types of activities. There may be a continuum in which some children learn more rapidly using child-initiated activities while others may benefit from using planned activities. It is also possible that initially, some children may need the support of a planned activity for development of certain skills, and then use child-initiated activities for continued practice and maintenance of the skill.

Effective use of this approach in an early intervention center-based or home-based program is dependent on several factors. For a center-based program these factors include a program structure that:

- permits identification of individual child goals and objectives
- ensures adequate intervention time is available for reaching participating children's goals and objectives
- permits staff adequate time to observe children's behavior, determine their interests and plan interventions to meet their needs;
- ensures staff can capitalize on child-initiated, routine and planned activities to provide children sufficient opportunity to acquire and practice target skills
- permits systematic monitoring of child progress
- effective use of this approach in a home-based program is dependent on all of the above factors
- has program staff who are able to assist caregivers in learning how to use routine and child-initiated activities to assist their infant or child in acquiring target skills

Program Structure

Central to the use of activity-based intervention is the embedding of children's educational and therapeutic objectives in a variety of activities. The activities become the framework in which intervention occurs, thus making the development and implementation of activities critical to the learning process. For the most part, activities need to be fun and motivating, making them inherently reinforcing. To be effective, activities should be age and skill-level appropriate.

Well designed activities allow learning to proceed on a variety of different objectives for individual children, or when groups of children are involved, permits learning to occur on a variety of targets appropriate for participating children. Activities that effectively promote learning often require minimal adult direction—the emphasis is on the child producing the behavior and leading the activity as opposed to the adult doing the majority of talking and directing.

For children with special needs some activities may need to be planned to ensure sufficient opportunity for learning target skills. Planned activities tend to be more successful if they are not overly contrived or the instructional intent too obvious. Interventionists who are perceptive observers of human behavior will find that infants and children provide a huge array of discriminable cues about what they find interesting and what they do not.

Individual Program Plans

Prior to planning activities or being able to effectively use routine events or child-initiated actions, interventionists should develop individual program plans for children, whether in a center-based or home-based program.

Each long-range goal and associated training or treatment objective on a child's IEP or IFSP is developed into a program plan like the one shown on Table 12-1. The Program Plan Form describes the long-range goal, the associated objective, and lists more discrete program steps that may be necessary for some children. The section of the plan labeled "antecedents - response - consequences" contains the specific planning for children. Many different methods of providing antecedents are appropriate for activity-based intervention. Inherent in the approach is the use of motivating and reinforcing materials and arranging the environment in ways that facilitate child initiation. Incidental teaching and its variations, time delay and mand-model (Warren & Kaiser, 1988), are useful within the activities for all types of targeted objectives including communication. Techniques described by Fey (1986) as "hybrid approaches," including sabotage, forgetful clinician, and interruption, add variations which often lead to child initiations within activities. Interruption of behavior chains as described by Goetz, Gee and Sailor (1985) is effective with children who are more severely handicapped once routines have been established. The use of joint action routines (Snyder-McLean, Solomonson, McLean & Sack, 1984) is a useful strategy for establishing routines for children within an activity-based intervention model. The sequential ordering of antecedents from most-to-least intrusive is important to ensure children are acquiring independence in their use of targeted skills. Providing a wide range of antecedents as previously noted is one of the methods of planning for generalization within activity-based intervention.

Once a program plan is completed for each objective, the interventionist is ready to begin to capitalize on child-initiated and routine activities and to design planned activities in which objectives or program steps can be embedded.

For home-based programs in which the caregiver(s) are the primary interventionists, designing program plans is also important. These plans are used to assist the caregiver in identifying antecedents which can be incorporated in daily activities to teach their child's targeted objectives. In addition, plans can be used to encourage caregivers to follow and respond to activities initiated by the child by knowing how to use different approaches such as incidental teaching and modeling.

Program Activity Schedules

Use of activity-based intervention does not preclude the need for a schedule of events that are to occur during a specified time. Scheduling is more critical for center-based programs than for home based programs; however, even when services are delivered at home, some scheduling or planning is essential if the caregiver or interventionist is to ensure there are opportunities for working on targeted objectives.

Table 12-2 contains a classroom activity schedule form. For purposes of explanation, four objectives for a specific child, Joey, are listed at the top of the form, with the complete objectives written at the bottom of the form. The schedule of center-based activities is listed on the side. The X's indicate which scheduled activities will likely provide opportunities for learning to occur on the listed objectives. Completing

TABLE 12-1
Individual Program Plan Form

Child: ___Joey_____   **Interventionist:** ___Ms. Jones_____

Initiated:___10 / 2 / 88___   **Expected Completion:**___12 / 2 / 88___   **Completed:**____ / / ____

Domain: Fine Motor [ ]   Gross Motor [ ]   SocCom. [ ]   Cognitive [X]   Social [ ]   Self-Care [ ]

Intervention Setting(s): Small Group [ ]   Large Group [ ]   Individual [ ]   Home [ ]

Long Range Goal: Child will attempt to solve common problems by using different strategies.

Treatment Objective: The child will attempt to solve common problems by using more than one strategy.

Program Steps:

1) When objects are placed out of reach or inside difficult to open containers, child will use a "tool" 3 of 5 opportunities before receiving help from others.

2) When objects are placed out of reach or inside difficult to open containers, child will request help from adult; 3 of 5 opportunities.

3) When objects are placed out of reach or inside difficult to open containers, child will persist in attempts to access objects; 3 of 5 opportunities

Antecedents	Responses	Consequences
- Adult present	- request help	- gets help
- Environment arranged with materials partially obstructed or sabotaged	- child persists	- gets material
- Adult gestures or verbally suggests trying again	- child tries	- gets material
- Adult models	- child imitates	- gets material

Decision rule:
If performance does not improve consistently on each step as indicated by probe data, return to previous program step or modify program step or treatment objective.

TABLE 12-2
An example of a
Program Activity Schedule for a
Center-Based Program

Child: Joey

Classroom: Toddlers

Date: 10 / 89

	Objectives			
Schedule	1). Toilet Training[a]	2). Problem solving[b]	Picture 3). Identification[c]	Vocalization 4).Gesture Response[d]
9:00 Arrival Free Play	X	X	X	X
9:20 Opening Circle	X		X	X
9:30 Small Group #1	X	X	X	X
9:50 Choice, Art Music, Motor	X	X	X	X
10:10 Outside Play	X	X		
10:30 Toileting Self-Care	X			
10:45 Snack	X			X
11:00 Storytime Book Center	X		X	X
11:10 Small Group #2	X	X	X	X
11:30 Choice, Manipulation, Blocks, Sociodramatic	X	X	X	X
11:50 Closing Circle	X		X	X
12:00 Dismissal	X			

X - Indicates which scheduled activities are likely to provide opportunities to work on designated objective.

[a] **Objective 1**: Child will indicate soiled and wet pants and/or diapers by verbalizing/gesturing.

[b] **Objective 2**: Child will attempt to solve common problems by using more than one strategy.

[c] **Objective 3**: Child will locate at least 10 common objects, people, and/or events in familiar pictures when named by another person.

[d] **Objective 4**: Child will respond to simple questions with a vocalization and gesture.

TABLE 12-3
**An example of an
Activity Schedule for a Home**

<u>Treatment Objectives</u>

<u>Home Routine</u>	<u>Grasps Objects</u>	<u>Participates in Social Games</u>
Dressing	offer child one sock or shoe while you put other on [a]	play peek or gotcha
Changing	offer child closed powder, lotion or cream container to grasp	play a tickle game or soo-big
Mealtime/Snack	offer cracker for self-feeding, encourage helping hold bottle	
Clean-up	offer clothe or towel, wait for child to reach and grasp	play patty cake or peek
Car Travel	have toys attached to car seat for child—to encourage independent reaching and grasping	when buckling in car seat—wave bye-bye
Bathtime	see clean-up—have easy-to-grasp toys in tub, add sponges	play favorite games in tub, play games using a mirror
Playtime	have toys available	encourage child to initiate any favorite game
Bedtime		sing good night songs, rock quietly

[a] Indicates suggested activity that may occur during home routine that can be used to work on treatment objective.

such a schedule and having it readily available, assists interventionists in remembering that objectives can be targeted throughout the day. Specific times for data collection can be indicated by circling the X on the schedule.

Similar but more flexible activity schedules can be derived for caregivers in the home or other settings. An example is contained in Table 12-3. Such schedules can help to alert caregivers to the many opportunities for working on skills when engaged in routine, daily activities with the child. The schedule incorporates suggestions of activities for each objective which could be integrated into the daily routine. It is important to not impose a structured daily routine onto a caregiver, but rather, to suggest activities which can be integrated into whatever schedule of events already occurs during the day.

Activity Plans

If a program's structure requires children's participation in group activities, it is essential to develop activity plans. Using the information provided in children's individual program plans, interventionists can design a series of activity plans which will complement child-initiated and routine activities. Incorporating a variety of training or treatment objectives for children with different developmental levels into a common activity can be challenging.

Planning an activity and its sequence is necessary for logically embedding targets for participating children and for ensuring that there will be sufficient repetition for learning to occur. As the activity is written, the interventionist should indicate how the activity will be presented to meet the various targets and children' different developmental levels.

The level of detail for the description is determined by the varying children's needs and the complexity of the activity. Once the plan is written it can be used as a flexible "script." Key words and actions are identified to be sure every possible training opportunity is used to its fullest advantage during the activity and that any individual adaptations or augmentations are planned prior to the activity. In addition to describing the activity, the necessary materials for conducting the activity should be listed. This permits assembling the materials prior to the activity so it can proceed smoothly. The final aspect of writing of the activity is to list possible variations.

Variations should be planned for two reasons. First, variations provide an alternative activity that can be used if children evidence little interest in the original activity. Many variables affect childrens' interest and any well-planned or favorite activity may prove to be unappealing on a particular day. For logistical reasons, alternative activities should not require totally different settings or materials.

A second reason for developing alternative activities is that variations provide more and different opportunities to embed intervention objectives. This provides more practice time which should hasten acquisition. In addition, variations should enhance generalization of the response. If allowed, children often introduce variations into activities themselves. Interventionists often can use these variations in productive and useful ways. A sample activity plan is contained in Table 12-4.

Interdisciplinary Team Activity Planning

Activity-based intervention offers a vehicle for interdisciplinary team involvement in the center or home intervention plan. Given an activity with the potential to embed a variety of child objectives, team members can make contributions to enhance the performance of each involved child. For example, in a sand-play activity the occupational therapist can incorporate some functional practice of wrist rotation for a specific child by suggesting the toys for the sand play be stored in large plastic jars with lids that the children must open to get a toy. Toys, such as shovels and spoons, can also be included for additional practice. The physical therapist could determine optional positioning for motor-

TABLE 12-4
Example Activity Plan

Name of Activity: Water Play   **Written by:** Ms. Cripe   **Date:**   10 / 89

Activity Sequence	Variations	Key Action Key Words	Materials	Evaluation Comments
- Laying the tablecloth out on the floor is the beginning	- Cornmeal or sand can be used instead of water in tubs	tub, water, apron, spoon, cup, tablecloth, sponge, floatie, sifter, pitcher, more, pour, dry hands, want, squeeze, float, stirring, open, sink, splash, hard, soft	tablecloth	
- Children must then request aprons, tubs, water and play items.	- Add food coloring to the water. Bubbles can be made using rotary hand beaters and dish soap.		tubs, aprons, sifters, spoons, cups	
- When children request water, a problem has to be solved. The lid on the pitcher is closed and the water cannot be poured. The children are asked what to do. (Open!)	- Styrofoam pieces in various shapes to float		water	
- Now the water can be poured but only a small amount should be given out so that the children can request "more."	- Beans, corn, rice can be added for color and texture.		pitchers, floaties, sponges, squares and cylinders, towels	
- One toy item is requested at a time. The interventionist can then initiate turn-taking with the children while they play with the water.	- A wading pool can be used for all children to play around in a circle; either inside or outside.			
- Turns can be taken with pouring, stirring, splashing, pushing floaties, or squeezing sponges.				
- Opportunities should also be offered for conversational turn-taking by talking to the children about what you or they are doing.				
- The activity is drawn to a close by requesting the different toy items from the children.				
- The tubs are emptied and collected and the children are asked "What do you need?" (towels)				
- After giving them a towel, ask "What are you doing?" Ask them "What else needs drying?" (tablecloth)				
- The children then help fold the tablecloth and put the materials away on the shelf.				

impaired children to facilitate their active participation. Sand play can occur in tubs placed on a table or on the floor for children with special positioning needs as well as at a sand table which requires prolonged independent standing. The communication specialist can choose toys for the activity which contain children's articulation targets such as cups, cookie cutters, and cans for the child learning to use /k/ at the beginning of words.

Beyond the specific training targets for individual children, the team can work together to enhance the activity for all children. The communication specialist can offer suggestions that will be beneficial for the language development of all the children involved. For example, simply requiring the children to ask for the toys before receiving the jar holding the objects provides everyone with the opportunity to practice requesting and the use of appropriate language forms. Materials can be suggested by the motor specialists which will help all children develop fine and gross motor skills throughout the activity. The psychologist may have suggestions for structuring the activity which help children with behavior problems interact appropriately with their peers by waiting for a turn.

Working together benefits the team as well as the children through the exchange of professional expertise. This approach provides an excellent vehicle for professionals trained in more isolated-therapy models to integrate their specific therapies into functional activities which can occur within planned or routine daily schedule.

Monitoring Child Progress

A form, such as that shown in Table 12-5, may be useful to monitor child progress. The children's objectives to be targeted during the activity are written under the first column. The interventionist can list all the children's objectives or only those that the activity is likely to provide opportunity for practice. Listing all objectives can be useful when variations in the activity occur or when children initiate some action.

The particular events within an activity that provide children the chance to work on the objective are briefly listed in the second column - Opportunities (antecedents). Completing this column helps sensitize interventionists to times when training opportunities might occur as well as encourage active planning of such opportunities.

The third column - Target Behavior (response) - provides a space to define the behavior of interest. The fourth column - Outcome (consequences) - provides space to indicate what should happen following the child's response.

The final columns permit recording the number of times children produce the response correctly and incorrectly. These data can be examined in relationship to the number of opportunities that were available for children to respond during the activity. The Other column permits interventionists to record responses other than those specified in the criteria. For example, the interventionist offers a child two blocks (one big and one small) and asks if the child wants the big or small block. The child responds neither (block) by shaking her head. This is an appropriate response which is neither correct or incorrect, and therefore, should

Child's Name: _____   Date: _____

TABLE 12-5
CHILD PROGRESS MONITORING FORM

Objective	Opportunities (Antecedents)	Target Behavior (Response)	Outcome Consequences	Response			
				Correct+	Incorrect-	Other*	No Response

* Indicates an appropriate response other than the targeted response.

be recorded in the Other column. The last column - No Response - indicates the number of times an opportunity occurs for the child to practice the target response, but the opportunity was not used by the child. For example, if a child had the opportunity to request a needed article but did not (e.g., coat to go outside), this would require the interventionist to mark the No Response column.

Adding across the Correct, Incorrect, Other, and No Response columns will indicate the number of opportunities the child had to produce the target response. This number then can be compared to the number of correct or other type of responses to produce either a ratio or percentage score that can be used to monitor child progress.

Many other forms could be devised to monitor child progress. The format is not important provided that interventionists can collect data efficiently and reliably. When employing activity-based intervention, it is essential to monitor the number of opportunities children are given to learn target objectives. Such information is particularly critical if children are not systematically reaching objectives.

SUMMARY

This chapter presents a description of an approach to early intervention called activity-based intervention. The larger systems approach to early intervention which links assessment, intervention and, evaluation provides the structure and context for the implementation of activity-based intervention.

Activity-based intervention uses child-initiated, routine, and planned activities to assist infants and children in reaching their IEP or IFSP goals and objectives. The essence of the approach is to embed training on objectives in a wide range of activities. The desired outcome for children is the development of functional and generalizable skills across important developmental domains.

References

Bricker, D., & Veltman, M. (in press). Early intervention programs: Child focused approaches. In S. Meisels & J. Shonkoff (Eds.), *Early intervention: A handbook of theory, practice and analysis.* Cambridge, MA: Cambridge University Press.

Brinker, R. (1985). Curricula without recipes: A challenge to teachers and a promise to severely mentally retarded students. In D. Bricker & J. Filler (Eds.), *Severe mental retardation: From theory to practice.* Reston, VA: Council for Exceptional Children.

Brinker, R., & Bricker, D. (1980). Teaching a first language: Building complex structures from simpler components. In J. Hogg & P. Mittler (Eds.), *Advances in mental handicap research*, Vol. 1. Chichester, England: Wiley & Sons.

Fey, M. (1986). *Language intervention with young children.* San Diego, CA: College-Hill Press.

Goetz, L., Gee, K., & Sailor, W. (1985). Using a behavior chain interruption strategy to teach communication skills to students with severe disabilities.   *Journal of the Association for the Severely Handicapped, 10*(1), 21-30.

Guess, D., & Siegel-Causey, E. (1985). Behavior control and education of severely handicapped students: Who's doing what to whom? and why? In D. Bricker & J. Filler (Eds.), *Severe mental retardation: From theory to practice.* Reston, VA: Council for Exceptional Children.

MacDonald, J. (1989). *Becoming partners with children.* San Antonio, TX:.

Odom, S. (1988). Research in early childhood special education. In S. Odom & M. Karnes (Eds.), *Early intervention for infants and children with handicaps.* Baltimore, MD: Paul Brookes.

Stremel-Campbell, K., & Campbell, R. (1985). Training techniques that may facilitate generalization. In S. Warren & A. Rogers-Warren (Eds.), *Teaching functional language.* Baltimore, MD: University Park Press.

Snyder-McLean, L., Solomonson, B., McLean, J., & Sack, S. (1984). Structuring joint action routines: A strategy for facilitating communication and language development in the classroom. *Seminars in Speech and Language, 5*(3), 213-228.

Warren, S., & Kaiser, A. (1988). Research in early language intervention. In S. Odom & M. Karnes (Eds.), *Early intervention for infants and children with handicaps.* Baltimore, MD: Paul Brookes.

13.
Curricular Approaches and Content

The curricular content chosen for a program is of importance to the children, families, and staff. Selection of an appropriate curricular approach requires time and effort. Knowledge of the major differences to be found in various approaches seems essential to adopting curricular materials that are consonant with program goals and individual child objectives. The necessity for linking a program's philosophy, goals, content, intervention strategies, assessment and evaluation procedures has already been discussed in detail in Chapter 9. This chapter addresses some broad issues associated with early intervention curricula and describes the promising approach generally termed curriculum-based assessment. This approach is based on the use of assessment and evaluation tools that are tied directly to an associated curriculum.

Curriculum can be defined as the content of intervention. Although many different curricular approaches are available, each appear to share some important elements: planned activities, systematic presentation sequence, specified treatment or training objectives, and a guiding orientation or theoretical perspective.

Formal curricula are composed of planned activities to be conducted by a caregiver or an interventionist or arranged through environmental engineering. The activities that constitute a curriculum are generally sequenced in some systematic fashion from simple to increasingly more complex. Most curricula contain a number of areas or domains in which activities are hierarchically sequenced within each domain. Most curricular activities have been designed to assist a child in attaining a specific objective or generalized goal. Finally, the content and the nature of the presentation in a curriculum generally reflects the underlying orientation or theoretical persuasion of the curricular approach.

ISSUES SURROUNDING CURRICULAR CONTENT AND APPROACHES

There are several important issues associated with curricular content and approaches used in early intervention programs. These issues include: structure, child-directed versus adult-directed, consequences, generalization, curricular emphasis, and utility.

Structure

The historical roots of early intervention programs for children who are handicapped lie in programs designed for older children and adults. These early programs employed principles derived from the experimental analysis of behavior. Much of the early work was focused on devising educational programs for children who were seriously handicapped and residing in institutional settings.

Residential populations often required rigorous application of behavior modification techniques in order to gain control over the child's behavior before any attempt could be made to introduce an intervention program addressed to the acquisition of new skills. The work and technology derived from focusing on such deviant populations was then transferred to programs for children who were younger and were living at home (Bricker & Carlson, 1981). The application of the operant technology was found effective—that is, interventionists were able to control the children's behavior and assist them in acquiring a variety of skills.

Although the importance of this work should not be underestimated, researchers with more cognitive orientations began wondering about the utility and generalizability of the skills being taught to children under such rigorously controlled and structured regimes. These regimes minimized flexibility and adaptability because children were reinforced for careful adherence to the adult-imposed structure. Variations from specified routines were openly discouraged. Also the technology influenced the curricular content. Specific responses were targeted using task analytic approaches. Little attention was given to how content might overlap across domains or how the child might be assisted to develop generative repertoires that would lead to more complex problem-solving abilities and greater independent functioning. The problem was, of course, not in the behavioral technology but rather the manner in which it was applied.

In large measure, Piaget, his American interpreters, and some psycholinguists (see e.g., the volume edited by Schiefelbusch & Lloyd, 1974) provided the impetus for early interventionists to reconsider the impact of their intervention efforts with at-risk and handicapped populations. These theorists and investigators argued that rather than designing training and treatment efforts around structured individual skill acquisition, early intervention curricular efforts should be guided by sound theoretical frameworks. The theoretical frameworks should generate the content areas to be acquired, the interrelationship between areas, and the developmental sequences within areas. The initial efforts in undertaking such a process were perhaps predictable because many interventionists, as behavioral engineers, operationalized early sensorimotor and communicative behavior into a set of independent skills to be acquired response by response under structured conditions. Again, the child was viewed as a passive receptacle who contributed little to the training enterprise, even though Piaget (1970) had argued for the active involvement by the child in learning about the physical and social environment.

Contemporary views held by interventionists have further moderated or changed curricular approaches. Unfortunately, however, proposed changes are often formulated as a dichotomy which pits the behaviorist and structure against the developmentalist and openness. This dichotomy is unfortunate and does not accurately represent the nature of the disagreement between various curricular approaches (Brinker, 1985).

The polarization of behavioral and developmental positions has not assisted in clarifying issues.

What, then, are the differences between programs which follow structured arrangements of specific antecedents-responses-consequences and programs which rely more on naturally occurring events and arrangements of the environment to provide the necessary antecedents and consequences for effective instruction? The former programs usually can be identified by their carefully structured lesson plan format in which the interventionist's behavior as well as the child's response is specified. Often, it is assumed that programs that do not follow carefully specified sequences are less objective and precise. This, of course, is not necessarily accurate. The objectivity and precision of an intervention program are determined by its implementation. In addition, many assume that less structured approaches do not employ behavioral teaching principles. Again, this is not accurate. All intervention programs use behavioral technology; it is the manner and precision of implementation that varies.

Child-directed versus adult-directed

In curricular approaches where the daily lesson plans are predetermined, the child has little opportunity to affect the curricular content. Other approaches may specify the goals and objectives for the child but leave the implementation to be decided, in part, by events occurring in the environment and the interests of the child (e.g., activity-based intervention). For example, a treatment goal might be to assist the child in using more agent-action-object phrases throughout the day rather than conducting specific drills on a set number of predetermined phrases. The interventionist then uses opportunities that arise during the day to work on this objective. Looking at a book chosen by the child might provide the caregiver or interventionist many opportunities to assist the child in developing and using agent-action-object sequences.

Considerable work is underway in this area. For example, an edited volume describes a number of useful approaches for designing functional communication programs (Warren & Rogers-Warren, 1985). Using these approaches requires careful attention to the daily activities to ensure that each child is receiving adequate training on selected objectives. Often, it is difficult to monitor the amount of time the child has to work on treatment objectives. Successful employment of child-directed approaches requires systematic collection of data on the child's progress toward specific objectives. Programs that employ a specific lesson plan format can use other times of the day to allow the child to select activities and enhance generalization of specific responses. The reverse is also true because programs which generally do not employ specific lessons can use planned instructional regimes when and if desirable.

Consequences

The delivery of consequences is another issue associated with curricular approaches. Some programs focus on reinforcement of the desired response using some form of obvious feedback. Often, this feedback is verbal comments such as "good boy," "that's right," "you did that well," and so on.

If tasks are primarily selected by the adult, the children's motivation may be a consistent problem, and therefore, artificial contingencies may be needed. In programs where the child has more freedom to determine the activities in which the training exercises are embedded, reinforcement is often inherent in the activity (Mahoney & Weller, 1980). For example, searching for a desired toy promotes the concept of object permanence, and finding the toy may provide the reinforcement and subsequent motivation for further searches. It is probably not necessary or useful to tell the child, "good looking" when the child discovers the toy. Pouring juice into a cup provides practice in wrist rotation and self-help skills, and getting to drink the juice may be reward enough to continue to practice the behavior. Conversely, turning uninteresting objects back and forth to practice wrist rotation may require the delivery of some form of verbal praise to keep the child engaged in the training activity. All of us engage in activities and responses that are maintained through artificial contingencies, but much of our behavior is determined by events integrally linked to the activity. If movement towards independence is a major objective, curricular approaches that are overly reliant on artificial consequences may not assist in reaching this objective.

Generalization

Another dimension along which curricula differ is their approach to generalization. Some approaches place an emphasis first on establishing an antecedent-response relationship that is specific and discrete. Once this single-cue-single-response association is developed, the next step becomes generalization of the response to other appropriate exemplars of the class or antecedent events. In such approaches, establishing control over the child's behavior may inadvertently reduce the child's chance for generalization or development of a generative problem-solving strategy. By use of rigid programming, sources of unsystematic variation are reduced, and the child acquires a response as predetermined. Such procedures eliminate or greatly reduce the infusion of variability in the acquisition of new skills and concepts that might significantly enhance generalization of the action or concept over time. Of course, there are individuals so impaired that the acquisition of simple responses may require the development of specific associations between antecedents and responses. However, for most children, the future is far more optimistic, and thus the need, to rethink approaches to assist children in acquiring concepts and responses that lead to dynamic and generative repertoires.

Curricular Emphasis

Historically, the emphasis of early intervention curricula, particularly for preschool-age children, has been on acquiring self-help, motor, speech and "academic" skills. The presumption was that growth in academic areas is required for children's successive placements (Wolery & Brookfield-Norman, 1988). An examination of both curricular and measurement tools used by programs suggests the importance placed on pre-academic skills (see e.g., the *Inventory of Early Development* by Brigance, 1978). Indeed, the instructional format followed by many programs emphasizes an academic focus. That is, little children are required to sit in small groups around tables and work on selected school-like activities. Activities such as "free play" traditionally have been viewed as fillers between legitimate intervention activities.

In spite of Piaget's declarations on the importance of play for the young child, it has taken some relatively recent research to convince many early interventionists of the importance of play for children (Fewell & Kaminski, 1988). A growing body of work suggests that play is the work of little children and during periods of play, children acquire a number of important behaviors, such as appropriate role playing, interactional skills, and how to successfully engage the physical environment. It seems that play allows the young child the freedom to explore, vary, and rearrange without undue restriction or direction from the social environment.

Another area of curricular neglect has been social-communicative development. Early social-communicative exchanges between children and their social environment may serve as an important foundation for the conceptual and more advanced pragmatic structure of later language usage (Bricker & Schiefelbusch, 1984). The importance of acquiring nonacademic, social, and communicative skills to be successful both in school and later life is often underestimated. As MacMillan (1977) and Zigler (1984) report, the reasons that retarded populations fail to adjust to social and vocational environments are often noncognitive factors, such as social skills and personality variables.

Utility

The final curricular issue to be discussed is the usefulness, or functionality, of curricular content for children who are at-risk or handicapped. It is unclear whether early interventionists have consciously or unconsciously avoided the issue of the usefulness of what they attempt to teach infants and young children. For whatever reason, ignoring the usefulness of training or treatment objectives should no longer be tolerated. The usefulness of learned responses for the child underlies other issues of child versus adult-directed activities, consequences, generalization and curricular emphasis. If the responses selected for teaching are functional for the child—that is, functional in that they lead to greater independence and adaptability—then acquiring such responses may be largely child directed and naturally reinforcing. Children appear to strive to master behavior and information that offers means for greater control over their environment.

The usefulness of responses should be an important criterion in determining the content of the intervention program. For example, teaching the child to use a pincer grasp can be done in a variety of activities. Often, interventionists appear to choose having the child pick up small pegs and place them in containers. This might be the activity of choice, if for some reason, this activity is functional for the child. On the other hand, practicing the pincer grasp while picking up Cheerios, raisins, small beads for stringing, turning on light switches, and so on, may be more useful for the child because such responses produce a practical and desirable outcome which more likely enhances the child's independence and adaptability.

Summary

It seems that many administrators, researchers, interventionists, and even parents feel a program cannot be doing its job *if* children are enjoying themselves. The older the children, the more prevalent this attitude. The joy of exploration, invention, and innovation are largely eliminated from the curriculum, and children are required to engage in predetermined activities that may or may not be of interest to them. How unfortunate it is for young children, that highly structured programs are seen by many as programs of excellence, and those programs that permit flexibility, choice, and even some disorganization are viewed as less effective. Such judgements require the careful examination of program objectives. What are or should be the outcomes for children who participate in early intervention programs? Is the acquisition of specific skills paramount to all else? As Guess and Siegel-Causey (1985) ask: Should not children have the right of choice?

Approaches which have no structure or that permit children free rein are not being advocated here. Rather, it is important that program personnel find mechanisms that allow a balance between structure and choice for participating children. It is possible to design a curriculum that capitalizes on the children's motivation. The knowledgeable interventionist can often allow a child to set the pace and the direction and find ways to weave the child's selected educational or treatment targets into those activities. Is it possible to assist children in enhancing their conceptual and behavioral repertoires and still permit them to enjoy the process.

CURRICULUM-BASED ASSESSMENT AND EVALUATION APPROACH

Measurement tools that link assessment with curriculum have been traditionally referred to as curriculum-based assessment; however, when used in the context of a linked assessment, intervention (curriculum) and evaluation system, a more appropriate name is curriculum-based assessment *and* evaluation. In addition, discussions of curriculum-based assessment tend to emphasis the assessment while little attention is paid to the curriculum. In this discussion, curriculum-based assessment will be expanded to include evaluation and the importance of the associated curriculum will be addressed.

According to Bagnato, Neisworth and Capone (1986), curriculum-based assessment (CBA) uses a test-teach-test approach in which children are assessed on goals and objectives to be acquired, given intervention, and then re-assessed on their achievement of these goals and objectives. The re-assessment is, in fact, the evaluation of the child's progress toward the specified targets and is a vital portion of the CBA system.

Use of curriculum-based assessment and evaluation measures enhances program efficiency and accountability, and should result in greater child progress. Interventionists have available a variety of curriculum-based assessment and evaluation materials. Below are some general criteria that can be used for selecting the most useful CBA approach from among them.

Conceptual base

It is important that curricula content be guided by a theoretical sound framework. That framework should suggest the contents to be included and the sequence in which it should be presented. Developmental theory and research have been the most helpful in choosing the domains of behavior to be addressed in a comprehensive curriculum for infants and young children. In addition, developmental theory has assisted in determining the general hierarchically arrangement of the content which composes the domains.

Information provide by developmentalists has been used to establish, in a general sense, a hierarchy of relatively predictable steps (e.g., most children learn to sit up, creep, scoot, or crawl before acquiring mobility in an upright position). These data, in turn, have been used to structure general curricular sequences or materials. However, divergence within these curricular sequences should be expected, particularly for handicapped groups. Developmentally arranged sequences should be used only as general guidelines. Interventionists and caregivers should not expect that all children must necessarily acquire the same behaviors or acquire behaviors in the same pattern to become adaptive adults (e.g., a deaf child may adequately communicate using signs rather than speech). In addition, there are special skills or behaviors that may be essential for some children who are handicapped, that do not necessarily appear in the repertoires of normally developing youngsters (e.g., using augmentative communication systems). Although this reality requires that some nondevelopmental items be included and that all curricular content be adaptable, developmental theory and research still provide early interventionists with the most useful set of general guidelines for selecting curricular domains and sequences.

Comprehensive Content

Many infants and young children identified for early intervention services have an array of problems. Even children who have a specific etiology, such as cerebral palsy, may have communication, cognitive, and social problems in addition to motor disabilities. Consequently, a second criteria for choosing curricula for an early intervention program should be the domains included in the curriculum.

Content generated by developmental theorists, taken in tandem with collective knowledge about young children, suggests that at least seven content domains be included in a curriculum. These domains include: (1) Fine Motor; (2) Gross Motor; (3) Cognitive; (4) Self-Care; (5) Social; (6) Communication: and, (7) pre-academic for older children. It is helpful if the following information is provided for each domain:

1. The parameters of that domain
2. Organization of the domain into systematic, logical groups of hierarchical behaviors

3. Associated long-range goals and training or treatment objectives

4. Suggested training activities

5. Possible "adaptations" for training or treatment objectives for children who would be unable to execute the response in the typical or expected manner

Content Organization

A third criteria is that the curriculum-based assessment and evaluation be organized in a hierarchical manner. This organizational approach permits interventionists to plan and execute assessment, intervention, and evaluation efficiently. Most children will follow general developmental sequences, and therefore, if items and activities are designed in a hierarchical manner, the interventionist can more easily target where to begin training and what the succeeding intervention goals and objectives may be. An example is offered below:

Domain
↓
Strands
↓
Long-Range Goals
↓
Treatment or Training Objectives
↓
Training Activities

Each domain should be composed of several sub-groups or strands which refer to groups of related behaviors. Strands should be arranged hierarchically within a domain from simple to most difficult. Each strand should contain a set of long-range goals also arranged in a hierarchical or developmental sequence. Each long-range goal should have several training or treatment objectives that are arranged from simple to more difficult, with the most difficult objective leading directly to its associated long-range goal. Associated with each objective should be a series of appropriate activities that could potentially be used to assist the child in attaining the objective.

Arrangements and relationships, such as those suggested in the previous example, permits interventionists to see the hierarchical development from the domain to the training activities or the reverse. Having such an organizational system permits training to move to increasingly more difficult concepts or skills in a cohesive and coordinated manner. In addition, such organizational formats lead directly to the development of the IEP or IFSP.

Linking assessment, curriculum and evaluation

A fourth criteria to be considered when choosing a curriculum-based assessment and evaluation system is how well the content and organization permit linking these important components. By definition, CBA coordinates testing and intervention, and thus, the issue becomes the nature of the relationship between the assessment, curriculum and evaluation. As Bagnato, Neisworth and Capone (1986) indicate, not all CBA measures provide equally explicit or direct links to curriculum.

In the organizational format suggested above, the long-range goals, treatment and training objectives should be specified in the curriculum-based assessment and evaluation materials. The specification of the long-range goals and objectives on the assessment tool provide a strong and direct link to the development of the IEP or IFSP. That is, the IEP or IFSP can be developed directly from the assessment.

The direct relationship between the IEP or IFSP goals and objectives and the curricular training materials ensures a strong link between the IEP or IFSPs and the daily or weekly intervention activities. Finally, evaluation of the child's progress should be conducted by noting the progress toward selected IEP or IFSP targets. The clearer and more direct the ties between the assessment, the development of goals, the selection of curricular activities and evaluation of progress, the more useful interventionists will likely find the curriculum-based assessment and evaluation system.

Curricular focus

Flexible and useful curriculum-based assessment and evaluation materials should formulate their long-range goals and treatment or training objectives as conceptual or response classes, rather than as singular, specific responses. That is, the long-range goals and treatment objectives should be generic as opposed to specific. Most essential behaviors can and should be generalized conceptual or response classes that are both elicited by, and performed across, a variety of settings and conditions. For example, the demonstration of means-ends behavior should occur whenever the child is faced with a problem that necessitates the use of a person or object as a tool to attain a desired end, such as pulling a napkin to obtain a cookie, tugging on a string attached to a desired toy, turning a faucet to obtain water, or vocalizing and pointing for the adult to retrieve a dropped toy. Although the infant's response differs, the effect is the same—the use of some tool (broadly defined) to attain a desired end. The specific form is important only as an index of the infant's general problem-solving scheme as shown in the diagram below.

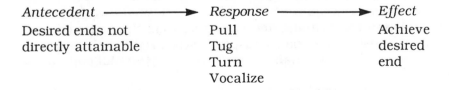

Antecedent ⟶	*Response* ⟶	*Effect*
Desired ends not	Pull	Achieve
directly attainable	Tug	desired
	Turn	end
	Vocalize	

In terms of conceptual classes, a similar situation exists for the infant or child in the sense that generally the desired outcome is the appropriate response to the indicated salient feature across stimuli rather than the establishment of one-to-one correspondences.   For example, to have a functional concept, children must identify a wide array of phenomena as cars. The child must be able to extract the salient features of "carness" in order to produce and understand the word appropriately under a seemingly infinite set of changing conditions.   The extraction of the essential features builds for the infant a conceptual class as indicated in the diagram.

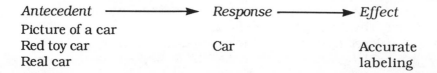

Antecedent ⟶ *Response* ⟶ *Effect*
Picture of a car
Red toy car   Car   Accurate
Real car   labeling

The goal should be to develop assessment and curriculum targets that are written in broad and functional terms.   Therefore, an objective that is focusing on prehension should be written as:

> "The child places and releases an object in a controlled fashion: onto a flat surface; into a container; and balanced on top of another object."

> Rather than, "The child puts pegs in the peg board." or "Builds a tower of 2 cubes."

The form of the assessment and curricular items should allow for maximum flexibility to take advantage of environmental variability and children's motivation.   In addition, the generic formulation of goals and objectives as response classes leads to the subsequent development of essential programming targets with important outcomes: for example, using the pincer grasp, not the placement of pegs in a board.

Adaptations

While using developmental hierarchies as general guidelines is recommended, there will be children who will require variations from proposed sequences and content.   Since these variation may require adaptations in assessment and curriculum materials, a sixth criteria to use in selecting materials is their adaptability.

Adaptations are changes in assessment or curricular materials to accommodate a child's particular handicapping condition(s).   Adaptations are not intended to change the difficulty of the item or activity. Functional equivalence, however, may not always be the same as developmental equivalence or equivalence in task difficulty. If the child must receive information through an alternate rather than the preferred sensory modality, or use an alternative response system, the problem posed to the child may be functionally more demanding or difficult in its adapted form.

There are three general classes of possible adaptations. First, there can be changes in the *stimulus presentation* for children whose handicapping condition interferes with the reception of the standard target's directions or cues. An example of such adaptation is the presentation of an object-permanence task to a child who is visually impaired. The stimulus presentation for this child may involve the use of auditory and tactual cues in place of visual ones. This is also an instance where the adaptation maintains functional equivalence (success is still defined in terms of retrieval of a perceptually absent object) but the tasks are not developmentally equivalent.

A second class of adaptations involves variation in the *acceptable response* for children whose handicapping condition interferes with production of the preferred response. An example of a situation that requires this kind of adaptation occurs in a child whose handicap includes oral-motor movement. The child's handicap precludes ordinary speech production, so manual signing may become an acceptable response.

The third kind of adaptation is simply a *combination* of the two previous classes. Both stimulus presentation and acceptable response must be modified because the child's handicap or handicaps interfere with both reception and production. An example of a situation requiring this dual adaptation may occur with a child who is hearing impaired and who must be presented linguistic information visually (e.g., with signs) and may only be able to respond manually. This third class of adaptations is in many cases the most difficult to make, since neither stimulus presentation nor response occur in the standard format.

Curriculum-based assessment and evaluation systems that need to be used across a broad range of children should provide options for adaptation of items and activities. The more generic the items, generally the more easily adaptations can be made by interventionists and caregivers.

COMPREHENSIVE CURRICULUM-BASED ASSESSMENT AND EVALUATION MATERIALS

The number of curriculum-based assessment and evaluation materials continues to grow. A list of available materials is contained at the end of this chapter. Interventionists would benefit from becoming familiar with these curriculum-assessment packages and comparing them against the criteria discussed above. Each of these packages have strengths and weaknesses, and the potential user is advised to explore these factors before selecting a particular approach.

SUMMARY

Issues associated with curriculum for early intervention populations have been addressed in this chapter. In addition, several criteria for selection of curriculum-based assessment and evaluation materials were suggested. Approaches that are most useful to interventionists and caregivers have a sound conceptual base, are comprehensive, have a hierarchical organization, support the linking of program components, have items and activities with a generic focus, and assist the user in making adaptations. A number of curriculum-based assessment and evaluation approaches and materials are available. The names, addresses and a brief description of selected curriculum-based assessment and evaluation materials are contained in Table 13-1. In addition, the following resources review early intervention curricula:

Bagnato, S., Neisworth, J., & Capone, A. (1986). Curriculum-based assessment for the young exceptional child: Rationale and review. *Topics in Early Childhood Special Education, 6*(2),97-110.

Bailey, D., Jens, K., & Johnson, N. (1983). Curricula for handicapped infants. In S. Garwood & R. Fewell (Eds.), *Educating handicapped infants*. Rockville, MD: Aspen.

Notari, A., Slentz, K., & Bricker, D. (in press). Assessment-curriculum systems for early childhood special education. In R. Brown & D. Mitchell (Eds.), *Early intervention for disabled and at-risk infants*. London: Croom Helm.

Robinson, C., Davey, K., & Esterling, L. (1982). *A Review and Catalog of Early Childhood Special Education Resources*. Omaha, NE: Meyers Children's Rehabilitation Institute, University of Nebraska Medical Center.

TABLE 13-1
Curriculum-Based Assessment and Evaluation Materials

Name and Author(s)	Components	Developmental Age Range	Domains
1. *Arizona Basic Assessment and Curriculum for Young Children with Special Needs (ABACUS)*; J.M. McCarthy, K.A. Lund, C.S. Bos & J. Glattke; Denver, CO: Love, 1986.	Screening Assessment manual Communication Sample Scoring Booklet Curriculum Parent Involvement and Home Teaching Manual Evaluation Manual	2 to 5 1/2 years	Body management Self-Care Communication Pre-academic Specialization
2. *Battelle Developmental Inventory*; J. Newborg, J.B. Stock, L. Wnek, J. Guidubaldi & J. Svinicki; Allen, TX: DLM Teaching Resources, 1984.	Assessment manual Scoring booklet Profile Screening test Testing cards	Birth to 8 years	Personal-Social Adaptive motor Communication Cognitive
3. *Brigance Diagnostic Inventory of Early Development*; A. Brigance; North Billerica, MA: Curriculum Assoc., 1978.	Assessment manual Scoring booklets Graphs Materials (pictures)	Birth to 6 years	Psychomotor Self-Help Speech & Language General knowledge and comprehension Early academic
4. *The Carolina Curriculum for Handicapped Infants and Infants At Risk*; N. Johnson-Martin, K. Jens & S.H. Attenmeier; Baltimore, MD: Brookes Publ., 1986.	Checklist Curriculum Individual activity sheets Progress Chart	Birth to 24 months	Cognition Communication- Language Social Self-Help Fine Motor Gross Motor

TABLE 13-1 [Continued]
Curriculum-Based Assessment and Evaluation Materials

Name and Author(s)	Components	Developmental Age Range	Domains
5. *Developmental Programming for Infants and Young Children-Early Intervention Developmental Programming and Profile* (Revised version); D.S. Schafer & M.S. Moersch (Eds.); Ann Arbor, MI: Univ. of Michigan Press, 1981.	Assessment manual Test booklet Stimulation activities	Birth to 36 months	Perceptual/Fine Motor Cognition Language Social-Emotional Self-Care Gross Motor
6. *Preschool Developmental Profile*; D.B. D'Eugenio & M.S. Moersch (Eds.); Ann Arbor, MI: Univ. of Michigan Press, 1981.	Assessment manual Test booklet Picture cards	3 to 6 years	Perceptual/Fine Motor Cognition Language Social-Emotional Self-Care Gross Motor
7. *Evaluation and Programming System (EPS)*; D. Bricker, D. Gentry & E. Bailey; Eugene, OR: Univ. of Oregon, 1985.	Assessment Manual Recording Form Parent Form Curriculum Computer Software	Birth to 3 years	Fine Motor Gross Motor Self-Care Cognitive Social-Communication Social
8. *The Portage Guide to Early Education*; A. Bluma, M. Shearer, A. Frohman & J. Hilliard; Portage, WI: The Portage Project, CESA, 1976.	Checklist Activity Cards	Birth to 6 years	Infant Stimulation Specialization Language Motor Self-Help Cognition
9. *Vineland Adaptive Behavior Scales*; S.S. Sparrow, D.A. Balla & D.V. Cicchetti; Circles Pines, MN: American Guidance Service, 1964.	Expanded Form Survey Form Classroom Form Computer Software Cassette Training Tape (English & Spanish)	Birth to 18 years	Communication Daily Living Skills Socialization Motor skills Maladaptive Behavior
10. *Hi Comp Curriculum*; S. Willoughby-Herb & J. Neisworth; San Antonio, TX: Psychological Corp., 1983.	Assessment Curriculum	Birth to 5 years	Communication Self-Care Motor Problem solving

References

Bagnato, S., Neisworth, J., & Capone, A. (1986). Curriculum-based assessment for the young exceptional child. *Topics in Early Childhood Special Education, 6*(2), 97-110.

Bricker, D., & Carlson, L. (1981). Issues in early language intervention. In R. Schiefelbusch & D. Bricker (Eds.), *Early language: Acquisition and intervention*. Baltimore, MD: University Park Press.

Bricker, D., & Schiefelbusch, R. (1984). Infants at risk. In L. McCormick & R. Schiefelbusch (Eds.), *Early language intervention*. Columbus, OH: Charles E. Merrill.

Brigance, A. (1978). *Inventory of early development*. North Billerica, MA: Curriculum Associates.

Brinker, R. (1985). Curricula without recipes: A challenge to teachers and a promise to severely mentally retarded students. In D. Bricker & J. Filler (Eds.), *The severely mentally retarded: From research to practice*. Reston, VA: The Council for Exceptional Children.

Fewell, R. & Kaminski, R. (1988). Play skills development and instruction for young children with handicaps. In S. Odom & M. Karnes (Eds.), *Early intervention for infants and children with handicaps*. Baltimore, MD: Paul Brookes.

Guess, D., & Siegel-Causey, E. (1985). Behavioral control and education of severely handicapped students: Who's doing what to whom? And why? In D. Bricker & J. Filler (Eds.), *The severely mentally retarded: From research to practice*. Reston, VA: The Council for Exceptional Children.

MacMillan, D. (1977). *Mental retardation in school and society*. Boston, MA: Little, Brown & Co.

Mahoney, G., & Weller, E. (1980). An ecological approach to language intervention. In D. Bricker (Ed.), *A resource book on language intervention with children*. San Francisco: Jossey-Bass.

Piaget, J. (1970). Piaget's theory. In P. Mussen (Ed.), *Carmichael's manual of child psychology* (Vol. 1). New York: Wiley & Sons.

Schiefelbusch, R., & Lloyd, L. (Eds.). (1974). *Language perspectives: Acquisition, retardation and intervention*. Baltimore, MD: University Park Press.

Warren, S., & Rogers-Warren, A. (Eds.) (1985). *Teaching functional language*. Baltimore, MD: University Park Press.

Wolery, M., & Brookfield-Norman, J. (1988). (Pre)Academic instruction for handicapped preschool children. In S. Odom & M. Karnes (Eds.), *Early intervention for infants and children with handicaps*. Baltimore, MD: Paul Brookes.

Zigler, E. (1984). A developmental theory on mental retardation. In B. Blatt & R. Morris (Eds.), *Perspectives in special education: Personal orientations*. Glenview, IL: Scott, Foresman & Co.

14.
Environmental
Engineering

While the focus of Chapter 13 is primarily on the content of intervention, this chapter is aimed at suggesting how to arrange and use elements of the physical and social environment to enhance learning. As such, it may be useful to view this chapter as the reciprocal of Chapter 13. Intervention content and the strategies employed to present that content should be complementary. Rather than restrict this chapter to a discussion of intervention techniques, the larger context of environmental engineering will be adopted.

In the present context, environmental engineering refers to the management of the environment's physical and social attributes to efficiently assist children in acquiring and using targeted skills and information. In particular, the following areas are addressed: use of physical space and equipment, management of staff, implementation of intervention strategies, and use of other children as change agents.

As a number of writers have noted (for example, Rogers-Warren, 1982), little empirical work has been conducted to determine the environmental elements that are essential for effective learning or how to deploy those elements with at-risk or handicapped populations less than five years of age. State and federal regulations specify health and safety features of environments that house young children, but rarely do such regulations describe the elements that are appropriate or useful in providing enriching contexts for children to play and learn. Most personnel who provide services for infants and young children are forced to resort to their experiential backgrounds or anecdotal reports from colleagues as to what approaches or strategies have been successful. Thus, it may not be surprising that current home and center-based programs pay little, if any, attention to the arrangement of the physical and social environments to assist in the intervention effort. The field of early intervention is in need of well-controlled investigations to determine the impact of various environmental elements.

Before discussing how to manage physical and social elements of the environment, three caveats should be acknowledged. First, it is unlikely that the "goodness" or "badness" of environmental arrangements can be determined using an absolute scale. Rather, the appropriateness is determined within the context of program goals and goals established for individual children and families. Program resources and other relevant variables (e.g., facilities) may also need consideration. Consequently, suggestions for environmental engineering strategies are offered as general guidelines that require individualization prior to their application.

A second caveat is that the environment should be seen as a dynamic interrelationship of social and physical elements. Changes in one set of elements may require adjustment in other elements. Remembering the dynamic nature of the environment should assist in instigating and accommodating change and adjustment.

Third, programs should be conducted in locations reasonably free from confusion, disorganization and intense, uncontrolled stimulation (Bailey & Wolery, 1984). Experience suggests that infants and young children can become distressed when the noise and confusion exceed their ability to filter out extraneous incoming stimulation. Observation of the general arousal state of children should determine whether the environmental stimulation is too intense (e.g., high levels of noise and movement by children and adults). Of course, it is also possible for the environment to become too muted and static, which also may be counterproductive. The young child who is handicapped should learn to adapt to more typical settings, which often are laced with noise and confusion. Learning to cope with such environments is necessary if the child is to have the opportunity to experience a broad range of settings and activities. Maintaining a training setting that is overly quiet, isolated, or unchanging may not enhance the child's ability to cope with a broad range of alternative environments.

As indicated, the location of the intervention environment can be the home, center, playground or elsewhere. The critical attribute of the environment is that the surroundings be arranged to consistently demand more from the child. Thus, the environmental engineering strategies suggested below should be seen as relevant to *all* of the child's surroundings.

USE OF PHYSICAL SPACE AND EQUIPMENT

Preschool environments for preschool-age children who are handicapped have often been described as cold, barren, and uninteresting (Olds, 1979). In fact, a study reported by Bailey, Clifford and Harms (1982) suggests that programs for children who are handicapped do differ from programs for nonhandicapped preschoolers. The nature of the reported differences suggests that a less "rich" environmental context is generally provided for children who are handicapped. Because children who are handicapped often have attention and learning problems, interventionists may believe that less stimulating environments—in the sense of fewer distractions—are preferred.

Focusing solely on the richness or stimulating value of the physical environment will not provide all the necessary information on the adequacy of an environment. The most important analysis should be based on the needs of the children and families that can be met within the context of program resources. Determination of the number of pictures, the variety of colors, or the placement of toys should not be done apart from the established program goals and IEP or IFSP goals for individual children and families.

Physical Space

Systematic observation of center programs and home environments—particularly areas where children play—strongly suggests that too little thought is given to the physical arrangement of furniture and pieces of equipment that constitute the infant's or child's world. Observation of center programs and homes often indicates no apparent planning of the physical environment or organization from the perspectives of efficiency, practicality, accessibility, and promotion of independence.

Efficiency. Environmental arrangements that enhance efficiency are often more pertinent for the caregiver or interventionist than for the child. Efficiency suggests that the physical space is arranged to make completion of tasks and activities smooth, easy, and quick. If art materials are stored some distance from where art activities are conducted, the interventionist may have to make many trips back and forth between storage and activity areas. Time spent bringing materials to the table where children are working on an art activity lessens instructional time with the children. A mother who must retrieve a dry diaper from a cabinet located away from the changing area or bathroom may expend valuable time moving back and forth between areas and run the risk of the child becoming injured during her absence. A study of the physical set-up can generate valuable information for arranging the environment to permit maximum efficiency in conducting the daily activities in which caregivers and interventionists engage.

Accessibility. Accessibility may often be an inherent aspect of efficiency; however, in some cases, the caregiver or interventionist may need to consider accessibility to equipment, materials, and the physical environment separately. A piece of equipment may be strategically located, yet inaccessible. For example, if small toys are dumped into a toy box rather than placed side by side on a shelf, the accessibility may be limited for young children with limited motor or cognitive skills. Retrieving a toy from the box may require motor skills or understanding of object permanence unavailable to the children. The adult may also have to spend needless time searching through the jumbled toy box in an effort to locate specific items. Cubbies for children may be appropriately located beside the door, but may be too high for use by small children. Lack of access may require that the adult retrieve the children's coats for each outdoor excursion. Requiring the adult to retrieve coats reduces the child's opportunity to learn and practice important self-help skills, and uses valuable adult time in a nonproductive manner.

Practicality. Practicality refers to using space and equipment in a manner that is useful for the child. For example, having a rocking horse available that children with physically impairments cannot access is not functional. Providing foam mats—although perhaps not as attractive as the rocking horse—for the physically disabled child may permit the child freedom of movement not otherwise possible. Picture books that lack haptic variety may not be particularly functional for visually impaired children, and toys that produce quiet sounds may not be functional for hearing impaired children. Toys with many small pieces that require considerable hand-eye coordination are generally not practical or safe for infants. Objects that are easy to grasp and maneuver are more functional and appropriate for infants who are developing grasping and manipulative skills.

Independence. The final general aspect to consider in arranging the physical environment is whether the arrangement assists in promoting independent functioning. If most objects and toys are not within a child's reach, the child must depend on adults or older children to obtain a desired object. Independent hand washing and toileting can be enhanced by placement of a sturdy stool that permits the child access to the sink and toilet without assistance. Materials placed at the child's level encourage self-selection and also allow the child to put materials away. Any arrangement that promotes independent functioning, even for the child with the most severe handicaps, should be encouraged.

Equipment

Equipment is the second aspect of the physical environment to be considered. Considerations should focus on safety, durability, flexibility, functionality, and the equipment's usefulness in arousing active participation from children. Selection of equipment should be determined by the nature of the population being served. The importance of safety and durability is self-evident; however, flexibility and functionality need further explanation. As a rule, the greater the number of different activities that a piece of equipment can be used for, the more satisfactory it is. Perhaps that is why so many classrooms have balls which bounce, roll, float, can be chewed, squeezed, or placed in containers. Learning to do a variety of activities with the same object promotes testing and exploratory behavior in young children—skills to be encouraged. Functionality refers to the equipment's capacity to assist the child in acquiring responses that will be useful in other environments; for example, use of a real telephone.

Equipment that elicits continued active participation by the child is clearly preferable to items that merely require activation and watching. Piaget (1970) contends that young children acquire their knowledge of the environment through active manipulation. When possible, it is essential for children to be actively engaged in their surroundings (Bailey & Wolery, 1984).

Equipment can be either general or specialized. General refers to items such as tables, chairs, small manipulables, climbing apparatus, and the like, that are found in most programs for young children. Specialized equipment refers to specific items essential to encourage more effective functioning of individual children. Often, the addition of some special equipment will make it possible for a child to execute a skill he could not otherwise perform (Campbell, Green, & Carlson, 1977). For example, the addition of a small wooden peg to the tray of his high chair allowed one young spastic child the stability to learn to feed himself. The child would grasp the peg with the left hand, pulling himself forward which allowed a flexed position that provided his upper torso with the additional stability required to feed himself with the right hand (Banerdt & Bricker, 1978). For more specific information on how toys and equipment can influence children's behavior, see Ross, 1982; Quiltich and Risley, 1973; and Day, 1983.

Arranging the Space and Equipment

The introductory section of this chapter was intended to provide some general guidelines to consider when arranging the physical and social environment. These guidelines are meant to serve as a foundation for the development of a systematic strategy to organize the environment to facilitate children's growth and development and to assist family members in acquiring targeted skills. The strategy suggested to organize and use physical space and equipment is composed of four steps: (1) develop goals; (2) devise a plan to meet the goals; (3) implement the plan; and (4) evaluate its effectiveness in meeting the established goals.

Develop Goals. A consistent theme throughout this book has been the need to develop goals and objectives for the program and participating children and families. The effective use of space and equipment requires the development of goals and objectives.

These goals should lead naturally from and be consistent with the program goals and the individual IEP or IFSP goals developed for participating children and families. If a program goal is to enhance communicative development in participating children, then the physical environment should be arranged to engage the children in communicative behavior. The equipment should also be purchased and used to encourage communication. Thus, the personnel operating a center-based program should give careful consideration to program and individual child goals when arranging the environment. Likewise, home interventionists should assist caregivers in arranging the environment, whenever possible, to assist in meeting the IEP or IFSP goals established for their child.

Devise a Plan. Given a set of operationalized goals and objectives, caregivers and interventionists are ready to devise a plan that will organize the physical space and available equipment to facilitate attainment of established goals. In devising a plan, personnel should remember the general features of efficiency, accessibility, practicality, and promoting independence. Space should be arranged to ensure these features are an integral part of the environmental arrangements. If a program goal is to enhance independent mobility for children who are severely motorically impaired, then a plan should be devised that is responsive to that goal. Adequate space should be available for children to practice their mobility skills, and support should be available for those youngsters who require assistance in moving about. If a goal for an infant in a home program is to enhance his concept of means-ends and object permanence, the caregivers should be encouraged to place toys and other desired objects *out* of their child's reach. The child can be then encouraged to develop skills to search for and obtain out-of-reach items.

Implement the Plan.   If an interventionist invests time in developing goals and devising plans for reaching established goals, the manner in which space and equipment are arranged will be done with cohesiveness and purpose. The arrangement of space shown in Figure 14-1 illustrates a design that takes into account the need for efficiency, accessibility, practicality, and independence.

In this design, the children's cubbies are located next to the entry door. Upon entry, children can immediately remove their wraps and stow their possessions in the appropriate cubby. Adjacent to the cubbies, but separated by low shelves appropriate to the height of the children, is an area designated for free play. Children should be able to freely access this area and play with toys located in this space. The shelves act as boundaries that help protect the children from those choosing to engage in activities appropriate to the large muscle activity area. On the other side of the free play area, separated by low shelves, is a designated quiet area. Children can look at books or engage in quiet activities in this area. Rugs and pillows should be available in this area. Next to the quiet area is an area that can be used for large-group activities. A blackboard and record player can be kept in this area. Adjacent to the large-group area is a section where small-group or individual activities can be conducted. This area is separated by medium-height cloth barriers that help protect the children from outside distractions but still enable the interventionist to see the rest of the classroom. There is a specific area for snacks which contains tables with appropriately sized chairs. The snack area is next to the bathroom.

Although the arrangement shown in Figure 14-1 may not be suitable for some programs, it does represent a well-designed plan for the following reasons. It is efficiently arranged because each area has adequate shelf space to store relevant and needed materials so that they are accessible. It is also efficient because the cubbies are situated close to the entry and exit ways, and the bathroom is near the snack area. This layout is arranged so that all areas are accessible to the staff and the children, and the cubbies and storage shelves are accessible to the children. In addition, the layout is practical because it permits easy movement from area to area, the staff can monitor children's activities throughout the room because no visual barriers exist, and the physical boundaries (e.g., shelves) help the children make discriminations about the match between activities and areas. This design fosters independence because the spacial arrangement provides the children with adequate structure for conducting activities in the appropriate areas. Finally, the accessibility of equipment and materials enhances the children's ability to engage in independent activities as appropriate.

Evaluation.   As with intervention programs, the determination of the effectiveness of environmental arrangements should be accomplished through objective evaluation procedure. Carta, Sainato, and Greenwood (1988) have devised an ecological assessment system that can be used to

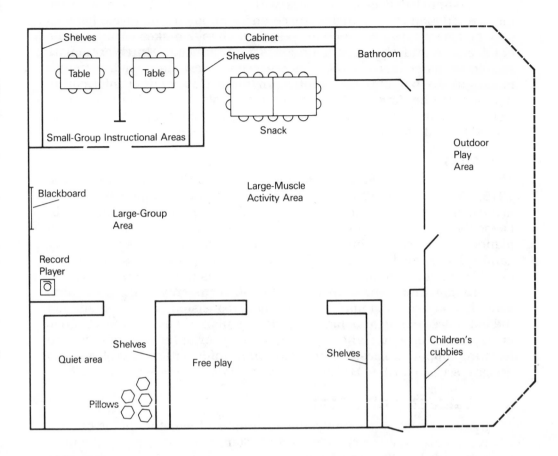

FIGURE 14-1. Classroom floor plan.

examine dynamic as well as static aspects of intervention programs. This system can be used to obtain a variety of information that can be used to evaluate ecological aspects (e.g.,time spent in various activities, type of materials, and equipment used) of the program. Collecting in-depth information on the effectiveness of the use of space and equipment across extended periods may exceed the resources of many intervention programs. However, most interventionists should be able to design a simple strategy for determining if the arrangement of space and equipment is producing the desired outcomes. It may be useful to have a staff member or caregiver observe certain child behaviors to ascertain if the arrangement is having the desired impact. For example, if a goal is communication between nonhandicapped children and children who are handicapped, observation of the number of contacts occurring after changing some aspects of the physical environment may be in order. The staff may choose to undertake some other systematic changes to see which physical arrangement produces greater interaction between the two groups of children.

Personnel delivering services within the child's home may have more restrictions in arranging space and equipment; however, families may be agreeable to some change, if such change makes caring for the child easier and the child's progress is enhanced. Interventionists should be as concerned with finding ways to evaluate environmental factors in the home as in a center program. Collection of information may have to be done on a more informal basis, but evaluation of how well the home environment is supporting the child and family goals should be undertaken.

Summary

There are those who believe "the environment is the curriculum" (Olds, 1979). The position advocated in this section of the chapter is that the arrangement of space and the type of available equipment are important elements of an intervention program. These elements can be used in a planned and purposeful manner to enhance learning in children, or they can be disregarded. Doing the latter eliminates a powerful set of factors capable of aiding the intervention staff as well as the learners.

To maximize the impact of the physical environment, a plan should be devised and implemented that is consistent with program and individualized child and family goals. A plan promotes the effective arrangement of space and equipment that can optimize teaching and learning opportunities. For additional information on classroom designs, see Olds, 1979; Bailey and Wolery, 1984, Rogers-Warren, 1982.

MANAGEMENT OF STAFF

A paramount goal is to arrange the environment, whether home or elsewhere, to maximize the caregiver's and interventionist's teaching opportunities and the child's and family's learning opportunities. The more opportunities to instruct and learn that are available, the more likely the child and other family members will progress toward established goals. An important requisite to developing the necessary learning opportunities is sound management of the intervention staff's time and resources. Much of a staff's expertise can be wasted if systems are not devised and executed for the utilization of that expertise. Time spent in designing a plan for how to use the staff is essential to a well-run and effective intervention program.

Center Programs

A plan for the use of center-based personnel should contain three elements: schedules for staff for intervention activities, schedules for transition periods, and contingency plans for unexpected events.

Intervention Activities Schedule.   Scheduling does not mean that a staff member is assigned to opening group from 9:00 to 9:15 and to an activity group from 9:15 to 9:45. Rather, each staff member should have a regular assignment schedule that indicates his or her role and responsibilities in the various program activities. For example, during opening group, John's assignment is to lead the group in singing songs and other relevant group activities. Inherent in this assignment are organizing the opening-group activities to include the children, caregivers, and staff; ensuring each staff member understands and executes his or her assigned responsibility; selecting appropriate activities; assembling the necessary equipment and ensuring that it functions properly; monitoring the children's participation; evaluating the activity; and adjusting the activity based on evaluative feedback.

After opening the group, John is responsible for children assigned to a small-group activity focused on enhancing communication and problem solving. Responsibilities for this activity would include: selecting activities which appropriately target the communicative and problem solving goals of the participating children; assembling the necessary equipment and materials and having them accessible to the children; selecting appealing strategies for presentation of the materials; ensuring that all children participate in ways that permit them to gain new skills and practice acquired responses; managing the children's behavior so that the activities can occur without disruption; evaluating the effectiveness of the activities and the children's progress; and, adjusting activities as indicated by the evaluative feedback. If each staff member carefully designs his or her activities throughout the day with an eye toward comprehensive organization and responsibility, then the probability exists that the effectiveness of the intervention is maximized. To properly execute the selected activities with the children requires preplanning that considers all relevant variables. In the process of planning, staff should also consider variations in activities that may be introduced by the children and how to use such variations to work on targeted goals and objectives.

In assigning activities to staff members, at least two options are available. Staff members can be assigned a specific group of children for whom they are responsible. Using such a system means the staff member moves with the children as they change activities throughout the day. This approach permits maximum familiarity with the children and their respective goals and may allow the interventionist to use many opportunities throughout the day to build and expand the children's repertoires. The major drawback may be children's more limited access to others. Interacting with a variety of people can help children generalize skills and learn to cope with variability.

An alternative strategy is to assign staff members a particular part of the room and specific activities. This plan permits the children more chance to interact with a variety of staff members. It may provide the staff members more variety as well. However, the staff members are required to be familiar with the goals of many more children and thus may not be as attuned to individual children's needs. The plan chosen should reflect the goals and resources of the program. Often, trying both procedures will result in a final plan that incorporates aspects of each approach.

Transition Schedules. In addition to designing a schedule for the various activities, it is essential to plan for transition points during the day. Often, when children are required to move from one activity to another, learning time is lost and considerable confusion occurs. Children may wander away, remove toys from designated areas, or engage in nonproductive activities, and other confusion may result. Problems arise during transitions because program personnel do not spend adequate time in planning for efficient, effective, and functional movement of children from activity to activity. Again, staff should be assigned specific responsibilities and develop strategies (e.g., cues to alert children that it is time to change activities) to ensure that transitions become times that are productive for children and staff.

Unexpected Events.   The advent of unexpected events requires staff to develop contingency plans for such occurrences. At least three types of contingency plans should be developed. First, plans to cover times when an activity for a child or a group of children is being particularly effective and the interventionist would like to continue the activity. In such cases, staff members should have developed some means to communicate with each other and implement an alternative plan for other, noninvolved children until the activity is completed. Second, the reverse may occur because a selected activity may be unsuccessful for some reason. Thus, staff members should have an alternative plan available to replace the planned activity for that day. Finally, emergencies may occur which require the temporary absence of a staff member. Plans developed for such occurrences should be familiar to all staff members. Planning for unexpected events by staff can often keep potentially disruptive events from negatively affecting the program's operation or, in some cases, can turn these events into meaningful learning opportunities for children.

Home Programs

The need for plans to assist home interventionists in organizing their visits may appear less necessary, but it is the illusion of the relaxed, informal "visit" that most jeopardizes effectiveness. Without consideration of the interventionist's time during the home visit, goals and objectives may not be attended to from visit to visit. Thus, the interventionist should carefully plan the activities to be conducted, assemble the necessary materials and equipment, and develop procedures for implementation and evaluation. In most cases, the caregiver will be involved, which requires that the interventionist and the caregiver jointly plan the nature of their involvement as well as strategies to accomplish that involvement. The interventionist needs to have backup suggestions to allow for situations in which the original activity is ineffective or some unforeseen circumstance, interferes with the execution of the original plan (e.g., the primary caregiver is ill and another family member participates).

The key to successful use of home-based staff is planning that will permit an organized approach to meeting the various staff responsibilities. Planning should include the caregiver unless the caregiver chooses not to participate. Even in these circumstances, the interventionist should continue to search for avenues that might build the caregiver's involvement in the planning efforts.

Summary

The effective use of staff in either center-based or home-based programs requires two considerations. First, a balance should be struck between change and routine. Neither too little nor too much change is facilitative for staff, caregivers, or children. Programs that change schedules too frequently can cause confusion and waste staff time and effort in learning new routines. Programs that rarely change may drift into routines that are uninteresting and unrewarding to children, families, and staff. Programs should be continually evaluated and change undertaken when feedback suggests that goals are not being met or not reached within expected time frames.

A second consideration is the need for communication among staff members and between staff and family members. Each member of the direct intervention staff and the support team needs to be knowledgeable about each other's activities. Without consistent sharing of information, problems will occur. Each staff and family member should be working in concert to assist the child if expected progress is to be maintained toward established goals. Functional communication will not occur without recognition of its importance and without formal mechanisms to ensure its occurrence.

IMPLEMENTATION OF INTERVENTION STRATEGIES

Since the advent of behaviorism, there have been disagreements about its appropriateness for explaining and modifying human behavior (Evans, 1971). Some have argued that the principles espoused by the behaviorist are inappropriately applied to the human organism, except, perhaps, to more seriously impaired individuals. Behaviorists' discussions of the control and manipulation of human behavior have often polarized people into camps of believers and critics. Believers tend to disregard concepts such as free will and argue that most forms of human behavior can be manipulated through environmental arrangement of antecedent and consequent events. Nonbelievers argue for the need to appreciate nonobservable variables from which human motivation, choice, and direction are derived. For interventionists, this polarization has tended to force people to take one side or the other. Debates and energy often have focused on areas that have produced little help for the problems confronting interventionists.

Whether one likes or dislikes the term *behaviorist* is secondary to the recognition that we are all behaviorists. Overt responses of individuals, whether motoric or verbal, provide the only data available from which to derive information and generate hypotheses for intervention activities. In addition to the recognition that the behavior of the individual is our primary data source, there is the need to understand and apply behavioral learning principles.

Considerable misunderstanding and ignorance of behavioral learning principles exists. This problem is, at least in part, the result of the polarization between behavioral and developmental or cognitively-oriented approaches. All interventionists arrange antecedent events to elicit responses, and consequences then follow (even ignoring is a consequence). The question is whether these arrangements are conducted in an unplanned, haphazard fashion or in a logical, cohesive manner. Again, we all employ behavioral learning principles; the issue is how effectively the principles are used. The psychotherapist who nods as a client discusses a problem is employing the same principle as an interventionist who hugs a child following the successful completion of a task.

Since most interventionists use observable behavior as a primary source of information, and since they also apply behavioral learning principles, what are the primary differences between philosophies and programs? The important differences between those programs that use a behavioral learning perspective versus those more focused on cognitive and motivational variables are: (1) the level of inference the intervention staff is willing to accept; and (2) the rigor with which the behavioral learning principles are applied.

Inferences

The level of inference refers to how removed explanations of cause and effect are from observable behavior. Behavior analysts observe behavior and attempt to record events as objectively as possible. For example, while observing an interaction between a child and his mother, the observer might record that Billy hit his mother on the arm with a toy car as she bent toward him. A more cognitively-oriented person might observe the same scene and add that Billy was angry with his mother, his anger causing him to strike her with the car. The determination that Billy was angry is an inference based on the child's behavior. Both descriptions use observable events; the difference lies in the level of inference drawn from the observable events.

Drawing inferences is a legitimate activity and one that most people use frequently. If we could not draw inferences, the world would be far less interesting. However, when operating in the professional realm, it is essential to recognize when inferences are made and the basis for drawing the inference. Too often, inferences are taken as fact, which can result in misguided intervention efforts. For example, a teacher's observations of Suzy's noncooperative behavior during large-group time leads to the inference that the child is obstinate. The interventionist designs a program to encourage cooperative behavior from Suzy. Implementation of the program leads to little change in Suzy's behavior, because, unknown to the interventionist, the child is hearing impaired and is unable to respond appropriately to verbal directions provided during group time. If the interventionist recognizes his or her inference about Suzy's behavior, then a suitable change in the program may occur in an efficient manner. If the interventionist treats the inference about Suzy as fact, then relevant program changes may be long in coming.

Rather than casting people into opposing camps, it is more useful to recognize that as interventionists we all use behavioral principles in our assessment, intervention, and evaluation strategies. The primary difference lies in the degree of inference one is willing to make from observable events. Drawing inferences is appropriate as long as one is able to discriminate between the inference and the observable events which serve as the basis for the inference.

Behavioral Principles of Learning

Behavioral principles of learning have been developed into the most effective intervention strategy currently available. No matter what one's theoretical orientation, it is important that early intervention personnel be knowledgeable about and competent users of these principles. Interventionists have the choice of understanding and applying these principles in a purposeful and organized manner or allowing events to occur in ways that may or may not serve the interests of children, families, and interventionists. The choice is easy. The basic equation that serves as a foundation for the intervention strategy advocated is:

A(antecedent) $\longrightarrow$ R(response) $\longrightarrow$ C(consequence).

Antecedent refers to any event that serves to set up and call forth the targeted response. Consequences are the events that follow the occurrence of the target response. These three elements—antecedents, responses, and consequences—work in tandem, and therein lies the strength of the strategy. Interventionists should think in terms of ARC units rather than of individual elements (e.g., consequences) when developing intervention programs.

It is important to understand the broad and generalized application of the ARC equation. Too often, ARC units are understood and conceptualized as one-to-one correspondences, such as the example illustrated here:

Antecedent	Response	Consequence
Picture of-a plane	verbal response plane	verbal response good boy

Using ARC units only to formulate specific and structured contingencies is an overly narrow application of the principles. Rather, the interventionist should be working to have the child respond appropriately across a range of appropriate and relevant antecedent events, such as different pictures of planes, toy planes of various sizes, colors and shapes, and real planes. Each of these antecedent events should be capable of eliciting the verbal label "plane." Maintaining the word in the child's repertoire is accomplished through the use of a variety of consequences, such as receiving affirmation, acquiring a toy, or initiating a conversation.

Although the initial training may focus on establishing a one-to-one correspondence between a specific antecedent and response, for most children it is essential to quickly vary the antecedent events and to tolerate variability in the response topography, (e.g., "plane", "airplane"). Consequences should vary and be functionally related to the response whenever possible.

Employing the Strategy

Employing behavioral intervention strategies has been addressed in a number of helpful books. The purpose of this section is not to replicate the information provided in these books, but to suggest a general plan of operation that sometimes does not accompany the more detailed accounts of how to employ the strategy.

Following is listed a set of general steps that provides a framework for selecting target responses, arranging program elements, and collecting outcome data.

Step 1: Write behavioral objectives (These should come directly from the IEP or IFSP.)

Step 2: Measure occurrence of the target response

Step 3: Implement the intervention program

Step 4: Collect and graph data

Step 5: Modify program as necessary

The objective of Step 1 is to define the response or behavior of interest in a particular domain. Using a curriculum-based assessment and evaluation measure will provide a set of long-range goals and training or treatment objectives. For many children, each objective should be further divided into a series of program steps. Each program step should be written as a behavioral objective. According to Halle and Sindelar (1982), behavioral objectives should be written in terms of: observable components, the context in which they occur, and the criterion level. For example:

> For eight consecutive days, Paul will independently indicate wants during snack time by saying, "more juice" and "more cracker." The production of words will be intelligible and produced at least once each day to receive a snack.

Once defined, Step 2 requires measuring the occurrence of the response. During the observation, the interventionist should note those antecedent and consequence events that appear to affect the occurrence or nonoccurrence of the targeted response. Measurement can yield a permanent or nonpermanent result. For example, a permanent outcome might be a Polaroid picture of the curve of the child's spine, while a nonpermanent record might be the number of times a child hits another child.

In most instances, the response will be measured using event recording, duration recording, or interval recording (e.g., time sampling). Event recording refers to systematically counting the number of times or the frequency that a response occurs. Using the example above, the observer would record the number of times Paul requests juice and crackers by independently saying "more juice, more cracker" during snack time. Placing checks on a recording form each time Mary cries is another example of event recording. In event recording, it may be important to note the length of the observation period.

Duration recording refers to noting the length of time a response occurs. For example, noting the frequency that a child has tantrums—if they occur infrequently—may be less useful than recording the duration of the tantrum. Interval recording refers to systematically selecting periods of time to note the occurrence of a response. Generally, a time period is pre-designated (10 seconds), and at the end of each interval, the recorder checks to see whether or not the target response is being exhibited. For more detail on data recording systems, see Alberto and Troutman, 1982; Axelrod, 1977; and Hall, 1971.

Step 3 is implementation of the program to meet the child's behavioral objective. This step focuses on applying behavioral learning principles to assist the child in acquiring the content (behavioral objective). Relevant learning principles can be divided into strategies for arranging antecedents, promoting responses, and providing consequences.

Effective management of antecedent events entails selection of events and activities that help elicit the target response. Two aspects need consideration: the sequence and the format in which events are presented. Following a well-designed curricular sequence, a set of program steps, or task analysis, generally ensures that the sequence of responses the child learns will move from least to most difficult. Intervention should generally begin where the child is currently responding and move progressively toward the more difficult level of responding. The presentation format advocated is activity-based, which has been described in detail in Chapter 12. The interventionist needs to consider the type of activities and materials that will be most appropriate for the child, setting, and behavioral objectives.

Promoting the occurrence of the target response can be done using a variety of instructional techniques including: shaping, various modeling and prompting techniques, and chaining. Shaping is the differential reinforcement of successive approximations to a target behavior. If the target behavior is walking using alternate steps, a successive approximation might be cruising using side steps. Prompts refer to additional aids that increase the likelihood a response will occur. Physical prompts can include various levels of physical assistance and modeling. Verbal prompts can be cues or full descriptions of the desired response. Chaining refers to sequences of linked behaviors. For example, shoe-tying is composed of a series of discrete responses that culminates in shoes being tied. Often it is helpful to teach a more complex response through the use of backward or forward chaining. The effective interventionist needs to be fluent in the application of these techniques.

Consequences can be classified as positive or punishing. Positive reinforcement increases the probability that a response will occur, while punishers inhibit or decrease the occurrence of a response. In most cases, interventionists should use punishing events infrequently. Positive consequences should not be construed to be only artificial contingencies, such as receiving candy or verbal praise. Rather, positive reinforcement consequences can and should be, an integral part of the activity. For example, saying "juice" should produce juice for the child and serve as sufficient reinforcement to maintain the response.

The discussion of intervention strategies offered here provides only cursory information that should be supplemented through other sources. There are a number of books designed specifically for interventionists that discuss these techniques. See for example, Alberto and Troutman, 1982; Axelrod, 1977; Sulzer-Azaroff and Mayer, 1977; Bailey and Wolery, 1984.

OTHER CHILDREN AS CHANGE AGENTS

Other children can serve as a valuable teaching resource. Unfortunately, this resource is often disregarded by adult interventionists. As argued earlier in this book, development of more complex repertoires is largely a function of progressive environmental demands. Consequently, programs should be designed to stimulate and demand progressively more sophisticated responses from participating children. Overly solicitous adults who respond for children, or arrange conditions so children do not have to change, are counterproductive to children's growth and development. Having children who are handicapped surrounded by children who have similar problems or deficits may not provide a maximally demanding environment. In addition, there is evidence that children who are handicapped as a group are less socially capable (Strain & Kohler, 1988). If other children can be effective change agents, then it would seem wise to include children that are socially adept and can serve as effective models for less competent children.

Integrating children who are handicapped and nonhandicapped children has the potential to create a more demanding environment for the child who is at-risk or handicapped—an environment that may assist in the continued development of the child's behavioral repertoire. It is possible that when young impaired and nonimpaired children are grouped together, interventionists and parents may develop more realistic expectations about what less competent children should be attempting to do. Furthermore, such an environment is likely to be more demanding. Not only may the physical environment be filled with more interesting objects, as indicated by the research reported by Bailey, Clifford and Harms (1982), but the nonhandicapped peers may expect and encourage behavior that could produce significant changes in the children who are handicapped.

It seems clear that children can learn through imitation (Bandura, 1971), but the willingness of children to imitate others is affected by a range of motivational and reinforcement variables. Programs that include nonhandicapped youngsters may enhance the possibility of imitation learning by the youngster who is handicapped for several reasons. First, in order for children to acquire new responses by observing and modeling other children's behavior, the opportunity for watching and imitating more complex behavior must be available. Isolation of young children who are handicapped from nonhandicapped peers may reduce an important avenue of stimulation and subsequent learning. For example, it seems unlikely that children with hearing impairment will benefit linguistically from exclusive associations with other children who are hearing impaired. Being exposed to appropriate language models should assist the child who is hearing impaired in developing better communication skills.

Second, active participation appears to enhance imitation learning, a finding which argues for programs to provide contact among handicapped and nonhandicapped children. Third, there are indications that children model selectively. That is, children tend to imitate the behavior of more competent individuals who are more skillful (Strichart, 1974).

Other children, particularly more competent children, can fill valuable teaching roles. Thus, program personnel should explore means for inclusion of nonhandicapped children in programs that serve children who are at-risk and handicapped. However, merely placing nonhandicapped children in a program will not ensure interaction between the two groups or that less competent children will observe and imitate the actions of the more competent children (O'Connell, 1984). Rather, the interventionists must plan and organize activities to encourage interaction between the groups of children. For descriptions of programs and procedures for integrating handicapped and nonhandicapped children see Vincent, Brown and Getz-Sheftel, 1981; Allen, 1981; O'Connell, 1984; Odom & McEvoy, 1988; Safford, 1989.

SUMMARY

This chapter has discussed four constellation of factors that can be arranged or engineered to facilitate learning. A major theme has been the numerous options available to assist children in acquiring targeted behaviors. Too often, intervention is viewed from an inordinately narrow perspective which dictates that learning occurs under specific conditions. The position advocated here is that a myriad of options are available for assisting children and families in the learning process.

The physical arrangement of space and equipment can serve as a teaching vehicle and can enhance intervention activities, or can deter the process through inappropriate and nonfunctional arrangements. The manner in which staff are deployed can also add or detract from the intervention process. Systems for the smooth and efficient use of the intervention staff can enhance learning opportunities. An equally important strategy is the use of other children as models and teaching resources. A vertical teaching model in which more competent children assist those less competent holds great appeal both from the point of view of husbanding resources and as an effective teaching method for the child-teacher and the child-learner.

Finally, a variety of carefully developed intervention strategies is available for use. Interventionists have the choice of understanding and employing these procedures in efficient, effective ways or using these valuable strategies in less effective ways. The better the interventionist understands these principles of learning and the more flexibly these principles can be applied, the greater becomes the potential benefit to participating children and their families.

References

Alberto, P., & Troutman, A. (1982). *Applied behavior analysis for teachers.* Columbus, OH: Charles E. Merrill.

Allen, K. (1981). Curriculum models for successful mainstreaming. *Topics in Early Childhood Special Education, 1,* 45-55.

Axelrod, S. (1977). *Behavior modification for the classroom teacher.* NY: McGraw-Hill.

Bailey, D., Clifford, R., & Harms, T. (1982). Comparison of preschool environments for handicapped and nonhandicapped children. *Topics in Early Childhood Special Education, 2*(1), 9-20.

Bailey, D., & Wolery, M. (1984). *Tracking infants and preschoolers with handicaps.* Columbus, OH: Charles E. Merrill.

Bandura, A. (1971). Influence of models' reinforcement contingencies on the acquisition of imitative responses. In E. McGinnies & C. Ferster (Eds.), *The reinforcement of social behavior.* Boston, MA: Houghton Mifflin Co.

Banerdt, B., & Bricker, D. (1978). A training program for selected self-feeding skills for the motorically impaired. *AAESPH Review, 3,* 222-229.

Campbell, P., Green, K., & Carlson, L. (1977). Approximating the norm through environmental and child-centered prosthetics and adaptive equipment. In E. Sontag, J., Smith, & N. Certo (Eds.), *Educational programming for the severely and profoundly handicapped.* Reston, VA: The Council for Exceptional Children.

Carta, J., Sainato, D., & Greenwood, C. (1988). Advances in the ecological assessment of classroom instruction for young children with handicaps. In S. Odom & M. Karnes (Eds.), *Early intervention for infants and children with handicaps.* Baltimore, MD: Paul Brookes.

Day, D. (1983). *Early childhood education.* Glenview, IL: Scott, Foresman & Company.

Evans, R. (1971). Aversive versus positive control of behavior. (Interview with B.F. Skinner). In E. McGinnies & C. Ferster (Eds.), *The reinforcement of social behavior.* NY: Houghton Mifflin Co.

Hall, R. (1971). *Managing behavior* (5 vols.). Lawrence, KS: H. & H. Enterprises, Inc.

Halle, J., & Sindelar, P. (1982). Behavioral observation methodologies for early childhood education. *Topics in Early Childhood Special Education, 2*(1), 43-54.

O'Connell, J. (1984). Preschool integration and its effects on the social interactions of handicapped and nonhandicapped children: A review. *Journal of the Division for Early Childhood, 8,* 38-48.

Odom, S., & McEvoy, M. (1988). Integration of young children with handicaps and normally developing children. In S. Odom & M. Karnes (Eds.), *Early intervention for infants and children with handicaps.* Baltimore, MD: Paul Brookes.

Olds, A. (1979). Designing developmentally optimal classrooms for children with special needs. In S. Meisels (Ed.), *Special education and development.* Baltimore, MD: University Park Press.

Piaget, J. (1970). Piaget's theory. In P. Mussen (Ed.), *Carmichael's manual of child psychology* (Vol. 1). NY: Wiley.

Quiltich, M., & Risley, T. (1973). The effects of play materials on social play. *Journal of Applied Behavior Analysis, 6,* 573-578.

Rogers-Warren, A. (1982). Behavioral ecology in classrooms for young, handicapped children. *Topics in Early Childhood Special Education, 2*(1), 21-32.

Ross, D. (1982). Selecting materials for mainstreamed preschools. *Topics in Early Childhood Special Education, 2*(1), 33-42.

Safford, P. (1989). *Integrated teaching in early childhood.* White Plains, NY: Longman.

Strain, P., & Kohler, F. (1988). Social skill intervention with young children with handicaps: Some new conceptualizations and directions. In S. Odom & M. Karnes (Eds.), *Early intervention for infants and children with handicaps.* Baltimore, MD: Paul Brookes.

Strichart, S. (1974). Effects of competence and nurturance on imitation of nonretarded peers by retarded adolescents. *American Journal of Mental Deficiency, 78,* 665-673.

Sulzer-Azaroff, B., & Mayer, R. (1977). *Applying behavior-analysis procedures with children and youth.* NY: Holt, Rinehart & Winston.

Vincent, L., Brown, L., & Getz-Sheftel, M. (1981). Integrating handicapped and typical children during the preschool years: The definition of best educational practice. *Topics in Early Childhood Special Education, 1*(1), 17-24.

15.
Program Evaluation

Evaluation is essential for effective intervention, and generally, effective evaluation cannot be separated from assessment. The assessment and evaluation of individual change and programmatic impact requires that intervention methods and systems be based on procedures that are appropriate for evaluating their efficacy. Assessment and evaluation should determine the format and success of intervention for individual children and determine the impact of programs on groups of children. These objectives require that assessment and evaluation procedures serve three distinct but complementary functions: (1) guidance for the development of individual and family program plans; (2) feedback about the success of individual programming for children and families; and (3) a means for determining the value of an intervention program for groups or subgroups of program participants. Underlying these three functions is the important concept that these separate assessment-evaluation objectives be linked into a unified approach.

For a number of reasons, a strong relationship between program philosophy, program goals, assessment procedures, curricular content, and subsequent evaluation of individual and group progress should exist. This linked system was described in detail in Chapter 11, and was graphically represented in Figure 11-1.

If the assessment procedures used do not yield information necessary to develop effective long-range goals and training or treatment objectives, then one might ask, why use them? The generation of data that do not lend themselves to the development of relevant IEPs or IFSPs are of questionable value. Rather, the assessment procedures employed should produce data that can be used directly to formulate individual child goals and objectives and family outcomes. Further, these goals and outcomes should relate directly to the curricular content and emphasis employed by a program. Ensuring these direct relationships requires that there be a strong link between the assessment procedures, the development of IEPs or IFSPs, and the subsequent curricular materials used to meet the selected objectives.

The assessment-intervention linkage should be extended to include evaluation. To appropriately determine the impact of the selected intervention content and procedures, it is necessary to employ methods of comparison that take into account the child's behavior prior to and following intervention. If the purpose is to determine the impact of an intervention program, then it is only sensible that the content of the intervention be reflected in the evaluation procedures. This reality requires that there be a strong and continuing linkage from assessment to IEP or IFSP development to curricular emphasis to evaluation. Interestingly, such approaches are seldom found in intervention programs. As Bagnato and Neisworth (1981) suggest, often little relationship appears to exist between the assessment, curricular focus, and evaluation that programs employ. The use of assessment and evaluation procedures that do not reflect program emphasis explains, in part, one major difficulty in the generation of useful efficacy data for early intervention programs (Bricker, Bailey, & Bruder, 1984).

One might logically ask why more programs do not employ linked assessment-intervention-evaluation systems. Two reasons are apparent. First, many personnel who operate early intervention programs did not receive preservice or inservice training on methods for linking assessment-intervention-evaluation. In fact, many received little training on the topic of evaluation, and thus, must struggle to establish any form of accountability. Thus, less than adequate linked systems often reflect the program personnel's lack of training and information in the areas of evaluation.

A second reason one finds few operationally linked assessment-intervention-evaluation systems is that descriptions of such approaches are seldom found in the literature. Most frequently, descriptions focus on one element such as assessment and fail to extend the descriptions to other program elements. Other descriptions, which may be more relevant, remain at the theoretical level and fail to provide interventionists with strategies for implementing the type of linked system being advocated. A book by Bagnato and Neisworth (1981) is an exception and provides both a model and extensive description of how to implement a linked assessment-curricular system. More recently, Hutinger (1988) has described a linked screening-assessment- and curriculum system.

The organizational framework for a linked assessment-intervention-evaluation system proposed in this chapter includes the three functions of assessment-evaluation already described. In particular, the focus is on using the initial assessment data to develop appropriate intervention objectives and as a baseline for evaluation of progress and program effectiveness at the group or aggregate level. Prior to discussing this linked approach to assessment, intervention, and evaluation, definitions and examples of screening, norm-referenced, and criterion-referenced tests are presented. In addition, the major assessment and evaluation dilemmas facing early interventionists are described.

MEASUREMENT: SCREENING, ASSESSMENT AND EVALUATION

An examination of the assessment and evaluation procedures employed by many early intervention programs reveals discrepancies even in terminology. Verbal and written descriptions suggest that discriminations between the processes of screening, diagnosis, program assessment, and evaluation often fail to occur. Thus, a brief delineation of these four processes may be useful.

As indicated in Figure 15-1, these processes are separate but can be and often are related. Screening should occur first, and during this process, which can be formal or informal, a binary decision is reached as to whether the child requires further testing.

If the child fails the screening, he or she should be referred to the next level. This level which is called diagnosis is designed to determine if there is a problem (e.g., yes, the child has a problem, or is ok) and the nature of the problem. The diagnostic process is generally conducted by a multidisciplinary team of professionals. If a problem is identified, the child's eligibility for services should be determined and referral to an appropriate program made.

Upon entry into a program, assessment measures should be administered to determine what specific intervention goals and objectives and outcomes should be established for the child and the family. Assessment and evaluation differ because the assessment process provides baseline information, but no comparison. The process of evaluation requires a comparison—most frequently comparing the child's and family's performance before and after intervention as indicated by arrows in Figure 15-1.

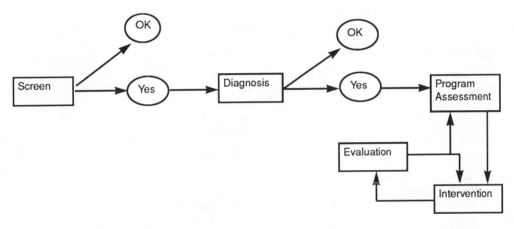

FIGURE 15-1. *Relationship between screening, diagnosis, program assessment and evaluation.*

Screening Tests

Frankenburg, Emde and Sullivan (1985) define screening as: "The application of quick and relatively simple procedures to a relatively asymptomatic population in order to identify persons who have a high likelihood of harboring the problem in question." (p.xiii)

Table 15-1 contains a list of screening instruments frequently used with infants and young children. This table contains the name of the test, the age range, domains covered, availability of psychometric data and type of test outcomes.

TABLE 15-1
Selected Screening Instruments

Name	Age Range	Domains	Psychometric Data Available	Outcomes
1. *Early Screening Inventory*; Meisels & Wiske; 1988.	4 to 6 years	Visual Motor Adaptive Language & Cognition Gross Motor Body awareness	Yes	Domains & Total scores
2. *Minneapolis Preschool Screening Inventory*; Lichtenstein; 1982.	3.7 to 5.4 years	Building, copying, matching shapes Naming colors, counting, etc.	Yes	Total scores, cut-offs given
3. *Developmental Indicators for the Assessment of Learning (Revised) (DIAL-R)*; Mardell-Czudnowski & Goldenberg, 1983.	2.6 to 5.6 years	Fine Motor Gross Motor Concepts Communication	Yes	Domain & Total scores
4. *Infant Monitoring Questionnaires*; Center on Human Development, 1989.	4 to 48 months	Fine Motor Gross Motor Adaptive Communication Personal-Social	Yes	Domain & Total scores; cut-off points
5. *Denver Developmental Screening Test*; Frankenburg & Dodds, 1970.	Birth to 6 years	Gross Motor Language Fine Motor/ Adaptive Personal-Social	Yes	Age level
6. *Developmental Activities Screening Inventory (DAS)*; Dubose & Langley, 1977.	Sensory impaired preschoolers 6-60 months	Fine Motor Causality- Means/Ends Number Concepts Size Discrimination Seriation	Yes, but limited validty data	Skill inventory

Norm-Referenced Tests

Norm-referenced tests are designed to compare an individual's performance with his or her peers (Salvia & Ysseldyke, 1981). This type of test emphasizes the relationship of the individual to the norm-group. Does the child perform similiar to, less well, or better than the norm group? Norm-referenced tests are useful in determining if children are functioning at the level of their age-mates, but are generally not helpful in developing intervention goals and objectives.

Table 15-2 contains a list of the norm-referenced tests frequently used with infants and young children. This table contains the test's name, age range, domains covered, availability of psychometric data, and type of test outcomes.

TABLE 15-2
Selected Norm-Referenced Tests

Name	Age Range	Domains	Psychometric Data Available	Outcomes
1. *Bayley Scales of Infant Development (BSID)*; Bayley, 1969.	2 to 30 months	Mental Psychomotor	Yes	Developmental quotient, Developmental age
2. *The Gesell Developmental Schedules*; Knobloch, Stevens & Malone, 1980.	1 to 72 months	Communication Gross Motor Fine Motor Adaptive Personal-Social	Yes	Developmental quotient, Maturity age
3. *Battelle Developmental Inventory*; Newborg, Stock, Wnek, Guidubaldi & Svinicki, 1988.	Birth to 8 years	Personal-Social Adaptive Motor Communication Cognitive	Yes	Percentiles Standard score Age equivalents Profiles
4. *Stanford-Binet Intelligence Scale*; Thorndike, Hagen & Sattler, 1985.	2 years to Adult	General intelligence	Yes	Mental age; IQ
5. *McCarthy Scales of Children's Abilities*; McCarthy, 1972.	2.5 to 8.5 years	Verbal Perceptual Quantitative Cognitive Memory Motor	Yes, but limited validity data	Scale index, General cognitive index
6. *The Developmental Profile II* (Rev. ed.); Alpern & Shearer, 1980.	Birth to 9 years	Physical Self-Help Social Academic Communication	Yes	Inventory of skills; Profile of functional developmental-age levels

Criterion-Referenced Tests

According to U.S. Office of Education validation guidelines (Tallmadge & Horst 1976):

> The dominant characteristic of tests that are labeled "criterion-referenced" is that their content is clearly defined in terms of some performance dimension or interest. This relationship permits direct interpretation of individual scores in ways which have immediate practical implications. (p. 55)

Table 15-3 contains a list of selected criterion-referenced tests used with infants and young children. This Table contains the test name, age range, domains covered, availability of psychometric data, and type of test outcomes.

ASSESSMENT/EVALUATION DILEMMAS

Substantial problems exist in accurately, and perhaps more importantly, usefully assessing baseline behavior and monitoring subsequent change in populations of infants and children who are at-risk and handicapped. In-depth discussions of these problems exist elsewhere (e.g., see Simeonsson, Huntington, & Parse, 1980; Fewell, 1983; Sheehan & Keogh, 1982; Weatherford, 1986); consequently, they will be only highlighted here. The nature of these problems can be conveniently categorized as:

1. Target population

2. Instruments

3. Expectancies

4. Relationship of assessment to programming

Target Population

An immense problem that pervades the field of early intervention is the heterogeneity of the target population. As indicated in Chapter 6, the at risk and handicapped populations have disabilities that range from mild to profound. Programs must serve children with sensory impairments, motoric disabilities, cognitive deficits, communication disorders, and general behavioral disturbances. Often children have a combination of problems or have a disability so significant that it pervades all aspects of the child's behavioral repertoire. For example, infants, toddlers, and young children may be unable to understand directions or unwilling to perform certain tasks. Young children are often wary and uncommunicative until they come to know the adult and the setting. Other factors that lead to diversity include variations in socioeconomic background, families' educational levels, and general parental perceptions and expectations for children. Diverse ethnic backgrounds of families require that assessment and evaluation strategies take into account different values and customs. All of these factors conspire to produce a diverse group of infants and young children and their families, making the accurate assessment and evaluation of individual children a difficult exercise and the evaluation of group performances extremely vulnerable to outcomes that may not be valid.

TABLE 15-3
Selected Criterion-Referenced Tests

Name	Age Range	Domains	Psychometric Data Available	Outcomes
1. *The Learning Accomplishment Profile-Diagnostic Edition* (revised) (LAP-D); LeMay, Griffin & Sanford, 1978.	Birth to 5.5 years	Language & Cognition Gross Motor Self-Help Social Fine Motor	Yes	Diagnostic profile; Initial developmental task analysis
2. *The Brigance Diagnostic Inventory of Early Development*; Brigance, 1978.	Birth to 6 years	Motor Speech/Language Preacademic	None	Performance level and developmental age levels
3. *Hawaii Early Learning Profile (HELP)*; Furuno, O'Reilly, Hosaka, Inatsuka, Allman & Zeisloft, 1979.	Birth to 36 months	Cognitive Language Fine Motor Gross Motor Social-Emotional Self-Help	Limited	Profile of skill level; approximate age levels
4. *Sewall Early Education Developmental Profiles (S.E.E.D.)*; Herst, Wolfe, Jorgensen & Pallan, 1976.	Birth to 4 years	Social-Emotional Fine Motor Gross Motor Adaptive Language Feeding Self-Help	No	Profile of abilities
5. *The Evaluation and Programming System: For Infants and Young Children (EPS)*; Bricker, Bailey & Gentry, 1985.	Birth to 36 months	Gross Motor Fine Motor Communication Cognitive Social Self-Help	Yes	Profile of skill level
6. *The Callier-Azusa Scale*; Stillman, 1975.	Birth-9 years	Motor Perceptual Language Daily Living Social	None	Diagnostic profile of level of functioning
7. *Uniform Performance Assessment System (UPAS)*; White, Edgar, Haring, Affleck, Hayden & Bendersky, 1980.	Birth to 6 years	Preacademic/ Fine Motor Communication Social/Self-Help Gross Motor Behavior Management	Yes	Profile of skill level
8. *Help for Special Preschoolers;* Santa Cruz County Office of Education, 1987.	3 to 6 years	Self-Help Motor Skills Communication Social Skills Cognitive	No	Skills/behaviors for intervention

Instruments

A remarkably large number of screening, norm-referenced, criterion-referenced, checklists, and other types of tests are available. Unfortunately, few meet the necessary requirements for a linked assessment-intervention-evaluation system. In addition, many existing instruments are not useful for assessing and evaluating program effectiveness for a variety of reasons.

As indicated previously, screening instruments are designed to quickly sort the target population into two groups: those who appear to not have a problem and those who might have. Screening tools do not provide adequate information for developing intervention plans or for monitoring progress.

Most norm-referenced tests were developed using populations of normally developing children. Many of the available instruments have little or no normative data reflecting an at-risk or handicapped population's performance on the measure. Although many of these instruments can be used for purposes of identification and diagnosis, they are not appropriate to chart the progress of children who are at-risk or handicapped because no norms or benchmarks exist for these groups of infants and children (Johnson, 1982). The further children's performances differ from normal development, the less applicable are such instruments for establishing baseline behavior and monitoring subsequent progress. Adequate documentation of progress for the child with more severe impairments requires instruments that can reflect small changes in behavior.

Often, the content found in norm-referenced instruments may not be useful in developing IEPs or IFSPs for children. For example, Bayley Scale items, "Manipulates table edge actively" or "Discriminates strangers" or "Playful response to mirror," do not lend themselves to development of useful intervention goals. In addition, significant gaps between items may preclude systematic programming unless the interventionist is extremely knowledgeable about developmental sequences.

A further obstacle to using many existing measures is the population variability discussed earlier. Standardized tests require that items be presented precisely as specified. If test protocols are not followed, the results are invalid. Equally troublesome is the specification of the form of the response, which generally permits little latitude; for instance, the child with limited hand use would be penalized on items that require execution of fine motor responses within a given time period. The limitations and diversity within populations of children who are handicapped require a basic reformulation of the approach to assessment and monitoring (Robinson, 1982).

This is not to imply that norm-referencing or standardization of testing procedures is undesirable. Rather, the intent and the content of the currently existing norm-referenced instruments are generally inappropriate for the purpose of assessing the impact of intervention procedures on infants and children who are at-risk and handicapped. The majority of presently available norm-referenced tests were constructed to reflect the degree to which children approximate the behavior typical to their chronological-age peers.

Criterion-referenced tests avoid many of the problems associated with standardized tests but often have other difficulties. A review of Table 15-3 suggests that many criterion-referenced tests have little psychometric data; thus, the data they generate on individual child performances may be suspect in terms of validity and reliability. If a test indicates the child has made progress from September to June, should the data be considered an accurate reflection of change in the child or the result of test error?

A second problem associated with criterion-referenced tests is that the content may not reflect the program emphasis. Thus, a child's performance may not show change because the instrument is focused on areas not taught in the intervention program. This common problem has, in the past, lead many interventionists to develop "homemade" tests. Although such tests may better represent the content of a program, this approach is somewhat shortsighted. Most homemade instruments are not used with sample sizes large enough to collect adequate psychometric data, and thus, one is again faced with resulting information about change in children that is suspect.

These dilemmas often complicate the choice of an instrument. The interventionist may be faced with a choice between a psychometrically sound instrument that does not reflect the program's goals and a criterion-referenced instrument that reflects program goals but whose psychometric properties are unknown. Finally, many norm-referenced or criterion-referenced tests do not lend themselves to the development of a linked assessment-intervention-evaluation system.

"Although many instruments are available for assessing various aspects of family functioning, most suffer from several limitations" (Bailey, 1988). According to Bailey, these limitations include: measures designed to examine hypothetical constructs (e.g., stress) that have questionable usefulness for developing services, and intrusive measures that are deficit-oriented which again, are not helpful in identifying and providing appropriate services. Thus, many of the problem associated with instruments available for children are also present in family measures.

Expectancies

There are several issues inherent in the evaluation of a program's worth, but two questions are of major concern: (1) Are the children and families who are involved in the program making "acceptable" progress, and if so, (2) is there reasonable evidence to indicate that observed progress is greater than if the children and families had been in alternative programs? In order to answer these questions, meaningful standards for "acceptable" progress must be established, and it must be possible to estimate what progress *would* have been if the family had *not* been associated with the program in question.

Inherent in making estimations is the need for a set of relevant benchmarks or expectancies against which child and family progress can be measured. Unfortunately, no agreed-upon set of standards exists

which permits universal comparison of children and families to determine progress; there is no operationally defined prototype that is generally acceptable. For example, agreement might be forthcoming that
children should do well in school, however, attempts to operationally
define "do well in school" highlight the necessity for qualifiers.
Benchmarks are established or defined in relation to personal, family,
and cultural values, as well as by the individual's environmental and
biological resources. It is apparent that the standards of progress for a
biologically normal child would be different from those for a youngster
with Down syndrome or possibly those for a child from a background of
poverty. These examples clarify the need for establishing agreed-upon
and useful reference points (e.g., content areas, intervention targets) for
measuring progress if meaningful analyses are to be conducted.

In the absence of functionally-derived and empirically-verified
expectancies for infants and children who are at-risk and handicapped,
a normal developmental model has often been adopted. Many interventionists have reasoned that while children with handicaps may never
master all of the skills normal children are capable of performing, the
skills which they learn should be acquired in essentially the same order
and brought to at least a reasonable approximation of the normative
response. To assess the degree and significance of atypical children's
progress, it should only be necessary to note how far along the normal
developmental sequence the children have moved. Unlike items in a
norm-referenced test, scale items would not be chosen simply for their
ability to discriminate between children, but would be chosen because
they represent an ordered series of significant milestones along a
continuum of normal growth and learning. Also, it would not be necessary for children to actually *reach* normal levels of performance before
some change in children's performances were noted; sequential progress
toward goals could be recorded.

Up until the age of at least two years, the sequence of normal
human development is surprisingly consistent (Cohen & Gross, 1979).
The actual time when certain skills appear will vary, but the order of
their emergence is governed for the most part by apparent physiological
interdependencies (e.g., before a child is able to sit for long periods without support, the child must be able to lift his head). Between the years of
two and six, the picture is a little less certain, primarily due to the
increasing impact of experience upon development. Beyond the age of
six, developmental patterns begin to vary even more, becoming increasingly dependent upon arbitrary curricula, instructional emphases, and
many other variables in the child's environment (Fischer, 1980; McCall,
1981).

Such increasing variance from normal patterns of development
has several implications. First, it underlines the importance of avoiding
assessment devices which place total reliance on what is "normal." Such
approaches may be insensitive to the significant and functional progress
a child can still make when deviating from the norm becomes necessary.
Second, attention is focused on the need to become more precise in the
differentiation between what is "necessary" or "functional" and what is
simply "usual." Certain motor development *is* necessary for walking,

but this developmental sequence is not necessary for locomotion per se. Obviously, whenever a child can be taught skills which approximate the norm, an attempt should be made to achieve those aims. However, failure to move toward normality must not be equated with failure to develop functionally useful skills or to progress in any meaningful way.

The above statements should not be interpreted as a disavowal of the usefulness of developmental theory or models. Rather, they caution against the wholesale adaptation of normal developmental models as the only or most appropriate source to establish benchmarks or reasonable expectancies for infants and children who are at-risk and handicapped. Nevertheless, because few other useful models currently exist, the use of normal developmental sequences used as a general reference are often the best available resource for establishing expectancies. However, interventionists should be prepared for children who will deviate significantly from established norms and have strategies for ensuring that such deviation becomes as functional as possible.

Relationship of Assessment, Intervention and Evaluation

The final problems associated with existing assessment-evaluation systems is the lack of continuity between assessment-evaluation and subsequent intervention efforts. These problems include: assessment-evaluation measures that have no relationship to program objectives; assessment information that does not lead to the development of an appropriate and useful IEP or IFSP; assessment and evaluation measures that do not reflect intervention efforts; and evaluation measures that do not adequately reflect change.

An examination of many existing tests reveals significant inadequacies when considered from the perspective of targets for intervention programs. As discussed in Chapter 11, there should be a direct relationship between program objectives and the assessment and evaluation instrument. In addition, assessment information should provide the basis for developing the IEP or IFSP. Many currently available instruments may not reflect program goals and may not provide the necessary information for the development of a useful IEP or IFSP.

A related issue of significant concern, particularly for more severely impaired populations, is the usefulness of intervention content in terms of enhancing children's repertoires. Many interventionists are becoming increasingly attentive to the formulation of curricular materials from a programmatic perspective. The responses that will be of most use to the individual or build towards repertoires of independent functioning are becoming the focus. Rather than working on specific toy skills, such as puzzles, peg boards, or other similar toys, many interventionists are directing training efforts towards functional skills and behaviors, such as turning switches and knobs, labeling essential objects or events, and communication of needs (e.g., thirst).

Assessment and evaluation measures should reflect the program emphasis and individual children's goals and family outcomes if reasonable information about effectiveness is to be derived. Using evaluation measures that examine content that is not the focus of the program will provide little helpful feedback in the way of program impact.

Ideally, evaluation efforts should be linked directly to the assessment and intervention components of a program.

Finally, evaluation measures should be able to reflect the change that occurs in children and families as a result of intervention. This requires that the evaluation efforts capture the program focus and are sensitive enough to reflect change. Although substantial item intervals may be appropriate for children developing within normal limits, or even populations of children who are at-risk, problems may arise when working with groups of infants and children with more serious problems. For example, children who are severely handicapped involved in intensive intervention over a period of several months may show negligible change on standardized instruments, but may show clear improvement on measures with more fine-grained item intervals. A need exists for instruments which have relatively small intervals between items to assist the interventionist in programming, and also to reflect changes in the entire target population.

Summary

Early intervention services for at-risk and handicapped populations have expanded dramatically in the last decade. With the expansion of services has come the need to develop assessment and evaluation tools to assess the incoming behavioral repertoires of these target populations and to monitor subsequent program impact on both individuals and groups. Subsequent progress has been made in both areas. Because of new assessment-intervention-evaluation models, early intervention personnel are increasingly able to conduct effective assessments, generate relevant IEPs or IFSPs, and complete useful individual and group evaluations.

A LINKED APPROACH TO PROGRAM EVALUATION

The evaluation plans and strategies undertaken by many early intervention programs appear to lack a guiding theoretical rationale or focus. That is, there seems to be no articulated plan as to what type of data to collect or analysis to be conducted. The need for a well-structured plan becomes clear when one considers the implications of following a nontheoretical documentation process in which measures are selected and analysis conducted because they might show something. Under such a regime, program personnel can be overwhelmed.

Figure 15-2 offers an organizational framework for the three functions of assessment and evaluation necessary to ensure effective intervention efforts. Though not all service-delivery programs will be able to allocate sufficient resources at each level, the field as a whole must consider each level of evaluation if progress is to be made in refining theory, content, and technology for early intervention efforts across diverse populations. The proposed plan reflected in Figure 15-2 suggests that assessment-intervention-evaluation systems may be divided into four phases:

• initial assessment and formulation of IEP or IFSP

- weekly monitoring for immediate feedback on individual intervention programs
- quarterly evaluation of individual children and families
- annual evaluation of individual child and family progress and program effectiveness for subgroups of children and families

The scematic presented in Figure 15-2 was designed to emphasize the direct and continuing links between assessment, intervention and evaluation. Upon entry into the program, an initial assessment is conducted on the child and family. The data generated from this assessment are used to develop the IEP or IFSP. A weekly monitoring system directly related to the IEP or IFSP is established and the data obtained from this monitoring are used for quarterly evaluations. Quarterly evaluations also require that program personnel readminister the initial assessment tests. Based on the child's and families' charted progress, the IEP or IFSP are modified as necessary. The child and

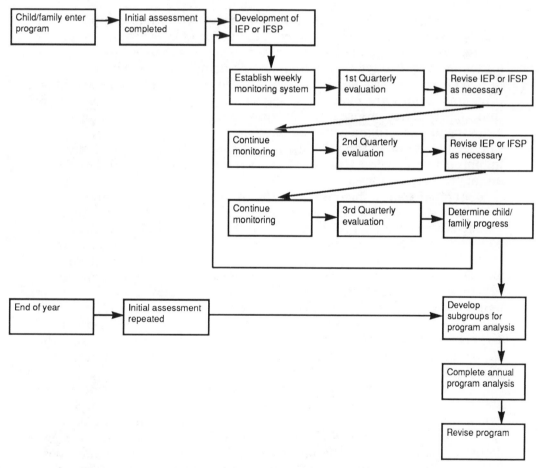

FIGURE 15-2. Framework for a linked approach to evaluaton.

family continue to cycle through this system until the end of the year or until they exit from the program. The annual evaluation is completed by readministering the initial assessments. The data are compared to initial and quarterly performances to establish program impact for individual children and families and subgroups of children and families. This system ensures continuity from the initial assessment to the annual evaluation and should assist in obtaining maximum impact from program involvement.

Initial Assessments

The link between assessment, intervention and evaluation begins with the entry of the child into a service program. Initial assessments can influence the delivery of services in three ways. First, determining the appropriateness of the program for children and families can be addressed. Second, determining the match between the program's goals and those of the family must be assessed to lay the groundwork for development of family involvement in the program. Third, an appropriate IEP or IFSP can be formulated for the child.

Programs are frequently oriented toward children with particular deficits. Every program cannot serve the needs of every child. Programs treating hearing-impaired children, for example, may be inappropriate for children with physical disabilities. Although diagnostic and evaluation services may assist in placing children in appropriate intervention programs, errors are made, and service-delivery agencies should verify that appropriate services can be provided to the child. The initial assessment may enhance annual outcome data because data on children who should not be in the program and who may not improve as a result of inappropriate placement will not skew the evaluations of children who are appropriately placed.

Another major objective of initial assessment is the formulation of a realistic and appropriate IEP or IFSP that has an accompanying individual evaluation plan. The initial assessment should: (1) provide a picture of the historical, social, and medical factors that may be relevant to the delivery of services to the child; (2) determine the child's beginning skill level so that an intervention plan directed toward improving areas in which the child is deficient can be developed; and 3) determine the family's involvement as reflected in stated family outcomes.

An effective IEP or IFSP is the heart of an intervention program. The content of the IEP or IFSP provides the road map for getting from the child's beginning skill repertoire to the skills specified as annual goals in the IEP or IFSP. The development of the IEP or IFSP goals epitomizes the inseparable mix of assessment and intervention. Poor initial assessment will lead to inappropriate or unrealistic IEPs or IFSPs, which will in turn lead to a failure to show improvement. The formulation of an IEP or IFSP is as crucially dependent on appropriate assessment as the weaving of the best cloth is on the selection of the finest fibers. In developing the IFSP, the same care should be given to the selection of family outcomes. These outcomes should form the basis of the intervention efforts directed to the family.

The IEP or IFSP should be based primarily on information accumulated during the initial assessment period, though this first testing should be validated at the first quarterly evaluation. The initial information should be used to develop a plan of action for the interventionists and to identify the specific content areas that the IEP or IFSP will address. An IEP or IFSP should contain long-range goals, training or treatment objectives, behavioral prescriptions, and time-frames, criteria and procedures for meeting those goals. In addition, the IFSP should contain statements of outcomes for the family, name of the case manager, and transitional procedures for movement to the next program. The operationalization of the IEP or IFSP should be straightforward so it can be used as a guide for the interventionist working with the child, and as a criterion against which the success of intervention may be evaluated in quantitative terms.

Weekly Monitoring of Child Progress

A useful IEP or IFSP specifies both the tasks to be carried out and the manner in which the success of the program will be evaluated. An inadequate IEP or IFSP training goal might state, "Language will be targeted." A more useful goal might state:

"John's use of nouns in structured group settings will be targeted. He will be rewarded for each use of a noun in a group. The number of times he uses nouns in groups will be plotted every other day. Each week the average number of noun use will be determined. If the noun use has not increased 25 percent by the end of two weeks, the intervention strategy will be reevaluated."

This goal is specific in two important ways. First, the goal clearly states the targets and the data to be collected. Second, and equally important, the goal incorporates the IEP or IFSP into the feedback system. The results of weekly monitoring should have an impact on the IEP or IFSP and on the delivery of services to the child. Failure to use weekly data to revise methods and intervention content will almost surely lead to poor progress at quarterly and annual evaluations.

The amount and type of data collected should be determined by the severity of the child's disability and the resources of the program. A project designed to demonstrate the effectiveness of a systematic program must devote extensive resources to monitoring and evaluation; a project primarily concerned with the delivery of services to large numbers of youngsters must of necessity balance data collection with timely delivery of services to all the children.

With planning, the collection of information on child progress can usually be done in conjunction with service delivery. That is, the interventionist can monitor child behavior and prompt or shape a new response at the same time. Interventionists many collect trial-by-trial data or administer brief probes before and after training activities. In some situations, collecting data may be difficult, though with some ingenuity, it is possible. For example, an interventionist may use a wrist counter to record the number of communication gestures produced by the child during the training period each day. These daily data may then be used to monitor weekly progress as well as quarterly progress.

A variety of strategies may be used for weekly monitoring of children. The strategies selected should balance the resources of the program, the intervention efforts, and the necessity to use weekly monitoring as a source of feedback to keep the intervention effort on track. Weekly data should be viewed by the interventionist as a source of information rather than as a burden. Just as physicians are expected to make the best use of medical information in determining whether surgery or some other form of treatment is succeeding, interventionists should consider the collection of data to be part of their responsibility to children and their families. In addition to the benefits weekly monitoring has for the child, adjustments in the program resulting from these data may enhance the prospects of demonstrating individual improvement and program efficacy at quarterly and annual evaluations.

The intervals at which progress toward family outcomes is monitored should be a joint decision between interventionists and family members. With planning, strategies may be found that permit the systematic monitoring of progress toward family outcomes that family find acceptable. The nature of the monitoring will depend upon the outcomes. For example, if an outcome is to permit the mother more time away from her child, progress data may involve the mother telling the interventionist about her weekly outings from the home. The frequency of weekly outings can then be charted over time.

Quarterly Evaluation

Quarterly evaluation should focus on determining the effect of intervention efforts on quarterly objectives specified in the IEP or IFSP. This can be done by using the initial assessment measures in conjunction with the weekly data. Quarterly evaluation should be used to compare the child's and family's progress with some standard or expectation. Without assigning expected dates of completion to objectives, interventionists and caregivers may not be able to determine if the progress made by the child and family is acceptable or unacceptable.

For example, quarterly objectives should have automatic timelines; the child is expected to reach criterion on quarterly objectives within three months. Projections as shown in Figure 15-3 enhance intervention-evaluation efforts by comparing the expected rate of progress with the child's actual rate of progress. Through frequent plotting of the child's progress toward the established quarterly objectives, interventionists can establish more realistic objectives. In addition, comparisons between expected and attained outcomes will generate information that may eventually allow the establishment of relevant norms for subgroups of children who are at-risk and handicapped.

Quarterly evaluations provide information for revising the IEP or IFSP. For example, if all children fail to reach their established quarterly objectives in the motor domain, the program may not be providing enough training time in this area, or the training time may be used ineffectively. In either case, the quarterly evaluation may suggest that a modification of the program is in order. Information from the quarterly evaluations provides feedback about child and family progress and needed modifications or revisions in the IEP or IFSP.

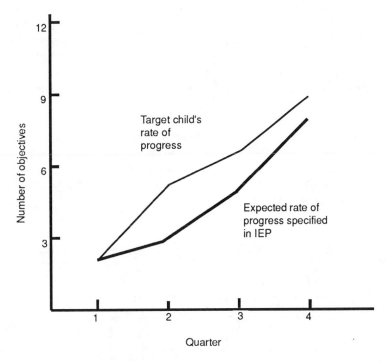

FIGURE 15-3. Comparing expected and actual child progress across quarters during one year.

Annual Evaluation of Program Impact

Annual evaluations can be used to evaluate the progress of individual children and families and the generic impact of the program (e.g., subgroup analysis). That is, annual evaluation addresses both the impact of the program on individual children and families and the effectiveness of the program on subgroups. Without the latter comparisons, it is difficult to improve the development and implementation of effective intervention strategies with subpopulations of children. Methodological design and measurement problems facing the field of early intervention make subgroup evaluations difficult. However, conducting analyses of subgrouping yields important findings on generalization of impact for certain constellations of children (e.g., all Down syndrome children) and families (e.g., parents with different educational levels). Annual evaluation is the point of maximum intersection between evaluation of individual children and evaluation of programmatic effectiveness.

IMPLEMENTATION MODEL FOR DETERMINING CHILD AND FAMILY PROGRESS

Content of Progress

An effective strategy for establishing the content areas for measuring child and family progress is through the use of a framework composed of three independent, yet interrelated, levels of evaluation. Figure 15-4 provides a schematic of this approach. The greater the consistency between the three levels, the more efficient, appropriate, and useful will be the selected areas for measuring child and family change and program impact. The selection of program goals for children and families should be predicated upon the underlying philosophy or rationale that sets the general structure and atmosphere for the program. A frequent rationale for early intervention is that it facilitates: (1) growth and development in important behavioral areas; and (2) acceptance and enjoyment of the child by the family. Based on this rationale, a set of related program goals might include enhancing: (1) children's acquisition and use of sensorimotor skills; (2) children's acquisition and use of social skills; (3) children's acquisition and use of communication skills; (4) children's acquisition and use of motor skills; (5) positive family interaction; and (6) parent's attitudes about their children.

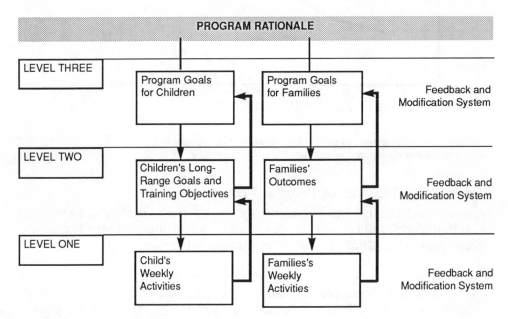

FIGURE 15-4.   *Three interrelated levels of program evaluation.*

Such program goals (Level 3), in conjunction with initial assessment information, provide the professional staff and family members with a content framework from which to select and develop the individual child's goals and objectives and family outcomes (Level 2). For a specific child, such related objectives based on program goals might be:

1. *Long-Range Goal:* The child will appropriately use social-communicative signals to indicate labels, requests, greetings, and to gain attention.

> *Training Objective* (which is based on the long-range goal): The child will look at adult, point to objects, and vocalize to gain desired objects, actions, or events.

2. *Long-Range Goal*: The child will initiate appropriate interactions with peers.

> *Training Objective*: The child will respond appropriately to interactions initiated towards him or her by peers.

The long-range goals and training objectives and outcomes (Level 2) developed for each participating child and family provide the basis for the development of the child's individual weekly activities and the family's weekly activities (Level 1). Weekly activity plans for the child's training objectives might be:

1. During opening and closing group time, a desired object or event will be withheld while the child is prompted to look at adult, point, and vocalize.

2. During snack time, juice and crackers will be placed out of the child's reach and the child will be prompted to make eye contact, reach, and vocalize.

3. During small group activities, peers will be prompted to initiate towards the child (e.g., share a crayon, throw a ball to) and the child will be prompted to reciprocate the action (e.g., give peer his or her crayon, roll the ball back).

4. During any program activity, the child will be immediately reinforced (e.g., given desired object, event, person) when he or she spontaneously makes eye contact, reaches, and vocalizes.

5. During any program activity, the child will be immediately reinforced (e.g., praised, given another turn) for responding appropriately to a peer's actions.

These examples reflect a nested series of training targets that evolve from global goals at Level 3 to increasingly more specific targets at Level 2 and Level 1. Such an organized nest of progressively more global training objectives provides a useful system for selecting the content to measure child progress at each of the three levels of evaluation. The measurement strategy and the comprehensiveness of the measurement target may change at these three levels, but the basic content remains the same. This content consistency provides a set of guidelines which directs measurement of child and family change and program impact.

Measurement of Progress

To evaluate child and family change, comparison with previous performances may be sufficient. However, to evaluate progress toward program goals, comparisons such as a standardized test, a set of norms, or a statistical analysis of change may need to be employed. The three-level framework offered in Figure 15-5 can also provide a useful system for measuring child and family change and program impact. Figure 15-5 parallels Figure 15-4 and suggests appropriate procedures and type of instruments for measuring progress at each of the three levels.

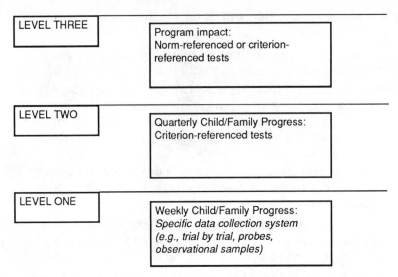

FIGURE 15-5.   A three-level framework to direct selection of instruments for
measuring progress.

Level 1: Measuring Weekly Progress

The measurement of the child's and family's acquisition and use of specific targets will, in most cases, have to be conducted without the benefit of a standardized or criterion-referenced instrument. To measure child or family change at this level, most interventionists will need to devise or adapt a specific data collection format (e.g., trial-by-trial, probes, observational sample) appropriate to the objective or outcomes. Measurement approaches will vary across objectives and outcomes. For example, data collected on the child's use of vocalizations and gestures, or social interactions, might be monitored through a weekly observation of the child at play, while monitoring a mother's acquisition of a specific child management skill might be done by conducting weekly probes.

The amount and type of data collected should be determined by the severity of the problem, the specific objective or outcomes, and program resources. Planning the collection of information on progress can be done in conjunction with the intervention program. That is, the caregiver or interventionist can usually record the behavior and work on a new response simultaneously if the data collection system has been properly devised.

Level 2: Measuring Progress Toward Long-Range Goals and Training or Treatment Objectives and Outcomes

The data acquired on specific targets for child and family change are essential to the formulation and implementation of a sound intervention program. The data collected on child and family progress towards more global long-range goals and outcomes can be employed to measure change as well. These data can also be used to evaluate program impact if the outcomes can be aggregated for total or subgroup analyses. For measuring child progress towards long-range goals and objectives, published instruments with reliability and validity information may be useful. The instrument selected should be the same used during the initial assessment phase that provides the information used to formulate the IEP or IFSP. Selection of an instrument should be based on several factors:

1. The test will likely reflect the long-range goals and treatment or training objectives selected for participating children.

2. The test reflects the program's goals.

3. The test can be administered and scored by staff without undue difficulty.

4. The test's results are interpretable and useful.

If an instrument is available that meets these program-relevant criteria, or with some modification meet the criteria, serious consideration should be given to the adoption of this test for a number of reasons. First, a published or broadly disseminated instrument may have psychometric information not available for most "homemade" instruments. Second, more widely used instruments may have been developed with more care contributing to their face validity and usefulness. Third, such instruments may permit meaningful comparisons across children, groups, and programs.

Because most family outcomes will be individualized, it is unlikely that any one instrument will be available to monitor family progress. It is more likely that adaptable systems such as Goal Attainment Scaling will be more useful (Bailey, Simeonsson, Winton, Huntington, Comfort, Isbell, O'Donnell & Helm, 1986).

Level 3: Measuring Progress Toward Program Goals

Assessing attainment of program goals can be used to monitor child and family change but is generally more useful for assessing the more generic impact of the program on participating children. The generic nature of this level of assessing progress and impact makes the adoption of a norm-referenced and standardized test generally the most desirable choice. The interventionist must decide the type(s) of child-progress goals for all children or subgroups of children. These goals may be: (1) normal development in all areas; (2) normal development in several areas; (3) any development in all areas; or (4) any development in some areas (Sheehan, 1979). If the program goal is normality in the sensori-motor domain, then the Bayley Scales of Infant Development (Bayley, 1969) may be an appropriate instrument to select to measure progress toward that program goal. Standardized tests are a wise choice when evaluating program outcomes because of their long-term summative nature (Green, Ginsberg, & Hyman, 1974). However, programmatic evaluation using norm-referenced tests poses problems similar to those of individual assessment. These problems include population variability, suitability of existing instruments, and design/analytic strategies (Bricker & Littman, 1982). Interventionists should be aware of the limitations of norm-referenced tests and appropriately qualify their results (see Garwood, 1982; Ramey, Campbell, & Wasik, 1982).

It is important to establish criteria for selecting a test to measure attainment of program goals. Again, the test generally should have the following features:

1. Appropriate for the population, although the population on which the test was normed may be different;

2. Administration and interpretation of the test are within the resources of the program; and

3. Results are useable for program evaluation.

The first criterion suggests that the measure selected should be sensitive enough to detect change in children's performance and should also have reasonable agreement with program goals and objectives (Hamilton & Swan, 1981). The third criterion implies that outcomes will not be useful for developing individual intervention procedures, but rather may offer general information on changes in the group or subgroups of children served by the program.

Analysis of Progress

Again, it is useful to use the three-level evaluation framework found in Figure 15-4 to discuss appropriate designs and analytical procedures. Designs and analyses should vary depending upon the purpose, content, and level at which progress is being monitored or program impact is being assessed.

Level 1: Analysis of Weekly Progress

At this level, progress towards the acquisition and use of specific training targets is of primary interest. For children, some form of weekly information should be collected and then systematic comparisons made between these data and those collected previously. Such comparisons require some consistent system for acquiring these data if the comparison is to be valid. A number of different strategies can be employed. For example, the number of objectives reached within a given time period or length of time to reach criteria can be indicated. Data can be plotted on individual graphs to illustrate percent, proportion, frequency, or rate change over time. The most appropriate design for this level is probably single subject analysis. If possible, programs should attempt to demonstrate functional relationships between the intervention programs and changes in responses or patterns of behavior. However, some programs may not have the necessary resources to effectively carry out reversal or multiple baseline procedures, and then charting weekly progress may have to suffice. Program personnel should select a pragmatic and useful way to examine and display their weekly data to monitor progress and to make sound decisions.

Analysis of progress toward family outcomes will need to match the adopted evaluation strategy. A goal should be to develop some strategy that permits gauging progress toward outcomes that can be managed by staff and families and that is acceptable to families.

Level 2: Analysis of Progress Toward Long-Range Goals and Treatment or Training Objectives and Outcomes

This level of analysis can be conducted in much the same way as described in Level 1 for individual children and family members. Use of a group design approach would be equally appropriate if the children and families can be meaningfully assigned to subgroups. Program staff have at least two general options available. The first procedure involves the statistical comparison of predicted progress with actual progress. The predicted progress can be derived in several ways, including reference to existing norms, correlation between performance on pretest and posttest, and correlations between posttest of one year and posttest of the next year. An alternative to a statistical comparison is to establish expectancies or timelines for which children and family members will reach criteria on training objectives, long-range goals, and outcomes. Then the actual progress can be plotted against the pretest timelines for each long-range goal and training objective. Problems with these approaches include assumptions of linear growth and stable estimates of progress.

The second alternative requires the comparison of one intervention program with other programs. This design also has problems which include: (1) ensuring the comparability of children and families across programs; (2) variability in critical program dimensions (e.g., staff); and (3) assessments that favor one group over another (e.g., communication assessment that requires only an oral response may unduly penalize children in programs where alternative communication strategies are encouraged).

These problems make it apparent that currently no perfect strategy exists for measuring progress. Programs must evaluate their goals and resources and then select the design that offers the best compromise for their population.

Level 3: Analysis of Progress Toward Program Goals

The analytic designs discussed for Level 2 are equally appropriate for this level of determining progress and program effectiveness. At this level, some form of comparison seems mandatory if program impact is to be implied. As with Level 2, a number of serious barriers exist when evaluating progress towards program goals. These problems, discussed earlier, are population variability, suitability of available measures, lack of appropriate assessment models and the relationship of assessment to programming.

The populations served by early intervention programs range from at-risk to profoundly impaired, and the impairments are extremely diverse. In addition, great variability may be found in educational and socioeconomic levels of families involved in programs. Often, this diversity creates extremely small numbers of children and families who can be meaningfully grouped. This heterogeneity affects the measures and designs that are applicable for examining program impact (Lewis & Wehren, 1982).

The barriers facing interventionists in documenting program impact are significant and are underlined with another pervasive difficulty. The majority of early intervention programs do not have adequate resources to permit the conduct of elaborate and controlled comparisons of program effectiveness (Johnson, 1988). This reality should not provide a cover that allows interventionists to eliminate attempts at documenting program impact, nor should this reality condone poorly conceived and executed measurement plans. Rather, limited resources should require: (1) thoughtful compromise; (2) extensive planning in order to use limited resources most effectively; and (3) dedication to searching for acceptable alternatives to present designs and analytical problems.

SUMMARY

This chapter has presented an approach to evaluation of child and family progress that is based upon the conceptual position that assessment, intervention, and evaluation should be directly linked to each other. This interrelated system directly employs the information produced by the initial assessment to develop IEPs or IFSPs. Data generated by quarterly evaluation of progress toward the IEP or IFSP goals and outcomes are used to modify intervention efforts and revise IEPs or IFSPs as necessary. Annual evaluations entail comparisons with the child's and family's entry behavior and quarterly progress. The assessment, intervention, and evaluation phases are dependent on and directly linked to one another.

Although linked assessment-intervention-evaluation approaches assist significantly in the field's attempt to document progress and impact, there can be little doubt that the evaluation problems still to be overcome are enormous. Currently, the best we can do is to adopt compromise strategies that produce the greatest benefits. Limitations continue to exist in measuring child and family change and the impact of early intervention programs. As noted by Bailey and Bricker (1984), the field of early intervention has made significant progress during its short life. We have moved from wondering if we could intervene with infants and young children to developing systems that enhance our efforts and accountability. Continued work will yield assessment and evaluation measures, designs, and analytical techniques that will improve our ability to determine program effectiveness for children and families.

References

Alpern, G., & Shearer, M. (1980). *The developmental profile II (Rev. ed.).* Aspen, CO: Psychological Development Publications.

Bagnato, S., & Neisworth, J. (1981). *Linking developmental assessment and curricula.* Rockville, MD: Aspen Publications.

Bailey, D. (1988). Rationale and model for family assessment in early intervention. In D. Bailey & R. Simeonsson (Eds.), *Family assessment in early intervention.* Columbus, OH: Merrill.

Bailey, D., Simeonsson, R., Winton, P., Huntington, G., Comfort, M., Isbell, P., O'Donnell, K., & Helm, J. (1986). Family-focused intervention: A functional model for planning, implementing, and evaluating individualized family services in early intervention. *Journal of the Division for Early Childhood, 10*, 156-171.

Bailey, E., & Bricker, D. (1984). The efficacy of early intervention for severely handicapped infants and young children. *Topics in Early Childhood Special Education, 4*(3), 30-51.

Bayley, N. (1969). *The Bayley scales of infant development.* New York: The Psychological Corporation.

Bricker, D., Bailey, E., & Bruder, M. (1984). The efficacy of early intervention and the handicapped infant: A wise or wasted resource? *Advances in Developmental and Behavioral Pediatrics*, Vol. V. Greenwich, CT: JAI Press.

Bricker, D., Gentry, D., & Bailey, E. (1985). *The Evaluation and Programming System: For Infants and Young Children.* Eugene, OR: Center on Human Development, University of Oregon.

Bricker, D., & Littman, D. (1982). Intervention and evaluation: The inseparable mix. *Topics in Early Childhood Special Education, 1*, 23-33.

Brigance, A. (1978). *Brigance diagnostic inventory of early development.* Worcester, MA: Curriculum Associates, Inc.

Cohen, M., & Gross, P. (1979). *The developmental resource: Behavioral sequences for assessment and program planning.* New York: Grune & Stratton.

Dubose, R., & Langley, M. (1977). *The developmental activities screening inventory.* NY: Teaching Resouces.

Fewell, R. (1983). Assessing handicapped infants. In S. Garwood & R. Fewell (Eds.), *Educating handicapped infants.* Rockville, MD: Aspen.

Fischer, K. (1980). A theory of cognitive development: The control and construction of hierarchies of skills. *Psychological Review, 87*, 477-531.

Frankenburg, W., & Dodds, J. (1970). *Denver developmental screening test (DDST).* Denver, CO: Ladoca Project and Publishing Foundation, Inc.

Frankenburg, W., Emde, R., & Sullivan, J. (1985). Preface. In W. Frankenburg, R. Emde & J. Sullivan (Eds.), *Early identification of children at risk.* New York: Plenum Press.

Furuno, S., O'Reilly, K., Hosaka, C., Inatsuka, T., Allman, T., & Zeisloft, B. (1985). *HELP: Hawaii Early Learning Profile Activity Guide.* Palo Alto, CA: VORT Corporation.

Garwood, G. (1982). Early childhood intervention: Is it time to change outcome variables? *Topics in Early Childhood Special Education, 1*, ix-xi.

Green, D., Ginsberg, N., & Hyman, H. (1974). *The nature and uses of criterion and norm-referenced achievement tests.* Monterey, CA: McGraw-Hill.

Hamilton, J., & Swan, W. (1981). Measurement references in the assessment of preschool handicapped children. *Topics in Early Childhood Special Education, 1*(2), 41-48.

Herst, J., Wolfe, S., Jorgensen, G., & Pallan, S. (1976). *S.E.E.D.* (Sewall early education development profiles). Denver, CO: Sewall Rehabilitation Center.

Hutinger, P. (1988). Linking screening, identification, and assessment with curriculum. In J. Jordan, J. Gallagher, P., Hutinger & M. Karnes (Eds.), *Early childhood special education: Birth to three.* Reston, VA: Council for Exceptional Children.

Infant Monitoring Questionnaires. (1989). Center on Human Development, University of Oregon.

Johnson, L. (1988). Program evaluation: The key to quality programming. In J. Jordan, J. Gallagher, P. Hutinger & M. Karnes (Eds.), *Early childhood special education: Birth to three.* Reston, VA: Council for Exceptional Children.

Johnson, N. (1982). An interventionist's perspective. In D. Bricker (Ed.), *Intervention with at-risk and handicapped infants: From research to application.* Baltimore, MD: University Park Press.

Knobloch, H., Stevens, F., & Malone, A. (1980). *Manual of developmental diagnosis: The administration and interpretation of the revised Gesell and Armatruda developmental and neurologic examination.* Hagerstown, MD: Harper & Row.

LeMay, D., Griffin, P., & Sanford, A. (1978). *Learning accomplishment profile: Diagnostic edition* (Rev. ed.). Winston-Salem, NC: Kaplan School Supply.

Lewis, M., & Wehren, A. (1982). The central tendency in study of the handicapped child. In D. Bricker (Ed.), *Intervention with at-risk and handicapped infants: From research to application.* Baltimore, MD: University Park Press.

Lichtenstein, R. (1982). *Minneapolis Preschool Screening Instrument.* Minneapolis, Minn.: Prescriptive Instruction Center, Minneapolis Public Schools.

McCall, R. (1981). Nature-nurture and the two realms of development: A proposed integration with respect to mental development. *Child Development, 52*(1), 1-12.

McCarthy, D. (1972). *McCarthy scales of children's abilities.* NY: The Psychological Corporation.

Mardell-Czudnowski, C., & Goldenberg, D. (1983). *Developmental Indicators for the Assessment of Learning-Revised* (DIAL-R). Edison, NJ: Childcraft Corp.

Meisels, S., & Wiske, M. (1988). Early screening inventory, Second Edition. New York: Teachers College Press.

Newborg, J., Stock, J., Wnek, L., Guidabaldi, J., & Svinicki, J. (1988). *Battelle Developmental Inventory*. Allen, TX: DLM Teaching Resources.

Ramey, C., Campbell, F., & Wasik, B. (1982). Use of standardized tests to evaluate early childhood special education programs. *Topics in Early Childhood Special Education, 1*, 51-60.

Robinson, C. (1982). Questions regarding the effects of neuromotor problems on sensorimotor development. In D. Bricker (Ed.), *Intervention with at-risk and handicapped infants: From research to application*. Baltimore, MD: University Park Press.

Salvia, J., & Ysseldyke, J. (1981). *Assessment in special and remedial education*, Second Edition. Dallas: Houghton Mifflin.

Sheehan, R., & Keogh, B. (1982). Design and analysis in the evaluation of early childhood special education programs. *Topics in Early Childhood Special Education, 1*, 81-88.

Sheehan, R. (1979). Measuring child progress: Large group design and norm-referenced alternatives. In M. May (Ed.), *Evaluating handicapped children's early education program*. Seattle, WA: WESTAR.

Simeonsson, R., Huntington, G., & Parse, S. (1980). Assessment of children with severe handicaps: Multiple problems—Multivariate goals. *Journal of the Association for the Severely Handicapped, 5*, 55-72.

Stillman, R. (1975). *The Callier-Azusa scale: Assessment of deaf-blind children*. Reston, VA: Council for Exceptional Children.

Tallmadge, G., & Horst, D. (1976). *A procedural guide for validating achievement gains in educational projects*. Washington, DC: U.S. Department of Health, Education, and Welfare, U.S. Office of Education. U.S. Government Printing Office.

Thorndike, R., Hagen, E., & Sattler, J. (1985). *Stanford-Binet intelligence Scale*, Ed. 4. Chicago: Riverside Publishing.

Weatherford, D. (1986). The challenge of evaluating early intervention programs for severely handicapped children and their families. In L. Bickman & D. Weatherford (Eds.), *Evaluating early intervention programs for severely handicapped children and their families*. Austin, TX: Pro-Ed.

White, O., Edgar, E., Haring, N., Affleck, J., & Hayden, A. (1980). *Uniform performance assessment system*. Columbus, OH: Charles E. Merrill.

Name Index

Subject Index